Beginning Java™ EE 6 Platform with GlassFish™ 3

From Novice to Professional

Second Edition

ANTONIO GONCALVES

Apress®

Beginning Java™ EE 6 Platform with GlassFish™ 3: From Novice to Professional, Second Edition

ISBN-13 (pbk): 978-1-4302-2889-9

ISBN-13 (electronic): 978-1-4302-2890-5

Printed and bound in the United States of America 9 8 7 6 5 4 3 2 1

President and Publisher: Paul Manning
Lead Editors: Steve Anglin, Tom Welsh
Technical Reviewer: Jim Farley
Editorial Board: Clay Andres, Steve Anglin, Mark Beckner, Ewan Buckingham, Gary Cornell,
    Jonathan Gennick, Jonathan Hassell, Michelle Lowman, Matthew Moodie, Duncan Parkes,
    Jeffrey Pepper, Frank Pohlmann, Douglas Pundick, Ben Renow-Clarke, Dominic Shakeshaft,
    Matt Wade, Tom Welsh
Coordinating Editor: Mary Tobin
Copy Editor: Ami Knox
Compositor: Kimberly Burton
Indexer: Potomac Indexing, LLC
Artist: April Milne
Cover Designer: Anna Ishchenko

Distributed to the book trade worldwide by Springer Science+Business Media, LLC., 233 Spring Street, 6th Floor, New York, NY 10013. Phone 1-800-SPRINGER, fax (201) 348-4505, e-mail orders-ny@springer-sbm.com, or visit www.springeronline.com.

For information on translations, please e-mail rights@apress.com, or visit www.apress.com.

Apress and friends of ED books may be purchased in bulk for academic, corporate, or promotional use. eBook versions and licenses are also available for most titles. For more information, reference our Special Bulk Sales–eBook Licensing web page at www.apress.com/info/bulksales.

To Eloïse, who fills my heart with love.

Contents at a Glance

Contents

Foreword

While Java EE 5 is considered by everyone to be the most important enterprise release, Java EE 6 has a lot in store for you and every server-side Java developer. The most widely spread technology to write enterprise-class applications just got better with enhanced EJB 3.1, Java Persistence API (JPA) 2.0, the new, yet already very successful, Java API for RESTful web services (JAX-RS), and the made-over JavaServer Faces (JSF) 2.0 specification. The enterprise Java platform has now matured to a degree where it can be both complete and lightweight.

Now you could spend quality time with your favorite search engine and blog reader to navigate through the numerous blogs, wikis, and documentation covering all or parts of Java EE 6, but I'd like to suggest that you'd be better off starting with this book. It is concise, pragmatic, and offers an all-in-one experience.

Having the open source GlassFish application server as the underlying platform for this book makes a lot of sense for two reasons: first, GlassFish v3 is the Reference Implementation (RI) and thus is aligned with Java EE 6, and second, using an RI does not mean you can't please developers and scale to production deployments. The skills acquired with GlassFish in conjunction with those of the most recent technologies are portable in the enterprise.

Antonio Goncalves is a rare combination of friendly Java enthusiast and precise yet no-nonsense Java EE expert. His role as a consultant combined with his involvement chairing the successful Java User Group in Paris and, of course, his role as a member of several key Java EE 6 expert groups makes him the ideal author for *Beginning Java EE 6 Platform with GlassFish 3*.

When you are done reading this book, I'd like to suggest that the greatest value of Java EE is not the sum of its features but rather the community that created it, as well as the very nature of it being a standard that lets you choose or change your implementation as you wish. Freedom is not simply about open source but also about open standards.

Alexis Moussine-Pouchkine
GlassFish Team, Oracle

About the Author

■ **Antonio Goncalves** is a senior software architect living in Paris. Initially focused on Java development since the late 1990s, his career has taken him to different countries and companies where he works now as a Java EE consultant in software architecture. As a former BEA consultant, he has great expertise in application servers such as WebLogic, JBoss, and, of course, GlassFish. He is particularly fond of open source and is a member of the OSSGTP (Open Source Solution Get Together Paris). He is also the cocreator and coleader of the Paris Java User Group.

Antonio wrote his first book on Java EE 5, in French, back in 2007. Since then he has joined the JCP and is an Expert Member of various JSRs (Java EE 6, JPA 2.0, and EJB 3.1). For the last few years, Antonio has given talks at international conferences mainly about Java EE, including JavaOne, The Server Side Symposium, Devoxx, Jazoon and many Java User Groups. He has also written numerous technical papers and articles for IT web sites (DevX) and IT magazines (*Programmez, Linux Magazine*). Since 2009, he has been part of the French Java podcast called Les Cast Codeurs (influenced by the Java Posse). For all his work for the Java Community, Antonio has been elected Java Champion.

Antonio is a graduate of the Conservatoire National des Arts et Métiers in Paris (with an engineering degree in IT) and the Brighton University (with an MSc in object-oriented design).

About the Technical Reviewer

■ **Jim Farley** is a technology architect, strategist, writer, and manager. His career has touched a wide array of domains, from commercial to nonprofit, finance to higher education. In addition to his day job, Jim teaches enterprise development at Harvard University. Jim is the author of several books on technology, and contributes articles and commentary to various online and print publications.

Acknowledgments

Writing a book about a new specification such as Java EE 6 is an enormous task that requires the talent of different people. First of all, I really want to thank Steve Anglin from Apress for giving me the opportunity to contribute to the Apress *Beginning* series, which I greatly appreciated as a reader. Throughout the writing process, I was constantly in contact with Mary Tobin and Tom Welsh who reviewed the book as well as reassured me when I had doubt about finishing on time. Thanks to Jim Farley who did an excellent job of giving me good technical advice to improve the book.

I also need to thank Alexis Midon and Sebastien Auvray, who coauthored the RESTful web services chapter (Chapter 15). Alexis is a passionate software engineer and a REST enthusiast, and Sebastien is a talented developer and a pragmatic adopter of REST. Thanks, guys, for your precious help.

A special thanks to Alexis Moussine-Pouchkine, who kindly agreed to write the foreword of this book as well as the section on GlassFish. He was also a big help in contacting the right person to give me a hand on a particular topic. I'm thinking of Ryan Lubke for JSF 2.0, Paul Sandoz for JAX-RS 1.1, and François Orsini for Derby.

Thanks to Damien Gouyette for his help on JSF 2.0. Damien has great experience in web development as a whole and JSF in particular. Thanks to Arnaud Heritier, who wrote the section on Maven, as well as Nicolas de Loof, who did a last proofread on the topic.

Sebastien Moreno helped me on JUnit as well as reviewing the entire manuscript with David Dewalle and Pascal Graffion. They had to put up with a tight schedule. Thank you very much for the hard work.

Thanks to the proofreader Stefano Costa, who tried to add a Shakespearean touch to the book.

The diagrams in this book were made using the Visual Paradigm plug-in for IntelliJ IDEA. I would like to thank both Visual Paradigm and JetBrains for providing me with a free license for their excellent products.

I could not have written this book without the help and support of the Java community: people who gave a bit of their time to help me through e-mails, mailing lists, or forums. Of course, the mailing lists of the JCP expert groups are the first that come to mind; thanks to the expert members and the spec leads (Roberto Chinnici, Bill Shannon, Kenneth Saks, Linda DeMichiel, Michael Keith, Reza Rahman, Adam Bien, etc.).

And a big kiss to my daughter Eloïse, who is growing up and such a wonderful loving kid.

A book is conceived with the help of a never-ending list of people you want to thank for having contributed, in one way or another: technical advice, a beer at the bar, an idea, or a piece of code (Bernard Pons, Youness Teimoury, Mariane Hufschmitt, Jean-Louis Dewez, Frédéric Drouet, the Paris JUG geeks, the OSSGTP guys, Les Cast Codeurs, FIP, Marion, Les Connards, Vitalizen, La Fontaine, Ago, La Grille, les Eeckman, Yaya, Rita, os Navalhas, La Commune Libre d'Aligre, etc.).

Thank you all!

Preface

In today's business world, applications need to access data, apply business logic, add presentation layers, and communicate with external systems. That's what companies are trying to achieve while minimizing costs, using standard and robust technologies that can handle heavy loads. If that's your case, you have the right book in your hands.

Java Enterprise Edition appeared at the end of the 1990s and brought to the Java language a robust software platform for enterprise development. Challenged at each new version, badly understood or misused, overengineered, and competing with open source frameworks, J2EE was seen as a heavyweight technology. Java EE benefited from these criticisms to improve and is today focused on simplicity.

If you are part of the group of people who still think that "EJBs are bad, EJBs are evil," read this book, and you'll change your mind. EJBs (Enterprise Java Beans) are great, as is the entire Java EE 6 technology stack. If, on the contrary, you are a Java EE adopter, you will see in this book how the platform has found equilibrium, through its ease of development in all the stacks, new specifications, lighter EJB component model, profiles, and pruning. If you are a beginner in Java EE, this is also the right book: it covers the most important specifications in a very understandable manner and is illustrated with a lot of code and diagrams to make it easier to follow.

Open standards are collectively one of the main strengths of Java EE. More than ever, an application written with JPA, EJB, JSF, JMS, SOAP web services, or RESTful web services is portable across application servers. Open source is another of Java EE's strengths. As you'll see in this book, most of the Java EE 6 Reference Implementations use open source licensing (GlassFish, EclipseLink, Mojarra, OpenMQ, Metro, and Jersey).

This book explores the innovations of this new version, and examines the various specifications and how to assemble them to develop applications. Java EE 6 consists of nearly 30 specifications and is an important milestone for the enterprise layer (EJB 3.1, JPA 2.0), for the web tier (Servlet 3.0, JSF 2.0), and for interoperability (SOAP web services and RESTful services). This book covers a broad part of the Java EE 6 specifications and uses the JDK 1.6 and some well-known design patterns, as well as the GlassFish application server, the Derby database, JUnit, and Maven. It is illustrated abundantly with UML diagrams, Java code, and screenshots.

How Is This Book Structured?

This book is not meant to be an exhaustive reference on Java EE 6. It concentrates on the most important specifications and highlights the new features of this release. The structure of the book follows the architecture layering of an application:

```
Presentation

Chapter 10: JavaServer Faces
Chapter 11: Pages and Components
Chapter 12: Processing & Navigation
```

```
Business logic

Chapter 6: Enterprise Java Beans
Chapter 7: Session Beans & Timer Service
Chapter 8: Callbacks & Interceptors
Chapter 9: Transactions & Security
```

```
Interoperability

Chapter 13: Sending Messages
Chapter 14: SOAP Web Services
Chapter 15: RESTful Web Services
```

```
Persistence

Chapter 2: Java Persistence
Chapter 3: Object-Relational Mapping
Chapter 4: Managing Persistent Objects
Chapter 5: Callbacks & Listeners
```

Chapter 1 briefly presents Java EE 6 essentials and the tools used throughout the book (JDK, Maven, JUnit, Derby, and GlassFish).

The persistent tier is described from Chapter 2 to Chapter 5 and focuses on JPA 2.0. After a general overview with some hands-on examples in Chapter 2, Chapter 3 dives into object-relational mapping (mapping attributes, relationships, and inheritance). Chapter 4 shows you how to manage and query entities, while Chapter 5 presents their life cycle, callback methods, and listeners.

To develop a transaction business logic layer with Java EE 6, you can naturally use EJBs. This will be described from Chapter 6 to Chapter 9. After an overview of the specification, its history, and a hands-on example in Chapter 6, Chapter 7 will concentrate on session beans and their programming model, as well as the new timer service. Chapter 8 focuses on the life cycle of EJBs and interceptors, while Chapter 9 explains transactions and security.

From Chapter 10 to Chapter 12, you will learn how to develop a presentation layer with JSF 2.0. After an overview of the specification in Chapter 10, Chapter 11 will focus on how to build a web page with JSF and Facelets components. Chapter 12 will show you how to interact with an EJB back end and navigate through pages.

Finally, the last chapters will present different ways to interoperate with other systems. Chapter 13 will show you how to exchange asynchronous messages with Java Message Service (JMS) and Message-Driven Beans (MDBs). Chapter 14 focuses on SOAP web services, while Chapter 15 covers RESTful web services.

Downloading and Running the Code

The examples used in this book are designed to be compiled with the JDK 1.6, deployed to the GlassFish V3 application server, and stored in Derby. Chapter 1 shows you how to install all these software programs, and each chapter explains how to build, deploy, run, and test components depending on the technology used. The code has been tested on the Windows platform, but not on Linux nor on OS X. The source code of the examples in the book is available from the Source Code page of the Apress web site at www.apress.com. You can also download the code straight from the public Subversion at http://beginningee6.kenai.com.

Contacting the Author

If you have any questions about the content of this book, the code, or any other topic, please contact me at antonio.goncalves@gmail.com. You can also visit my web site at www.antoniogoncalves.org and follow me on Twitter at @agoncal.

CHAPTER 1

■ ■ ■

Java EE 6 at a Glance

Enterprises today live in a global competitive world. They need applications to fulfill their business needs, which are getting more and more complex. In this age of globalization, companies are distributed over continents, they do business 24/7 over the Internet and across different countries, and their systems have to be internationalized and ready to deal with different currencies and time zones. All that while reducing their costs, lowering the response times of their services, storing business data on reliable and safe storage, and offering several graphical user interfaces to their customers, employees, and suppliers.

Most companies have to combine these innovative challenges with their existing Enterprise Information Systems (EIS) while at the same time developing business-to-business applications to communicate with partners. It is also not rare for a company to have to coordinate in-house data stored in different locations, processed by multiple programming languages, and routed through different protocols. And, of course, it has to do this without losing money, which means preventing system crashes and being highly available, scalable, and secure. Enterprise applications have to face change and complexity, and be robust. That's precisely why Java Enterprise Edition (Java EE) was created.

The first version of Java EE (originally known as J2EE) focused on the concerns that companies were facing back in 1999: distributed components. Since then, software applications have had to adapt to new technical solutions like SOAP or RESTful web services. The platform has evolved to respond to these technical needs by providing various standard ways of working through specifications. Throughout the years, Java EE has changed and become richer, simpler, easier to use, and more portable.

In this chapter, I'll give you an overview of Java EE. After an introduction of its internal architecture, I'll cover what's new in Java EE 6. The second part of this chapter focuses on setting up your development environment so you can do some hands-on work by following the code snippets listed in these pages.

Understanding Java EE

When you want to handle collections of objects, you don't start by developing your own hashtable; you use the collection API. Similarly, if you need a transactional, secure, interoperable, and distributed application, you don't want to develop all the low-level APIs: you use the Enterprise Edition of Java. Just as Java Standard Edition (Java SE) provides an API to handle collections, Java EE provides a standard way to handle transactions with Java Transaction API (JTA), messaging with Java Message Service (JMS), or persistence with Java Persistence API (JPA). Java EE is a set of specifications intended for enterprise applications. It can be seen as an extension of Java SE to facilitate the development of distributed, robust, powerful, and highly available applications.

1

Java EE 6 is an important milestone. Not only does it follow the steps of Java EE 5 by focusing on an easier development model, it also adds new specifications and brings profiles and pruning to make it lighter. The release of Java EE 6 coincides closely with the tenth anniversary of the enterprise platform. It combines the advantages of the Java language with experience gained over the last ten years. Moreover, it profits from the dynamism of open source communities as well as the rigor of the JCP. Today Java EE is a well-documented platform with experienced developers, a large community, and many deployed applications running on companies' servers. Java EE is a suite of APIs to build standard component-based multitier applications. These components are deployed in different containers offering a series of services.

A Bit of History

Ten years is a good time to look back at the evolution of Java EE (see Figure 1-1), which was formerly called J2EE. J2EE 1.2, first developed by Sun, was released in 1999 as an umbrella specification containing ten Java Specification Requests (JSRs). At that time people were talking about CORBA, so J2EE 1.2 was created with distributed systems in mind. Enterprise Java Beans (EJBs) were introduced with support for remote stateful and stateless service objects, and optional support for persistent objects (entity beans). They were built on a transactional and distributed component model using RMI-IIOP (Remote Method Invocation–Internet Inter-ORB Protocol) as the underlying protocol. The web tier had servlets and JavaServer Pages (JSPs), and JMS was used for sending messages.

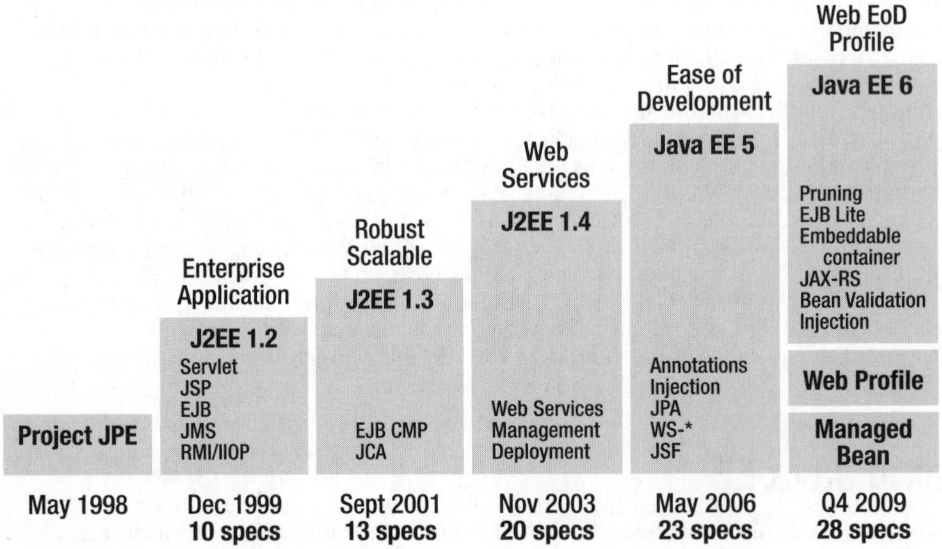

Figure 1-1. History of J2EE/Java EE

■ **Note** CORBA originated about 1988 precisely because enterprise systems were beginning to be distributed (e.g., Tuxedo, CICS). EJBs and then J2EE followed on with the same assumptions, but ten years later. By the time J2EE was begun, CORBA was fully baked and industrial strength, but companies found simpler, more decoupled ways to connect distributed systems, like web services. So CORBA became redundant for most enterprise systems.

Starting with J2EE 1.3, the specification was developed by the Java Community Process (JCP) under JSR 58. Support for entity beans was made mandatory, and EJBs introduced XML deployment descriptors to store metadata (which was serialized in a file in EJB 1.0). This version addressed the overhead of passing arguments by value with remote interfaces, by introducing local interfaces and passing arguments by reference. J2EE Connector Architecture (JCA) was introduced to connect Java EE to EIS.

■ **Note** The JCP is an open organization, created in 1998, that is involved in the definition of future versions and features of the Java platform. When the need for a new component or API is identified, the initiator (a.k.a. specification lead) creates a JSR and forms a group of experts. This group, made of companies' representatives, organizations, universities or private individuals, is responsible for the development of the JSR and has to deliver 1) one or more specifications that explain the details and define the fundamentals of the JSR, 2) a Reference Implementation (RI), which is an actual implementation of the specification, and 3) a Compatibility Test Kit (a.k.a. Technology Compatibility Kit, or TCK), which is a set of tests every implementation needs to pass before claiming to conform to the specification. Once approved by the Executive Committee (EC), the specification is released to the community for implementation. Java EE is called an Umbrella JSR, or a Platform Edition Specification (such as Profiles), because it ties together other JSRs.

J2EE 1.4 (JSR 151) included 20 specifications in 2003 and added support for web services. EJB 2.1 allowed session beans to be invoked over SOAP/HTTP. A timer service was created to allow EJBs to be invoked at designated times or intervals. This version provided better support for application assembly and deployment.

Although its supporters predicted a great future for it, not all of J2EE's promise materialized. The systems created with it were too complicated, and development time was frequently out of all proportion to the complexity of the user's requirements. J2EE was seen as a heavyweight component model: difficult to test, difficult to deploy, difficult to run. That's when frameworks such as Struts, Spring, or Hibernate emerged and showed a new way of developing enterprise application. Fortunately, in the second quarter of 2006, Java EE 5 (JSR 244) was released and turned out to be a remarkable improvement. It took some inspiration from open source frameworks by bringing back a Plain Old Java Object (POJO) programming model. Metadata could be defined with annotations, and XML descriptors became optional. From a developer's point of view, EJB 3 and the new JPA were more of a quantum leap than an evolution of the platform. JavaServer Faces (JSF) was introduced as the standard presentation tier framework, and JAX-WS 2.0 replaced JAX-RPC as the SOAP web services API.

Today, Java EE 6 (JSR 316) follows the path of ease of development by embracing the concepts of annotations, POJO programming, and the configuration-by-exception mechanism throughout the platform, including the web tier. It comes with a rich set of innovations such as the brand-new JAX-RS 1.1; it simplifies mature APIs like EJB 3.1, and enriches others such as JPA 2.0 or the timer service. But the major themes for Java EE 6 are portability (through standardizing global JNDI naming, for example), deprecation of some specifications (via pruning), and creating subsets of the platform through profiles. In this book, I want to show you these improvements and how much easier and richer Java Enterprise Edition has become.

Standards

As you can see, Java EE is based on standards. It is an umbrella specification that bundles together a number of other JSRs. You might ask why standards are so important, as some of the most successful Java frameworks are not standardized (Struts, Spring, etc.). Throughout history, humans have created standards to ease communication and exchange. Some notable examples are language, currency, time, navigation, measurements, tools, railways, electricity, telegraphs, telephones, protocols, and programming languages.

In the early days of Java, if you were doing any kind of web or enterprise development, you were living in a proprietary world by creating your own frameworks or locking yourself to a proprietary commercial framework. Then came the days of open source frameworks, which are not always based on open standards. You can use open source and be locked to a single implementation, or use open source that implements standards and be portable. Java EE provides open standards that are implemented by several commercial (WebLogic, Websphere, MQSeries, etc.) or open source (GlassFish, JBoss, Hibernate, Open JPA, Jersey, etc.) frameworks for handling transactions, security, stateful components, object persistence, and so on. Today, more than ever in the history of Java EE, your application is deployable to any compliant application server with very few changes.

Architecture

Java EE is a set of specifications implemented by different containers. Containers are Java EE runtime environments that provide certain services to the components they host such as life-cycle management, dependency injection, and so on. These components use well-defined contracts to communicate with the Java EE infrastructure and with the other components. They need to be packaged in a standard way (following a defined directory structure that can be compressed, we talk about archive files) before being deployed. Java EE is a superset of the Java SE platform, which means Java SE APIs can be used by any Java EE components.

Figure 1-2 shows the logical relationships between containers. The arrows represent the protocols used by one container to access another. For example, the web container hosts servlets, which can access EJBs through RMI-IIOP.

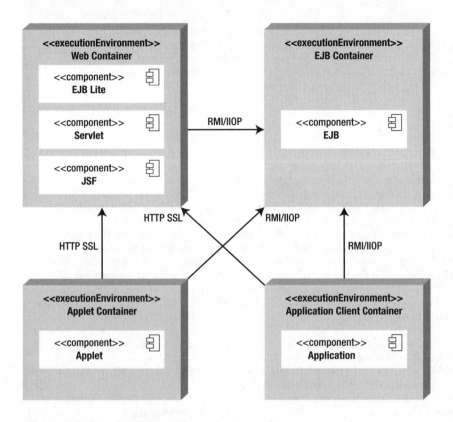

Figure 1-2. *Standard Java EE containers*

Components

The Java EE runtime environment defines four types of components that an implementation must support:

- *Applets* are GUI applications that are executed in a web browser. They use the rich Swing API to provide powerful user interfaces.

- *Applications* are programs that are executed on a client. They are typically GUIs or batch-processing programs that have access to all the facilities of the Java EE middle tier.

- *Web applications* (made of servlets, servlet filters, web event listeners, JSP pages, and JSF) are executed in a web container and respond to HTTP requests from web clients. Servlets also support SOAP and RESTful web service endpoints. Starting with Java EE 6, web applications can also contain EJBs Lite (more on that in Chapter 6).

- *Enterprise applications* (made of Enterprise Java Beans, Java Message Service, Java Transaction API, asynchronous calls, timer service, RMI/IIOP) are executed in an EJB container. EJBs are container-managed components for processing transactional business logic. They can be accessed locally and remotely through RMI (or HTTP for SOAP and RESTful web services).

Containers

The Java EE infrastructure is partitioned into logical domains called containers (see Figure 1-2). Each container has a specific role, supports a set of APIs, and offers services to components (security, database access, transaction handling, naming directory, resource injection). Containers hide technical complexity and enhance portability. Depending on the kind of application you want to build, you will have to understand the capabilities and constraints of each container in order to use one or more. For example, if you need to develop a web application, you will develop a JSF tier with an EJB Lite tier and deploy them into a web container. But if you want a web application to invoke a business tier remotely and use messaging and asynchronous calls, you will need both the web and EJB containers.

Applet containers are provided by most web browsers to execute applet components. When you develop applets, you can concentrate on the visual aspect of the application while the container gives you a secure environment. The applet container uses a sandbox security model where code executed in the "sandbox" is not allowed to "play outside the sandbox." This means that the container prevents any code downloaded to your local computer from accessing local system resources, such as processes or files.

The application client container (ACC) includes a set of Java classes, libraries, and other files required to bring injection, security management, and naming service to Java SE applications (Swing, batch processing, or just a class with a `main()` method). ACC communicates with the EJB container using RMI-IIOP and the web container with HTTP (e.g., for web services).

The web container provides the underlying services for managing and executing web components (servlets, EJBs Lite, JSPs, filters, listeners, JSF pages, and web services). It is responsible for instantiating, initializing, and invoking servlets and supporting the HTTP and HTTPS protocols. It is the container used to feed web pages to client browsers.

The EJB container is responsible for managing the execution of the enterprise beans containing the business logic tier of your Java EE application. It creates new instances of EJBs, manages their life cycle, and provides services such as transaction, security, concurrency, distribution, naming service, or the possibility to be invoked asynchronously.

Services

Containers provide underlying services to their deployed components. As a developer, you can concentrate on implementing business logic rather than solving technical problems faced in enterprise applications. Figure 1-3 shows you the services provided by each container. For example, web and EJB containers provide connectors to access EIS, but not the applet container or the ACCs. Java EE offers the following services:

- *Java Transaction API (JTA)*: This service offers a transaction demarcation API used by the container and the application. It also provides an interface between the transaction manager and a resource manager at the Service Provider Interface (SPI) level.

- *Java Persistence API (JPA)*: Standard API for object-relational mapping (ORM). With its Java Persistence Query Language (JPQL), you can query objects stored in the underlying database.

- *Validation*: Bean Validation provides a class level constraint declaration and validation facility.

- *Java Message Service (JMS)*: This allows components to communicate asynchronously through messages. It supports reliable point-to-point (P2P) messaging as well as the publish-subscribe (pub-sub) model.

- *Java Naming and Directory Interface (JNDI)*: This API, included in Java SE, is used to access naming and directory systems. Your application uses it to associate (bind) names to objects and then to find these objects (lookup) in a directory. You can look up datasources, JMS factories, EJBs, and other resources. Omnipresent in your code until J2EE 1.4, JNDI is used in a more transparent way through injection.

- *JavaMail*: Many applications require the ability to send e-mails, which can be implemented through use of the JavaMail API.

- *JavaBeans Activation Framework (JAF)*: The JAF API, included in Java SE, provides a framework for handling data in different MIME types. It is used by JavaMail.

- *XML processing*: Most Java EE components can be deployed with optional XML deployment descriptors, and applications often have to manipulate XML documents. The Java API for XML Processing (JAXP) provides support for parsing documents with SAX and DOM APIs, as well as for XSLT. The Streaming API for XML (StAX) provides a pull-parsing API for XML.

- *Java EE Connector Architecture (JCA)*: Connectors allow you to access EIS from a Java EE component. These could be databases, mainframes, or Enterprise Resource Planning (ERP) programs.

- *Security services*: Java Authentication and Authorization Service (JAAS) enables services to authenticate and enforce access controls upon users. The Java Authorization Service Provider Contract for Containers (JACC) defines a contract between a Java EE application server and an authorization service provider, allowing custom authorization service providers to be plugged into any Java EE product.

- *Web services*: Java EE provides support for SOAP and RESTful web services. The Java API for XML Web Services (JAX-WS), replacing the Java API for XML-based RPC (JAX-RPC), provides support for web services using the SOAP/HTTP protocol. The Java API for RESTful Web Services (JAX-RS) provides support for web services using the REST style.

- *Dependency injection*: Since Java EE 5, some resources (datasources, JMS factories, persistence units, EJBs…) can be injected in managed components. Java EE 6 goes further by using CDI (Context and Dependency Injection) as well as the DI (Dependency Injection for Java) specifications.

- *Management*: Java EE defines APIs for managing containers and servers using a special management enterprise bean. The Java Management Extensions (JMX) API is also used to provide some management support.

- *Deployment*: The Java EE Deployment Specification defines a contract between deployment tools and Java EE products to standardize application deployment.

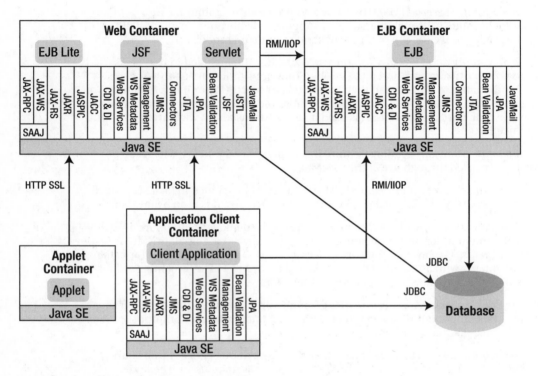

Figure 1-3. Services provided by containers

Network Protocols

As shown in Figure 1-3 (see the "Platform Overview" section of the Java EE 6 specification), components deployed in containers can be invoked through different protocols. For example, a servlet deployed in a web container can be called with HTTP as well as a web service with an EJB endpoint deployed in an EJB container. Here is the list of protocols supported by Java EE:

- *HTTP*: HTTP is the Web protocol and is ubiquitous in modern applications. The client-side API is defined by the `java.net` package in Java SE. The HTTP server-side API is defined by servlets, JSPs, and JSF interfaces, as well as SOAP and RESTful web services. HTTPS is a combination of HTTP and the Secure Sockets Layer (SSL) protocol.

- *RMI-IIOP*: Remote Method Invocation (RMI) allows you to invoke remote objects independently of the underlying protocol. The Java SE native RMI protocol is Java Remote Method Protocol (JRMP). RMI-IIOP is an extension of RMI used to integrate with CORBA. Java interface description language (IDL) allows Java EE application components to invoke external CORBA objects using the IIOP protocol. CORBA objects can be written in many languages (Ada, C, C++, Cobol, etc.) as well as Java.

Packaging

To be deployed in a container, components have first to be packaged in a standard formatted archive. Java SE defines Java Archive (jar) files, which are used to aggregate many files (Java classes, deployment descriptors, resources, or external libraries) into one compressed file (based on the ZIP format). As seen in Figure 1-4, Java EE defines different types of modules that have their own packaging format based on this common jar format.

An application client module contains Java classes and other resource files packaged in a jar file. This jar file can be executed in a Java SE environment or in an application client container. Like any other archive format, the jar file contains an optional `META-INF` directory for meta information describing the archive. The `META-INF/MANIFEST.MF` file is used to define extension- and package-related data. If deployed in an ACC, the deployment descriptor can optionally be located at `META-INF/application-client.xml`.

An EJB module contains one or more session and/or message-driven beans (MDBs) packaged in a jar file (often called an EJB jar file). It contains an optional `META-INF/ejb-jar.xml` deployment descriptor and can be deployed only in an EJB container.

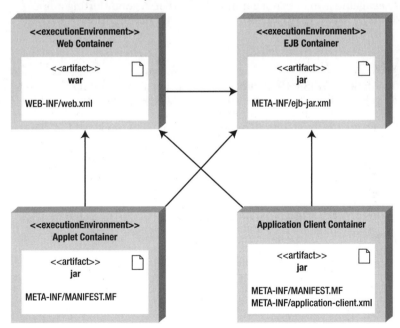

Figure 1-4. Archives in containers

A web application module contains servlets, JSPs, JSF pages, and web services, as well as any other web-related files (HTML and XHTML pages, Cascading Style Sheets (CSS), Java-Scripts, images, videos, and so on). Since Java EE 6, a web application module can also contain EJB Lite beans (a subset of the EJB API described in Chapter 6). All these artifacts are packaged in a jar file with a `.war` extension (commonly referred to as a war file, or a Web Archive). The optional web deployment descriptor is defined in the `WEB-INF/web.xml` file. If the war contains EJB Lite beans, an optional deployment descriptor can be set at `WEB-INF/ejb-jar.xml`. Java.`class` files are placed under the `WEB-INF/classes` directory and dependent jar files in the `WEB-INF/lib` directory.

An enterprise module can contain zero or more web application modules, zero or more EJB modules, and other common or external libraries. All this is packaged into an enterprise archive (a jar file with an `.ear` extension) so that the deployment of these various modules happens simultaneously and coherently. The optional enterprise module deployment descriptor is defined in the `META-INF/application.xml` file. The special `lib` directory is used to share common libraries between the modules.

Java Standard Edition

It's important to stress that Java EE is a superset of Java SE (Java Standard Edition). This means that all the features of the Java language are available in Java EE as well as the APIs.

Java SE 6 was officially released on December 11, 2006. It was developed under JSR 270 and brought many new features as well as continuing the ease of development introduced by Java SE 5 (autoboxing, annotations, generics, enumeration, etc.). Java SE 6 provides new tools for diagnosing, managing, and monitoring applications. It improves the existing JMX API and simplifies execution of scripting languages in the Java Virtual Machine (JVM). This book does not explicitly cover Java SE 6, so you should refer to the extensive Java literature available if you are not comfortable with it. A good starting point would be *Beginning Java™ SE 6 Platform: From Novice to Professional* by Jeff Friesen (Apress, 2007).

Java EE 6 Specifications

Java EE 6 is an umbrella specification defined by JSR 316 that contains 33 other specifications. An application server that aims to be Java EE 6 compliant has to implement all these specifications. Tables 1-1 to 1-5 list them all, grouped by technological domain, with their version and JSR numbers. Some specifications have been pruned, which means that they will possibly be removed from Java EE 7.

Table 1-1. Java Enterprise Edition Specification

Specification	Version	JSR	URL
Java EE	6.0	316	http://jcp.org/en/jsr/detail?id=316
Web Profile	6.0	316	http://jcp.org/en/jsr/detail?id=316
Managed Beans	1.0	316	http://jcp.org/en/jsr/detail?id=316

Table 1-2. *Web Services Specifications*

Specification	Version	JSR	URL	Pruned
JAX-RPC	1.1	101	http://jcp.org/en/jsr/detail?id=101	X
JAX-WS	2.2	224	http://jcp.org/en/jsr/detail?id=224	
JAXB	2.2	222	http://jcp.org/en/jsr/detail?id=222	
JAXM	1.0	67	http://jcp.org/en/jsr/detail?id=67	
StAX	1.0	173	http://jcp.org/en/jsr/detail?id=173	
Web Services	1.2	109	http://jcp.org/en/jsr/detail?id=109	
Web Services Metadata	1.1	181	http://jcp.org/en/jsr/detail?id=181	
JAX-RS	1.1	311	http://jcp.org/en/jsr/detail?id=311	
JAXR	1.1	93	http://jcp.org/en/jsr/detail?id=93	X

Table 1-3. *Web Specifications*

Specification	Version	JSR	URL	Pruned
JSF	2.0	314	http://jcp.org/en/jsr/detail?id=314	
JSP	2.2	245	http://jcp.org/en/jsr/detail?id=245	
Debugging Support for Other Languages	1.0	45	http://jcp.org/en/jsr/detail?id=45	
JSTL (JavaServer Pages Standard Tag Library)	1.2	52	http://jcp.org/en/jsr/detail?id=52	
Servlet	3.0	315	http://jcp.org/en/jsr/detail?id=315	
Expression Language	2.2	245	http://jcp.org/en/jsr/detail?id=245	

Table 1-4. Enterprise Specifications

Specification	Version	JSR	URL	Pruned
EJB	3.1	318	http://jcp.org/en/jsr/detail?id=318	Entity CMP
Interceptors	1.1	318	http://jcp.org/en/jsr/detail?id=318	
JAF	1.1	925	http://jcp.org/en/jsr/detail?id=925	
JavaMail	1.4	919	http://jcp.org/en/jsr/detail?id=919	
JCA	1.6	322	http://jcp.org/en/jsr/detail?id=322	
JMS	1.1	914	http://jcp.org/en/jsr/detail?id=914	
JPA	2.0	317	http://jcp.org/en/jsr/detail?id=317	
JTA	1.1	907	http://jcp.org/en/jsr/detail?id=907	

Table 1-5. Management, Security, and Other Specifications

Specification	Version	JSR	URL	Pruned
JACC	1.1	115	http://jcp.org/en/jsr/detail?id=115	
Bean Validation	1.0	303	http://jcp.org/en/jsr/detail?id=303	
Contexts and Dependency Injection	1.0	299	http://jcp.org/en/jsr/detail?id=299	
Dependency Injection for Java	1.0	330	http://jcp.org/en/jsr/detail?id=330	
Common Annotations	1.1	250	http://jcp.org/en/jsr/detail?id=250	
Java EE Application Deployment	1.2	88	http://jcp.org/en/jsr/detail?id=88	X
Java EE Management	1.1	77	http://jcp.org/en/jsr/detail?id=77	
Java Authentication Service Provider Interface for Containers	1.0	196	http://jcp.org/en/jsr/detail?id=196	

What's New in Java EE 6?

Now that you've seen the internal architecture of Java EE, you might be wondering what the novelties are in Java EE 6. The main goal of this release is to continue the improved ease of development introduced with Java EE 5. In Java EE 5, EJBs, persistent entities, and web services were remodeled to follow a more object-oriented approach (Java classes implementing Java interfaces) and to use annotations as a new way of defining metadata (XML deployment descriptors becoming optional). Java

EE 6 follows this path and applies the same paradigms to the web tier. Today, a JSF managed bean is an annotated Java class with an optional XML descriptor.

Java EE 6 focuses also on bringing simplicity to the platform by introducing profiles, and pruning some outdated technologies. It adds more features to the existing specification (e.g., standardizing singleton session beans) while adding new ones (such as JAX-RS). More than before, Java EE 6 applications are portable across containers with standard JNDI names and a specified embedded EJB container.

Lighter

The Java EE 6 expert group had to face an interesting challenge: how to make the platform lighter while adding more specifications? Today, an application server has to implement 33 specifications in order to be compliant with Java EE 6. A developer has to know thousands of APIs, some not even relevant anymore because they are being pruned. To make the platform more lightweight, the group introduced profiles, pruning, and EJB Lite (a subset of the full EJB features focusing on local interfaces, interceptors, transactions, and security only). EJB Lite is explained in greater detail in Chapter 6.

Pruning

Java EE was first released in 1999, and ever since new specifications have been added at each release (as shown previously in Figure 1-1). This became a problem in terms of size, implementation, and adoption. Some features were not well supported or not widely deployed because they were technologically outdated or other alternatives were made available in the meantime. So the expert group decided to propose the removal of some features through pruning.

Java EE 6 has adopted the pruning process (also known as marked for deletion) already adopted by the Java SE group. It consists of proposing a list of features for possible removal in Java EE 7. Note that none of the proposed removal items will actually be removed from Java EE 6 but could be from Java EE 7. Some features will be replaced by newer specifications (such as entity beans being replaced by JPA), and others will just leave the Java EE 7 umbrella and keep on evolving as individual JSRs (e.g., JSR 88). Here is the list of pruned features:

- *EJB 2.x Entity Beans CMP (part of JSR 318)*: The complex and heavyweight persistent component model of EJB 2.*x* entity beans has been replaced by JPA.

- *JAX-RPC (JSR 101)*: This was the first attempt to model SOAP web services as RPC calls. It has now been replaced by the much easier to use and robust JAX-WS.

- *JAXR (JSR 93)*: JAXR is the API dedicated to communicating with UDDI registries. Because UDDI is not widely used, JAXR would leave Java EE and evolve as a separate JSR.

- *Java EE Application Deployment (JSR 88):* JSR 88 is a specification that tool developers can use for deployment across application servers. This API hasn't gained much vendor support, so it would leave Java EE and evolve as a separate JSR.

Profiles

Profiles are a major new feature in the Java EE 6 environment. Their main goal is to reduce the size of the platform to suit the developer's needs more efficiently. No matter the size or complexity of the application you develop today, you will deploy it in an application server that offers you APIs and services for 33 specifications. A major criticism leveled against Java EE was that it was too large. Profiles are designed precisely to address this issue. As shown in Figure 1-5, profiles are subsets of the platform or supersets of it, and may overlap with the platform or with other profiles.

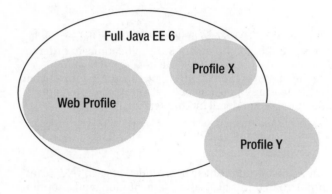

Figure 1-5. Profiles in the Java EE platform

Java EE 6 defines a single profile called the Web Profile. Its aim is to allow developers to create web applications with the appropriate set of technologies. Web Profile 1.0 is specified in a separate JSR and is the first profile of the Java EE 6 platform. Others might be created in the future (you could think of a minimal profile or a portal profile). The Web Profile will evolve at its own pace, and we might end up with a Web Profile 1.1 or 1.2 before Java EE 7 is released. Also, we will see application servers being Web Profile 1.0 compliant as opposed to fully Java EE 6 compliant. Table 1-6 lists the specifications that are included in the Web Profile.

Table 1-6. Web Profile 1.0 Specifications

Specification	Version	JSR	URL
JSF	2.0	314	http://jcp.org/en/jsr/detail?id=314
JSP	2.2	245	http://jcp.org/en/jsr/detail?id=245
JSTL	1.2	52	http://jcp.org/en/jsr/detail?id=52
Servlet	3.0	315	http://jcp.org/en/jsr/detail?id=315
Expression Language	2.2	245	http://jcp.org/en/jsr/detail?id=245
EJB Lite	3.1	318	http://jcp.org/en/jsr/detail?id=318
JPA	2.0	317	http://jcp.org/en/jsr/detail?id=317
JTA	1.1	907	http://jcp.org/en/jsr/detail?id=907
Bean Validation	1.0	303	http://jcp.org/en/jsr/detail?id=303
Managed Beans	1.0	316	http://jcp.org/en/jsr/detail?id=316
Interceptors	1.1	318	http://jcp.org/en/jsr/detail?id=318
Contexts and Dependency Injection	1.0	299	http://jcp.org/en/jsr/detail?id=299
Dependency Injection for Java	1.0	330	http://jcp.org/en/jsr/detail?id=330
Debugging Support for Other Languages	1.0	45	http://jcp.org/en/jsr/detail?id=45
Common Annotations	1.1	250	http://jcp.org/en/jsr/detail?id=250

Easier to Use

Besides making the platform lighter, one aim of Java EE 6 was also to make it easier to use. A direction taken by this version was to apply the ease-of-use paradigm to the web tier. Java EE components need metadata to instruct the container about components' behavior. Before Java EE 5, the only format you could use for metadata was XML (in deployment descriptor file). Since Java EE 5, you can also use annotations directly in your code. With less XML to write, components would be easier to package and deploy. In Java EE 5, the enterprise tier was rearchitected, and the components moved toward POJOs and interfaces. But the web tier didn't benefit from these improvements.

Today in Java EE 6, servlets, JSF managed beans, JSF converters, validators, and renderers are also annotated classes with optional XML deployment descriptors. Listing 1-1 shows a JSF managed bean that turns out to be a Java class with a single annotation. If you are already familiar with JSF, you will be pleased to know that, in most cases, the `faces-config.xml` file `faces-config.xml` file becomes optional (if you don't know JSF, you will learn about it in Chapters 10 through 12).

Listing 1-1. A JSF Managed Bean

```
@ManagedBean
public class BookController {

    @EJB
    private BookEJB bookEJB;

    private Book book = new Book();
    private List<Book> bookList = new ArrayList<Book>();

    public String doCreateBook() {
        book = bookEJB.createBook(book);
        bookList = bookEJB.findBooks();
        return "listBooks.xhtml";
    }

    // Getters, setters
}
```

EJBs also become easier to develop in Java EE 6. As shown in Listing 1-2, if you need to access an EJB locally, a simple annotated class with no interface is enough. EJBs can also be deployed directly in a war file without being previously packaged in a jar file. This makes EJBs the simplest transactional component that can be used from simple web applications to complex enterprise ones.

Listing 1-2. A Stateless EJB

```
@Stateless
public class BookEJB {

    @PersistenceContext(unitName = "chapter01PU")
    private EntityManager em;

    public Book findBookById(Long id) {
        return em.find(Book.class, id);
    }

    public Book createBook(Book book) {
        em.persist(book);
        return book;
    }
}
```

Richer

On one hand, Java EE 6 is becoming lighter by introducing profiles, and on the other it's also becoming richer by adding new specifications and improving existing ones. RESTful web services have been making their way into modern applications. Java EE 6 follows the needs of enterprises by adding the new

JAX-RS specification. As shown in Listing 1-3, a RESTful web service is an annotated Java class that responds to HTTP actions. You will learn more about JAX-RS in Chapter 15.

Listing 1-3. A RESTful Web Service

```
@Path("books")
public class BookResource {

    @PersistenceContext(unitName = "chapter01PU")
    private EntityManager em;

    @GET
    @Produces({"application/xml", "application/json"})
    public List<Book> getAllBooks() {
        Query query = em.createNamedQuery("findAllBooks");
        List<Book> books = query.getResultList();
        return books;
    }
}
```

The new version of the persistence API (JPA 2.0) is improved by adding collections of simple data types (`String`, `Integer`, etc.), pessimistic locking, a richer JPQL syntax, a brand-new Criteria API, and support for a caching API. JPA is discussed in Chapter 2 through Chapter 5.

EJBs are easier to develop (with optional interfaces) and to package (in a war file), but they also have new features, such as the possibility to use asynchronous calls or a richer timer service for scheduling tasks. There is also a new singleton session bean component. As shown in Listing 1-4, a single annotation can turn a Java class into a container-managed singleton (one instance of the component per application). You will learn more about these new features in Chapter 6 through Chapter 9.

Listing 1-4. A Singleton Session Bean

```
@Singleton
public class CacheEJB {

    private Map<Long, Object> cache = new HashMap<Long, Object>();

    public void addToCache(Long id, Object object) {
        if (!cache.containsKey(id))
            cache.put(id, object);
    }

    public Object getFromCache(Long id) {
        if (cache.containsKey(id))
            return cache.get(id);
        else
            return null;
    }
}
```

The presentation tier also gets richer. JSF 2.0 adds support for Ajax and for Facelets (see Chapter 10 through Chapter 12).

More Portable

From its creation, the aim of Java EE was to enable the development of an application and its deployment to any application server without changing the code or the configuration files. This was never as easy as it seemed. Specifications don't cover all the details, and implementations end up providing nonportable solutions. That's what happened with JNDI names, for example. If you deployed an EJB to GlassFish, JBoss, or WebLogic, the JNDI name was different because it wasn't part of the specification, so you had to change your code depending on the application server you used. That particular problem has now been fixed, because Java EE 6 specifies a syntax for JNDI names that is the same across application servers (see Chapter 7).

Another difficult point with EJBs was the ability to test them, or use them in a Java SE environment. Some application servers (such as JBoss) had specific implementations to do it. EJB 3.1 specifies an embedded container that is a standard API for executing EJBs within a Java SE environment (see Chapter 7).

The CD-BookStore Application

Throughout the book, you will see snippets of code dealing with entities, EJBs, JSF pages, JMS listeners, and SOAP or RESTful web services. They all belong to the CD-BookStore application. This application is an e-commerce web site that allows customers to browse a catalog of books and CDs on sale. The application has external interactions with a bank system to validate credit card numbers. The use case diagram in Figure 1-6 describes the system's actors and functionalities.

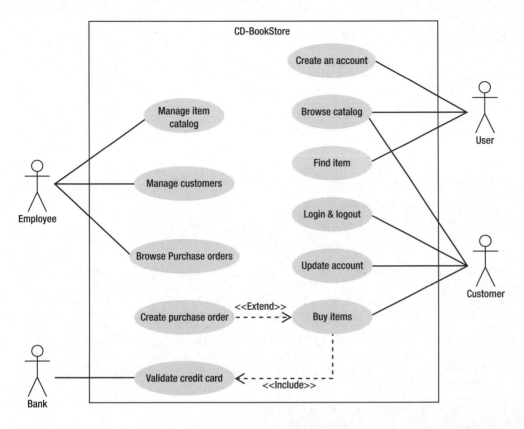

Figure 1-6. Use case diagram of the CD-BookStore application

The actors interacting with the system described in Figure 1-6 are:

- *Employees* of the company who need to manage both the catalog of items and the customers' details. They can also browse the purchase orders.

- *Users* who are anonymous persons visiting the web site and consulting the catalog of books and CDs. If they want to buy an item, they need to create an account to become customers.

- *Customers* who can browse the catalog, update their account details, and buy items online.

- The *external bank* to which the system delegates credit card validations.

■ **Note** You can download the code examples of this book from the Apress web site (http://www.apress.com) or straight from the Subversion repository at http://beginningee6.kenai.com.

Setting Up Your Environment

This book shows you lots of code, and most of the chapters have a "Putting It All Together" section. These sections provide step-by-step examples showing you how to develop, compile, deploy, execute, and unit test a component. To run these examples, you need to install the required software:

- JDK 1.6

- Maven 2

- JUnit 4

- Derby 10.6 database (a.k.a. Java DB)

- GlassFish v3.0.1 application server

JDK 1.6

Essential for the development and the execution of the examples in the book is the Java Development Kit (JDK). It includes several tools such as a compiler (`javac`), a virtual machine, a documentation generator (`javadoc`), monitoring tools (Visual VM), and so on. To install the JDK 1.6, go to the official Sun web site (`http://java.sun.com/javase/downloads`), select the appropriate platform and language, and download the distribution.

   If you are running on Windows (Linux and OS X are not supported in this book but the code should be portable), double-click the `jdk-6u20-windows-i586.exe` file. The first screen invites you to accept the license of the software, and then the second screen, shown in Figure 1-7, lists the modules of the JDK you can choose to install (JDK, JRE, Derby database, sources).

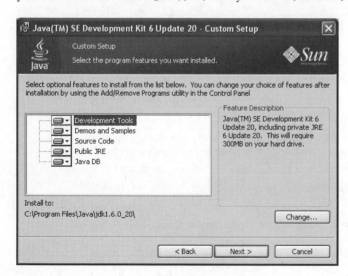

Figure 1-7. Setting up the JDK installation

Once the installation is complete, it is necessary to set the JAVA_HOME variable and the %JAVA_HOME%\bin directory to the PATH variable. Check that Java is recognized by your system by entering java -version (see Figure 1-8).

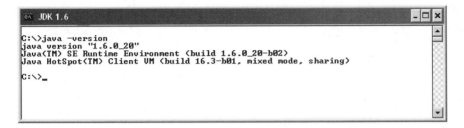

Figure 1-8. Displaying the JDK version

Maven 2

To reflect what you'll find in the real development world, I've decided to use Apache Maven (http://maven.apache.org) to build the examples of this book. The purpose of this book is not to explain Maven. You will find plenty of resources for Maven on the Internet or in bookstores. But I will introduce some elements so that you can easily understand and use the examples.

A Bit of History

Building a Java EE application requires different operations:

- Generating code and resources

- Compiling Java classes and test classes

- Packaging the code in an archive (jar, ear, war, etc.) with potentially external jar libraries

Doing these tasks manually can be time-consuming and can generate errors. Thus, development teams have looked for ways of automating these tasks.

In 2000, Java developers started to use Apache Ant (http://ant.apache.org), allowing them to create scripts for building applications. Ant itself is written in Java and offers a range of commands that, unlike a Unix Make tool, are portable across platforms. Development teams started to create their own scripts to fulfill their needs. Yet Ant was quickly pushed to its limits when projects had to start encompassing complex heterogeneous systems. Companies faced difficulties to industrialize their build system. There was no real tool to easily reuse a build script between different projects (copy/paste was the only way).

In 2002, Apache Maven was born, and this project not only addressed these issues, but also went beyond being a simple building tool. Maven offers projects a building solution, shared libraries, and a plug-in platform, allowing you to do quality control, documentation, teamwork, and so forth. Based on the "convention over configuration" principle, Maven brings a standard project description and a number of conventions such as a standard directory structure (as shown in Figure 1-9). With an extensible architecture based on plug-ins (a.k.a. mojos), Maven can offer many different services.

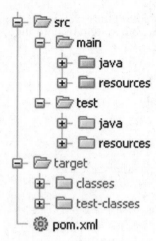

Figure 1-9. Standard Maven directory structure

Project Descriptor

Maven is based on the fact that a majority of Java and Java EE projects face similar needs when building applications. A Maven project needs to follow standards as well as define specific features in a project descriptor, or Project Object Model (POM). The POM is an XML file (`pom.xml`) placed at the root of the project. As shown in Listing 1-5, the minimum required information to describe the identity of the project is the `groupId`, the `artifactId`, the version, and the packaging type.

Listing 1-5. Minimal pom.xml

```
<?xml version="1.0" encoding="UTF-8"?>
<project xmlns="http://maven.apache.org/POM/4.0.0" ↪
        xmlns:xsi="http://www.w3.org/2001/XMLSchema-instance"↪
        xsi:schemaLocation="http://maven.apache.org/POM/4.0.0 ↪
        http://maven.apache.org/xsd/maven-4.0.0.xsd">

    <modelVersion>4.0.0</modelVersion>
    <groupId>com.apress.javaee6</groupId>
    <artifactId>chapter01</artifactId>
    <version>2.0-SNAPSHOT</version>
    <packaging>jar</packaging>
</project>
```

A project is often divided into different artifacts. These artifacts are then grouped under the same `groupId` (similar to packages in Java) and uniquely identified by the `artifactId`. Packaging allows Maven to produce the artifact following a standard format (jar, war, ear, etc.). Finally, the version allows identifying an artifact during its lifetime (version 1.1, 1.2, 1.2.1, etc.). Maven imposes versioning so a team can manage the life of its project development. Maven also introduces the concept of SNAPSHOT versions (the version number ends with the string -SNAPSHOT) to identify an artifact when it's being developed.

The POM defines much more information about your project. Some is purely descriptive (name, description, etc.); other information concerns the application execution such as the list of external libraries used, and so on. Finally, the pom.xml defines environmental information to build the project (versioning tool, continuous integration server, artifacts repositories) and any other specific process to build your project.

Managing Artifacts

Maven goes beyond building artifacts; it also offers a genuine approach to archive and share these artifacts. Maven uses a local repository on your hard drive (by default in %USER_HOME%\.m2\repository) where it stores all the artifacts that the project's descriptor manipulates. The local repository (see Figure 1-10) is filled either by the local developer's artifacts (e.g., myProject-1.1.jar) or by external ones (e.g., glassfish-3.0.1.jar) that Maven downloads from remote repositories. By default, Maven uses a main repository at http://repo1.maven.org/maven2 to download the missing artifacts.

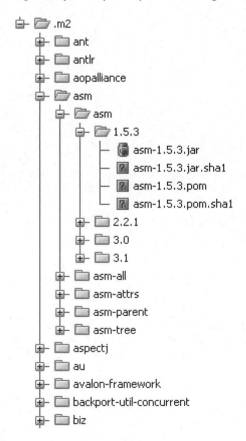

Figure 1-10. Example of a local repository

23

A Maven project defines in a declarative way its dependencies in the POM (`groupId`, `artifactId`, `version`, type) as shown in Listing 1-6. If necessary, Maven will download them to the local repository from remote repositories. Moreover, using the POM descriptors of these external artifacts, Maven will also download the artifacts they need and so on. Therefore, the development team doesn't have to manually deal with project dependencies. The necessary libraries are added automatically by Maven.

Listing 1-6. Dependencies in the `pom.xml`

```
...
<dependencies>
    <dependency>
        <groupId>org.eclipse.persistence</groupId>
        <artifactId>javax.persistence</artifactId>
        <version>2.0.0</version>
        <scope><provided></scope>
    </dependency>
    <dependency>
        <groupId>org.glassfish</groupId>
        <artifactId>javax.ejb</artifactId>
        <version>3.0.1</version>
        <scope>provided</scope>
    </dependency>
</dependencies>
...
```

Dependencies may have limited visibility (called scope):

- `test`: The library is used to compile and run test classes but is not packaged in the produced artifact.

- `provided`: The library is provided by the environment (persistence provider, application server, etc.) and is only used to compile the code.

- `compile`: The library is necessary for compilation and execution.

- `runtime`: The library is only required for execution but is excluded from the compilation (e.g., JSF components, JSTL tag libraries).

Project Modularity

To address project modularity, Maven provides a mechanism based on modules. Each module is a Maven project in its own right. Maven is able to build a project with different modules by calculating the dependencies they have between them (see Figure 1-11). To facilitate reusing common parameters, POM descriptors can inherit from parent POM projects.

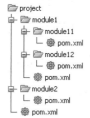

Figure 1-11. A project and its modules

Plug-ins and Life Cycle

Maven uses a life cycle made of several phases (see Figure 1-12): it cleans the resources, validates the project, generates any needed sources, compiles Java classes, runs test classes, packages the project, and installs it to the local repository. This life cycle is the vertebral column on which Maven plug-ins (a.k.a. mojos) hang. Depending on the type of project you build, the associated mojos can be different (a mojo to compile, another to test, another to build, etc.). In the project description, you can link new plug-ins to a life-cycle phase, change the configuration of a plug-in, and so on. For example, when you build a web service client, you might add a mojo that generates web service artifacts during the generate-sources phase.

Figure 1-12. Project life cycle

Installation

The examples of this book have been developed with Apache Maven 2.2.1. Once you have installed JDK 1.6, make sure the JAVA_HOME environment variable is set. Then download Maven from http://maven.apache.org/, unzip the file on your hard drive, and add the apache-maven\bin directory to your PATH variable.

Once you've done this, open a DOS command line and enter mvn -version to validate your installation. Maven should print its version and the JDK version as shown in Figure 1-13.

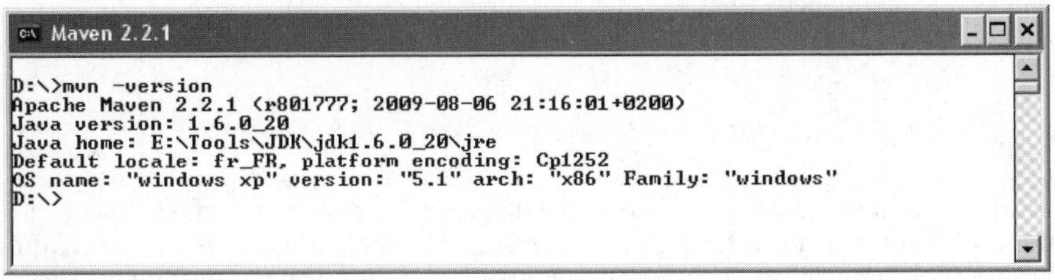

Figure 1-13. Maven displaying its version

Be aware that Maven needs Internet access so it can download plug-ins and project dependencies from the main repository. If you are behind a proxy, see the documentation to configure your settings.

Usage

Here are some commands that you will be using to run the examples in the book. They all invoke a different phase of the project life cycle (clean, compile, install, etc.) and use the pom.xml to dd libraries, customize the compilation, or extend some behaviors with plug-ins:

- mvn clean: Deletes all generated files (compiled classes, generated code, artifacts, etc.)

- mvn compile: Compiles the main Java classes

- mvn test-compile: Compiles the test classes

- mvn test: Compiles the test classes and executes the tests

- mvn package: Compiles and executes the tests and packages in an archive

- mvn install: Builds and installs the artifacts in your local repository

- mvn clean install: Cleans and installs (Note that you can add several commands separated by a space.)

■ **Note** Maven allows you to compile, run, and package the examples of this book. But, to develop the code, you need an integrated development environment (IDE). I use IntelliJ IDEA from JetBrains, and you will see some screenshots of it throughout these pages. But you can use any IDE you want because this book only relies on Maven, not on specific IntelliJ IDEA features.

JUnit 4

JUnit is an open source framework to write and run repeatable tests. JUnit features include

- Assertions for testing expected results

- Fixtures for sharing common test data

- Runners for running tests

JUnit is the de facto standard unit testing library for the Java language, and it stands in a single jar file that you can download from `http://www.junit.org/` (or use Maven dependency management to do it). The library contains a complete API to help you write your unit tests and a tool to execute them. Unit tests help your code to be more robust, bug free, and reliable.

A Bit of History

JUnit was originally written by Erich Gamma and Kent Beck in 1998. It was inspired by Smalltalk's SUnit test framework, also written by Kent Beck. It quickly became one of the most popular frameworks in the Java world.

Bringing the benefits of unit testing to a wide range of languages, JUnit has inspired a family of *x*Unit tools like nUnit (.NET), pyUnit (Python), CppUnit (C++), dUnit (Delphi), and others. JUnit took an important place in achieving test-driven development (TDD).

How Does It Work?

Since JUnit 4, writing unit tests is simplified by using annotations, static import, and other Java features. Compared to the previous versions of JUnit, it provides a simpler, richer, and easier testing model, as well as introducing more flexible initialization, cleanup, timeouts, and parameterized test cases.

Let's see some of the JUnit features through a simple example. Listing 1-7 represents a `Customer` POJO. It has some attributes, including a date of birth, constructors, getters, and setters.

Listing 1-7. A Customer Class

```
public class Customer {
  private Long id;
  private String firstName;
  private String lastName;
  private String email;
```

```
  private String phoneNumber;
  private Date dateOfBirth;
  private Date creationDate;

  // Constructors, getters, setters
}
```

The CustomerHelper class, shown in Listing 1-8, provides a utility method to calculate the age of a given customer (calculateAge()).

Listing 1-8. The CustomerHelper Class

```
public class CustomerHelper {
  private int ageCalcResult;
  private Customer customer;

  public void calculateAge() {
    Date dateOfBirth = customer.getDateOfBirth();
    Calendar birth = new GregorianCalendar();
    birth.setTime(dateOfBirth);
    Calendar now = new GregorianCalendar(2001, 1, 1);
    ageCalcResult = now.get(Calendar.YEAR) - birth.get(Calendar.YEAR);
  }

  // Not implemented yet
  public Date getNextBirthDay() {
    return null;
  }

  public void clear() {
    ageCalcResult=0;
    customer=null;
  }

  // Getters, setters
}
```

The calculateAge() method uses the dateOfBirth attribute to return the customer's age. The clear() method resets the CustomerHelper state, and the getNextBirthDay() method is not implemented yet. This helper class has some flaws: it looks like there is a bug in the age calculation. To test the calculateAge() method, we could use the JUnit class CustomerHelperTest described in Listing 1-9.

Listing 1-9. A Test Class for CustomerHelper

```
import org.junit.Before;
import org.junit.Ignore;
import org.junit.Test;

import static org.junit.Assert.*;
```

```java
public class CustomerHelperTest {

  private static CustomerHelper customerHelper = new CustomerHelper();

  @Before
  public void clearCustomerHelper() {
    customerHelper.clear();
  }

  @Test
  public void notNegative() {
    Customer customer = new Customer();
    customer.setDateOfBirth(new GregorianCalendar(1975, 5, 27).getTime());

    customerHelper.setCustomer(customer);
    customerHelper.calculateAge();

    int calculatedAge = customerHelper.getAgeCalcResult();

    assert calculatedAge >= 0;
  }

  @Test
  public void expectedValue() {
    int expectedAge = 33;

    Calendar birth = new GregorianCalendar();
    birth.roll(Calendar.YEAR, expectedAge * (-1));
    birth.roll(Calendar.DAY_OF_YEAR, -1);

    Customer customer = new Customer();
    customer.setDateOfBirth(birth.getTime());

    customerHelper.setCustomer(customer);
    customerHelper.calculateAge();

    assertTrue(customerHelper.getAgeCalcResult() == expectedAge);
  }

  @Test(expected = NullPointerException.class)
  public void emptyCustomer() {
    Customer customer = new Customer();

    customerHelper.setCustomer(customer);
    customerHelper.calculateAge();

    assertEquals(customerHelper.getAgeCalcResult(), -1);
  }
```

```
@Ignore("not ready yet")
@Test
public void nextBirthDay() {
  // some work to do
  }
}
```

The test class in Listing 1-9 contains four test methods. The `expectedValue()` method will fail because there is a bug in the `CustomerHelper` age calculation. The `nextBirthDay()` method is ignored because it is not yet implemented. The two other test methods will succeed. `emptyCustomer()` expects the method to throw a `NullPointerException`.

Test Methods

In JUnit 4, test classes do not have to extend anything. To be executed as a test case, a JUnit class needs at least one method annotated with `@Test`. If you write a class without at least one `@Test` method, you will get an error when trying to execute it (`java.lang.Exception: No runnable methods`).

A test method must use the `@Test` annotation, return `void`, and take no parameters. This is controlled at runtime and throws an exception if not respected. The `@Test` annotation supports the optional `expected` parameter, which declares that a test method should throw an exception. If it doesn't or if it throws a different exception than the one declared, the test fails. In this example, trying to calculate the age of an empty `customer` object should throw a `NullPointerException`.

In Listing 1-9, the `nextBirthDay()` method is not implemented. However, you don't want the test to fail; you just want to ignore it. You can add the `@Ignore` annotation in front or after `@Test`. Test runners will report the number of ignored tests, along with the number of tests that succeeded and failed. Note that `@Ignore` takes an optional parameter (a `String`) in case you want to record why a test is being ignored.

Assert Methods

Test cases must assert that objects conform to an expected result. For that, JUnit has an `Assert` class that contains several methods. In order to use it, you can either use the prefixed syntax (e.g., `Assert.assertEquals()`) or import statically the `Assert` class (shown in Listing 1-9). As you can see in the `notNegative()` method, you can also use the Java `assert` keyword.

Fixtures

Fixtures are methods to initialize and release any common object during tests. JUnit uses `@Before` and `@After` annotations to execute code before or after each test. These methods can be given any name (`clearCustomerHelper()` in this example), and you can have multiple methods in one test class. JUnit uses `@BeforeClass` and `@AfterClass` annotations to execute specific code only once per class. These methods must be unique and static. `@BeforeClass` and `@AfterClass` can be very useful if you need to allocate and release expensive resources.

Launching JUnit

To run the JUnit launcher, you must add the JUnit jar file to your **CLASSPATH** variable (or add a Maven dependency). After that, you can run your tests through the Java launcher as shown in the following code. Note that, when using **assert**, you must specify the **–ea** parameter; if you don't, assertions are ignored.

```
java -ea org.junit.runner.JUnitCore com.apress.javaee6.CustomerHelperTest
```

The preceding command will provide the following result:

```
JUnit version 4.8
..E.I
Time: 0.016
There was 1 failure:
1) expectedValue(com.apress.javaee6.CustomerHelperTest)
java.lang.AssertionError: at CustomerHelperTest.expectedValue(CustomerHelperTest.java:52)

FAILURES!!!
Tests run: 3, Failures: 1
```

The first displayed information is the JUnit version number (4.8 in this case). Then JUnit gives the number of executed tests (here, three) and the number of failures (one in this example). The letter **I** indicates that a test has been ignored.

JUnit Integration

JUnit is currently very well integrated with most IDEs (IntelliJ IDEA, Eclipse, NetBeans, etc.). When working with these IDEs, in most cases, JUnit highlights in green to indicate successful tests and in red to indicate failures. Most IDEs also provide facilities to create test classes.

JUnit is also integrated to Maven through the Surefire plug-in used during the test phase of the build life cycle. It executes the JUnit test classes of an application and generates reports in XML and text file formats. The following Maven command runs the JUnit tests through the plug-in:

```
mvn test
```

Derby 10.6

Initially called Cloudscape, the Derby database developed in Java was given to the Apache foundation by IBM and became open source. Sun Microsystems has released its own distribution called JavaDB. Of small footprint (2MB), Derby is a fully functional relational database, supporting transactions, that can easily be embedded in any Java-based solution.

Derby provides two different modes: embedded and network server. The embedded mode refers to Derby being started by a simple single-user Java application. With this option, Derby runs in the same JVM as the application. In this book, I will use this mode during unit testing. The network server mode refers to Derby being started as a separate process and providing multiuser connectivity. I will use this mode throughout the book when running applications.

Installation

Installing Derby is very easy; in fact, you may find it is already installed because it is bundled with the JDK 1.6. During the installation of JDK 1.6 (refer back to Figure 1-7), the wizard proposed you install Java DB. And by default it does. If you don't have it installed, you can download the binaries from http://db.apache.org.

Once installed, set the DERBY_HOME variable to the path where you've installed it, and add %DERBY_HOME%\bin to your PATH variable. Start the Derby network server by launching the %DERBY_HOME%\bin\startNetworkServer.bat script. Derby displays some information to the console such as the port number it listens to (1527 by default).

Derby comes with several utilities, one of them being sysinfo. Open a DOS command line, enter sysinfo, and you should see information about your Java and Derby environment, as shown in Figure 1-14.

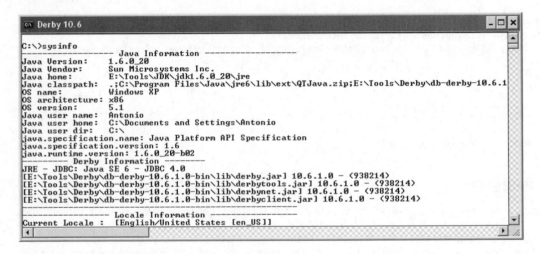

Figure 1-14. sysinfo output after installing Derby

Usage

Derby provides several tools (located under the bin subdirectory) to interact with the database. The simplest are probably ij, which allows you to enter SQL commands at a command prompt, and dblook, which lets you view all or part of a database's data definition language (DDL).

Make sure you've started the Derby network server, and type the command ij to enter the command prompt and run interactive queries against a Derby database. Then, enter the following commands to create a database and a table, insert data into the table, and query it:

```
ij> connect 'jdbc:derby://localhost:1527/Chapter01DB;create=true';
```

This connects to the Chapter01DB database. Because it doesn't exist already, the create=true parameter forces its creation.

```
ij> create table customer (custId int primary key, firstname varchar(20),
 lastname varchar(20));
```

This creates a **customer** table with a primary key column and two **varchar(20)** columns for the first name and last name. You can display the description of the table by entering the following command:

```
ij> describe customer;
COLUMN_NAME     |TYPE_NAME     |DEC&    |NUM&    |COLUM&   |COLUMN_DEF   |CHAR_OCTE&   |IS_NULL&
--------------------------------------------------------------------------------------------------
CUSTID          |INTEGER       |0       |10      |10       |NULL         |NULL         |NO
FIRSTNAME       |VARCHAR       |NULL    |NULL    |20       |NULL         |40           |YES
LASTNAME        |VARCHAR       |NULL    |NULL    |20       |NULL         |40           |YES
```

Now that the table is created, you can add data using the **insert** SQL statement as follows:

```
ij> insert into customer values (1, 'Fred', 'Chene');
ij> insert into customer values (2, 'Sylvain', 'Verin');
ij> insert into customer values (3, 'Robin', 'Riou');
```

You can then use all the power of the SQL **select** statement to retrieve, order, or aggregate data.

```
ij> select count(*) from customer;
1
-----------
3

ij> select * from customer where custid=3;
CUSTID |FIRSTNAME |LASTNAME
-------------------------------------------------------
3      |Robin     |Riou
ij> exit;
```

To get the DDL of the created table, you can exit **ij** and run **dblook** against the **Chapter01DB** database.

```
C:\> dblook -d 'jdbc:derby://localhost:1527/Chapter01DB'
-- Source database is: Chapter01DB
-- Connection URL is: jdbc:derby://localhost:1527/Chapter01DB
-- appendLogs: false
-- ------------------------------------------------
-- DDL Statements for tables
-- ------------------------------------------------
CREATE TABLE "APP"."CUSTOMER" ("CUSTID" INTEGER NOT NULL, "FIRSTNAME" ↪
VARCHAR(20), "LASTNAME" VARCHAR(20));
-- ------------------------------------------------
-- DDL Statements for keys
-- ------------------------------------------------
-- primary/unique
ALTER TABLE "APP"."CUSTOMER" ADD CONSTRAINT "SQL0903154616250" PRIMARY KEY ("CUSTID");
```

GlassFish v3.0.1

While a fairly new application server, GlassFish is already used by a large number of developers and corporations. Not only is it the Reference Implementation (RI) for the Java EE technology, it is also what you get when downloading the Java EE SDK. You can also deploy critical production applications on the GlassFish application server. Besides being a product, GlassFish is also a community that has gathered around the open source code and lives on `http://glassfish.org`. The community is quite responsive on mailing lists and forums.

A Bit of History

The origins of GlassFish take us back to the early Tomcat days when Sun and the JServ group donated this technology to Apache. Ever since, Sun has been reusing Tomcat in its various products. In 2005, Sun created the GlassFish project. The initial main goal was to produce a fully certified Java EE application server. GlassFish version 1.0 shipped in May 2006. At its core, the web container part of GlassFish has a lot of Tomcat heritage (in fact, an application running on Tomcat should run unmodified on GlassFish).

GlassFish v2 was released in September 2007 and has since had several updates. This is the most widely deployed version to date. GlassFish tends to be pretty good at maintaining the same user experience across major releases, not breaking code nor changing developers' habits. Also, there is no quality difference between the "community" and "supported" versions of GlassFish. While paying customers have access to patches and additional monitoring tools (GlassFish Enterprise Manager), the open source version available from `http://glassfish.org` and the supported version available from `http://www.oracle.com/goto/glassfish` have undergone the same amount of testing, making it easy to switch to a supported version at any time in the project cycle.

In March 2010, soon after the acquisition of Sun Microsystems by Oracle, a roadmap for the community was published with version 3.0.1, and 3.1, 3.2 and 4.0 planned for the next few years and clustering being brought back into the 3.1 version (it was not initially in the 3.0 release, which had full Java EE 6 support and modularity as higher priorities).

For the purpose of this book, I'll be using GlassFish Open Source Edition 3.0.1 which shipped in June 2010 and the first release of the "Oracle era." The main goals of GlassFish 3 are modularization of the core features with the introduction of an OSGi-based kernel and full support for Java EE 6. A number of developer-friendly features such as fast startup time and session preservation across redeployments are also part of this release.

■ **Note** The GlassFish team has put a tremendous effort toward having rich and up-to-date documentation, making available many different guides: Quick Start Guide, Installation Guide, Administration Guide, Administration Reference, Application Deployment Guide, Developer's Guide, and more. Check them out at `http://glassfish.org/docs`. Also check the FAQs, how-tos, and the GlassFish forum for more information.

GlassFish v3 Architecture

As an application programmer (and not one of the GlassFish developers), you do not need to understand the internal architecture of GlassFish v3, but you might be interested in the main architectural choices and guiding principles. Being built on a modular kernel powered by OSGi, GlassFish ships and runs straight on top of the Apache Felix implementation. It also runs with Equinox or Knopflerfish OSGi runtimes. HK2 (the Hundred-Kilobyte Kernel) abstracts the OSGi module system to provide components, which can also be viewed as services. Such services can be discovered and injected at runtime. OSGi is not exposed to Java EE developers for the time being but it is quite possible to inject OSGi Declarative Services into Java EE components using the standard @Resource annotation.

■ **Note** OSGi is a standard for dynamic component management and discovery. Applications or components can be remotely installed, started, stopped, updated, and uninstalled without requiring a reboot. Components can also detect the addition or removal of new services dynamically and adapt accordingly. Apache Felix, Equinox, and Knopflerfish are OSGi implementations.

This modularity and extensibility is how GlassFish v3 can grow from a simple web server listening to administrative commands to a more capable runtime by simply deploying artifacts such as war files (a web container is loaded and started, and the application deployed) or EJB jar files (which will dynamically load and start the EJB container). Additionally, the bare-bones server starts in just a few seconds (less than 5 seconds on reasonably modern hardware), and you only pay for what you use in terms of startup time and memory consumption. Starting the web container on the fly takes about 3 more seconds, and deployments are often less than 1 second. This all makes GlassFish v3 a very developer-friendly environment.

No matter how many modules GlassFish v3 dynamically loads, the administration console, the command-line interface, and the centralized configuration file are all extensible, and each remains unique. Also worth mentioning is the Grizzly framework, which started out as a nonblocking, I/O-based HTTP server to become one of the key elements in GlassFish as shown in Figure 1-15.

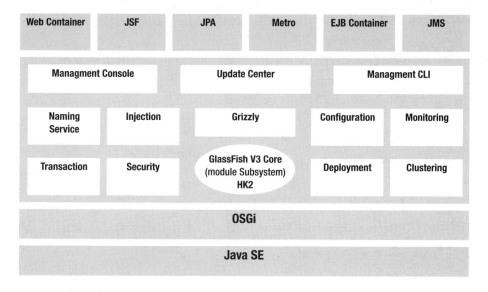

Figure 1-15. GlassFish v3 architecture

Update Center

Once you're given a modular application server, you can start to mix and match various modules to build your own environment just like you would with IDEs and Linux distributions, or similar to the way Firefox lets you manage your extensions. The GlassFish Update Center is a set of graphical and command-line tools to manage your runtime. The technology behind this is the Image Packaging System (IPS, also known as **pkg**), which is what the OpenSolaris project uses for package management. GlassFish v3 is available in two distributions: Web Profile (defined by the Java EE 6 Web Profile) and Full Profile. These distributions each ship with a specific set of modules, the web profile being a strict subset of the full profile. Beyond this default combination, a user can connect to one or more repositories to update the existing features (such as move from the Web Profile to the Full Java EE 6 Profile), add new features (Grails support, a JDBC driver, a portlet container, etc.) or even add new third-party applications. In a corporate environment, you can set up your own repository and use the update center **pkg** command-line tool to provision and bootstrap the installation of GlassFish-based software.

In practice, with GlassFish v3, the update center can be accessed via the admin console, the graphical client available at `%GLASSFISH_HOME%\bin\updatetool`, or the **pkg** command line. All three allow you to list, add, and remove components available from a set of multiple repositories (although, in the case of the admin console, a number of operations are not available since the application server should not be running at the time of install). In the case of **pkg** (also located in `%GLASSFISH_HOME%\bin`), the most common commands are `pkg list`, `pkg install`, `pkg uninstall`, and `pkg image-update`.

GlassFish Subprojects

There are many different parts to the GlassFish application server, so the project was broken up into subprojects. This helps you to further understand not only the different pieces, but also the adoption of individual features outside of the GlassFish environment, in stand-alone mode or within another container. Figure 1-16 shows a high-level architecture of the functional parts of the application server.

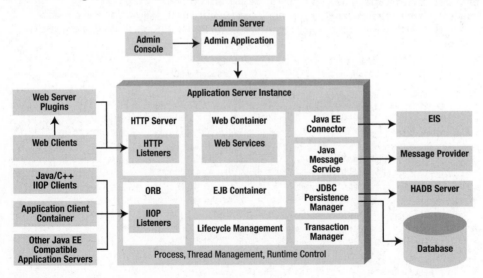

Figure 1-16. *Functional parts of GlassFish*

OpenMQ, for instance, is a production-quality open source implementation of JMS. Although it is often used stand-alone for message-oriented architectures, OpenMQ can also be integrated in various ways with GlassFish (in-process, out-of-process, or remote). The administration of OpenMQ can be done via the GlassFish admin console or the `asadmin` command-line interface (see the upcoming "The asadmin CLI" section). The community web site is at `http://openmq.dev.java.net`.

Metro is the one-stop shop for web services. This complete stack builds on the JAX-WS development paradigm and augments it with advanced features such as trusted, end-to-end security; optimized transport (MTOM, FastInfoset); reliable messaging; and transactional behavior for SOAP web services. Such quality of service (QoS) for web services is based on standards (OASIS, W3C), is expressed in the form of policies, and does not require the use of a new API in addition to JAX-WS. Metro is also regularly tested with Microsoft against .NET implementations to ensure interoperability between the two technologies. The community web site is at `http://metro.dev.java.net`.

Mojarra is the name of the JSF 1.2 and 2.0 implementation in GlassFish and is available at `http://mojarra.dev.java.net`. It is certainly one of the most often reused projects by other application servers.

Jersey is the production-quality Reference Implementation for the new JAX-RS specification. Both the specification and the implementation were the early comers to Java EE 6 and GlassFish. In fact, Jersey 1.0 has been available in the update center for GlassFish v2 and v3 since it was released in 2008. Jersey is also used internally by GlassFish v3 to offer a RESTful administration API which complements the existing tools described in the next section. The Jersey community web site is at `http://jersey.dev.java.net`.

Administration

Obviously, being a compliant application server means that GlassFish implements 100 percent of the Java EE 6 specifications, but it also has additional features that make it a polished product, such as its administrative capabilities, be it through the admin console or via a powerful `asadmin` command-line interface. Almost all the configuration is stored in a file called `domain.xml` (located in `domains\domain1\config`), which can be useful for troubleshooting, but this file should not be edited by hand; instead, one of these two administration tools should be used. Both of them rely on the extensive JMX instrumentation provided by GlassFish.

Admin Console

The admin console is a browser-based administration user interface (see Figure 1-17) for the application server. This tool is for both administrators and developers. It provides graphical representation of the objects under management, enhanced log file viewing, system status, and monitoring data. At a minimum, the console manages the creation and modification of configurations (JVM tuning, log level, pool and cache tuning, etc.), JDBC, JNDI, JavaMail, JMS, and connector resources, as well as applications (deployment). At any time in the navigation of the tool, contextual help is available via the top-right Help button. With a default installation, the admin console is available upon GlassFish startup at `http://localhost:4848`. Starting with GlassFish v3, an anonymous user can be set up at install time, removing the need to log in. Previous versions of GlassFish used `admin` as the user name and `adminadmin` as the default password. Note that the admin console is loaded in the application server on the first hit to the URL above, thus illustrating the load-on-demand feature of GlassFish v3.

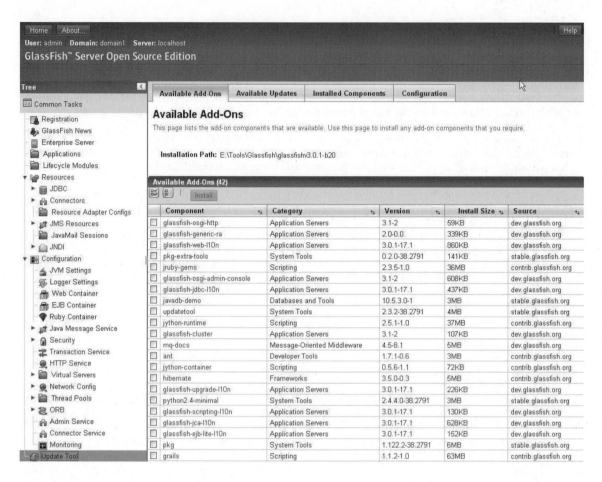

Figure 1-17. Web administration console

The asadmin CLI

The `asadmin` command-line interface (CLI) is quite powerful and often what people use in production, as it can be scripted to create instances and resources, deploy applications, and provide monitoring data on a running system. The command is located under the `bin` subdirectory of GlassFish and can manage multiple local or remote application server domains. `asadmin` offers several hundred commands, but you should get away with using only a small subset of these. If you are curious about the commands, try `asadmin help`. Useful commands in a simple developer profile include `asadmin start-domain`, `asadmin stop-domain`, `asadmin deploy`, `asadmin deploydir`, and `asadmin undeploy`. In case of a typo, `asadmin` will give you a choice of the closest matching command. Try `asadmin resource`, for instance, and `asadmin` will give you the related commands as shown in Figure 1-18.

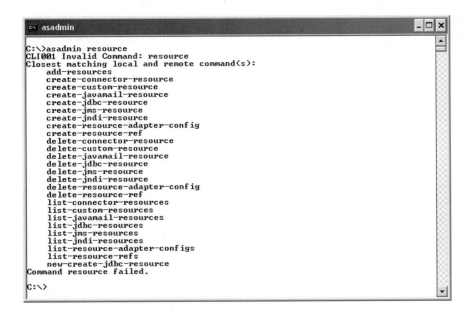

Figure 1-18. asadmin CLI

Installing GlassFish

GlassFish can be downloaded via multiple distribution mechanisms. The most obvious choices are to get it from `http://glassfish.org`, or with the Java EE SDK (it also ships with the NetBeans IDE 6.9 and above as well as with the Eclipse Tools Bundle for GlassFish available from http://download.java.net/glassfish/eclipse). I'll document here how to download and install GlassFish from the community web site.

Go to the main download page, `http://glassfish.org/downloads`, and select the download link for "GlassFish Open Source Edition 3.0.1". You are then offered the choice of both a graphical installer download and a simple Zip download. Each option further offers the choice between the Java EE 6 Full Profile and Web Profile. I will document here the installer version of the Full Profile. Note that GlassFish is available for Windows, Linux, Solaris, and Mac OS X. Executing the shell will start the graphical installer, which will:

- Ask you to agree to the license.

- Request an install location.

- Let you configure an admin username and password (or default to an anonymous user).

- Let you configure HTTP and admin ports (while checking that they're not already in use).

- Install and enable the update tool (**pkg** and **updatetool** clients). With the Zip installer, the updatetool is not installed by default and will be installed from the network on the first run.

39

It will then decompress a simple preconfigured GlassFish install with default settings: admin port is 4848, HTTP port is 8080, and no explicit admin user configured. Once properly installed, GlassFish can be started with the `asadmin` command line (see Figure 1-19).

```
asadmin start-domain
```

Figure 1-19. Starting GlassFish

You can then go to the admin console (shown earlier in Figure 1-17) at `http://localhost:4848` or to the default welcome page at `http://localhost:8080`.

■ **Tip** If you only have one domain, you can omit the default domain name and start GlassFish with only `asadmin` `start-domain`. If you'd like to have the log file appear inline rather than checking the content of the dedicated log file (`domains/domain1/logs/server.log`), you can use `asadmin` `start-domain` `--verbose`.

There are many more things that GlassFish has to offer; I'll show you some of them in this book, but I'll leave it to you to explore its support for session preservation across redeployments, incremental deployment in NetBeans and Eclipse, advanced OSGi hybrid application support, diagnostic services, RESTful management, monitoring, and the various security configurations.

Summary

When a company develops a Java application and needs to add enterprise features such as transaction management, security, concurrency, or messaging, Java EE is an attractive choice. It is standard, components are deployed to different containers, which gives you many services, and it works with various protocols. Java EE 6 follows the path of its previous version by adding ease of use to the web tier. This version of the platform is lighter (thanks to pruning, profiles, and EJB Lite), easier to use (no need for interfaces on EJBs or annotations on the web tier), richer (it includes new specifications and new features), and more portable (it includes standardized embedded EJB container and allows for JNDI names).

In the second part of this chapter, I concentrated on setting up the development environment. The book has several snippets of code and "Putting It All Together" sections. You need several tools and frameworks to compile, deploy, run, and test the code: JDK 1.6, Maven 2, JUnit 4, Derby 10.6, and GlassFish v3.0.1.

In this chapter, I gave you a very quick overview of Java EE 6. The remaining chapters will be dedicated to a closer study of the Java EE 6 specifications.

CHAPTER 2

■ ■ ■

Java Persistence

Applications are made up of business logic, interaction with other systems, user interfaces . . . and persistence. Most of the data that our applications manipulate has to be stored in databases, retrieved, and analyzed. Databases are important: they store business data, act as a central point between applications, and process data through triggers or stored procedures. Persistent data is everywhere, and most of the time it uses relational databases as the underlying persistence engine. *Relational databases* store data in tables made of rows and columns. Data is identified by *primary keys*, which are special columns with uniqueness constraints and, sometimes, indexes. The relationships between tables use *foreign keys* and *join tables* with integrity constraints.

All this vocabulary is completely unknown in an object-oriented language such as Java. In Java, we manipulate objects that are instances of classes. Objects inherit from others, have references to collections of other objects, and sometimes point to themselves in a recursive manner. We have concrete classes, abstract classes, interfaces, enumerations, annotations, methods, attributes, and so on. Objects encapsulate state and behavior in a nice way, but this state is only accessible when the Java Virtual Machine (JVM) is running: if the JVM stops or the garbage collector cleans its memory content, objects disappear, as well as their state. Some objects need to be persistent. By persistent data, I mean data that is deliberately stored in permanent form on magnetic media, flash memory, and so forth. An object that can store its state to get reused later is said to be persistent.

There are different ways to persist state within Java. One way is through the mechanism of serialization, which is the process of converting an object into a sequence of bits. Objects can be serialized on a disk, or over a network connection (including Internet), in an independent format that can be reused across different operating systems. Java provides a simple, transparent, and standard mechanism to serialize objects by implementing the `java.io.Serializable` interface. This mechanism, although very simple, is poor. It has neither a query language nor an infrastructure supporting heavy concurrent access or clustering.

Another means of persisting state is through Java Database Connectivity (JDBC), which is the standard API to access relational databases. It can connect to a database, execute Structured Query Language (SQL) statements, and get back a result. This API has been part of the Java platform since version 1.1. Although still widely used, it has tended to be eclipsed by the more powerful object-relational mapping (ORM) tools.

The principle of ORM involves delegating access to relational databases to external tools or frameworks, which in turn give an object-oriented view of relational data, and vice versa. Mapping tools have a bidirectional correspondence between the database and objects. Several frameworks achieve this, such as Hibernate, TopLink, and Java Data Objects (JDO), but Java Persistence API (JPA) is the preferred technology, as it has been included in Java EE 6.

JPA Specification Overview

JPA 1.0 was created with Java EE 5 to solve the problem of data persistence. It brings the object-oriented and relational models together. In Java EE 6, JPA 2.0 follows the same path of simplicity and robustness, and adds new functionalities. You can use this API to access and manipulate relational data from Enterprise Java Beans (EJBs), web components, and Java SE applications.

JPA is an abstraction above JDBC that makes it possible to be independent of SQL. All classes and annotations of this API are in the `javax.persistence` package. The main components of JPA are as follows:

- ORM, which is the mechanism to map objects to data stored in a relational database.

- An entity manager API to perform database-related operations, such as Create, Read, Update, Delete (CRUD) operations.

- The Java Persistence Query Language (JPQL), which allows you to retrieve data with an object-oriented query language.

- Transactions and locking mechanisms when accessing data concurrently provided by Java Transaction API (JTA). Resource-local (non-JTA) transactions are also supported by JPA.

- Callbacks and listeners to hook business logic into the life cycle of a persistent object.

A Brief History of the Specification

ORM solutions have been around for a long time, even before Java. Products such as TopLink originally started with Smalltalk in 1994 before switching to Java. Commercial ORM products like TopLink have been available since the earliest days of the Java language. They were successful, but were never standardized for the Java platform. A similar approach to ORM was standardized in the form of JDO, which failed to gain any significant market penetration.

In 1998, EJB 1.0 was created and later shipped with J2EE 1.2. It was a heavyweight, distributed component used for transactional business logic. Entity Container Managed Persistence (CMP) was introduced in EJB 1.0, enhanced through versions up to EJB 2.1 (J2EE 1.4). Persistence could only be done inside the container through a complex mechanism of instantiation using home, local, or remote interfaces. The ORM capabilities were also very limited, as inheritance was difficult to map.

Parallel to the J2EE world was a popular open source solution that led to some surprising changes in the direction of persistence: Hibernate, which brought back a lightweight, object-oriented persistent model.

After years of complaints about Entity CMP 2.*x* components and in acknowledgment of the success and simplicity of open source frameworks such as Hibernate, the persistence model of the Enterprise Edition was completely rearchitected in Java EE 5. JPA 1.0 was born with a very lightweight approach that adopted many Hibernate design principles. The JPA 1.0 specification was bundled with EJB 3.0 (JSR 220).

Today, with Java EE 6, JPA in its second version follows the path of ease of development and brings new features. It has evolved with its own dedicated specification, JSR 317.

What's New in JPA 2.0?

If JPA 1.0 was a completely new persistence model from its Entity CMP 2.*x* ancestor, JPA 2.0 is a continuation of JPA 1.0. It keeps the object-oriented approach with annotation and optional XML mapping files. This second version brings new APIs, extends JPQL, and adds these new functionalities:

- Collections of simple data types (`String`, `Integer`, etc.) and of embeddable objects can now be mapped in separate tables. Previously, you could only map collections of entities.

- Map support has been extended so that maps can have keys and values of basic types, entities, or embeddables.

- Maintaining a persistent ordering is now possible with the `@OrderColumn` annotation.

- Orphan removal allows child objects to be removed from a relationship if the parent object is removed.

- Optimistic locking was already supported, but now pessimistic locking has been introduced.

- A brand-new Criteria API has been introduced to allow queries to be constructed in an object-oriented manner rather than using a string-based approach.

- JPQL syntax is richer (e.g., it now allows case expressions).

- Embeddable objects can now be nested into other embeddable objects and have relationships to entities.

- The dot (`.`) navigation syntax has been extended to handle embeddables with relationships and embeddables of embeddables.

- Support for a new caching API has been added.

- Some properties in the persistence.xml file have been standardized, increasing the portability of your application.

I will discuss these functionalities in detail in Chapters 3, 4, and 5.

Reference Implementation

EclipseLink 2.0 is an open source implementation of JPA 2.0. It provides a powerful and flexible framework for storing Java objects in a relational database. EclipseLink is a JPA implementation, but it also supports XML persistence through Java XML Binding (JAXB) and other means such as Service Data Objects (SDO). It provides support not only for ORM, but also for object XML mapping (OXM), object persistence to Enterprise Information Systems (EIS) using Java EE Connector Architecture (JCA), and database web services.

EclipseLink's origins stem from the Oracle TopLink product given to the Eclipse Foundation in 2006. EclipseLink is the JPA reference implementation and is the persistence framework used in this book. It is also referred to as the *persistence provider*, or simply the *provider*.

Understanding Entities

When talking about mapping objects to a relational database, persisting objects, or querying objects, the term "entity" should be used rather than "objects." Objects are instances that just live in memory. Entities are objects that live shortly in memory and persistently in a database. They have the ability to be mapped to a database; they can be concrete or abstract; and they support inheritance, relationships, and so on. These entities, once mapped, can be managed by JPA. You can persist an entity in the database, remove it, and query it using a query language (Java Persistence Query Language, or JPQL). ORM lets you manipulate entities, while under the covers the database is being accessed. And, as you will see, an entity follows a defined life cycle. With callback methods and listeners, JPA lets you hook some business code to life-cycle events.

Object-Relational Mapping

The principle of ORM is to delegate to external tools or frameworks (in our case, JPA) the task of creating a correspondence between objects and tables. The world of classes, objects, and attributes can then be mapped to relational databases made of tables containing rows and columns. Mapping gives an object-oriented view to developers who can transparently use entities instead of tables. And how does JPA map objects to a database? Through *metadata*.

Associated with every entity is metadata that describes the mapping. This metadata enables the persistence provider to recognize an entity and to interpret the mapping. This metadata can be written in two different formats:

- *Annotations*: The code of the entity is directly annotated with all sorts of annotations that are described in the `javax.persistence` package.

- *XML descriptors*: Instead of (or in addition to) annotations, you can use XML descriptors. The mapping is defined in an external XML file that will be deployed with the entities. This can be very useful when database configuration changes depending on the environment, for example.

To make the mapping easier, JPA (like many other Java EE 6 specifications) uses the concept of *configuration by exception* (sometimes referred to as *programming by exception*). The idea is that JPA has certain default mapping rules (e.g., the table name is the same as the entity name). If you are happy with them, you don't need to use extra metadata (no annotation or XML is needed), but, if you don't want the provider to apply the default rules, you can customize the mapping to your own needs using metadata. In other words, having to supply a configuration is the exception to the rule.

So let's see how this applies to an entity. Listing 2-1 shows a `Book` entity with some attributes. As you can see, some of them are annotated (`id`, `title`, and `description`), and some are not.

Listing 2-1. A Simple Book Entity

```
@Entity
public class Book {

    @Id @GeneratedValue
    private Long id;
    @Column(nullable = false)
    private String title;
    private Float price;
    @Column(length = 2000)
    private String description;
    private String isbn;
    private Integer nbOfPage;
    private Boolean illustrations;

    // Constructors, getters, setters
}
```

To be recognized as an entity, the `Book` class must be annotated with `@javax.persistence.Entity` (or the XML equivalent). The `@javax.persistence.Id` annotation is used to denote the primary key, and the value of this identifier is automatically generated by the persistence provider (`@GeneratedValue`). The `@Column` annotation is used in some attributes to customize the default column mapping (`title` becomes not nullable, and `description` has a length of 2,000 characters). The persistence provider will then be able to map the `Book` entity to a `BOOK` table (which is a default mapping rule), generate a primary key, and synchronize the values of the attributes to the table columns. Figure 2-1 shows the mapping between the entity and the table.

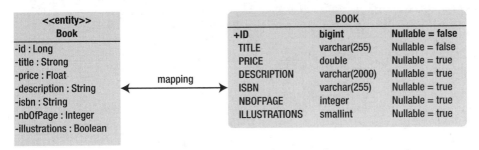

Figure 2-1. The Book entity is mapped to the BOOK table.

As you will see in Chapter 3, mapping is very rich, allowing you to map all kinds of things from objects to relationships. The world of object-oriented programming abounds with classes and associations between classes (and collections of classes). Databases also model relationships, only differently: using foreign keys or join tables. JPA has a set of metadata to manage the mapping of relationships. Even inheritance can be mapped. Inheritance is commonly used by developers to reuse code, but this concept is natively unknown in relational databases (as they have to emulate inheritance using foreign keys and constraints). Even if inheritance mapping throws in several twists, JPA supports it and gives you three different strategies to choose from. These strategies will be described in Chapter 3.

Querying Entities

JPA allows you to map entities to databases and also to query them using different criteria. JPA's power is that it offers the ability to query entities and their relationships in an object-oriented way without having to use the underlying database foreign keys or columns. The central piece of the API responsible for orchestrating entities is the entity manager. Its role is to manage entities, read from and write to a given database, and allow simple CRUD operations on entities as well as complex queries using JPQL. In a technical sense, the entity manager is just an interface whose implementation is done by the persistence provider, EclipseLink. The following snippet of code shows you how to create an entity manager and persist a **Book** entity:

```
EntityManagerFactory emf = Persistence.createEntityManagerFactory("chapter02PU");
EntityManager em = emf.createEntityManager();
em.persist(book);
```

In Figure 2-2, you can see how the **EntityManager** interface can be used by a class (here **Main**) to manipulate entities (in this case, **Book**). With methods such as **persist()** and **find()**, the entity manager hides the JDBC calls to the database and the **INSERT** or **SELECT** SQL statement.

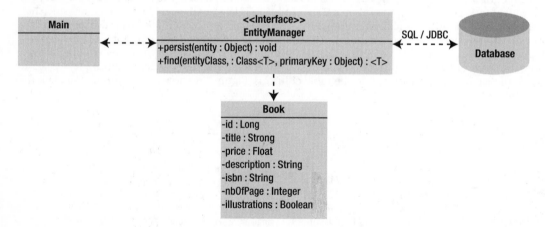

Figure 2-2. The entity manager interacts with the entity and the underlying database.

The entity manager also allows you to query entities. A *query* in this case is similar to a database query, except that, instead of using SQL, JPA queries over entities using JPQL. Its syntax uses the familiar object dot (.) notation. To retrieve all the books that have the title *H2G2*, you can write the following:

```
SELECT b FROM Book b WHERE b.title = 'H2G2'
```

A JPQL statement can be executed with dynamic queries (created dynamically at runtime), static queries (defined statically at compile time), or even with a native SQL statement. Static queries, also known as named queries, are defined using either annotations or XML metadata. The previous JPQL statement can, for example, be defined as a named query on the Book entity.

Listing 2-2 shows a Book entity defining the findBookByTitle named query using the @NamedQuery annotation.

Listing 2-2. A findBookByTitle Named Query

```
@Entity
@NamedQuery(name = "findBookByTitle", ↪
            query = "SELECT b FROM Book b WHERE b.title ='H2G2'")
public class Book {

    @Id @GeneratedValue
    private Long id;
    @Column(nullable = false)
    private String title;
    private Float price;
    @Column(length = 2000)
    private String description;
    private String isbn;
    private Integer nbOfPage;
    private Boolean illustrations;

    // Constructors, getters, setters
}
```

As you will see in Chapter 4, the EntityManager.createNamedQuery() method is used to execute the query and return a list of Book entities that match the search criteria.

Callbacks and Listeners

Entities are just Plain Old Java Objects (POJOs). When they are managed by the entity manager, they have a persistence identity, and their state is synchronized with the database. When they are not managed (i.e., they are detached from the entity manager), they can be used like any other Java class. This means that entities have a life cycle, as shown in Figure 2-3. When you create an instance of the Book entity with the new operator, the object exists in memory, and JPA knows nothing about it (it can even end up being garbage collected). When it becomes managed by the entity manager, its state is mapped and synchronized with the BOOK table. Calling the EntityManager.remove() method deletes the data from the database, but the Java object continues living in memory until it gets garbage collected.

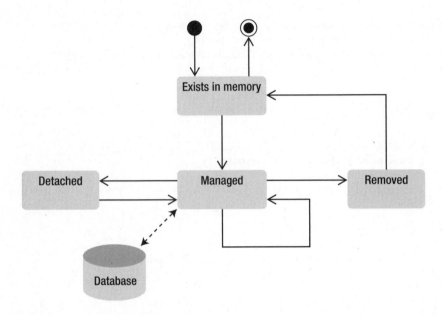

Figure 2-3. The life cyle of an entity

The operations made to entities fall into four categories: persisting, updating, removing, and loading, which correspond to the database operations of inserting, updating, deleting, and selecting, respectively. Each operation has a "Pre" and "Post" event (except for loading, which only has a "Post" event) that can be intercepted by the entity manager to invoke a business method. As you will see in Chapter 5, you will have @PrePersist and @PostPersist annotations, and so on. JPA allows you to hook business logic to the entity when these events occur. These annotations can be set on entity methods (a.k.a. callback methods) or in external classes (a.k.a. listeners). You can think of callback methods and listeners as analogous triggers in a relational database.

Putting it all Together

Now that you know a little bit about JPA, EclipseLink, entities, the entity manager, and JPQL, let's put them all together and write a small application that persists an entity to a database. The idea is to write a simple Book entity and a Main class that persists a book. You'll then compile it with Maven 2 and run it with EclipseLink and a Derby client database. To show how easy it is to unit test an entity, I will show you how to write a test class (BookTest) with a JUnit 4 test case and use the embedded mode of Derby for persisting data using an in-memory database.

This example follows the Maven directory structure, so classes and files have to be placed in the following directories:

- src/main/java: For the Book entity and the Main class

- src/main/resources: For the persistence.xml file used by the Main class

- src/test/java: For the BookTest class, which is used for unit testing

- `src/test/resources`: For the `persistence.xml` file used by the test cases

- `pom.xml`: For the Maven Project Object Model (POM), which describes the project and its dependencies on other external modules and components

Writing the Book Entity

The `Book` entity, shown in Listing 2-3, needs to be developed under the `src/main/java` directory. It has several attributes (a title, a price, etc.) of different data types (`String`, `Float`, `Integer`, and `Boolean`) and some JPA annotations:

- `@Entity` informs the persistence provider that this class is an entity and that it should manage it.

- `@Id` defines the `id` attribute as being the primary key.

- The `@GeneratedValue` annotation informs the persistence provider to autogenerate the primary key using the underlying database `id` utility.

- The `@Column` annotation is used to specify that the `title` property must be not null when persisted and to change the default maximum length of the column `description`.

- The `@NamedQuery` annotation defines a named query that uses JPQL to retrieve all the books from the database.

Listing 2-3. A Book Entity with a Named Query

```
package com.apress.javaee6.chapter02;
@Entity
@NamedQuery(name = "findAllBooks", query = "SELECT b FROM Book b")
public class Book {

    @Id @GeneratedValue
    private Long id;
    @Column(nullable = false)
    private String title;
    private Float price;
    @Column(length = 2000)
    private String description;
    private String isbn;
    private Integer nbOfPage;
    private Boolean illustrations;

    // Constructors, getters, setters
}
```

Note that for better readability I've omitted the constructor, getters, and setters of this class. As you can see in this code, except for a few annotations, Book is a simple POJO. Now let's write a Main class that persists a book to the database.

Writing the Main Class

The Main class, shown in Listing 2-4, is under the same directory as the Book entity. It commences by creating a new instance of the Book entity (using the Java keyword new) and sets some values to its attributes. There is nothing special here, just pure Java code. It then uses the Persistence class to get an instance of an EntityManagerFactory that refers to a persistence unit called chapter02PU, which I'll describe later in the section "Persistence Unit for the Main Class." This factory creates an instance of an EntityManager (em variable). As mentioned previously, the entity manager is the central piece of the JPA in that it is able to create a transaction, persist the Book object using the EntityManager.persist() method, and then commit the transaction. At the end of the main() method, both the EntityManager and EntityManagerFactory are closed to release the provider's resources.

Listing 2-4. A Main Class Persisting a Book Entity

```java
package com.apress.javaee6.chapter02;
public class Main {

    public static void main(String[] args) {

        // Creates an instance of book
        Book book = new Book();
        book.setTitle("The Hitchhiker's Guide to the Galaxy");
        book.setPrice(12.5F);
        book.setDescription("Science fiction comedy book");
        book.setIsbn("1-84023-742-2");
        book.setNbOfPage(354);
        book.setIllustrations(false);

        // Gets an entity manager and a transaction
        EntityManagerFactory emf = ↪
                Persistence.createEntityManagerFactory("chapter02PU");
        EntityManager em = emf.createEntityManager();

        // Persists the book to the database
        EntityTransaction tx = em.getTransaction();
        tx.begin();
        em.persist(book);
        tx.commit();

        em.close();
        emf.close();
    }
}
```

Again, for readability I've omitted exception handling. If a persistence exception occurs, you would have to roll back the transaction and log a message.

Persistence Unit for the Main Class

As you can see in the Main class, the EntityManagerFactory needs a persistence unit called chapter02PU. This persistence unit has to be defined in the persistence.xml file under the src/main/resources/META-INF directory (see Listing 2-5). This file, required by the JPA specification, is important as it links the JPA provider (EclipseLink in our case) to the database (Derby). It contains all the necessary information to connect to the database (target, URL, JDBC driver, user, and password) and informs the provider of the database-generation mode (create-tables means that tables will be created if they don't exist). The <provider> element defines the persistence provider, in our case, EclipseLink.

Listing 2-5. persistence.xml File Used by the Main Class

```xml
<?xml version="1.0" encoding="UTF-8"?>
<persistence xmlns="http://java.sun.com/xml/ns/persistence"
             xmlns:xsi="http://www.w3.org/2001/XMLSchema-instance"
             xsi:schemaLocation="http://java.sun.com/xml/ns/persistence
             http://java.sun.com/xml/ns/persistence/persistence_2_0.xsd"
             version="2.0">

  <persistence-unit name="chapter02PU" transaction-type="RESOURCE_LOCAL">
    <provider>org.eclipse.persistence.jpa.PersistenceProvider</provider>
    <class>com.apress.javaee6.chapter02.Book</class>
    <properties>
      <property name="eclipselink.target-database" value="DERBY"/>
      <property name="eclipselink.ddl-generation" value="create-tables"/>
      <property name="eclipselink.logging.level" value="INFO"/>
      <property name="javax.persistence.jdbc.driver" ↪
                value="org.apache.derby.jdbc.ClientDriver"/>
      <property name="javax.persistence.jdbc.url" ↪
          value="jdbc:derby://localhost:1527/chapter02DB;create=true"/>
      <property name="javax.persistence.jdbc.user" value="APP"/>
      <property name="javax.persistence.jdbc.password" value="APP"/>
    </properties>
  </persistence-unit>
</persistence>
```

This persistence unit lists all the entities that should be managed by the entity manager. Here, the <class> tag refers to the Book entity.

> ■ **Note** Listings 2-5 and 2-8 show a subset of the elements allowed in a `persistence.xml` file (`persistence-unit`, `provider`, `class`, `properties`...). Others elements can be used and are defined in chapter 8 of the JPA 2.0 specification. Note that, in the `properties` element, the ones named `javax.persistence` are standard and portable across implementations. The ones named `eclipselink` (such as the logging level for instance) are specific to EclipseLink.

Compiling with Maven

You have all the ingredients to run the application: the `Book` entity that you need to persist, the `Main` class, which does so using an entity manager, and the persistence unit binding the entity to the Derby database. To compile this code, instead of using the `javac` compiler command directly, you will use Maven. You first must create a `pom.xml` file that describes the project and its dependencies such as the JPA API. You also need to inform Maven that you are using Java SE 6 by configuring the `maven-compiler-plugin` as shown in Listing 2-6.

Listing 2-6. Maven `pom.xml` *File to Compile, Build, Execute, and Test the Application*

```xml
<?xml version="1.0" encoding="UTF-8"?>
<project xmlns="http://maven.apache.org/POM/4.0.0" ➥
        xmlns:xsi="http://www.w3.org/2001/XMLSchema-instance"➥
        xsi:schemaLocation="http://maven.apache.org/POM/4.0.0 ➥
        http://maven.apache.org/xsd/maven-4.0.0.xsd">

    <modelVersion>4.0.0</modelVersion>
    <groupId>com.apress.javaee6</groupId>
    <artifactId>chapter02</artifactId>
    <version>2.0</version>
    <name>chapter02</name>

    <dependencies>
        <dependency>
            <groupId>org.eclipse.persistence</groupId>
            <artifactId>javax.persistence</artifactId>
            <version>2.0.0</version>
        </dependency>
        <dependency>
            <groupId>org.eclipse.persistence</groupId>
            <artifactId>eclipselink</artifactId>
            <version>2.0.0</version>
        </dependency>
        <dependency>
            <groupId>org.apache.derby</groupId>
            <artifactId>derbyclient</artifactId>
            <version>10.6.1.0</version>
        </dependency>
```

```xml
        <dependency>
            <groupId>org.apache.derby</groupId>
            <artifactId>derby</artifactId>
            <version>10.6.1.0</version>
            <scope>test</scope>
        </dependency>
        <dependency>
            <groupId>junit</groupId>
            <artifactId>junit</artifactId>
            <version>4.8.1</version>
            <scope>test</scope>
        </dependency>
    </dependencies>

    <build>
        <plugins>
            <plugin>
                <groupId>org.apache.maven.plugins</groupId>
                <artifactId>maven-compiler-plugin</artifactId>
                <inherited>true</inherited>
                <configuration>
                    <source>1.6</source>
                    <target>1.6</target>
                </configuration>
            </plugin>
        </plugins>
    </build>
</project>
```

First, to be able to compile the code, you need the JPA API that defines all the annotations and classes that are in the `javax.persistence` package. You will get these classes in a jar referred by the `javax.persistence` artifact ID and stored in the Maven repository. The EclipseLink runtime (i.e., the persistence provider) is defined in the `eclipselink` artifact ID. You then need the JDBC drivers to connect to Derby. The `derbyclient` artifact ID refers to the jar that contains the JDBC driver to connect to Derby running in server mode (the database runs in a separate process and listens to a port) and the `derby` artifact ID contains the classes to use Derby as an embedded database. Note that this artifact ID is scoped for testing (`<scope>test</scope>`) and has a dependency on JUnit 4.

To compile the classes, open a command-line interpreter in the root directory that contains the `pom.xml` file and enter the following Maven command:

```
mvn compile
```

You should see the BUILD SUCCESSFUL message informing you that the compilation was successful. Maven creates a `target` subdirectory with all the class files as well as the `persistence.xml` file.

Running the Main Class with Derby

Before executing the Main class, you need to start Derby. The easiest way to do this is to go to the %DERBY_HOME%\bin directory and execute the startNetworkServer.bat script. Derby starts and displays the following messages in the console:

```
Security manager installed using the Basic server security policy.
Apache Derby Network Server - 10.6.1.0 - (802917) started and ready to accept
connections on port 1527
```

The Derby process is listening on port 1527 and waiting for the JDBC driver to send any SQL statement. To execute the Main class, you can use the java interpreter command or use Maven as follows:

```
mvn exec:java -Dexec.mainClass="com.apress.javaee6.chapter02.Main"
```

When you run the Main class, several things occur. First, Derby will automatically create the chapter02DB database once the Book entity is initialized. That is because in the persistence.xml file you've added the create=true property to the JDBC URL:

```
<property name="eclipselink.jdbc.url" ➥
        value="jdbc:derby://localhost:1527/chapter02DB;create=true"/>
```

This shortcut is very useful when you are in development mode, as you do not need any SQL script to create the database. Then, the eclipselink.ddl-generation property informs EclipseLink to automatically create the BOOK table. Finally, the book is inserted into the table (with an automatically generated ID).

```
em.persist(book);
```

Let's use Derby commands to display the table structure: enter the ij command in a console (as explained previously in Chapter 1, the %DERBY_HOME%\bin directory has to be in your PATH variable). This runs the Derby interpreter, and you can execute commands to connect to the database, show the tables of the chapter02DB database (show tables), check the structure of the BOOK table (describe book), and even show its content by entering SQL statements such as SELECT * FROM BOOK.

```
C:\> ij
version ij 10.6.1.0

ij> connect 'jdbc:derby://localhost:1527/chapter02DB';

ij> show tables;
TABLE_SCHEM     |TABLE_NAME      |REMARKS
------------------------------------------------------------------------
APP             |BOOK            |
APP             |SEQUENCE        |
```

```
ij> describe book;
COLUMN_NAME      |TYPE_NAME|DEC&|NUM&|COLUM&|COLUMN_DEF|CHAR_OCTE&|IS_NULL&
-------------------------------------------------------------------------
ID               |BIGINT   |0   |10  |19    |NULL      |NULL      |NO
TITLE            |VARCHAR  |NULL|NULL|255   |NULL      |510       |NO
PRICE            |DOUBLE   |NULL|2   |52    |NULL      |NULL      |YES
ILLUSTRATIONS    |SMALLINT |0   |10  |5     |0         |NULL      |YES
DESCRIPTION      |VARCHAR  |NULL|NULL|2000  |NULL      |4000      |YES
ISBN             |VARCHAR  |NULL|NULL|255   |NULL      |510       |YES
NBOFPAGE         |INTEGER  |0   |10  |10    |NULL      |NULL      |YES
```

Coming back to the code of the Book entity, because you've used the @GeneratedValue annotation (to automatically generate an ID), EclipseLink has created a sequence table to store the numbering (the SEQUENCE table). For the BOOK table structure, JPA has followed certain default conventions to name the table and the columns after the entity name and attributes. The @Column annotation has overridden some of these defaults such as the length of the description column, which is set to 2000.

Writing the BookTest Class

One complaint made about the previous versions of Entity CMP 2.x was the difficulty of unit testing persistent components. One of the major selling points of JPA is that you can easily test entities without requiring a running application server or live database. But what can you test? Entities themselves usually don't need to be tested in isolation. Most methods on entities are simple getters or setters with only a few business methods. Verifying that a setter assigns a value to an attribute and that the corresponding getter retrieves the same value does not give any extra value (unless a side effect is detected in the getters or the setters).

What about testing the database queries? Some developers would argue that this is not unit testing, as a real database is needed to run these tests. Testing in isolation with mock objects to simulate a database could be a lot of work. Also, testing an entity outside of any container (EJB or servlet container) would have an impact on the code, since transaction management has to be changed. Using an in-memory database and non-JTA transactions are a good compromise. CRUD operations and JPQL queries can be tested with a very lightweight database that doesn't need to run in a separated process (just by adding a jar file to the classpath). This is how you will run our BookTest class, by using the embedded mode of Derby.

Maven uses two different directories, one to store the main application code and another for the test classes. The BookTest class, shown in Listing 2-7, goes under the src/test/java directory and tests that the entity manager can persist a book and retrieve it from the database.

Listing 2-7. Test Class That Creates a Book and Retrieves All the Books from the Database

```
public class BookTest {

    private static EntityManagerFactory emf;
    private static EntityManager em;
    private static EntityTransaction tx;
```

```
@BeforeClass
public static void initEntityManager() throws Exception {
    emf = Persistence.createEntityManagerFactory("chapter02PU");
    em = emf.createEntityManager();
}

@AfterClass
public static void closeEntityManager() throws SQLException {
    em.close();
    emf.close();
}

@Before
public void initTransaction() {
    tx = em.getTransaction();
}

@Test
public void shouldCreateABook() throws Exception {

    // Creates an instance of book
    Book book = new Book();
    book.setTitle("The Hitchhiker's Guide to the Galaxy");
    book.setPrice(12.5F);
    book.setDescription("Science fiction comedy book");
    book.setIsbn("1-84023-742-2");
    book.setNbOfPage(354);
    book.setIllustrations(false);

    // Persists the book to the database
    tx.begin();
    em.persist(book);
    tx.commit();
    assertNotNull("ID should not be null", book.getId());

    // Retrieves all the books from the database
    List<Book> books = ↪
            em.createNamedQuery("findAllBooks").getResultList();
    assertEquals(1, books.size());
    }
}
```

Like the Main class, BookTest needs to create an EntityManager instance using an
EntityManagerFactory. To initialize these components, you can use the JUnit 4 fixtures. The
@BeforeClass and @AfterClass annotations allow executions of some code only once, before and after
the class is executed. That's the perfect place to create and close an EntityManager instance. The @Before
annotation allows you to run code before each test, which is where you get a transaction.

The should`CreateABook()` method is the test case, as it is annotated with the JUnit `@Test` annotation. This method persists a book (using the `EntityManager.persist()` method) and checks whether the `id` has been automatically generated by EclipseLink (with `assertNotNull`). If so, the `findAllBooks` named query is executed and checks whether the returned list size is equal to one.

Persistence Unit for the BookTest Class

Now that the test class is written, you need another `persistence.xml` file to use Derby embedded. The previous `persistence.xml` file defines a JDBC driver and a URL connection for Derby Server, which has to be started in a separate process. The `src/test/resources/META-INF/ persistence.xml` in Listing 2-8 uses an embedded JDBC driver.

Listing 2-8. persistence.xml File Used by the BookTest Class

```xml
<?xml version="1.0" encoding="UTF-8"?>
<persistence xmlns="http://java.sun.com/xml/ns/persistence"
             xmlns:xsi="http://www.w3.org/2001/XMLSchema-instance"
             xsi:schemaLocation="http://java.sun.com/xml/ns/persistence
             http://java.sun.com/xml/ns/persistence/persistence_2_0.xsd"
             version="2.0">

  <persistence-unit name="chapter02PU" transaction-type="RESOURCE_LOCAL">
    <provider>org.eclipse.persistence.jpa.PersistenceProvider</provider>
    <class>com.apress.javaee6.chapter02.Book</class>
    <properties>
      <property name="eclipselink.target-database" value="DERBY"/>
      <property name="eclipselink.ddl-generation" ↪
              value="drop-and-create-tables"/>
      <property name="eclipselink.logging.level" value="FINE"/>
      <property name="javax.persistence.jdbc.driver" ↪
              value="org.apache.derby.jdbc.EmbeddedDriver"/>
      <property name="javax.persistence.jdbc.url" ↪
              value="jdbc:derby:memory:chapter02DB;create=true"/>
      <property name="javax.persistence.jdbc.user" value="APP"/>
      <property name="javax.persistence.jdbc.password" value="APP"/>
    </properties>
  </persistence-unit>
</persistence>
```

There are other changes between the `persistence.xml` files. For example, the DDL generation is `drop-and-create-tables` instead of `create-tables`, because before testing you need the tables to be dropped and re-created so you have a fresh database structure. Also note that the logging level is `FINE` instead of `INFO`. Again, this is good for testing as you can obtain more information in case something goes wrong.

Running the BookTest Class with Embedded Derby

Nothing is easier than running the test: you rely on Maven. Open a console in the directory where the `pom.xml` file is located and enter the following command:

```
mvn test
```

Because the logging level has been set to `FINE`, you should see verbose information about Derby creating a database and tables in memory. The `BookTest` class is then executed, and a Maven report should inform you that the test is successful.

```
Tests run: 1, Failures: 0, Errors: 0, Skipped: 0, Time elapsed: 9.415 sec
Results :
Tests run: 1, Failures: 0, Errors: 0, Skipped: 0

[INFO] ------------------------------------------------------------
[INFO] BUILD SUCCESSFUL
[INFO] ------------------------------------------------------------
[INFO] Total time: 19 seconds
[INFO] Finished
[INFO] Final Memory: 4M/14M
[INFO] ------------------------------------------------------------
```

Summary

This chapter contains a quick overview of JPA 2.0. Like most of the other Java EE 6 specifications, JPA focuses on a simple object architecture, leaving its ancestor, a heavyweight component model (a.k.a. EJB CMP 2.x), behind. The chapter also covered entities, which are persistent objects that use mapping metadata through annotations or XML.

Thanks to the "Putting It All Together" section, you have seen how to run a JPA application with EclipseLink and Derby. Unit testing is an important topic in projects, and, with JPA and in memory databases such as Derby, it is now very easy to test persistence.

In the following chapters, you will learn more about the main JPA components. Chapter 3 will show you how to map entities, relationships, and inheritance to a database. Chapter 4 will focus on the entity manager API, the JPQL syntax, and how to use queries and locking mechanisms. Chapter 5, the last chapter of this JPA section, will explain the life cycle of entities and how to hook business logic in callback methods in entities and listeners.

CHAPTER 3

Object-Relational Mapping

In this chapter, I will go through the basics of object-relational mapping (ORM), which is basically mapping entities to tables and attributes to columns. I will then concentrate on more complex mappings such as relationships, composition, and inheritance. A domain model is made of objects interacting with each other. Objects and databases have different ways to store relationship information (through pointers or foreign keys). Inheritance is not a feature that relational databases naturally have, and therefore the mapping is not as obvious. I will go into some detail and show examples that will demonstrate how attributes, relationships, and inheritance are mapped from a domain model to a database.

Previous chapters have shown how annotations have been used extensively in the Enterprise Edition since Java EE 5 (mostly on EJBs, JPA, and web services). JPA 2.0 follows this path and introduces new mapping annotations as well as their XML equivalent. I will mostly use annotations to explain the different mapping concepts, but I will also introduce XML mapping.

How to Map an Entity

As a first example, let's start with the simplest mapping that we can possibly have. In the JPA persistence model, an entity is a Plain Old Java Object (POJO). This means an entity is declared, instantiated, and used just like any other Java class. An entity has attributes (its state) that can be manipulated via getters and setters. Each attribute is stored in a table column. Listing 3-1 shows a simple entity.

Listing 3-1. Simple Example of a Book Entity

```
@Entity
public class Book {

    @Id
    private Long id;
    private String title;
    private Float price;
    private String description;
    private String isbn;
    private Integer nbOfPage;
    private Boolean illustrations;
```

```
    public Book() {
    }

    // Getters, setters
}
```

This example of code from the CD-BookStore application represents a `Book` entity from which I've omitted the getters and the setters for clarity. As you can see, except for some annotations, this entity looks exactly like any Java class: it has several attributes (`id`, `title`, `price`, etc.) of different types (`Long`, `String`, `Float`, `Integer`, and `Boolean`), a default constructor, and getters and setters for each attribute. So how does this map to a table? The answer is thanks to annotations.

First of all, the class is annotated with `@javax.persistence.Entity`, which allows the persistence provider to recognize it as a persistent class and not just as a simple POJO. Then, the annotation `@javax.persistence.Id` defines the unique identifier of this object. Because JPA is about mapping objects to relational tables, objects need an ID that will be mapped to a primary key. The other attributes (`title`, `price`, `description`, etc.) are not annotated, so they will be made persistent by applying a default mapping.

This example of code has only attributes, but, as you will see in Chapter 5, an entity can also have business methods. Note that this `Book` entity is a Java class that does not implement any interface or extend any class. In fact, to be an entity, a class must follow these rules:

- The entity class must be annotated with `@javax.persistence.Entity` (or denoted in the XML descriptor as an entity).

- The `@javax.persistence.Id` annotation must be used to denote a simple primary key.

- The entity class must have a no-arg constructor that has to be public or protected. The entity class may have other constructors as well.

- The entity class must be a top-level class. An enum or interface cannot be designated as an entity.

- The entity class must not be final. No methods or persistent instance variables of the entity class may be final.

- If an entity instance has to be passed by value as a detached object (e.g., through a remote interface), the entity class must implement the `Serializable` interface.

Since the `Book` entity (shown previously in Listing 3-1) follows these simple rules, the persistence provider can synchronize the data between the attributes of the `Book` entity and the columns of the `BOOK` table. Therefore, if the attribute `isbn` is modified by the application, the `ISBN` column will be synchronized (if the entity is managed, if the transaction context is set, etc.).

As Figure 3-1 shows, the `Book` entity is stored in a `BOOK` table, and each column is named after the attribute of the class (e.g., the `isbn` attribute of type `String` is mapped to a column named `ISBN` of type `VARCHAR`). These default mapping rules are an important part of the principle known as *configuration by exception.*

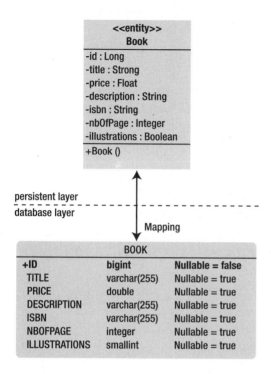

Figure 3-1. Data synchronization between the entity and the table

Configuration by Exception

Java EE 5 introduced the idea of configuration by exception (sometimes referred to as *programming by exception* or *convention over configuration*). This means, unless specified differently, the container or provider should apply the default rules. In other words, having to supply a configuration is the exception to the rule. This allows you to write the minimum amount of code to get your application running, relying on the container and provider defaults.

Let's return to the previous code example (see Listing 3-1). Without any annotation, the Book entity would be treated just like a POJO and not be persisted. That is the rule: if no special configuration is given, the default should be applied, and the default for the persistence provider is that the Book class has no database representation. But because you need to change this default behavior, you annotate the class with @Entity. It is the same for the identifier. You need a way to tell the persistence provider that the id attribute has to be mapped to a primary key, so you annotate it with @Id. This type of decision characterizes the configuration-by-exception approach, in which annotations are not required for the more common cases and are only used when an override is needed. This means that, for all the other attributes, the following default mapping rules will apply:

- The entity name is mapped to a relational table name (e.g., the Book entity is mapped to a BOOK table). If you want to map it to another table, you will need to use the @Table annotation, as you'll see later in the "Elementary Mapping" section.

- Attribute names are mapped to a column name (e.g., the id attribute, or the getId() method, is mapped to an ID column). If you want to change this default mapping, you will need to use the @Column annotation.

- JDBC rules apply for mapping Java primitives to relational data types. A String will be mapped to VARCHAR, a Long to a BIGINT, a Boolean to a SMALLINT, and so on. The default size of a column mapped from a String is 255 (a String is mapped to a VARCHAR(255)). But keep in mind that the default mapping rules are different from one database to another. For example, a String is mapped to a VARCHAR in Derby and a VARCHAR2 in Oracle. An Integer is mapped to an INTEGER in Derby and a NUMBER in Oracle. The information of the underlying database is provided in the persistence.xml file, which you'll see later in Chapter 4 in the "Persistence Context" section.

Following these rules, the Book entity will be mapped to a Derby table that has the structure described in Listing 3-2.

Listing 3-2. *Structure of the BOOK Table*

```
CREATE TABLE BOOK (
    ID BIGINT NOT NULL,
    TITLE VARCHAR(255),
    PRICE DOUBLE(52, 0),
    DESCRIPTION VARCHAR(255),
    ISBN VARCHAR(255),
    NBOFPAGE INTEGER,
    ILLUSTRATIONS SMALLINT,
    PRIMARY KEY (ID)
);
```

This is an example of a very simple mapping. Relationships and inheritance also have default mapping, as you'll see later in the "Relationship Mapping" section.

Most persistence providers, including EclipseLink, allow you to generate the database automatically from the entities. This feature is very convenient when you are in developing mode. By using all the defaults, you can map your data easily with only the @Entity and @Id annotations. However, most of the time you need to connect to a legacy database or follow strict database naming conventions. To do this, JPA gives you a rich set of annotations (or the XML equivalent) that allows you to customize each part of the mapping (table, column names, primary keys, column size, null or not null, and so on).

Elementary Mapping

There are significant differences in the way data is handled in Java and in a relational database. In Java, we use classes to describe both attributes for holding data and methods to access and manipulate that data. Once a class is defined, we can create as many instances as we need with the new keyword. In a relational database, data is stored in non-object structures (columns and rows), and dynamic behavior is stored functionally as table triggers and stored procedures that are not bound tightly to the data structures, as they are with objects. Sometimes mapping Java objects to the underlying database can be easy, and the default rules can be applied. At other times, these rules do not meet your needs, and you must customize the mapping. Elementary mapping annotations focus on customizing the table, the primary key, and the columns, and they let you modify certain naming conventions or typing (not-null column, length, etc.).

Tables

Rules for configuration-by-exception mapping state that the entity and the table name are the same (a Book entity is mapped to a BOOK table, an AncientBook entity is mapped to an ANCIENTBOOK table, and so on). This might suit you in most cases, but you may want to map your data to a different table, or even map a single entity to several tables.

@Table

The @javax.persistence.Table annotation makes it possible to change the default values related to the table. For example, you can specify the name of the table in which the data will be stored, the catalog, and the database schema. If this annotation is omitted, the name of the table will be the name of the entity. If you want to change the name to T_BOOK instead of BOOK, you would do as shown in Listing 3-3.

Listing 3-3. The Book Entity Being Mapped to a T_BOOK Table

```
@Entity
@Table(name = "t_book")
public class Book {

    @Id
    private Long id;
    private String title;
    private Float price;
    private String description;
    private String isbn;
    private Integer nbOfPage;
    private Boolean illustrations;

    public Book() {
    }

    // Getters, setters
}
```

■ **Note** In the @Table annotation, I include a lowercase table name (t_book). By default, most databases will map the entity to an uppercase table name (and that's the case with Derby) except if you configure them to honor case.

@SecondaryTable

Up to now, I have assumed that an entity gets mapped to a single table, also known as a *primary table*. But sometimes when you have an existing data model, you need to spread the data across multiple tables, or *secondary tables*. To do this, you need to use the annotation @SecondaryTable to associate a secondary table to an entity or @SecondaryTables (with an "s") for several secondary tables. You can distribute the data of an entity across columns in both the primary table and the secondary tables simply by defining the secondary tables with annotations and then specifying for each attribute which table it is in (with the @Column annotation, which I'll describe in the "Attributes" section in more detail). Listing 3-4 shows an Address entity mapping its attributes in one primary table and two secondary tables.

Listing 3-4. Attributes of the Address Entity Mapped in Three Different Tables

```
@Entity
@SecondaryTables({
    @SecondaryTable(name = "city"),
    @SecondaryTable(name = "country")
})
public class Address {

    @Id
    private Long id;
    private String street1;
    private String street2;
    @Column(table = "city")
    private String city;
    @Column(table = "city")
    private String state;
    @Column(table = "city")
    private String zipcode;
    @Column(table = "country")
    private String country;

    // Constructors, getters, setters
}
```

By default, the attributes of the Address entity are mapped to the primary table (which has the default name of the entity, so the table is called ADDRESS). The annotation @SecondaryTables informs you that there are two secondary tables: CITY and COUNTRY. You then need to specify which attribute is stored in which secondary table (using the annotation @Column(table="city") or @Column(table="country")). Figure 3-2 shows the tables structure to which the Address entity will be mapped. Each table contains different attributes but they all have the same primary key (to join the tables together). Again, remember that Derby translates lowercase table names (city) into uppercase (CITY).

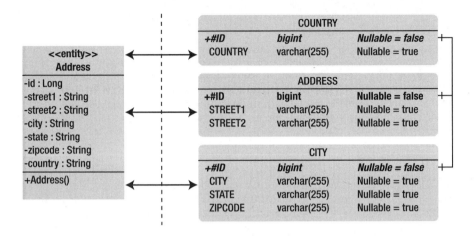

Figure 3-2. The `Address` *entity is mapped to three tables.*

As you probably understand by now, you can have several annotations in the same entity. If you want to rename the primary table, you can add the `@Table` annotation as demonstrated in Listing 3-5.

Listing 3-5. The Primary Table Is Renamed to `T_ADDRESS`

```
@Entity
@Table(name = "t_address")
@SecondaryTables({
    @SecondaryTable(name = "t_city"),
    @SecondaryTable(name = "t_country")
})
public class Address {

    // Attributes, constructor, getters, setters
}
```

■ **Note** When you use secondary tables, you must consider the issue of performance. Every time you access an entity, the persistence provider accesses several tables and has to join them. On the other hand, secondary tables can be a good thing when you have expensive attributes such as binary large objects (BLOBs) that you want to isolate in a different table.

Primary Keys

In relational databases, a primary key uniquely identifies each row in a table. It comprises either a single column or set of columns. Primary keys must be unique, as they identify a single row (a null value is not allowed). Examples of primary keys are a customer identifier, a telephone number, an order reference, and an ISBN. JPA requires entities to have an identifier mapped to a primary key, which will follow the same rule: uniquely identify an entity by either a single attribute or a set of attributes (composite key). This entity's primary key value cannot be updated once it has been assigned.

@Id and @GeneratedValue

A simple (i.e., noncomposite) primary key must correspond to a single attribute of the entity class. The `@Id` annotation that you've seen before is used to denote a simple primary key. `@javax.persistence.Id` annotates an attribute as being a unique identifier. It can be one of the following types:

- *Primitive Java types*: `byte`, `int`, `short`, `long`, `char`

- *Wrapper classes of primitive Java types*: `Byte`, `Integer`, `Short`, `Long`, `Character`

- *Arrays of primitive or wrapper types*: `int[]`, `Integer[]`, etc.

- *Strings, numbers, and dates*: `java.lang.String`, `java.math.BigInteger`, `java.util.Date`, `java.sql.Date`

When creating an entity, the value of this identifier can be generated either manually by the application or automatically by the persistence provider using the `@GeneratedValue` annotation. This annotation can have four possible values:

- `SEQUENCE` and `IDENTITY` specify use of a database SQL sequence or identity column, respectively.

- `TABLE` instructs the persistence provider to store the sequence name and its current value in a table, increasing the value each time a new instance of the entity is persisted. As an example, Derby creates a `SEQUENCE` table with two columns: the sequence name (which is an arbitrary name) and the sequence value (an integer automatically incremented by Derby).

- The generation of a key is done automatically (`AUTO`) by the underlying database, which will pick an appropriate strategy for a particular database. `AUTO` is the default value of the `@GeneratedValue` annotation.

If the `@GeneratedValue` annotation is not defined, the application has to create its own identifier by applying any algorithm that will return a unique value. The code in Listing 3-6 shows how to have an automatically generated identifier. `GenerationType.AUTO` being the default value, I could have omitted the `strategy` element. Note that the attribute `id` is annotated twice with `@Id` and `@GeneratedValue`.

Listing 3-6. The Book Entity with an Automatically Generated Identifier

```
@Entity
public class Book {

    @Id
    @GeneratedValue(strategy = GenerationType.AUTO)
    private Long id;
    private String title;
    private Float price;
    private String description;
    private String isbn;
    private Integer nbOfPage;
    private Boolean illustrations;

    // Constructors, getters, setters
}
```

Composite Primary Keys

When mapping entities, it is good practice to designate a single dedicated column as the primary key. However, there are cases where a composite primary key is required (such as having to map to a legacy database or when the primary keys have to follow certain business rules, for example a date and a value or a country code and a time stamp need to be included). To do this, a primary key class must be defined to represent the composite key. Then, we have two available annotations for defining this class, depending on how we want to structure the entity: @EmbeddedId and @IdClass. As you'll see, the final result is the same, and you will end up having the same database schema, but the way to query the entity is slightly different.

For example, the CD-BookStore application needs to post news frequently on the main page where you can see daily news about books, music, or artists. The news has content, a title, and, because it can be written in several languages, a language code (EN for English, PT for Portuguese, and so on). The primary key of the news could then be the title and the language code because an article can be translated into multiple languages but keep its original title. So the primary key class NewsId is composed of two attributes of type String: title and language. Primary key classes must include method definitions for equals() and hashCode() in order to manage queries and internal collections (equality for these methods must be consistent with the database equality), and their attributes must be in the set of valid types listed previously. They must also be public, implement Serializable if they need to cross architectural layers (e.g., they will be managed in the persistent layer and used in the presentation layer), and have a no-arg constructor.

@EmbeddedId

As you will see later in this chapter, JPA uses different sorts of embedded objects. To summarize, an embedded object doesn't have any identity (no primary key of its own), and its attributes will end up as columns in the table of the entity that contains it.

Listing 3-7 shows the NewsId class as an embeddable class. It is just an embedded object (annotated with @Embeddable) that happens to be composed of two attributes (title and language). This class must have no-arg constructor, getter, setter, `equals()`, and `hashCode()` implementations, i.e., it needs to use the JavaBean conventions. The class itself doesn't have an identity of its own (no `@Id` annotation). That's a characteristic of an embeddable.

Listing 3-7. The Primary Key Class Is Annotated with @Embeddable

```
@Embeddable
public class NewsId {

    private String title;
    private String language;

    // Constructors, getters, setters, equals, and hashcode
}
```

The `News` entity, shown in Listing 3-8, then has to embed the primary key class `NewsId` with the `@EmbeddedId` annotation. With this approach, there is no need to use `@Id`. Every `@EmbeddedId` must refer to an embeddable class marked with `@Embeddable`.

Listing 3-8. The Entity Embeds the Primary Key Class with @EmbeddedId

```
@Entity
public class News {

    @EmbeddedId
    private NewsId id;
    private String content;

    // Constructors, getters, setters
}
```

In Chapter 4, I will describe how to find entities using their primary key. Just as a first glimpse, here is how it works: the primary key is a class with a constructor. You have to instantiate this class with the values that form your unique key, and pass this object to the entity manager (the em attribute) as shown in Listing 3-9.

Listing 3-9. Simplified Code to Find an Entity Through Its Composite Primary Key

```
NewsId pk = new NewsId("Richard Wright has died", "EN")
News news = em.find(News.class, pk);
```

@IdClass

The other method of declaring a composite key is through the `@IdClass` annotation. It's a different approach whereby each attribute on the primary key class also needs to be declared on the entity class and annotated with `@Id`.

The composite primary key in the example `NewsId` in Listing 3-10 is just a POJO that does not require any annotation (in the previous example, the primary key class needs to be annotated with `@EmbeddedId`).

Listing 3-10. The Primary Key Class Is Not Annotated

```
public class NewsId {

    private String title;
    private String language;

    // Constructors, getters, setters, equals, and hashcode
}
```

Then, the entity News, shown in Listing 3-11, has to define the primary key using the @IdClass annotation and annotate each key with @Id. To persist the News entity, you will have to set a value to the title and the language attributes.

Listing 3-11. The Entity Defines Its Primary Class with the @IdClass Annotation

```
@Entity
@IdClass(NewsId.class)
public class News {

    @Id private String title;
    @Id private String language;
    private String content;

    // Constructors, getters, setters, equals, and hashcode
}
```

Both approaches, @EmbeddedId and @IdClass, will be mapped to the same table structure. This structure is defined in Listing 3-12 using the data definition language (DDL). The attributes of the entity and the primary key will end up in the same table, and the primary key will be formed with the attributes of the composite class (title and language).

Listing 3-12. DDL of the NEWS Table with a Composite Primary Key

```
create table NEWS (
    CONTENT VARCHAR(255),
    TITLE VARCHAR(255) not null,
    LANGUAGE VARCHAR(255) not null,
    primary key (TITLE, LANGUAGE)
);
```

The @IdClass approach is more prone to error, as you need to define each primary key attribute in both the @IdClass and the entity, taking care to use the same name and Java type. The advantage is that you don't need to change the code of the primary key class (no annotation is needed). For example, you could use a legacy class that, for legal reasons, you are not allowed to change but that you can reuse.

One visible difference is in the way you reference the entity in JPQL. In the case of @IdClass, you would do something like this:

```
select n.title from News n
```

With @EmbeddedId, you would have something like this:

```
select n.newsId.title from News n
```

Attributes

An entity must have a primary key (simple or compound) to be able to have an identity in a relational database. It also has all sorts of different attributes, making up its state, that have to be mapped to the table. This state can include almost every Java type that you could want to map:

- Java primitive types (int, double, float, etc.) and the wrapper classes (Integer, Double, Float, etc.)

- Arrays of bytes and characters (byte[], Byte[], char[], Character[])

- String, large numeric, and temporal types (java.lang.String, java.math.BigInteger, java.math.BigDecimal, java.util.Date, java.util.Calendar, java.sql.Date, java.sql.Time, java.sql.Timestamp)

- Enumerated types and user-defined types that implement the Serializable interface

- Collections of basic and embeddable types

Of course, an entity can also have entity attributes, collections of entities, or embeddable classes. This requires introducing relationships between entities (which will be covered in the "Relationship Mapping" section).

As you've seen, with configuration by exception, attributes are mapped using default mapping rules. However, sometimes you need to customize parts of this mapping. That's where JPA annotations (or their XML equivalent) come into play.

@Basic

The optional @javax.persistence.Basic annotation (see Listing 3-13) is the simplest type of mapping to a database column, as it overrides basic persistence.

Listing 3-13. @Basic Annotation Elements

```
@Target({METHOD, FIELD}) @Retention(RUNTIME)
public @interface Basic {
    FetchType fetch() default EAGER;
    boolean optional() default true;
}
```

This annotation has two parameters: optional and fetch. The optional element gives a hint as to whether the value of the attribute may be null. It is disregarded for primitive types. The fetch element can take two values: LAZY or EAGER. It gives a hint to the persistence provider runtime that data should be fetched lazily (only when the application asks for the property) or eagerly (when the entity is initially loaded by the provider).

For example, take the Track entity shown in Listing 3-14. A CD album is made up of several tracks, and each track has a title, a description, and a WAV file of a certain duration that you can listen to. The WAV file is a BLOB that can be a few megabytes long. When you access the Track entity, you don't want to eagerly load the WAV file; you can annotate the attribute with @Basic(fetch = FetchType.LAZY) so the data will be retrieved from the database lazily (only when you access the wav attribute using its getter, for example).

Listing 3-14. The Track Entity with Lazy Loading on the wav Attribute

```
@Entity
public class Track {

    @Id
    @GeneratedValue(strategy = GenerationType.AUTO)
    private Long id;
    private String title;
    private Float duration;
    @Basic(fetch = FetchType.LAZY)
    @Lob
    private byte[] wav;
    private String description;

    // Constructors, getters, setters
}
```

Note that the wav attribute of type byte[] is also annotated with @Lob to store the value as a large object (LOB). Database columns that can store these types of large objects require special JDBC calls to be accessed from Java. To inform the provider, an additional @Lob annotation must be added to the basic mapping.

@Column

The @javax.persistence.Column annotation, shown in Listing 3-15, defines the properties of a column. You can change the column name (which by default is mapped to an attribute of the same name); specify the size; and authorize (or not) the column to have a null value, to be unique, or to allow its value to be updatable or insertable. Listing 3-15 shows the @Column annotation API with the elements and their default values.

Listing 3-15. @Column Annotation Elements

```
@Target({METHOD, FIELD}) @Retention(RUNTIME)
public @interface Column {
    String name() default "";
    boolean unique() default false;
    boolean nullable() default true;
    boolean insertable() default true;
```

```
        boolean updatable() default true;
        String columnDefinition() default "";
        String table() default "";
        int length() default 255;
        int precision() default 0; // decimal precision
        int scale() default 0; // decimal scale
}
```

To redefine the default mapping of the original Book entity, you can use the @Column annotation in various ways (see Listing 3-16). For example, you can change the name of the title and nbOfPage column or the length of the description, and not allow null values. Note that not all the combinations of attributes on datatypes are valid (e.g., length only applies to string-valued column, scale and precision only to decimal column).

Listing 3-16. *Customizing Mapping for the Book Entity*

```
@Entity
public class Book {

    @Id
    @GeneratedValue(strategy = GenerationType.AUTO)
    private Long id;
    @Column(name = "book_title", nullable = false, updatable = false)
    private String title;
    private Float price;
    @Column(length = 2000)
    private String description;
    private String isbn;
    @Column(name = "nb_of_page", nullable = false)
    private Integer nbOfPage;
    private Boolean illustrations;

    // Constructors, getters, setters
}
```

The Book entity in Listing 3-16 will get mapped to the table definition in Listing 3-17.

Listing 3-17. *BOOK Table Definition*

```
create table BOOK (
    ID BIGINT not null,
    BOOK_TITLE VARCHAR(255) not null,
    PRICE DOUBLE(52, 0),
    DESCRIPTION VARCHAR(2000),
    ISBN VARCHAR(255),
    NB_OF_PAGE INTEGER not null,
    ILLUSTRATIONS SMALLINT,
    primary key (ID)
);
```

Most of the elements of the @Column annotation have an influence on the mapping. If you change the length of the description attribute to 2000, the destination column length will also be set at 2000. The updatable and insertable settings default to true, which means that any attribute can be inserted or updated in the database. You can set them to false when you want the persistence provider to ensure that it will not insert or update the data to the table in response to changes in the entity. Note that this does not imply that the entity attribute will not change in memory. You can still change the value in memory, but it will not be synchronized with the database. That's because the generated SQL statement (INSERT or UPDATE) will not include the columns. In other words, these elements do not affect the relational mapping; they affect the dynamic behavior of the entity manager when accessing the relational data.

@Temporal

In Java, you can use java.util.Date and java.util.Calendar to store data and then have several representations of it such as a date, an hour, or milliseconds. To specify this in ORM, you can use the @javax.persistence.Temporal annotation. This has three possible values: DATE, TIME, or TIMESTAMP. Listing 3-18 defines a Customer entity that has a date of birth and a technical attribute that stores the exact time it was created in the system (this uses the TIMESTAMP value).

Listing 3-18. The Customer Entity with Two @Temporal Attributes

```
@Entity
public class Customer {

    @Id
    @GeneratedValue
    private Long id;
    private String firstName;
    private String lastName;
    private String email;
    private String phoneNumber;
    @Temporal(TemporalType.DATE)
    private Date dateOfBirth;
    @Temporal(TemporalType.TIMESTAMP)
    private Date creationDate;

    // Constructors, getters, setters
}
```

The Customer entity in Listing 3-18 will get mapped to the table defined in Listing 3-19. The dateOfBirth attribute is mapped to a column of type DATE and the creationDate attribute to a column of type TIMESTAMP.

Listing 3-19. CUSTOMER Table Definition

```
create table CUSTOMER (
    ID BIGINT not null,
    FIRSTNAME VARCHAR(255),
    LASTNAME VARCHAR(255),
    EMAIL VARCHAR(255),
    PHONENUMBER VARCHAR(255),
    DATEOFBIRTH DATE,
    CREATIONDATE TIMESTAMP,
    primary key (ID)
);
```

@Transient

With JPA, as soon as a class is annotated with @Entity, all its attributes are automatically mapped to a table. If you do not need to map an attribute, you can use the @javax.persistence.Transient annotation or the java transient keyword. For example, let's take the same Customer entity and add an age attribute (see Listing 3-20). Because age can be automatically calculated from the date of birth, the age attribute does not need to be mapped, and therefore can be transient.

Listing 3-20. The Customer Entity with a Transient Age

```
@Entity
public class Customer {

    @Id
    @GeneratedValue
    private Long id;
    private String firstName;
    private String lastName;
    private String email;
    private String phoneNumber;
    @Temporal(TemporalType.DATE)
    private Date dateOfBirth;
    @Transient
    private Integer age;
    @Temporal(TemporalType.TIMESTAMP)
    private Date creationDate;

    // Constructors, getters, setters
}
```

As a result, the age attribute doesn't need any AGE column to be mapped to.

@Enumerated

Java SE 5 introduced enumeration types, which are now so frequently used that they are commonly part of the developer's life. The values of an enum are constants and have an implicit ordinal assignment that is determined by the order in which they are declared. This ordinal cannot be modified at runtime but can be used to store the value of the enumerated type in the database. Listing 3-21 shows a credit card type enumeration.

Listing 3-21. Credit Card Type Enumeration

```
public enum CreditCardType {
    VISA,
    MASTER_CARD,
    AMERICAN_EXPRESS
}
```

The ordinals assigned to the values of this enumerated type at compile time are 0 for VISA, 1 for MASTER_CARD, and 2 for AMERICAN_EXPRESS. By default, the persistence providers will map this enumerated type to the database assuming that the column is of type Integer. Looking at the code in Listing 3-22, you see a CreditCard entity that uses the previous enumeration with the default mapping.

Listing 3-22. Mapping an Enumerated Type with Ordinals

```
@Entity
@Table(name = "credit_card")
public class CreditCard {

    @Id
    private String number;
    private String expiryDate;
    private Integer controlNumber;
    private CreditCardType creditCardType;

    // Constructors, getters, setters
}
```

Because the defaults are applied, the enumeration will get mapped to an integer column, and it will work fine. But imagine introducing a new constant to the top of the enumeration. Because ordinal assignment is determined by the order in which values are declared, the values already stored in the database will no longer match the enumeration. A better solution would be to store the name of the value as a string instead of storing the ordinal. You can do this by adding an @Enumerated annotation to the attribute and specifying a value of STRING (ORDINAL is the default value), as shown in Listing 3-23.

Listing 3-23. Mapping an Enumerated Type with `String`

```
@Entity
@Table(name = "credit_card")
public class CreditCard {

    @Id
    private String number;
    private String expiryDate;
    private Integer controlNumber;
    @Enumerated(EnumType.STRING)
    private CreditCardType creditCardType;

    // Constructors, getters, setters
}
```

Now the `CreditCardType` database column will be of type `VARCHAR` and a Visa card will be stored with the string `"VISA"`.

Access Type

Until now I have shown you annotated classes (`@Entity` or `@Table`) and attributes (`@Basic`, `@Column`, `@Temporal`, etc.), but the annotations applied on an attribute (or field access) can also be set on the corresponding getter method (or property access). For example, the annotation `@Id` can be set on the `id` attribute or on the `getId()` method. As this is largely a matter of personal preference, I tend to use property access (annotate the getters), as I find the code more readable. This allows me to quickly read the attributes of an entity without drowning in annotations. In this book, for easy readability, I've decided to annotate the attributes. But in some cases, for example, with inheritance, it is not simply a matter of personal taste, as it can have an impact upon your mapping.

■ **Note** Java defines a field as an instance attribute. A property is any field with accessor (getter and setter) methods that follow the Java bean pattern (starts with getXXX, setXXX, or isXXX for a `Boolean`).

When choosing between field access (attributes) or property access (getters), you are specifying *access type*. By default, a single access type applies to an entity: it is either field access or property access, but not both (i.e., the persistence provider accesses persistent state either via attributes or via the getter methods). The specification states that the behavior of an application that mixes the placement of annotations on fields and properties without explicitly specifying the access type is undefined.

When field-based access is used (see Listing 3-24), the persistence provider maps the attributes. All nontransient instance variables that are not annotated with the `@Transient` annotation are persistent.

Listing 3-24. The Customer Entity with Annotated Fields

```
@Entity
public class Customer {

    @Id @GeneratedValue
    private Long id;
    @Column(name = "first_name", nullable = false, length = 50)
    private String firstName;
    @Column(name = "last_name", nullable = false, length = 50)
    private String lastName;
    private String email;
    @Column(name = "phone_number", length = 15)
    private String phoneNumber;

    // Constructors, getters, setters
}
```

When property-based access is used, as shown in Listing 3-25, the mapping is based on the getters rather than the attributes. All getters not annotated with the @Transient annotation are persistent.

Listing 3-25. The Customer Entity with Annotated Properties

```
@Entity
public class Customer {

    private Long id;
    private String firstName;
    private String lastName;
    private String email;
    private String phoneNumber;

    // Constructors

    @Id @GeneratedValue
    public Long getId() {
        return id;
    }
    public void setId(Long id) {
        this.id = id;
    }

    @Column(name = "first_name", nullable = false, length = 50)
    public String getFirstName() {
        return firstName;
    }
```

```java
    public void setFirstName(String firstName) {
        this.firstName = firstName;
    }

    @Column(name = "last_name", nullable = false, length = 50)
    public String getLastName() {
        return lastName;
    }
    public void setLastName(String lastName) {
        this.lastName = lastName;
    }

    public String getEmail() {
        return email;
    }
    public void setEmail(String email) {
        this.email = email;
    }

    @Column(name = "phone_number", length = 15)
    public String getPhoneNumber() {
        return phoneNumber;
    }
    public void setPhoneNumber(String phoneNumber) {
        this.phoneNumber = phoneNumber;
    }
}
```

In terms of mapping, the two entities in Listings 3-24 and 3-25 are completely identical because the attribute names happen to be the same as the getter names. But instead of using the default access type, you can explicitly specify the type by means of the @javax.persistence.Access annotation.

This annotation takes two possible values, FIELD or PROPERTY, and can be used on the entity itself and/or on each attribute or getter. For example, when an @Access(AccessType.FIELD) is applied to the entity, only mapping annotations placed on the attributes will be taken into account by the persistence provider. It is then possible to selectively designate individual getters for property access with @Access(AccessType.PROPERTY).

Explicit access types can be very useful (for example, with embeddables and inheritance) but mixing them often results in errors. Listing 3-26 shows an example of what might happen when you mix access types.

Listing 3-26. The Customer Entity That Explicitly Mixes Access Types

```java
@Entity
@Access(AccessType.FIELD)
public class Customer {

    @Id @GeneratedValue
    private Long id;
    @Column(name = "first_name", nullable = false, length = 50)
```

```
    private String firstName;
    @Column(name = "last_name", nullable = false, length = 50)
    private String lastName;
    private String email;
    @Column(name = "phone_number", length = 15)
    private String phoneNumber;

    // Constructors, getters, setters

    @Access(AccessType.PROPERTY)
    @Column(name = "phone_number", length = 555)
    public String getPhoneNumber() {
        return phoneNumber;
    }
    public void setPhoneNumber(String phoneNumber) {
        this.phoneNumber = phoneNumber;
    }
}
```

This example explicitly defines the access type as being FIELD at the entity level. This indicates to the persistence manager that it should only process annotations on attributes. The phoneNumber attribute is annotated with @Column, which restricts its length to 15. Reading this code, you expect to end up with a VARCHAR(15) in the database, but this is not what happens. The getter method shows the access type for the getPhoneNumber() method has been explicitly changed, and so has the length of the phone number (to 555). In this case, the entity AccessType.FIELD is overwritten by AccessType.PROPERTY. You will then get a VARCHAR(555) in the database.

Collection of Basic Types

Collections of things are extremely common in Java. In the upcoming text, you will learn about relationships between entities (which can be collections of entities). Basically, this means that one entity has a collection of other entities or embeddables. In terms of mapping, each entity is mapped to its own table, and references between primary and foreign keys are created. As you know, an entity is a Java class with an identity and many other attributes. But what if you need to store only a collection of Java types such as Strings or Integers? Since JPA 2.0, you can easily do this without having to go through the trouble of creating a separate class by using the @ElementCollection and @CollectionTable annotations.

The @ElementCollection annotation is used to indicate that an attribute of type java.util.Collection contains a collection of instances of basic types (i.e., nonentities) or embeddables (more on that in the "Embeddables" section). In fact, this attribute can be of the following types:

- java.util.Collection: Generic root interface in the collection hierarchy.

- java.util.Set: Collection that prevents the insertion of duplicate elements.

- java.util.List: Collection used when the elements need to be retrieved in some user-defined order.

In addition, the @CollectionTable annotation allows you to customize details of the collection table (i.e., the table that will join the entity table with the basic types table) such as its name. If this annotation is missing, the table name will be the concatenation of the name of the containing entity and the name of the collection attribute, separated by an underscore.

Once again, using the example Book entity, let's see how to add an attribute to store tags. Today, tags and tag clouds are everywhere; these tend to be very useful for sorting data, so imagine for this example you want to add as many tags as you can to a book to describe it and to find it quickly. A tag is just a string, so the Book entity could have a collection of strings to store this information, as shown in Listing 3-27.

Listing 3-27. *The Book Entity with a Collection of Strings*

```
@Entity
public class Book {

    @Id
    @GeneratedValue(strategy = GenerationType.AUTO)
    private Long id;
    private String title;
    private Float price;
    private String description;
    private String isbn;
    private Integer nbOfPage;
    private Boolean illustrations;
    @ElementCollection(fetch = FetchType.LAZY)
    @CollectionTable(name = "Tag")
    @Column(name = "Value")
    private List<String> tags = new ArrayList<String>();

    // Constructors, getters, setters
}
```

The @ElementCollection annotation is used to inform the persistence provider that the tags attribute is a list of strings and should be fetched lazily. If @CollectionTable is missing, the table name defaults to BOOK_TAGS (a concatenation of the name of the containing entity and the name of the collection attribute, separated by an underscore) instead of TAG as specified in the name element (name = "Tag"). Notice that I've added a complementary @Column annotation to rename the column to VALUE (if not, the column would be named like the attribute, TAGS). The result is shown in Figure 3-3.

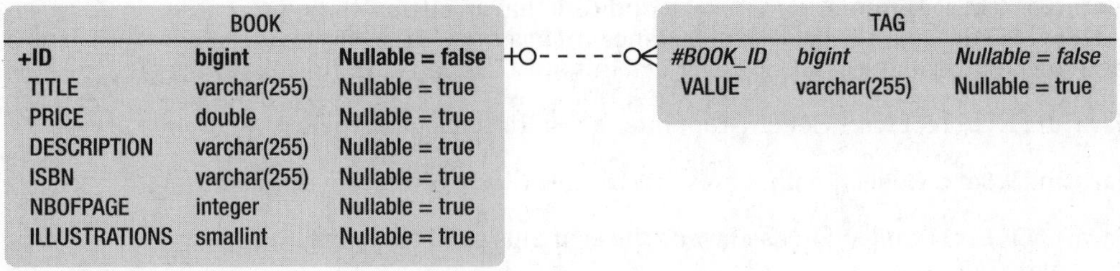

BOOK				TAG		
+ID	bigint	Nullable = false		#BOOK_ID	bigint	Nullable = false
TITLE	varchar(255)	Nullable = true		VALUE	varchar(255)	Nullable = true
PRICE	double	Nullable = true				
DESCRIPTION	varchar(255)	Nullable = true				
ISBN	varchar(255)	Nullable = true				
NBOFPAGE	integer	Nullable = true				
ILLUSTRATIONS	smallint	Nullable = true				

Figure 3-3. *Relationship between the BOOK and the TAG tables*

■ **Note** In JPA 1.0, these annotations didn't exist. However, you were still able to store a list of primitive types as a BLOB in the database. Why? Because `java.util.ArrayList` implements `Serializable`, and JPA can map `Serializable` objects to BLOBs automatically. However, if you used `java.util.List` instead, you would have an exception as it doesn't extend `Serializable`. The `@ElementCollection` is a more elegant and useful way of storing lists of basic types. Storing lists in an inaccessible binary format makes it opaque to queries and not portable to other languages (since only Java runtimes can make use of the underlying serialized object—not Ruby, PHP...).

Map of Basic Types

Like collections, maps are very useful to store data. In JPA 1.0, keys could only be a basic data type and values only entities. Now, maps can contain any combination of basic types, embeddable objects, and entities as keys or values, which brings significant flexibility to the mapping. But let's focus on maps of basic types.

When the map employs basic types, the `@ElementCollection` and `@CollectionTable` annotations can be used in the same way as you saw previously with collections. A collection table is then used to store the data of the map.

Let's take an example with a CD album that contains tracks (see Listing 3-28). A track can be seen as a title and a position (the first track of the album, the second track of the album, etc.). You could then have a map of tracks with an integer for the position (the key of the map) and a string for the title (the value of the map).

Listing 3-28. A CD Album with a Map of Tracks

```java
@Entity
public class CD {

    @Id
    @GeneratedValue
    private Long id;
    private String title;
    private Float price;
    private String description;
    @Lob
    private byte[] cover;
    @ElementCollection
    @CollectionTable(name="track")
    @MapKeyColumn (name = "position")
    @Column(name = "title")
    private Map<Integer, String> tracks = new HashMap<Integer, String>();

    // Constructors, getters, setters
}
```

As discussed previously, the @ElementCollection annotation is used to indicate the objects in the map that are stored in a collection table. The @CollectionTable annotation changes the default name of the collection table to TRACK.

The difference with collections is the introduction of a new annotation: @MapKeyColumn. This annotation is used to specify the mapping for the key column of the map. If it is not specified, the column is named with the concatenation of the name of the referencing relationship attribute and _KEY. Listing 3-28 shows the annotation renamed to POSITION from the default (TRACK_KEY) to be clearer.

The @Column annotation indicates that the column containing the map value should be renamed TITLE. The result is shown in the Figure 3-4.

CD				TRACK		
+ID	bigint	Nullable = false		#CD_ID	bigint	Nullable = false
TITLE	varchar(255)	Nullable = true		POSITION	integer	Nullable = true
PRICE	double	Nullable = true		TITLE	varchar(255)	Nullable = true
DESCRIPTION	varchar(255)	Nullable = true				
COVER	blob(64000)	Nullable = true				

Figure 3-4. *Relationship between the* CD *and the* TRACK *tables*

Mapping with XML

Now that you are more familiar with elementary mapping using annotations, let's take a look at XML mapping. If you have used an object-relational framework such as Hibernate, you will be familiar with how to map your entities in a separate XML deployment descriptors file. Since the beginning of this chapter, you haven't seen a single line of XML, just annotations. JPA also offers, as an option, an XML syntax to map entities. I will not go into too much detail about the XML mapping, as I've decided to focus on annotations (because they are easier to use in a book and most developers choose them over XML mapping). Keep in mind that every single annotation you see in this chapter has an XML equivalent, and this section would be huge if I covered them all. I encourage you to check Chapter 12 (XML Object/Relational Mapping Descriptor) of the JPA 2.0 specification, which covers all the XML tags in more detail.

XML deployment descriptors are an alternative to using annotations. However, although each annotation has an equivalent XML tag and vice versa, there is a difference in that the XML overrides annotations. If you annotate an attribute or an entity with a certain value, and at the same time you deploy an XML descriptor with a different value, the XML will take precedence.

The question is, when should you use annotations over XML and why? First of all, it's a matter of taste, as the behavior of both is exactly the same. When the metadata is really coupled to the code (for example, a primary key), it does make sense to use annotations, since the metadata is just another aspect of the program. Other kinds of metadata, such as the column length or other schema details, can be changed depending on the deployment environment (e.g., the database schema is different in the development, test, or production environment). A similar situation arises when a JPA-based product needs to support several different database vendors. Certain id generation, column options, etc. may need to be adjusted depending on the database type in use. This may be better expressed in external XML deployment descriptors (one per environment) so the code doesn't have to be modified.

Let's again turn to the Book entity example. This time imagine you have two environments, and you want to map the Book entity to the BOOK table in the development environment and to the BOOK_XML_MAPPING table in the test environment. The class will only be annotated with @Entity (see Listing 3-29) and not include information about the table it should be mapped to (i.e., it will have no

@Table annotation). The @Id annotation defines the primary key as being autogenerated, and a @Column annotation sets the size of the description to 500 characters long.

Listing 3-29. The Book Entity with Only a Few Annotations

```
@Entity
public class Book {

    @Id
    @GeneratedValue(strategy = GenerationType.AUTO)
    private Long id;
    private String title;
    private Float price;
    @Column(length = 500)
    private String description;
    private String isbn;
    private Integer nbOfPage;
    private Boolean illustrations;

    // Constructors, getters, setters
}
```

In a separate book_mapping.xml file (see Listing 3-30), following a specified XML schema, you can change the mapping for any data of the entity. The <table> tag allows you to change the name of the table to which the entity will be mapped (BOOK_XML_MAPPING instead of the default BOOK). Inside the <attributes> tag, you can customize the attributes, specifying not only their name and length, but also their relationships with other entities. For example, you can change the mapping for the title column and the number of pages (nbOfPage).

Listing 3-30. Mapping the File META-INF/book_mapping.xml

```xml
<?xml version="1.0" encoding="UTF-8"?>
<entity-mappings xmlns="http://java.sun.com/xml/ns/persistence/orm"
                 xmlns:xsi="http://www.w3.org/2001/XMLSchema-instance"
                 xsi:schemaLocation="http://java.sun.com/xml/ns/persistence/orm
                 http://java.sun.com/xml/ns/persistence/orm_2_0.xsd"
                 version="2.0">

  <entity class="com.apress.javaee6.chapter05.Book">
    <table name="book_xml_mapping"/>
    <attributes>
      <basic name="title">
        <column name="book_title" nullable="false" updatable="false"/>
      </basic>
      <basic name="description">
        <column length="2000"/>
      </basic>
```

```
    <basic name="nbOfPage">
      <column name="nb_of_page" nullable="false"/>
    </basic>
  </attributes>
</entity>

</entity-mappings>
```

An important notion to always have in mind is that the XML takes precedence on annotations. Even if the `description` attribute is annotated by `@Column(length = 500)`, the length of the column used is the one in the `book_mapping.xml` file, which is 2000. This can be confusing as you look at the code and see 500 and then check the DDL and see 2000; always remember to check the XML deployment descriptor.

A result of merging the XML metadata and the annotations metadata is that the `Book` entity will get mapped to the `BOOK_XML_MAPPING` table structure defined in Listing 3-31. If you want to completely ignore the annotations and define your mapping with XML only, you can add the `<xml-mapping-metadata-complete>` tag to the `book_mapping.xml` file (in this case, all the annotations will be ignored even if the XML does not contain an override).

Listing 3-31. `BOOK_XML_MAPPING` Table Structure

```
create table BOOK_XML_MAPPING (
    ID BIGINT not null,
    BOOK_TITLE VARCHAR(255) not null,
    DESCRIPTION VARCHAR(2000),
    NB_OF_PAGE INTEGER not null,
    PRICE DOUBLE(52, 0),
    ISBN VARCHAR(255),
    ILLUSTRATIONS SMALLINT,
    primary key (ID)
);
```

There is only one piece of information missing to make this work. In your `persistence.xml` file, you need to reference the `book_mapping.xml` file, and for this you have to use the `<mapping-file>` tag. The `persistence.xml` defines the entity persistence context and the database it should be mapped to. It is the central piece of information that the persistence provider needs to reference external XML mapping. Deploy the `Book` entity with both XML files in the `META-INF` directory, and you are done (see Listing 3-32).

Listing 3-32. A persistence.xml File Referring to an External Mapping File

```
<?xml version="1.0" encoding="UTF-8"?>
<persistence xmlns="http://java.sun.com/xml/ns/persistence"
             xmlns:xsi="http://www.w3.org/2001/XMLSchema-instance"
             xsi:schemaLocation="http://java.sun.com/xml/ns/persistence
             http://java.sun.com/xml/ns/persistence/persistence_2_0.xsd"
             version="2.0">

  <persistence-unit name="javaee6PU" transaction-type="RESOURCE_LOCAL">
    <provider>org.eclipse.persistence.jpa.PersistenceProvider</provider>
      <class>com.apress.javaee6.chapter05.Book</class>
```

```
    <mapping-file>META-INF/book_mapping.xml</mapping-file>
    <properties>
      <!--Persistence provider properties-->
    </properties>
  </persistence-unit>
</persistence>
```

Embeddables

In the "Composite Primary Keys" section earlier in the chapter, you quickly saw how a class could be embedded and used as a primary key with the @EmbeddedId annotation. Embeddables are objects that don't have a persistent identity on their own; they can be embedded only within owning entities. The owning entity can have collections of embeddables as well as a single embeddable attribute. They are stored as an intrinsic part of an owning entity and share the identity of this entity. This means each attribute of the embedded object is mapped to the table of the entity. It is a strict ownership relationship (a.k.a. composition), so that, if the entity is removed, the embedded object is also.

This composition between two classes uses annotations. The included class uses the @Embeddable annotation, whereas the entity that includes the class uses @Embedded. Let's take the example of a customer that has an identifier, a name, an e-mail address, and an address. All these attributes could be in a Customer entity (see Listing 3-34 a little later in the chapter), but, for object-modeling reasons, they are split into two classes: Customer and Address. Because Address has no identity of its own, but is merely part of the Customer state, it is a good candidate to become an embeddable object instead of an entity (see Listing 3-33).

Listing 3-33. The Address Class Is an Embeddable

```
@Embeddable
public class Address {

    private String street1;
    private String street2;
    private String city;
    private String state;
    private String zipcode;
    private String country;

    // Constructors, getters, setters
}
```

As you can see in Listing 3-33, the Address class is not annotated as being an entity but as an embeddable. The @Embeddable annotation specifies that Address can be embedded in another entity class (or another embeddable). On the other side of the composition, the Customer entity has to use the @Embedded annotation to specify that Address is a persistent attribute that will be stored as an intrinsic part and share its identity (see Listing 3-34).

Listing 3-34. The Customer Entity Embedding an Address

```
@Entity
public class Customer {

    @Id @GeneratedValue
    private Long id;
    private String firstName;
    private String lastName;
    private String email;
    private String phoneNumber;
    @Embedded
    private Address address;

    // Constructors, getters, setters
}
```

Each attribute of `Address` is mapped to the table of the owning entity `Customer`. There will only be one table with the structure defined in Listing 3-35. As you'll see later in the section "Overriding Attributes," entities can override the attributes of embeddables (using the `@AttributeOverrides` annotation).

Listing 3-35. Structure of the CUSTOMER Table with All the Address Attributes

```
create table CUSTOMER (
  ID BIGINT not null,
  LASTNAME VARCHAR(255),
  PHONENUMBER VARCHAR(255),
  EMAIL VARCHAR(255),
  FIRSTNAME VARCHAR(255),
  STREET2 VARCHAR(255),
  STREET1 VARCHAR(255),
  ZIPCODE VARCHAR(255),
  STATE VARCHAR(255),
  COUNTRY VARCHAR(255),
  CITY VARCHAR(255),
  primary key (ID)
);
```

■ **Note** In the previous sections I showed you how to map collections and maps of basic data types. In JPA 2.0, the same is possible with embeddables. You can map collections of embeddables as well as maps of embeddables (the embeddable can be either the key or the value of the map).

Access Type of an Embeddable Class

The access type of an embeddable class is determined by the access type of the entity class in which it exists. If the entity explicitly uses a property access type, an embeddable object will implicitly use property access as well. A different access type for an embeddable class can be specified by means of the @Access annotation.

The Customer entity (see Listing 3-36) and Address entity (see Listing 3-37) use different access types.

Listing 3-36. The Customer Entity with Field Access Type

```java
@Entity
@Access(AccessType.FIELD)
public class Customer {

    @Id @GeneratedValue
    private Long id;
    @Column(name = "first_name", nullable = false, length = 50)
    private String firstName;
    @Column(name = "last_name", nullable = false, length = 50)
    private String lastName;
    private String email;
    @Column(name = "phone_number", length = 15)
    private String phoneNumber;
    @Embedded
    private Address address;

    // Constructors, getters, setters
}
```

Listing 3-37. The Embeddable Object with Property Access Type

```java
@Embeddable
@Access(AccessType.PROPERTY)
public class Address {

    private String street1;
    private String street2;
    private String city;
    private String state;
    private String zipcode;
    private String country;

    // Constructors

    @Column(nullable = false)
    public String getStreet1() {
        return street1;
    }
```

```java
    public void setStreet1(String street1) {
        this.street1 = street1;
    }

    public String getStreet2() {
        return street2;
    }
    public void setStreet2(String street2) {
        this.street2 = street2;
    }

    @Column(nullable = false, length = 50)
    public String getCity() {
        return city;
    }
    public void setCity(String city) {
        this.city = city;
    }

    @Column(length = 3)
    public String getState() {
        return state;
    }
    public void setState(String state) {
        this.state = state;
    }

    @Column(name = "zip_code", length = 10)
    public String getZipcode() {
        return zipcode;
    }
    public void setZipcode(String zipcode) {
        this.zipcode = zipcode;
    }

    public String getCountry() {
        return country;
    }
    public void setCountry(String country) {
        this.country = country;
    }
}
```

Explicitly setting the access type on embeddables is strongly recommended to avoid mapping errors when an embeddable is embedded by multiple entities. Let's extend our model by adding an Order entity as shown in Figure 3-5. Address is now embedded by Customer (the home address of the customer) and Order (the delivery address).

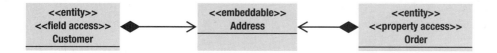

Figure 3-5. Address is embedded by Customer and Order.

Each entity defines a different access type: Customer uses field access, whereas Order uses property access. As an embeddable object's access type is determined by the access type of the entity class in which it is declared, Address will be mapped in two different ways, which can cause mapping problems. To avoid this, the Address access type should be set explicitly.

■ **Note** Explicit access types are also very helpful in inheritance. By default, the leaf entities inherit the access type of their root entity. In a hierarchy of entities, each can be accessed differently from the other classes in the hierarchy. Including an @Access annotation will cause the default access mode in effect for the hierarchy to be locally overridden.

Relationship Mapping

The world of object-oriented programming abounds with classes and associations between classes. These associations are structural in that they link objects of one kind to objects of another, allowing one object to cause another to perform an action on its behalf. Several types of associations can exist between classes.

First of all, an association has a direction. It can be *unidirectional* (i.e., one object can navigate toward another) or *bidirectional* (i.e., one object can navigate toward another and vice versa). In Java, you use the dot (.) syntax to navigate through objects. For example, when you write customer.getAddress().getCountry(), you navigate from the object Customer to Address and then to Country.

In Unified Modeling Language (UML), to represent a unidirectional association between two classes, you use an arrow to indicate the orientation. In Figure 3-6, Class1 (the source) can navigate to Class2 (the target), but not the inverse.

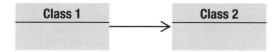

Figure 3-6. A unidirectional association between two classes

To indicate a bidirectional association, no arrows are used. As demonstrated in Figure 3-7, Class1 can navigate to Class2 and vice versa. In Java, this is represented as Class1 having an attribute of type Class2 and Class2 having an attribute of type Class1.

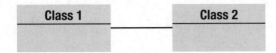

Figure 3-7. *A bidirectional association between two classes*

An association also has a *multiplicity* (or *cardinality*). Each end of an association can specify how many referring objects are involved in the association. The UML diagram in Figure 3-8 shows that one `Class1` refers to zero or more instances of `Class2`.

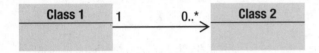

Figure 3-8. *Multiplicity on class associations*

In UML, a cardinality is a range between a minimum and a maximum number. So `0..1` means that you will have at minimum zero objects and at maximum one object. `1` means that you have one and only one instance. `1..*` means that you can have one or many instances, and `3..6` means that you have a range of between three and six objects. In Java, an association that represents more than one object uses collections of type `java.util.Collection`, `java.util.Set`, `java.util.List`, or even `java.util.Map`.

A relationship has an ownership (i.e., the owner of the relationship). In a unidirectional relationship, ownership is implied: in Figure 3-6, no doubt the owner is `Class1`, but in a bidirectional relationship, as depicted in Figure 3-7, the owner has to be specified explicitly. You then show the owning side, which specifies the physical mapping, and the inverse side (the non-owning side).

In the next sections, you'll see how to map collections of objects with JPA annotations.

Relationships in Relational Databases

In the relational world, things are different because, strictly speaking, a relational database is a collection of *relations* (also called *tables*), which means anything you model is a table. To model an association, you don't have lists, sets, or maps, you have tables. In JPA when you have an association between one class and another, in the database you will get a table reference. This reference can be modeled in two different ways: by using a *foreign key* (a *join column*) or by using a *join table*. In database terms, a column that refers to a key of another table is a *foreign key column*.

As an example, consider that a customer has one address, which is a *one-to-one relation*. In Java, you would have a `Customer` class with an `Address` attribute. In a relational world, you could have a `CUSTOMER` table pointing to an `ADDRESS` through a foreign key column (or join column), as described in Figure 3-9.

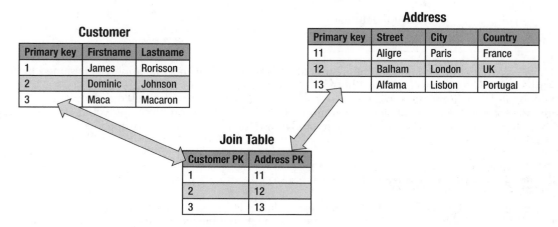

Customer

Primary key	Firstname	Lastname	Foreign key
1	James	Rorisson	11
2	Dominic	Johnson	12
3	Maca	Macaron	13

Address

Primary key	Street	City	Country
11	Aligre	Paris	France
12	Balham	London	UK
13	Alfama	Lisbon	Portugal

Figure 3-9. A relationship using a join column

There is a second way of modeling—using a join table. The CUSTOMER table in Figure 3-10 doesn't store the foreign key of the ADDRESS anymore. An intermediate table is created to hold the relationship information by storing the foreign keys of both tables.

Customer

Primary key	Firstname	Lastname
1	James	Rorisson
2	Dominic	Johnson
3	Maca	Macaron

Address

Primary key	Street	City	Country
11	Aligre	Paris	France
12	Balham	London	UK
13	Alfama	Lisbon	Portugal

Join Table

Customer PK	Address PK
1	11
2	12
3	13

Figure 3-10. A relationship using a join table

You wouldn't use a join table to represent a one-to-one relationship, as this could have performance issues (you always need to access a third table to get the address of a customer). Join tables are generally used when you have one-to-many or many-to-many cardinalities. As you will see in the following section, JPA uses these two modes to map object associations.

Entity Relationships

Now back to JPA. Most entities need to be able to reference, or have relationships with, other entities. This is what produces the domain model graphs that are common in business applications. JPA makes it possible to map associations so that an entity can be linked to another in a relational model. Like the elementary mapping annotations that you saw previously, JPA uses configuration by exception for associations. It has a default way of storing a relation, but, if this doesn't suit your database model, you have several annotations you can use to customize the mapping.

The cardinality between two entities may be one-to-one, one-to-many, many-to-one, or many-to-many. Each respective mapping is named after the cardinality of the source and target: @OneToOne,

@OneToMany, @ManyToOne, or @ManyToMany annotations. Each annotation can be used in a unidirectional or bidirectional way. Table 3-1 shows all the possible combinations between cardinalities and directions.

Table 3-1. All Possible Cardinality-Direction Combinations

Cardinality	Direction
One-to-one	Unidirectional
One-to-one	Bidirectional
One-to-many	Unidirectional
Many-to-one/one-to-many	Bidirectional
Many-to-one	Unidirectional
Many-to-many	Unidirectional
Many-to-many	Bidirectional

You will see that unidirectional and bidirectional are repetitive concepts that apply in the same way to all cardinalities. Next, you will see the difference between unidirectional and bidirectional relationships and then implement some of these combinations. I will not go through the complete catalog of the combinations but just focus on a subset. Explaining all the combinations would get repetitive. The important point is that you understand how to map cardinality and direction in relationships.

Unidirectional and Bidirectional

In an object-modeling point of view, direction between classes is natural. In a unidirectional association, object A points only to object B; in a bidirectional association, both objects refer to each other. However, some work is necessary when mapping a bidirectional relationship to a relational database, as is illustrated by the following example involving a customer who has a home address.

In a unidirectional relationship, a Customer entity has an attribute of type Address (see Figure 3-11). The relationship is one-way, navigating from one side to the other. Customer is said to be the owner of the relationship. In terms of the database, this means the CUSTOMER table will have a foreign key (join column) pointing to ADDRESS, and, when you own a relationship, you are able to customize the mapping of this relationship. For example, if you need to change the name of the foreign key, the mapping will be done in the Customer entity (i.e., the owner).

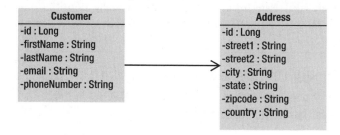

Figure 3-11. A unidirectional association between `Customer` *and* `Address`

As mentioned previously, relationships can also be bidirectional. To be able to navigate between `Address` and `Customer`, you need to transform a unidirectional relationship into a bidirectional one by adding a `Customer` attribute to the `Address` entity (see Figure 3-12). Note that, in UML class diagrams, attributes representing a relationship are not shown.

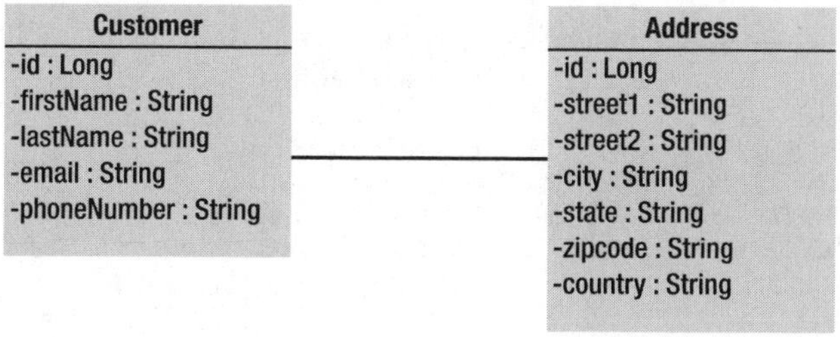

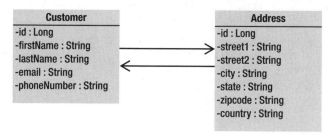

Figure 3-12. A bidirectional association between `Customer` *and* `Address`

In terms of Java code and annotations, it is similar to having two separate one-to-one mappings, one in each direction. You can think of a bidirectional relationship as a pair of unidirectional relationships, going both ways (see Figure 3-13).

Figure 3-13. A bidirectional association represented with two arrows

How do you map that? Who is the owner of this bidirectional relationship? Who owns the mapping information of the join column or the join table? If unidirectional relationships have an owning side, bidirectional ones have both an owning and an inverse side, which have to be explicitly specified with the mappedBy element of the @OneToOne, @OneToMany, and @ManyToMany annotations. mappedBy identifies the attribute that owns the relationship and is required for bidirectional relationships.

■ **Note** The foreign key attribute is not shown directly in the UML diagrams shown in Listings 3-11, 3-12 and 3-13. That's because in UML it is implied by the relationship. For example, in Listing 3-11, the arrow between Customer and Address implies that the Customer class has an attribute of type Address.

By way of explanation, let's compare the Java code (on one side) and the database mapping (on the other). As you can see on the left side of Figure 3-14, both entities point to each other through attributes: Customer has an address attribute annotated with @OneToOne, and the Address entity has a customer attribute also with an annotation. On the right side, the database mapping shows a CUSTOMER and an ADDRESS table. CUSTOMER is the owner of the relationship because it contains the ADDRESS foreign key.

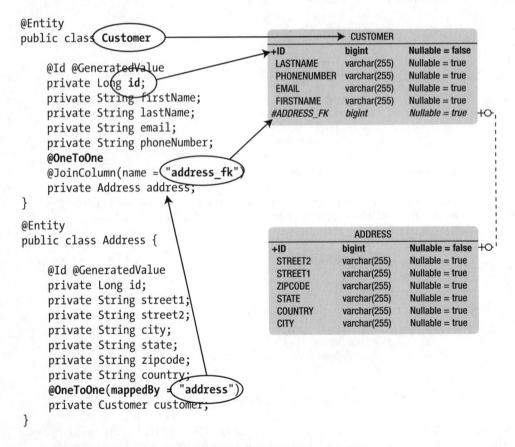

Figure 3-14. Customer and Address code with database mapping

The **Address** entity uses the **mappedBy** element on its **@OneToOne** annotation. **Address** is called the inverse owner of the relationship because it has a **mappedBy** element. The **mappedBy** element indicates that the join column (**address**) is specified at the other end of the relationship. In fact, at the other end, the **Customer** entity defines the join column by using the **@JoinColumn** annotation and renames the foreign key to **address_fk**. **Customer** is the owning side of the relationship, and, as the owner, it is the one to define the join column mapping. **Address** is the inverse side where the table of the owning entity contains the foreign key (the **CUSTOMER** table is the one with the **ADDRESS_FK** column).

There is a **mappedBy** element on the **@OneToOne**, **@OneToMany**, and **@ManyToMany** annotations, but not on the **@ManyToOne** annotation. You cannot have a **mappedBy** attribute on both sides of a bidirectional association. It would also be incorrect to not have it on either side as the provider would treat it as two independent unidirectional relationships. This would imply that each side is the owner and can define a join column.

■ **Note** If you are familiar with Hibernate, you might think of the JPA **mappedBy** as the equivalent of the Hibernate **inverse** attribute.

@OneToOne Unidirectional

A one-to-one unidirectional relationship between entities has a reference of cardinality **1**, which can be reached in only one direction. Referring to the example of a customer and her address, assume the customer has only one address (cardinality **1**). It is important to navigate from the customer (the source) toward the address (the target) to know where the customer lives. However, for some reason, in our model, shown in Figure 3-15, you don't need to be able to navigate in the opposite direction (i.e., you don't need to know which customer lives at a given address, for example).

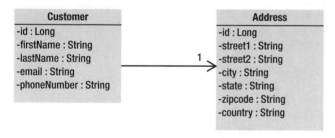

Figure 3-15. One customer has one address.

In Java, this means the **Customer** will have an **Address** attribute (see Listings 3-38 and 3-39).

Listing 3-38. A Customer with One Address

```
@Entity
public class Customer {

    @Id @GeneratedValue
    private Long id;
    private String firstName;
    private String lastName;
    private String email;
    private String phoneNumber;
    private Address address;

    // Constructors, getters, setters
}
```

Listing 3-39. An Address Entity

```
@Entity
public class Address {

    @Id @GeneratedValue
    private Long id;
    private String street1;
    private String street2;
    private String city;
    private String state;
    private String zipcode;
    private String country;

    // Constructors, getters, setters
}
```

As you can see in Listings 3-38 and 3-39, these two entities have the minimum required annotations: `@Entity` plus `@Id` and `@GeneratedValue` for the primary key, that's all. With configuration by exception, the persistence provider will map these two entities to two tables and a foreign key for the relationship (from the customer pointing to the address). A one-to-one mapping is triggered by the fact that `Address` is declared an entity and included in the `Customer` entity as an attribute. A relationship is automatically implied by using an entity as a property on another entity so no `@OneToOne` annotation is needed, as it relies on the defaults (see Listings 3-40 and 3-41).

Listing 3-40. The CUSTOMER Table with a Foreign Key to Address

```
create table CUSTOMER (
  ID BIGINT not null,
  FIRSTNAME VARCHAR(255),
  LASTNAME VARCHAR(255),
  EMAIL VARCHAR(255),
```

```
  PHONENUMBER VARCHAR(255),
  ADDRESS_ID BIGINT,
  primary key (ID),
  foreign key (ADDRESS_ID) references ADDRESS(ID)
);
```

Listing 3-41. The ADDRESS Table

```
create table ADDRESS (
  ID BIGINT not null,
  STREET1 VARCHAR(255),
  STREET2 VARCHAR(255),
  CITY VARCHAR(255),
  STATE VARCHAR(255),
  ZIPCODE VARCHAR(255),
  COUNTRY VARCHAR(255),
  primary key (ID)
);
```

As you now know, with JPA, if an attribute is not annotated, the default mapping rules are applied. So, by default, the foreign key column is named ADDRESS_ID (see Listing 3-40), which is the concatenation of the name of the relationship attribute (here address), the symbol _, and the name of the primary key column of the destination table (here it will be the column ID of the ADDRESS table). Also notice that, in the DDL, the ADDRESS_ID column is nullable by default, meaning that, by default, a one-to-one association is mapped to a zero (null value) or one.

To customize the mapping, you can use two annotations. The first one is @OneToOne (that's because the cardinality of the relation is one), and it can modify some attributes of the association itself such as the way is has to be fetched. The API of the @OneToOne annotation is defined in Listing 3-42.

Listing 3-42. @OneToOne Annotation API

```
@Target({METHOD, FIELD}) @Retention(RUNTIME)
public @interface OneToOne {
    Class targetEntity() default void.class;
    CascadeType[] cascade() default {};
    FetchType fetch() default EAGER;
    boolean optional() default true;
    String mappedBy() default "";
    boolean orphanRemoval() default false;
}
```

The other is @JoinColumn (its API is very similar to @Column). It is used to customize the join column, meaning the foreign key, of the owning side. Listing 3-43 shows how you would use these two annotations.

Listing 3-43. The Customer *Entity with Customized Relationship Mapping*

```
@Entity
public class Customer {

    @Id @GeneratedValue
    private Long id;
    private String firstName;
    private String lastName;
    private String email;
    private String phoneNumber;
    @OneToOne (fetch = FetchType.LAZY)
    @JoinColumn(name = "add_fk", nullable = false)
    private Address address;

    // Constructors, getters, setters
}
```

In JPA, a foreign key column is called a join column. The @JoinColumn annotation allows you to customize the mapping of a foreign key. It is used in Listing 3-43 to rename the foreign key column to ADD_FK and make the relationship obligatory by refusing the null value (nullable=false). The @OneToOne annotation gives the persistence provider a hint to fetch the relationship lazily.

@OneToMany Unidirectional

A one-to-many relationship is when one source object refers to an ensemble of target objects. For example, a purchase order is composed of several order lines (see Figure 3-16). The order line could refer to the purchase order with a corresponding @ManyToOne annotation. Order is the "one" side and the source of the relationship, and OrderLine is the "many" side and the target.

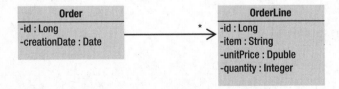

Figure 3-16. One order has several lines.

The cardinality is multiple, and the navigation is done only from Order toward OrderLine. In Java, this multiplicity is described by the Collection, List, and Set interfaces of the java.util package. Listing 3-44 shows the code of the Order entity with a one-way, one-to-many relationship toward OrderLine (see Listing 3-45).

Listing 3-44. An Order *Contains* OrderLines

```
@Entity
public class Order {

    @Id @GeneratedValue
    private Long id;
    @Temporal(TemporalType.TIMESTAMP)
    private Date creationDate;
    private List<OrderLine> orderLines;

    // Constructors, getters, setters
}
```

Listing 3-45. An OrderLine

```
@Entity
@Table(name = "order_line")
public class OrderLine {

    @Id @GeneratedValue
    private Long id;
    private String item;
    private Double unitPrice;
    private Integer quantity;

    // Constructors, getters, setters
}
```

The code in Listing 3-44 doesn't have any special annotation and relies on the configuration-by-exception paradigm. The fact that a collection of an entity type is being used as an attribute on this entity triggers a OneToMany relationship mapping by default. By default, one-to-many unidirectional relationships use a join table to keep the relationship information, with two foreign key columns. One foreign key column refers to the table ORDER and has the same type as its primary key, and the other refers to ORDER_LINE. The name of this joined table is the name of both entities, separated by the _ symbol. The join table is named ORDER_ORDER_LINE and will result in the schema structure illustrated in Figure 3-17.

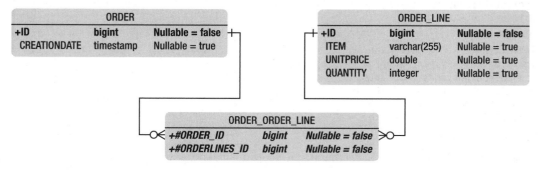

Figure 3-17. Join table between ORDER *and* ORDER_LINE

If you don't like the join table name and foreign key names, or, if you are mapping to an existing table, you can use JPA annotations to redefine these default values. The default value for a join column is the concatenation of the name of the entity, the symbol _, and the name of the referenced primary key. As the `@JoinColumn` annotation can be used to change the foreign key columns, the `@JoinTable` annotation can do the same for the join table mapping. You can also use the `@OneToMany` annotation (see Listing 3-46), which like `@OneToOne` customizes the relationship itself (using `fetch` mode and so on).

Listing 3-46. @JoinTable Annotation API

```
@Target({METHOD, FIELD}) @Retention(RUNTIME)
public @interface JoinTable {
    String name() default "";
    String catalog() default "";
    String schema() default "";
    JoinColumn[] joinColumns() default {};
    JoinColumn[] inverseJoinColumns() default {};
    UniqueConstraint[] uniqueConstraints() default {};
}
```

On the API of the `@JoinTable` annotation in Listing 3-46, you can see two attributes that are of type `@JoinColumn`: `joinColumns` and `inverseJoinColumns`. These two attributes are distinguished by means of the owning side and the inverse side. The owning side (the owner of the relationship) is described in the `joinColumns` element and, in our example, refers to the ORDER table. The inverse side, the target of the relationship, is specified by the `inverseJoinColumns` element and refers to ORDER_LINE.

Using the `Order` entity (see Listing 3-47), you can add the `@OneToMany` and `@JoinTable` annotations on the `orderLines` attribute by renaming the join table to JND_ORD_LINE (instead of ORDER_ORDER_LINE), as well as the two foreign key columns.

Listing 3-47. The Order Entity with Annotated One-to-Many Relationship

```
@Entity
public class Order {

    @Id @GeneratedValue
    private Long id;
    @Temporal(TemporalType.TIMESTAMP)
    private Date creationDate;
    @OneToMany
    @JoinTable(name = "jnd_ord_line",
        joinColumns = @JoinColumn(name = "order_fk"),
        inverseJoinColumns = @JoinColumn(name = "order_line_fk") )
    private List<OrderLine> orderLines;

    // Constructors, getters, setters
}
```

The `Order` entity in Listing 3-47 will get mapped to the join table described in Listing 3-48.

Listing 3-48. Structure of the Join Table

```
create table JND_ORD_LINE (
    ORDER_FK BIGINT not null,
    ORDER_LINE_FK BIGINT not null,
    primary key (ORDER_FK, ORDER_LINE_FK),
    foreign key (ORDER_LINE_FK) references ORDER_LINE(ID),
    foreign key (ORDER_FK) references ORDER(ID)
);
```

The default rule for a one-to-many unidirectional relationship is to use a join table, but it is very easy (and useful for legacy databases) to change to using foreign keys. The `Order` entity has to provide a `@JoinColumn` annotation instead of a `@JoinTable`, allowing the code to be changed as shown in Listing 3-49.

Listing 3-49. The `Order` Entity with a Join Column

```
@Entity
public class Order {

    @Id @GeneratedValue
    private Long id;
    @Temporal(TemporalType.TIMESTAMP)
    private Date creationDate;
    @OneToMany(fetch = FetchType.EAGER)
    @JoinColumn(name = "order_fk")
    private List<OrderLine> orderLines;

    // Constructors, getters, setters
}
```

The code of the `OrderLine` entity (shown previously in Listing 3-45) doesn't change. Notice that in Listing 3-49 the `@OneToMany` annotation is overriding the default `fetch` mode (turning it to `EAGER` instead of `LAZY`). By using `@JoinColumn`, the unidirectional association is then mapped using the foreign key strategy. The foreign key is renamed to `ORDER_FK` by the annotation and exists in the target table (`ORDER_LINE`). The result is the database structure shown in Figure 3-18. There is no join table, and the reference between both tables is through the foreign key `ORDER_FK`.

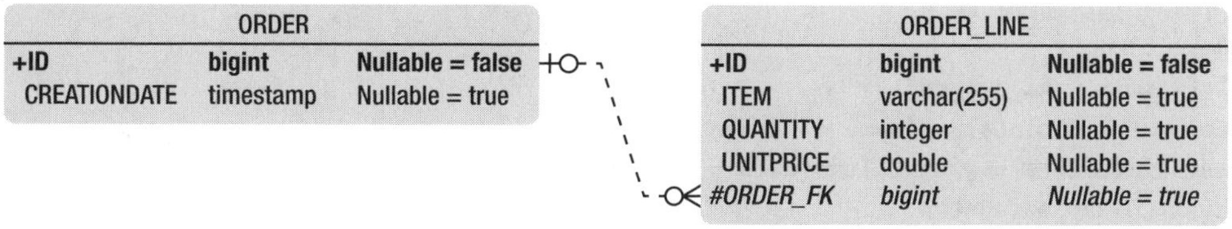

ORDER		
+ID	bigint	Nullable = false
CREATIONDATE	timestamp	Nullable = true

ORDER_LINE		
+ID	bigint	Nullable = false
ITEM	varchar(255)	Nullable = true
QUANTITY	integer	Nullable = true
UNITPRICE	double	Nullable = true
#ORDER_FK	bigint	Nullable = true

Figure 3-18. Join column between `Order` and `OrderLine`

@ManyToMany Bidirectional

A many-to-many bidirectional relationship exists when one source object refers to many targets, and when a target refers to many sources. For example, a CD album is created by several artists, and an artist appears on several albums. In the Java world, each entity will have a collection of target entities. In the relational world, the only way to map a many-to-many relationship is to use a join table (a join column would not work), and, as you've seen previously, in a bidirectional relationship you need to explicitly define the owner (with the mappedBy element).

Assuming the Artist entity is the owner of the relationship means that the CD is the reverse owner (see Listing 3-50) and needs to use the mappedBy element on its @ManyToMany annotation. mappedBy tells the persistence provider that appearsOnCDs is the name of the corresponding attribute of the owning entity.

Listing 3-50. One CD is Created by Several Artists

```
@Entity
public class CD {

    @Id @GeneratedValue
    private Long id;
    private String title;
    private Float price;
    private String description;
    @ManyToMany(mappedBy = "appearsOnCDs")
    private List<Artist> createdByArtists;

    // Constructors, getters, setters
}
```

So, if the Artist is the owner of the relationship, as shown in Listing 3-51, it is the one to customize the mapping of the join table via the @JoinTable and @JoinColumn annotations.

Listing 3-51. One Artist Appears on Several CD Albums

```
@Entity
public class Artist {

    @Id @GeneratedValue
    private Long id;
    private String firstName;
    private String lastName;
    @ManyToMany
    @JoinTable(name = "jnd_art_cd", ↪
        joinColumns = @JoinColumn(name = "artist_fk"), ↪
        inverseJoinColumns = @JoinColumn(name = "cd_fk"))
    private List<CD> appearsOnCDs;

    // Constructors, getters, setters
}
```

The join table between `Artist` and `CD` is renamed to `JND_ART_CD` as well as each join column. The `joinColumns` element refers to the owning side (the `Artist`) and the `inverseJoinColumns` refers to the inverse owning side (the `CD`). The database structure is shown in Figure 3-19.

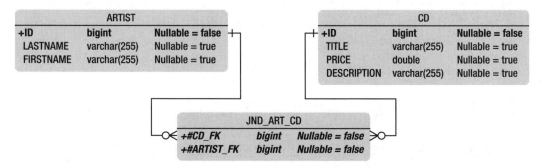

Figure 3-19. Artist, CD, and the join table

Note that, on a many-to-many and one-to-one bidirectional relationship, either side may be designated as the owning side. No matter which side is designated as the owner, the other side should include the `mappedBy` element. If not, the provider will think that both sides are the owner and will treat it as two separate one-to-many unidirectional relationships. That could result in four tables: `ARTIST` and `CD`, plus two joining tables, `ARTIST_CD` and `CD_ARTIST`. Neither would it be legal to have a `mappedBy` on both sides.

Fetching Relationships

All the annotations that you have seen (`@OneToOne`, `@OneToMany`, `@ManyToOne`, and `@ManyToMany`) define a fetching attribute, specifying the associated objects to be loaded immediately (eagerly) or deferred (lazily), with a resulting impact on performance. Depending on your application, certain relationships are accessed more often than others. In these situations, you can optimize performance by loading data from the database when the entity is initially read (eagerly) or when it is accessed (lazily). As an example, let's look at some extreme cases.

Imagine four entities all linked to each other with different cardinalities (one-to-one, one-to-many). In the first case (see Figure 3-20), they all have eager relationships. This means that, as soon as you load `Class1` (by a find by ID or a query), all the dependent objects are automatically loaded in memory. This can have an impact on the performance of your system.

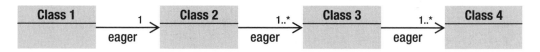

Figure 3-20. Four entities with eager relationships

Looking at the opposite scenario, all the relationships use a lazy `fetch` mode (see Figure 3-21). When you load `Class1`, nothing else is loaded (except the direct attributes of `Class1`, of course). You need to explicitly access `Class2` (by using the getter method, for example) to tell the persistence provider to load the data from the database, and so on. If you want to manipulate the entire object graph, you need to explicitly call each entity:

```
class1.getClass2().getClass3().getClass4()
```

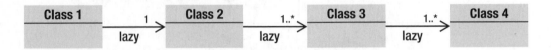

Figure 3-21. Four entities with lazy relationships

But don't think that `EAGER` is evil and `LAZY` is good. `EAGER` will bring all the data into memory using a small amount of database access (the persistence provider will probably use join queries to join the tables together and extract the data). With `LAZY`, you don't take the risk of filling up your memory because you control which object is loaded. But you have to access the database every time.

The `fetch` parameter is very important because, if it is misused, it can cause performance problems. Each annotation has a default `fetch` value that you have to be aware of and, if not appropriate, change (see Table 3-2).

Table 3-2. Default Fetching Strategies

Annotation	Default Fetching Strategy
@OneToOne	EAGER
@ManyToOne	EAGER
@OneToMany	LAZY
@ManyToMany	LAZY

If, when you load a purchase order in your application, you always need to access its order lines, then it may be efficient to change the default `fetch` mode of the `@OneToMany` annotation to `EAGER` (see Listing 3-52).

Listing 3-52. An Order with an Eager Relationship to `OrderLine`

```
@Entity
public class Order {

    @Id @GeneratedValue
    private Long id;
    @Temporal(TemporalType.TIMESTAMP)
```

```
    private Date creationDate;
    @OneToMany(fetch = FetchType.EAGER)
    private List<OrderLine> orderLines;

    // Constructors, getters, setters
}
```

Ordering Relationships

With one-to-many or many-to-many relationships, your entities deal with collections of objects. On the Java side, these collections are usually unordered. Neither do relational databases preserve any order in their tables. Therefore, if you want an ordered list, it is necessary to either sort your collection programmatically or use a JPQL query with an `Order By` clause. JPA has easier mechanisms, based on annotations that can help in ordering relationships.

@OrderBy

Dynamic ordering can be done with the `@OrderBy` annotation. "Dynamically" means that the ordering of the elements of a collection is made when the association is retrieved.

The example of the CD-BookStore application allows a user to write news about music and books. This news is text that is displayed on the web site. Once the news is published, people are allowed to add comments (see Listing 3-53). On the web site you want to display the comments chronologically, so ordering comes into account.

Listing 3-53. A Comment Entity with a Posted Date

```
@Entity
public class Comment {

    @Id @GeneratedValue
    private Long id;
    private String nickname;
    private String content;
    private Integer note;
    @Column(name = "posted_date")
    @Temporal(TemporalType.TIMESTAMP)
    private Date postedDate;

    // Constructors, getters, setters
}
```

The comments are modeled using the `Comment` entity, shown in Listing 3-53. It has content, is posted by an anonymous user (identified by a nickname) who leaves a note on the news, and has a posted date of type `TIMESTAMP` that is automatically created by the system. In the `News` entity, shown in Listing 3-54, you want to be able to arrange the list of comments ordered by posted date in descending order. To achieve this, you use the `@OrderBy` annotation in conjunction with the `@OneToMany` annotation.

Listing 3-54. The Comments of a News Entity Are Ordered by Descending Posted Date

```
@Entity
public class News {

    @Id @GeneratedValue
    private Long id;
    @Column(nullable = false)
    private String content;
    @OneToMany(fetch = FetchType.EAGER)
    @OrderBy("postedDate DESC")
    private List<Comment> comments;

    // Constructors, getters, setters
}
```

The `@OrderBy` annotation takes as parameters the names of the attributes on which the sorting has to be made (the `postedDate` attribute), as well as the method (ascending or descending). The string `ASC` or `DESC` can be used for sorting in either an ascending or descending manner, respectively. You can have several columns used in the `@OrderBy` annotation. If you need to order by posted date and note, you can use `OrderBy("postedDate DESC, note ASC")`.

The `@OrderBy` annotation doesn't have any impact on the database mapping. The persistence provider is simply informed to use an `order by` clause when the collection is retrieved.

@OrderColumn

JPA 1.0 supported dynamic ordering using the `@OrderBy` annotation but did not include support for maintaining a persistent ordering. JPA 2.0 addresses this by adding a new annotation: `@OrderColumn` (see Listing 3-55). This annotation informs the persistence provider that it is required to maintain the ordered list using a separate column where the index is stored. The `@OrderColumn` defines this separate column.

Listing 3-55. The @OrderColumn API Is Similar to @Column

```
@Target({METHOD, FIELD}) @Retention(RUNTIME)
public @interface OrderColumn {
    String name() default "";
    boolean nullable() default true;
    boolean insertable() default true;
    boolean updatable() default true;
    String columnDefinition() default "";
    int base() default 0;
    String table() default "";
}
```

Let's use the news and comments example and change it slightly. This time the `Comment` entity, shown in Listing 3-56, has no `postedDate` attribute, and therefore there is no way to chronologically sort the comments.

Listing 3-56. A Comment Entity with No Posted Date

```
@Entity
public class Comment {

    @Id @GeneratedValue
    private Long id;
    private String nickname;
    private String content;
    private Integer note;

    // Constructors, getters, setters
}
```

What the News entity, shown in Listing 3-57, *can* do is annotate the relationship with @OrderColumn. The persistence provider will then map the News entity to a table with an additional column to store the ordering.

Listing 3-57. The Ordering of Comments Is Persisted

```
@Entity
public class News {

    @Id @GeneratedValue
    private Long id;
    @Column(nullable = false)
    private String content;
    @OneToMany(fetch = FetchType.EAGER)
    @OrderColumn(name = "posted_index")
    private List<Comment> comments;

    // Constructors, getters, setters
}
```

In Listing 3-57, the @OrderColumn renames the additional column to POSTED_INDEX. If the name is not overridden, by default the column name is the concatenation of the name of the entity attribute and the _ORDER string (COMMENTS_ORDER in our example). The type of this column must be a numerical type. This ordered relationship will map to a separate join table as shown below:

```
create table NEWS_COMMENT (
    NEWS_ID BIGINT not null,
    COMMENTS_ID BIGINT not null,
    POSTED_INDEX INTEGER
);
```

There are performance impacts to be aware of; as with the @OrderColumn annotation, the persistence provider must also track changes to the index. It is responsible for maintaining the order upon insertion, deletion, or reordering. If data is inserted in the middle of an existing, sorted list of information, the persistence provider will have to reorder the entire index.

Portable applications should not expect a list to be ordered by the database, under the pretext that some database engines automatically optimize their indexes so that the data table appears as sorted. Instead, it should use either the @OrderColumn or @OrderBy construct. Note that you can't use both annotations at the same time.

Inheritance Mapping

Since their creation, object-oriented languages have used the inheritance paradigm. C++ allows multiple inheritance, and Java supports single-class inheritance. In object-oriented languages, developers commonly reuse code by inheriting attributes and behavior of root classes.

You have just studied relationships, and relationships between entities have a very straightforward mapping to a relational database. This is not the case with inheritance. Inheritance is a completely unknown concept and not natively implemented in a relational world. The concept of inheritance throws in several twists when saving objects into a relational database.

How do you organize a hierarchical model into a flat relational one? JPA has three different strategies you can choose from:

- A *single-table-per-class hierarchy strategy*: The sum of the attributes of the entire entity hierarchy is flattened down to a single table (this is the default strategy).

- A *joined-subclass strategy*: In this approach, each entity in the hierarchy, concrete or abstract, is mapped to its own dedicated table.

- A *table-per-concrete-class strategy*: This strategy maps each concrete entity hierarchy to its own separate table.

■ **Note** Support for the table-per-concrete-class inheritance mapping strategy is still optional in JPA 2.0. Portable applications should avoid using it until officially mandated.

Leveraging the easy use of annotations, JPA 2.0 delivers declarative support for defining and mapping inheritance hierarchies, including entities, abstract entities, mapped classes, and transient classes. The @Inheritance annotation is used on the root entity to dictate the mapping strategy to itself and to the leaf classes. JPA also transposes the object notion of overriding to the mapping, which allows root class attributes to be overridden by child classes. In the upcoming section, you will also see how the access type can be used with inheritance to mix field access and property access.

Inheritance Strategies

When it comes to mapping inheritance, JPA supports three different strategies. When an entity hierarchy exists, it always has an entity as its root. The root entity class can define the inheritance strategy by using the @Inheritance annotation. If it doesn't, the default single-table-per-class hierarchy strategy will be applied. To explore each strategy, I will discuss how to map a CD and a Book entity, both inheriting from the Item entity (see Figure 3-22).

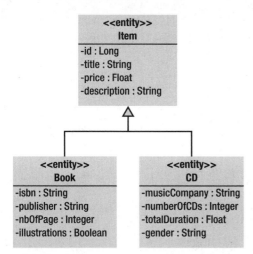

Figure 3-22. Inheritance hierarchy between CD, Book, and Item

The Item entity is the root entity and has an identifier, which will turn into a primary key, from which both the CD and Book entities inherit. Each of these leaf classes adds extra attributes such as an ISBN for the Book entity or a total time duration for the CD entity.

Single-Table-per-Class Hierarchy Strategy

The default inheritance mapping strategy is the single-table-per-class strategy, in which all the entities in the hierarchy are mapped to a single table. As it is the default, you can completely omit the @Inheritance annotation on the root entity (thanks to configuration by exception), and that's what the Item entity does (see Listing 3-58).

Listing 3-58. The Item Entity Defines a Single-Table-per-Class Strategy

```
@Entity
public class Item {

    @Id @GeneratedValue
    protected Long id;
    @Column(nullable = false)
    protected String title;
    @Column(nullable = false)
    protected Float price;
    protected String description;

    // Constructors, getters, setters
}
```

Item is the root class for the Book entity (see Listing 3-59) and CD entity (see Listing 3-60). These entities inherit the attributes of Item as well as the default inheritance strategy, and therefore don't have to use the @Inheritance annotation.

Listing 3-59. Book Extends Item

```
@Entity
public class Book extends Item {

    private String isbn;
    private String publisher;
    private Integer nbOfPage;
    private Boolean illustrations;

    // Constructors, getters, setters
}
```

Listing 3-60. CD Extends Item

```
@Entity
public class CD extends Item {

    private String musicCompany;
    private Integer numberOfCDs;
    private Float totalDuration;
    private String gender;

    // Constructors, getters, setters
}
```

With what you have seen so far, without inheritance, these three entities would be mapped into their own, separate tables, but with inheritance it's different. With the single-table-per-class strategy, they all end up in the same database table, which defaults to the name of the root class: ITEM. Figure 3-23 shows the ITEM table structure.

ITEM		
+ID	bigint	Nullable = false
DTYPE	varchar(31)	Nullable = true
TITLE	varchar(255)	Nullable = false
PRICE	double	Nullable = false
DESCRIPTION	varchar(255)	Nullable = true
ILLUSTRATIONS	smallinit	Nullable = true
ISBN	varchar(255)	Nullable = true
NBOFPAGE	integer	Nullable = true
PUBLISHER	varchar(255)	Nullable = true
MUSICCOMPANY	varchar(255)	Nullable = true
NUMBEROFCDS	integer	Nullable = true
TOTALDURATION	double	Nullable = true
GENDER	varchar(255)	Nullable = true

Figure 3-23. ITEM table structure

As you can see in Figure 3-23, the ITEM table sums all the attributes of the Item, Book, and CD entities. But there's an additional column that doesn't relate to any of the entities' attributes: it's the discriminator column, DTYPE.

The ITEM table will be filled with items, books, and CD albums. When accessing the data, the persistence provider needs to know which row belongs to which entity. This way, the provider will instantiate the appropriate object type (Item, Book, or CD) when reading the ITEM table. That's why a discriminator column is used to explicitly type each row.

Figure 3-24 shows a fragment of the ITEM table with some data. As you can see, the single-table-per-class strategy has some holes; not every column is useful for each entity. The first row is the data stored for an Item entity (the DTYPE column contains the name of the entity). Items only have a title, a price, and a description (see Listing 3-58 earlier); they don't have a music company, an ISBN, and so on. So these columns will always remain empty.

ID	DTYPE	TITLE	PRICE	DESCRIPTION	MUSIC COMPANY	ISBN	...
1	Item	Pen	2.10	Beautiful black pen			...
2	CD	Soul Train	23.50	Fantastic jazz album	Prestige		...
3	CD	Zoot Allures	18	One of the best of Zappa	Warner		...
4	Book	The robots of dawn	22.30	Robots everywhere		0-554-456	...
5	Book	H2G2	17.50	Funny IT book ;o)		1-278-983	...

Figure 3-24. Fragment of the ITEM table filled with data

The discriminator column is called DTYPE by default, is of type String (mapped to a VARCHAR), and contains the name of the entity. If the defaults don't suit, the @DiscriminatorColumn annotation allows you to change the name and the data type. By default, the value of this column is the entity name to which it refers, although an entity may override this value using the @DiscriminatorValue annotation.

In Listing 3-61, I rename the discriminator column to DISC (instead of DTYPE) and change its data type to Char instead of String; each entity should change its discriminator value to I for Item, B for Book (see Listing 3-62), and C for CD (see Listing 3-63).

Listing 3-61. Item Redefines the Discriminator Column

```
@Entity
@Inheritance(strategy = InheritanceType.SINGLE_TABLE)
@DiscriminatorColumn (name="disc", ↪
                    discriminatorType = DiscriminatorType.CHAR)
@DiscriminatorValue("I")
public class Item {

    @Id @GeneratedValue
    protected Long id;
    protected String title;
    protected Float price;
    protected String description;

    // Constructors, getters, setters
}
```

The root entity `Item` defines the discriminator column once for the entire hierarchy with `@DiscriminatorColumn`. It then changes its own default value to I with the `@DiscriminatorValue` annotation. Child items have to redefine their own discriminator value only.

Listing 3-62. Book Redefines the Discriminator Value to B

```
@Entity
@DiscriminatorValue("B")
public class Book extends Item {

    private String isbn;
    private String publisher;
    private Integer nbOfPage;
    private Boolean illustrations;

    // Constructors, getters, setters
}
```

Listing 3-63. CD Redefines the Discriminator Value to C

```
@Entity
@DiscriminatorValue("C")
public class CD extends Item {

    private String musicCompany;
    private Integer numberOfCDs;
    private Float totalDuration;
    private String gender;

    // Constructors, getters, setters
}
```

The result is shown in Figure 3-25. The discriminator column and its values are different from those shown earlier in Figure 3-24.

ID	DTYPE	TITLE	PRICE	DESCRIPTION	MUSIC COMPANY	ISBN	...
1	I	Pen	2.10	Beautiful black pen			...
2	C	Soul Train	23.50	Fantastic jazz album	Prestige		...
3	C	Zoot Allures	18	One of the best of Zappa	Warner		...
4	B	The robots of dawn	22.30	Robots everywhere		0-554-456	...
5	B	H2G2	17.50	Funny IT book ;o)		1-278-983	...

Figure 3-25. The ITEM table with a different discriminator name and values

The single-table-per-class strategy is the default, is the easiest to understand, and works well when the hierarchy is relatively simple and stable. However, it has some drawbacks; adding new entities to the hierarchy, or adding attributes to existing entities, involves adding new columns to the table, migrating data, and changing indexes. This strategy also requires the columns of the child entities to be nullable. If the ISBN of the Book entity happens to be nonnull, you cannot insert a CD anymore, because the CD entity doesn't have an ISBN.

Joined-Subclass Strategy

In the joined-subclass strategy, each entity in the hierarchy is mapped to its own table. The root entity maps to a table that defines the primary key to be used by all tables in the hierarchy, as well as the discriminator column. Each subclass is represented by a separate table that contains its own attributes (not inherited from the root class) and a primary key that refers to the root table's primary key. The nonroot tables do not hold a discriminator column.

You can implement a joined-subclass strategy by annotating the root entity with the @Inheritance annotation as shown in Listing 3-64 (the code of CD and Book is unchanged, the same as before).

Listing 3-64. The Item Entity with a Joined-Subclass Strategy

```
@Entity
@Inheritance(strategy = InheritanceType.JOINED)
public class Item {

    @Id @GeneratedValue
    protected Long id;
    protected String title;
    protected Float price;
    protected String description;

    // Constructors, getters, setters
}
```

From a developer's point of view, the joined-subclass strategy is natural, as each entity, abstract or concrete, will have its state mapped to a different table. Figure 3-26 shows how the Item, Book, and CD entities will be mapped.

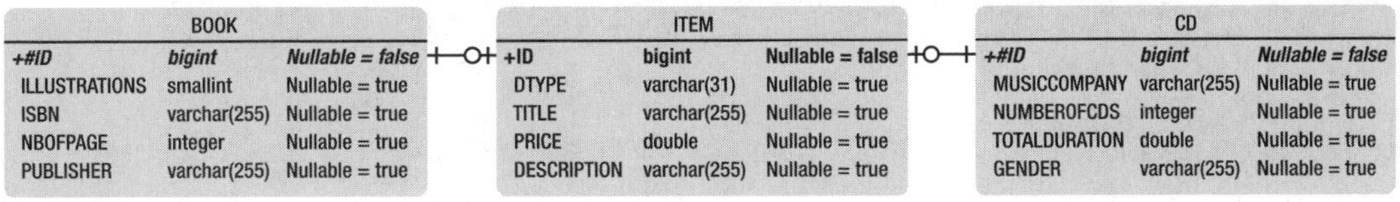

BOOK			ITEM			CD		
+#ID	*bigint*	*Nullable = false*	+ID	bigint	Nullable = false	*+#ID*	*bigint*	*Nullable = false*
ILLUSTRATIONS	smallint	Nullable = true	DTYPE	varchar(31)	Nullable = true	MUSICCOMPANY	varchar(255)	Nullable = true
ISBN	varchar(255)	Nullable = true	TITLE	varchar(255)	Nullable = true	NUMBEROFCDS	integer	Nullable = true
NBOFPAGE	integer	Nullable = true	PRICE	double	Nullable = true	TOTALDURATION	double	Nullable = true
PUBLISHER	varchar(255)	Nullable = true	DESCRIPTION	varchar(255)	Nullable = true	GENDER	varchar(255)	Nullable = true

Figure 3-26. Mapping inheritance with a joined-subclass strategy

You can still use @DiscriminatorColumn and @DiscriminatorValue annotations in the root entity to customize the discriminator column and values (the DTYPE column is in the ITEM table).

The joined-subclass strategy is intuitive and is close to what you know from the object inheritance mechanism. But querying can have a performance impact. This strategy is called joined because, to reassemble an instance of a subclass, the subclass table has to be joined with the root class table. The deeper the hierarchy, the more joins needed to assemble a leaf entity.

Table-per-Concrete-Class Strategy

In the table-per-class (or table-per-concrete-class) strategy, each entity is mapped to its own dedicated table like the joined-subclass strategy. The difference is that all attributes of the root entity will also be mapped to columns of the child entity table. From a database point of view, this strategy denormalizes the model and causes all root entity attributes to be redefined in the tables of all leaf entities that inherit from it. With the table-per-concrete-class strategy, there is no shared table, no shared columns, and no discriminator column. The only requirement is that all tables must share a common primary key that matches across all tables in the hierarchy.

Mapping our example to this strategy is a matter of specifying a TABLE_PER_CLASS on the @Inheritance annotation (see Listing 3-65) of the root entity (Item).

Listing 3-65. The Item Entity with a Table-per-Concrete-Class Strategy

```
@Entity
@Inheritance(strategy = InheritanceType.TABLE_PER_CLASS)
public class Item {

    @Id @GeneratedValue
    protected Long id;
    protected String title;
    protected Float price;
    protected String description;

    // Constructors, getters, setters
}
```

Figure 3-27 shows the ITEM, BOOK, and CD tables. You can see that BOOK and CD duplicate the ID, TITLE, PRICE, and DESCRIPTION columns of the ITEM table. Note that the tables are not linked.

BOOK		
+ID	bigint	Nullable = false
TITLE	varchar(255)	Nullable = true
PRICE	double	Nullable = true
ILLUSTRATIONS	smallint	Nullable = true
DESCRIPTION	varchar(255)	Nullable = true
ISBN	varchar(255)	Nullable = true
NBOFPAGE	integer	Nullable = true
PUBLISHER	varchar(255)	Nullable = true

ITEM		
+ID	bigint	Nullable = false
TITLE	varchar(255)	Nullable = true
PRICE	double	Nullable = true
DESCRIPTION	varchar(255)	Nullable = true

CD		
+ID	bigint	Nullable = false
MUSICCOMPANY	varchar(255)	Nullable = true
NUMBEROFCDS	integer	Nullable = true
TITLE	varchar(255)	Nullable = true
TOTALDURATION	double	Nullable = true
PRICE	double	Nullable = true
DESCRIPTION	varchar(255)	Nullable = true
GENDER	varchar(255)	Nullable = true

Figure 3-27. BOOK and CD tables duplicating ITEM columns

Each table can be redefined by annotating each entity with the @Table annotation.

The table-per-concrete-class strategy performs well when querying instances of one entity, as it is similar to using the single-table-per-class strategy: the query is confined to a single table. The downside is that it makes polymorphic queries across a class hierarchy more expensive than the other strategies (e.g., finding all the items, including CDs and books); it must query all subclass tables using a UNION operation, which is expensive when a large amount of data is involved. Support for this strategy is still optional in JPA 2.0.

Overriding Attributes

With the table-per-concrete-class strategy, the columns of the root class are duplicated on the leaf tables. They keep the same name. But what if a legacy database is being used and the columns have a different name? JPA uses the @AttributeOverride annotation to override the column mapping and @AttributeOverrides to override several.

To rename the ID, TITLE, and DESCRIPTION columns in the BOOK and CD tables, the code of the Item entity doesn't change, but the Book entity (see Listing 3-66) and CD entity (see Listing 3-67) have to use the @AttributeOverride annotation.

Listing 3-66. Book Overrides Some Item Columns

```
@Entity
@AttributeOverrides({
    @AttributeOverride(name = "id",↪
                    column = @Column(name = "book_id")),
    @AttributeOverride(name = "title",↪
                    column = @Column(name = "book_title")),
    @AttributeOverride(name = "description",↪
                    column = @Column(name = "book_description"))
})
public class Book extends Item {

    private String isbn;
    private String publisher;
    private Integer nbOfPage;
    private Boolean illustrations;

    // Constructors, getters, setters
}
```

Listing 3-67. CD Overrides Some Item Columns

```
@Entity
@AttributeOverrides({
    @AttributeOverride(name = "id",↪
                    column = @Column(name = "cd_id")),
    @AttributeOverride(name = "title",↪
                    column = @Column(name = "cd_title")),
    @AttributeOverride(name = "description",↪
                    column = @Column(name = "cd_description"))
})
public class CD extends Item {

    private String musicCompany;
    private Integer numberOfCDs;
```

```
        private Float totalDuration;
        private String gender;

        // Constructors, getters, setters
}
```

Because there is more than one attribute to override, you need to use @AttributeOverrides, which takes an array of @AttributeOverride annotations. Each annotation then points to an attribute of the Item entity and redefines the mapping of the column using the @Column annotation. So name = "title" refers to the title attribute of the Item entity, and @Column(name = "cd_title") informs the persistence provider that the title has to be mapped to a CD_TITLE column. The result is shown in Figure 3-28.

BOOK		
+BOOK_ID	bigint	Nullable = false
BOOK_TITLE	varchar(255)	Nullable = true
BOOK_DESCRIPTION	varchar(255)	Nullable = true
PRICE	double	Nullable = true
ILLUSTRATIONS	smallint	Nullable = true
ISBN	varchar(255)	Nullable = true
NBOFPAGE	integer	Nullable = true
PUBLISHER	varchar(255)	Nullable = true

ITEM		
+ID	bigint	Nullable = false
TITLE	varchar(255)	Nullable = true
PRICE	double	Nullable = true
DESCRIPTION	varchar(255)	Nullable = true

CD		
+CD_ID	bigint	Nullable = false
CD_TITLE	varchar(255)	Nullable = true
CD_DESCRIPTION	varchar(255)	Nullable = true
PRICE	double	Nullable = true
MUSICCOMPANY	varchar(255)	Nullable = true
NUMBEROFCDS	integer	Nullable = true
TOTALDURATION	double	Nullable = true
GENDER	varchar(255)	Nullable = true

Figure 3-28. BOOK and CD tables overriding ITEM columns

■ **Note** In the "Embeddables" section earlier in the chapter, you saw that an embeddable object can be shared by several entities (Address was embedded by Customer and Order). Because embeddable objects are an intrinsic part of an owning entity, their columns are also duplicated in each entity's table. The @AttributeOverrides can then be used if you need to override the embeddable columns.

Type of Classes in the Inheritance Hierarchy

The example used to explain the mapping strategies only uses entities. Item is an entity as well as Book and CD. But entities don't have to inherit from entities alone. A hierarchy of classes can mix all sorts of different classes: entities and also nonentities (or transient classes), abstract entities, and mapped superclasses. Inheriting from these different types of classes will have an impact on the mapping.

Abstract Entity

In the previous examples, the Item entity was concrete. It was annotated with @Entity and didn't have an abstract keyword, but an abstract class can also be specified as an entity. An abstract entity differs from a concrete entity only in that it cannot be directly instantiated with the new keyword. It provides a common data structure for its leaf entities (Book and CD) and follows the mapping strategies. For the persistence provider, an abstract entity is mapped as an entity. The only difference is in the Java space, not in the mapping.

Nonentity

Nonentities are also called transient classes, meaning they are POJOs. An entity may subclass a nonentity or may be extended by a nonentity. Why would you have nonentities in a hierarchy? Object modeling and inheritance are the means through which state and behavior are shared. Nonentities can be used to provide a common data structure to leaf entities. The state of a nonentity superclass is not persistent because it is not managed by the persistence provider (remember that the condition for a class to be managed by the persistence provider is the presence of an @Entity annotation).

For example, Book is an entity and, as shown in Listing 3-68, extends from an Item nonentity (Item doesn't have any annotation).

Listing 3-68. Item Is a Simple POJO with No @Entity

```
public class Item {

    protected String title;
    protected Float price;
    protected String description;

    // Constructors, getters, setters
}
```

The Book entity, shown in Listing 3-69, inherits from Item, so the Java code can access the title, price, and description attributes, plus any other method that is defined, in a normal, object-oriented way. Item can be concrete or abstract and does not have any impact on the final mapping.

Listing 3-69. The Book Entity Extends from a POJO

```
@Entity
public class Book extends Item {

    @Id @GeneratedValue
    private Long id;
    private String isbn;
    private String publisher;
    private Integer nbOfPage;
    private Boolean illustrations;

    // Constructors, getters, setters
}
```

Book is an entity and extends Item. But only the attributes of Book would be mapped to a table. No attributes from Item appear in the table structure defined in Listing 3-70. To persist a Book, you need to create an instance of Book, set values to any attributes you want (title, price, isbn, publisher, etc.), but only the Book's attributes (id, isbn, etc.) will get persisted.

Listing 3-70. The BOOK *Table Has No Attributes from* Item

```
create table BOOK (
    ID BIGINT not null,
    ILLUSTRATIONS SMALLINT,
    ISBN VARCHAR(255),
    NBOFPAGE INTEGER,
    PUBLISHER VARCHAR(255),
    primary key (ID)
);
```

Mapped Superclass

JPA defines a special kind of class, called a *mapped superclass*, to share state and behavior, as well as mapping information entities inherit from. However, mapped superclasses are not entities. They are not managed by the persistence provider, do not have any table to be mapped to, and cannot be queried or be part of a relationship, but they may provide persistent properties to any entities that extend it. They are similar to embeddable classes except they can be used with inheritance. A class is indicated as being a mapped superclass by annotating it with the @MappedSuperclass annotation.

Using the root class, Item is annotated with @MappedSuperclass, not @Entity, as shown in Listing 3-71. It defines an inheritance strategy (JOINED) and annotates some of its attributes with @Column, but because mapped superclasses are not mapped to tables, the @Table annotation is not permitted.

Listing 3-71. Item *Is a Mapped Superclass*

```
@MappedSuperclass
@Inheritance(strategy = InheritanceType.JOINED)
public class Item {

    @Id @GeneratedValue
    protected Long id;
    @Column(length = 50, nullable = false)
    protected String title;
    protected Float price;
    @Column(length = 2000)
    protected String description;

    // Constructors, getters, setters
}
```

As you can see in Listing 3-71, the title and description attributes are annotated with @Column. Listing 3-72 shows the Book entity extending Item.

Listing 3-72. Book Extends from a Mapped Superclass

```
@Entity
public class Book extends Item {

    private String isbn;
    private String publisher;
    private Integer nbOfPage;
    private Boolean illustrations;

    // Constructors, getters, setters
}
```

This hierarchy will be mapped into only one table. Item is not an entity and does not have any table. Attributes of Item and Book would be mapped to columns of the BOOK table, but mapped superclasses also share their mapping information. The @Column annotations of Item will be inherited. But, as mapped superclasses are not managed entities, you would not be able to persist or query them, for example. Listing 3-73 shows the BOOK table structure with customized TITLE and DESCRIPTION columns.

Listing 3-73. The BOOK Table Has all the Attributes from Item

```
create table BOOK (
    ID BIGINT not null,
    TITLE VARCHAR(50) not null,
    PRICE DOUBLE(52, 0),
    DESCRIPTION VARCHAR(2000),
    ILLUSTRATIONS SMALLINT,
    ISBN VARCHAR(255),
    NBOFPAGE INTEGER,
    PUBLISHER VARCHAR(255),
    primary key (ID)
);
```

Summary

Thanks to configuration by exception, not much is required to map entities to tables; inform the persistence provider that a class is actually an entity (using @Entity) and an attribute is its identifier (using @Id), and JPA does the rest. This chapter could have been much shorter if it stuck to the defaults. JPA has a very rich set of annotations to customize every little detail of ORM.

Elementary annotations can be used on attributes (@Basic, @Temporal, etc.) or classes to customize the mapping. You can change the table's name or the primary key type, or even avoid mapping with the @Transient annotation. With JPA 2.0, you can now map collections of basic types or embeddables. Depending on your business model, you can map relationships (@OneToOne, @ManyToMany, etc.) of different directions and multiplicity. Same thing with inheritance (@Inheritance, @MappedSuperclass, etc.) where you can use different strategies to map a hierarchy of entities and nonentities mixed together.

This chapter focused on the static part of JPA, or how to map entities to tables. The next chapter will deal with the dynamic aspects: how to query these entities.

Managing Persistent Objects

Java Persistence API has two sides. The first is the ability to map objects to a relational database. Configuration by exception allows persistence providers to do most of the work without much code, but the richness of JPA also allows customized mapping from objects to tables using either annotation or XML descriptors. From simple mapping (changing the name of a column) to more complex mapping (inheritance), JPA offers a wide spectrum of customizations. As a result, you can map almost any object model to a legacy database.

The other aspect of JPA is the ability to query these mapped objects. In JPA, the centralized service to manipulate instances of entities in a standard way is the entity manager. It provides an API to create, find, remove, and synchronize objects with the database. It also allows execution of different sorts of JPQL queries against entities such as dynamic, static, or native queries. Locking mechanisms are also possible with the entity manager.

The database world relies on Structured Query Language (SQL). This programming language is designed for managing relational data (retrieval, insertion, updating, and deletion), and its syntax is table oriented. You can select columns from tables made of rows, join tables together, combine the results of two SQL queries through unions, and so on. There are no objects here, only rows, columns, and tables. In the Java world, where we manipulate objects, a language made for tables (SQL) has to be twisted to suit a language made of objects (Java). This is where Java Persistence Query Language (JPQL) comes into play.

JPQL is the language defined in JPA to query entities stored in a relational database. JPQL syntax resembles SQL but operates against entity objects rather than directly with database tables. JPQL does not see the underlying database structure nor deal with tables or columns, but rather objects and attributes. And, for that, it uses the dot (.) notation that Java developers are familiar with.

In this chapter, you will learn how to manage persistent objects. This means you will learn how to do Create, Read, Update, and Delete (CRUD) operations with the entity manager as well as complex queries using JPQL. At the end of the chapter, you will see how concurrency is handled by JPA.

How to Query an Entity

Let's take as our first example a simple query: finding a book by its identifier. In Listing 4-1, you can see a Book entity that uses the @Id annotation to inform the persistence provider that the id attribute has to be mapped as a primary key.

Listing 4-1. A Simple Book Entity

```
@Entity
public class Book {

    @Id
    private Long id;
    private String title;
    private Float price;
    private String description;
    private String isbn;
    private Integer nbOfPage;
    private Boolean illustrations;

    // Constructors, getters, setters
}
```

The **Book** entity holds the mapping information. In this example, using most of the defaults, the data will be stored in a table whose name equals the name of the entity (**BOOK**), and each attribute will have an equivalent column mapping. You can use a separate **Main** class (see Listing 4-2) that uses the **javax.persistence.EntityManager** interface to store a **Book** instance in the table.

Listing 4-2. A Main Class Persisting and Retrieving a Book Entity

```
public class Main {

  public static void main(String[] args) {

    // 1-Create an instance of the Book entity
    Book book = new Book();
    book.setId(1234L);
    book.setTitle("The Hitchhiker's Guide to the Galaxy");
    book.setPrice(12.5F);
    book.setDescription("Science fiction created by Douglas Adams.");
    book.setIsbn("1-84023-742-2");
    book.setNbOfPage(354);
    book.setIllustrations(false);

    // 2-Get an entity manager and a transaction
    EntityManagerFactory emf = ↪
        Persistence.createEntityManagerFactory("chapter04PU");
    EntityManager em = emf.createEntityManager();
    EntityTransaction tx = em.getTransaction();
```

```
    // 3-Persist the book to the database
    tx.begin();
    em.persist(book);
    tx.commit();

    // 4-Retrieve the book by its identifier
    book = em.find(Book.class, 1234L);

    System.out.println(book);

    em.close();
    emf.close();
  }
}
```

The Main class in Listing 4-2 uses four different steps to persist a Book and retrieve it from the database:

1. Create an instance of the Book entity. Entities are annotated POJOs, managed by the persistence provider. From a Java viewpoint, an instance of a class needs to be created through the new keyword as any POJO. It is important to emphasize that, up to this point in the code, the persistence provider is not aware of the Book object.

2. Obtain an entity manager and a transaction. This is the important part of the code, as an entity manager is needed to manipulate entities. First, an entity manager factory is created for the "chapter04PU" persistence unit. This factory is then employed to obtain an entity manager (the em variable), used throughout the code to get a transaction (tx variable), and persist and retrieve a Book.

3. Persist the book to the database. The code starts a transaction (tx.begin()) and uses the EntityManager.persist() method to insert a Book instance. When the transaction is committed (tx.commit()), the data is flushed into the database.

4. Retrieve the book by its identifier. Again, the entity manager is used to retrieve the book using its identifier (EntityManager.find()).

Note in this code the absence of SQL queries, JPQL queries, or JDBC calls. Figure 4-1 shows the interaction between these components. The Main class interacts with the underlying database through the EntityManager interface, which provides a set of standard methods that allow you to perform operations on the Book entity. Behind the scenes, the EntityManager relies on the persistence provider to interact with the databases. When an EntityManager method is invoked, the persistence provider generates and executes a SQL statement through the corresponding JDBC driver.

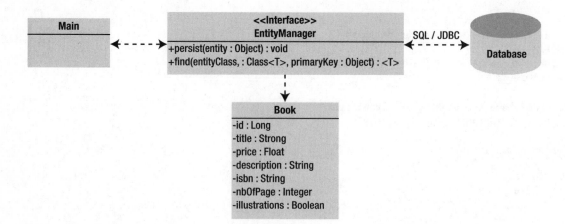

Figure 4-1. The entity manager interacts with the entity and the underlying database

Which JDBC driver to use? How to connect to the database? What's the database name? This information is missing from our previous code. When the Main class creates an EntityManagerFactory, it passes the name of a persistence unit as a parameter; in this case, it's called chapter04PU. The persistence unit indicates to the entity manager the type of database to use and the connection parameters, which are defined in the persistence.xml file, shown in Listing 4-3, that has to be deployed with the classes.

Listing 4-3. The persistence.xml File Defining the Persistence Unit

```xml
<?xml version="1.0" encoding="UTF-8"?>
<persistence xmlns="http://java.sun.com/xml/ns/persistence"
             xmlns:xsi="http://www.w3.org/2001/XMLSchema-instance"
             xsi:schemaLocation="http://java.sun.com/xml/ns/persistence
             http://java.sun.com/xml/ns/persistence/persistence_2_0.xsd"
             version="2.0">

  <persistence-unit name="chapter04PU" transaction-type="RESOURCE_LOCAL">
    <provider>org.eclipse.persistence.jpa.PersistenceProvider</provider>
    <class>com.apress.javaee6.chapter04.Book</class>
    <properties>
      <property name="eclipselink.target-database" value="DERBY"/>
      <property name="javax.persistence.jdbc.driver" ➥
              value="org.apache.derby.jdbc.ClientDriver"/>
      <property name="javax.persistence.jdbc.url" ➥
              value="jdbc:derby://localhost:1527/chapter04DB"/>
      <property name="javax.persistence.jdbc.user" value="APP"/>
      <property name="javax.persistence.jdbc.password" value="APP"/>
    </properties>
  </persistence-unit>
</persistence>
```

The **chapter04PU** persistence unit defines a JDBC connection for the **chapter04DB** Derby database. It connects with a user (**APP**) and a password (**APP**) at a given URL. The **<class>** tag tells the persistence provider to manage the **Book** class (there are other tags to implicitly or explicitly denote managed persistence classes such as **<mapping-file>**, **<jar-file>**, or **<exclude-unlisted-classes>**).

To make the code work, in addition to a Derby database running on port 1527, both a **Book** and **Main** class need to be compiled and deployed with this **META-INF/persistence.xml** file. By enabling logging, you might see some traces of SQL statements, but your code manipulates objects, in an object-friendly way, with no SQL statement or JDBC direct calls using the **EntityManager** API.

Entity Manager

The entity manager is a central piece in JPA. It manages the state and life cycle of entities as well as querying entities within a persistence context. The entity manager is responsible for creating and removing persistent entity instances and finding entities by their primary key. It can lock entities for protecting against concurrent access by using optimistic or pessimistic locking and can use JPQL queries to retrieve entities following certain criteria.

When an entity manager obtains a reference to an entity, it is said to be *managed*. Until that point, the entity is seen as a regular POJO (i.e., detached). The strength of JPA is that entities can be used as regular objects by different layers of an application and become managed by the entity manager when you need to load or insert data into the database. When an entity is managed, you can carry out persistence operations, and the entity manager will automatically synchronize the state of the entity with the database. When the entity is detached (i.e., not managed), it returns to a simple POJO and can then be used by other layers (e.g., a JSF presentation layer) without synchronizing its state with the database.

With the entity manager, the real work of persistence starts. **EntityManager** is an interface implemented by a persistence provider that will generate and execute SQL statements. The **javax.persistence.EntityManager** interface provides the API shown in Listing 4-4 to manipulate entities.

Listing 4-4. EntityManager API

```
public interface EntityManager {

    EntityTransaction getTransaction();
    EntityManagerFactory getEntityManagerFactory();
    void close();
    boolean isOpen();

    void persist(Object entity);
    <T> T merge(T entity);
    void remove(Object entity);
    <T> T find(Class<T> entityClass, Object primaryKey);
    <T> T find(Class<T> entityClass, Object primaryKey, Map<String, Object> properties);
    <T> T find(Class<T> entityClass, Object primaryKey, LockModeType lockMode);
    <T> T find(Class<T> entityClass, Object primaryKey,↪
                  LockModeType lockMode, Map<String, Object> properties);
    <T> T getReference(Class<T> entityClass, Object primaryKey);

    void flush();
    void setFlushMode(FlushModeType flushMode);
```

```
        FlushModeType getFlushMode();

        void lock(Object entity, LockModeType lockMode);
        void lock(Object entity, LockModeType lockMode, Map<String, Object> properties);
        LockModeType getLockMode(Object entity);

        void refresh(Object entity);
        void refresh(Object entity, LockModeType lockMode);
        void refresh(Object entity, Map<String, Object> properties);
        void refresh(Object entity, LockModeType lockMode, Map<String, Object> properties);

        void clear();
        void detach(Object entity);
        boolean contains(Object entity);

        Map<String, Object> getProperties();
        void setProperty(String propertyName, Object value);

        Query createQuery(String qlString);
        Query createNamedQuery(String name);
        Query createNativeQuery(String sqlString);
        Query createNativeQuery(String sqlString, Class resultClass);
        Query createNativeQuery(String sqlString, String resultSetMapping);

        <T> TypedQuery<T> createQuery(CriteriaQuery<T> criteriaQuery);
        <T> TypedQuery<T> createQuery(String qlString,Class<T> resultClass);
        <T> TypedQuery<T> createNamedQuery(String name,Class<T> resultClass);
        CriteriaBuilder getCriteriaBuilder();
        Metamodel getMetamodel();

        void joinTransaction();

        <T> T unwrap(Class<T> cls);
        Object getDelegate();

        QueryBuilder getQueryBuilder();
}
```

Don't get scared by the API in Listing 4-4, as this chapter will cover most of the methods. In the next section, I explain how to get an instance of an `EntityManager`.

Obtaining an Entity Manager

The entity manager is the central interface to interact with entities, but it first has to be obtained by an application. Depending on whether it is a container-managed environment (like you'll see in Chapter 6 with EJBs) or application-managed environment, the code can be quite different. For example, in a container-managed environment, the transactions are managed by the container. That means you don't need to explicitly write the commit or rollback, which you have to do in an application-managed environment.

The term "application-managed" means an application is responsible for explicitly obtaining an instance of `EntityManager` and managing its life cycle (it closes the entity manager when finished, for example). Listing 4-2, shown earlier, demonstrates how a class running in a Java SE environment gets an instance of an entity manager. It uses the `Persistence` class to bootstrap an `EntityManagerFactory` associated with a persistence unit (`chapter04PU`), which is then used to create an entity manager. Creating an application-managed entity manager is simple enough using a factory, but what differentiates application-managed from container-managed is how the factory is acquired.

A container-managed environment is when the application evolves in a servlet or an EJB container. In a Java EE environment, the most common way to acquire an entity manager is by the `@PersistenceContext` annotation injecting one, or by JNDI lookup. The component running in a container (servlet, EJB, web service, etc.) doesn't need to create or close the entity manager, as its life cycle is managed by the container. Listing 4-5 shows the code of a stateless session bean into which is injected a reference of the `chapter04PU` persistence unit.

Listing 4-5. A Stateless EJB Injected with a Reference of an Entity Manager

```
@Stateless
public class BookBean {

    @PersistenceContext(unitName = "chapter04PU")
    private EntityManager em;

    public void createBook() {
        // Create an instance of book
        Book book = new Book();
        book.setId(1234L);
        book.setTitle("The Hitchhiker's Guide to the Galaxy");
        book.setPrice(12.5F);
        book.setDescription("Science fiction created by Douglas Adams.");
        book.setIsbn("1-84023-742-2");
        book.setNbOfPage(354);
        book.setIllustrations(false);

        // Persist the book to the database
        em.persist(book);

        // Retrieve the book by its identifier
        book = em.find(Book.class, 1234L);

        System.out.println(book);
    }
}
```

Compared with Listing 4-2, the code in Listing 4-5 is much simpler. First, there is no `Persistence` or `EntityManagerFactory` as the entity manager instance is injected by the container. Second, because stateless beans manage the transactions, there is no explicit commit or rollback. This style of entity manager will be demonstrated in Chapter 6.

Persistence Context

Before exploring the `EntityManager` API in detail, you need to understand a crucial concept: the *persistence context*. A persistence context is a set of managed entity instances at a given time for a given user's transaction: only one entity instance with the same persistent identity can exist in a persistence context. For example, if a `Book` instance with an ID of 12 exists in the persistence context, no other book with this ID can exist within that same persistence context. Only entities that are contained in the persistence context are managed by the entity manager, meaning that changes will be reflected in the database.

The entity manager updates or consults the persistence context whenever a method of the `javax.persistence.EntityManager` interface is called. For example, when a `persist()` method is called, the entity passed as an argument will be added to the persistence context if it doesn't already exist. Similarly, when an entity is found by its primary key, the entity manager first checks whether the requested entity is already present in the persistence context. The persistence context can be seen as a first-level cache. It's a short, live space where the entity manager stores entities before flushing the content to the database. By default, objects just live in the persistent context for the duration of the transaction.

To summarize, let's look at Figure 4-2 where two users need to access entities whose data is stored in the database. Each user has his own persistence context that lasts for the duration of his own transaction. User 1 gets the `Book` entities with ID equals 12 and 56 from the database, so both get stored in his persistence context. User 2 gets the entities 12 and 34. As you can see, the entity with ID=12 is stored in each user's persistence context. While the transaction runs, the persistence context acts like a first-level cache storing the entities that can be managed by the `EntityManager`. Once the transaction ends, the persistence context ends and the entities are cleared.

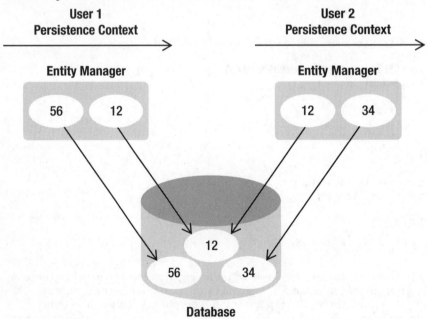

Figure 4-2. Entities living in different users' persistence context

The configuration for an entity manager is bound to the factory that created it. Whether application or container managed, the factory needs a persistence unit from which to create an entity manager. A persistence unit dictates the settings to connect to the database and the list of entities that can be managed in a persistence context. The persistence unit is defined in a `persistence.xml` file (see Listing 4-6) located in the `META-INF` directory. It has a name (`chapter04PU`) and a set of attributes.

Listing 4-6. A Persistence Unit with a Set of Manageable Entities

```xml
<?xml version="1.0" encoding="UTF-8"?>
<persistence xmlns="http://java.sun.com/xml/ns/persistence"
             xmlns:xsi="http://www.w3.org/2001/XMLSchema-instance"
             xsi:schemaLocation="http://java.sun.com/xml/ns/persistence
             http://java.sun.com/xml/ns/persistence/persistence_2_0.xsd"
             version="2.0">

  <persistence-unit name="chapter04PU" transaction-type="RESOURCE_LOCAL">
    <provider>org.eclipse.persistence.jpa.PersistenceProvider</provider>
    <class>com.apress.javaee6.chapter04.Book</class>
    <class>com.apress.javaee6.chapter04.Customer</class>
    <class>com.apress.javaee6.chapter04.Address</class>
    <properties>
      <property name="eclipselink.target-database" value="DERBY"/>
      <property name="javax.persistence.jdbc.driver" ↪
                value="org.apache.derby.jdbc.ClientDriver"/>
      <property name="javax.persistence.jdbc.url" ↪
                value="jdbc:derby://localhost:1527/chapter04DB"/>
      <property name="javax.persistence.jdbc.user" value="APP"/>
      <property name="javax.persistence.jdbc.password" value="APP"/>
    </properties>
  </persistence-unit>
</persistence>
```

The persistence unit is the bridge between the persistence context and the database. On one hand, the `<class>` tag lists all the entities that could be managed in the persistence context, and, on the other, it gives all the information to physically connect to the database (using properties). This is because you are in an application-managed environment (`transaction-type="RESOURCE_LOCAL"`). As you'll see in Chapter 6, in a container-managed environment, the `persistence.xml` would define a datasource instead of the database connection properties and set the transaction type to JTA (`transaction-type="JTA"`).

■ **Note** In JPA 2.0, some properties of the persistence.xml file have been standardized. They all start with `javax.persistence` such as `javax.persistence.jdbc.url`, `javax.persistence.jdbc.user` and so on. JPA providers are required to support these standard properties, but may provide custom properties of their own, such as the EclipseLink property in the example (e.g., `eclipselink.target-database`).

Manipulating Entities

The entity manager is also used to create complex JPQL queries to retrieve an entity or a list of entities. When manipulating single entities, the `EntityManager` interface can be seen as a generic Data Access Object (DAO), which allows CRUD operations on any entity (see Table 4-1).

Table 4-1. EntityManager Interface Methods to Manipulate Entities

Method	Description
`void persist(Object entity)`	Makes an instance managed and persistent
`<T> T find(Class<T> entityClass, Object primaryKey)`	Searches for an entity of the specified class and primary key
`<T> T getReference(Class<T> entityClass, Object primaryKey)`	Gets an instance, whose state may be lazily fetched
`void remove(Object entity)`	Removes the entity instance from the persistence context and from the underlying database
`<T> T merge(T entity)`	Merges the state of the given entity into the current persistence context
`void refresh(Object entity)`	Refreshes the state of the instance from the database, overwriting changes made to the entity, if any
`void flush()`	Synchronizes the persistence context to the underlying database
`void clear()`	Clears the persistence context, causing all managed entities to become detached
`void detach(Object entity)`	Removes the given entity from the persistence context, causing a managed entity to become detached
`boolean contains(Object entity)`	Checks whether the instance is a managed entity instance belonging to the current persistence context

To gain a better understanding of these methods, I will use a simple example of a one-way, one-to-one relationship between a `Customer` and an `Address`. Both entities have automatically generated identifiers (thanks to the `@GeneratedValue` annotation), and `Customer` (see Listing 4-7) has a lazy fetch to `Address` (see Listing 4-8).

Listing 4-7. The Customer Entity with a One-Way, One-to-One Address

```
@Entity
public class Customer {

    @Id @GeneratedValue
    private Long id;
    private String firstName;
    private String lastName;
    private String email;
    @OneToOne (fetch = FetchType.LAZY)
    @JoinColumn(name = "address_fk")
    private Address address;

    // Constructors, getters, setters
}
```

Listing 4-8. The Address Entity

```
@Entity
public class Address {

    @Id @GeneratedValue
    private Long id;
    private String street1;
    private String city;
    private String zipcode;
    private String country;

    // Constructors, getters, setters
}
```

These two entities will get mapped into the database structure shown in Figure 4-3. Note the ADDRESS_FK column is the foreign key to ADDRESS.

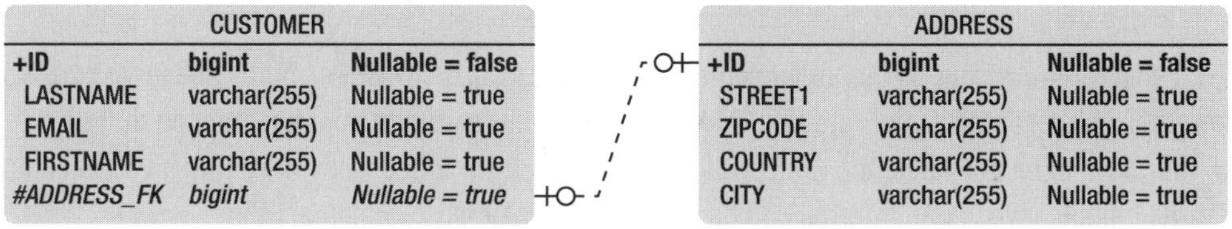

CUSTOMER					ADDRESS		
+ID	bigint	Nullable = false		+ID	bigint	Nullable = false
LASTNAME	varchar(255)	Nullable = true		STREET1	varchar(255)	Nullable = true
EMAIL	varchar(255)	Nullable = true		ZIPCODE	varchar(255)	Nullable = true
FIRSTNAME	varchar(255)	Nullable = true		COUNTRY	varchar(255)	Nullable = true
#ADDRESS_FK	bigint	Nullable = true		CITY	varchar(255)	Nullable = true

Figure 4-3. CUSTOMER and ADDRESS tables

For better readability, the fragments of code used in the upcoming section assume that the em attribute is of type EntityManager and tx of type EntityTransaction.

Persisting an Entity

Persisting an entity means inserting data into the database when the data doesn't already exist (otherwise an exception is thrown). To do so, it's necessary to create a new entity instance using the new operator, set the values of the attributes, bind one entity to another when there are associations, and finally call the EntityManager.persist() method as shown in the JUnit test case in Listing 4-9.

Listing 4-9. Persisting a Customer with an Address

```
Customer customer = new Customer("Antony", "Balla", "tballa@mail.com");
Address address = new Address("Ritherdon Rd", "London", "8QE", "UK");
customer.setAddress(address);

tx.begin();
em.persist(customer);
em.persist(address);
tx.commit();

assertNotNull(customer.getId());
assertNotNull(address.getId());
```

In Listing 4-9, customer and address are just two objects that reside in the JVM memory. Both become managed entities when the entity manager (variable em) takes them into account by persisting them (em.persist(customer)). At this time, both objects become eligible to be inserted in the database. When the transaction is committed (tx.commit()), the data is flushed to the database, and an address row is inserted into the ADDRESS table and a customer row into the CUSTOMER table. As the Customer is the owner of the relationship, its table holds the foreign key to ADDRESS. The assertNotNull expressions check that both entities have received a generated identifier (thanks to the persistence provider and the @Id and @GeneratedValue annotations).

Note the ordering of the persist() methods: a customer is persisted and then an address. If it were the other way round, the result would be the same. Earlier, the entity manager was described as a first-level cache. Until the transaction is committed, the data stays in memory and there is no access to the database. The entity manager caches data and, when ready, flushes the data in the order that the underlying database is expecting (respecting integrity constraints). Because of the foreign key in the CUSTOMER table, the insert statement for ADDRESS will be executed first, followed by that for CUSTOMER.

■ **Note** Most of the entities in this chapter do not implement the Serializable interface. That's because entities don't have to in order to get persisted in the database. They are passed by reference from one method to the other, and, when they have to be persisted, the EntityManager.persist() method is invoked. But, if you need to pass entities by value (remote invocation, external EJB container, etc.), they must implement the java.io.Serializable marker (no method) interface. It indicates to the compiler that it must enforce all fields on the entity class to be serializable, so that any instance can be serialized to a byte stream and passed using Remote Method Invocation (RMI).

Finding by ID

To find an entity by its identifier, you can use two different methods. The first is the EntityManager.find() method, which takes two parameters: the entity class and the unique identifier (see Listing 4-10). If the entity is found, it is returned; if it is not found, a null value is returned.

Listing 4-10. Finding a Customer by ID

```
Customer customer = em.find(Customer.class, 1234L)
if (customer!= null) {
    // Process the object
}
```

The second method is getReference() (see Listing 4-11). It is very similar to the find operation, as it takes the same parameters, but it retrieves a reference to an entity (via its primary key) and not its data. It is intended for situations where a managed entity instance is needed, but no data, other than potentially the entity's primary key, being accessed. With getReference(), the state data is fetched lazily, which means that, if you don't access state before the entity is detached, the data might not be there. If the entity is not found, an EntityNotFoundException is thrown.

Listing 4-11. Finding a Customer by Reference

```
try {
    Customer customer = em.getReference(Customer.class, 1234L)
    // Process the object
} catch(EntityNotFoundException ex) {
    // Entity not found
}
```

Removing an Entity

An entity can be removed with the EntityManager.remove() method. Once removed, the entity is deleted from the database, is detached from the entity manager, and cannot be synchronized with the database anymore. In terms of Java objects, the entity is still accessible until it goes out of scope and the garbage collector cleans it up. The code in Listing 4-12 shows how to remove an object after it has been created.

Listing 4-12. Creating and Removing Customer and Address Entities

```
Customer customer = new Customer("Antony", "Balla", "tballa@mail.com");
Address address = new Address("Ritherdon Rd", "London", "8QE", "UK");
customer.setAddress(address);

tx.begin();
em.persist(customer);
em.persist(address);
tx.commit();
```

```
tx.begin();
em.remove(customer);
tx.commit();

// The data is removed from the database
// but the object is still accessible
assertNotNull(customer);
```

The code in Listing 4-12 creates an instance of Customer and Address, links them together (customer.setAddress(address)), and persists them. In the database, the customer row is linked to the address through a foreign key; later on in the code, only the Customer is deleted. Depending on how the cascading is configured (discussed later in this chapter), the Address could be left with no other entity referencing it. The address row becomes an orphan.

Orphan Removal

For data consistency, orphans are not desirable, as they result in having rows in a database that are not referenced by any other table, without means of access. With JPA, you can inform the persistence provider to automatically remove orphans or cascade a remove operation as you'll see later. If a target entity (Address) is privately owned by a source (Customer), meaning a target must never be owned by more than one source, and that source is deleted by the application, the provider should also delete the target.

Associations that are specified as one-to-one or one-to-many support the use of the orphan-removal option. To include this option in the example, let's look at how the orphanRemoval=true element to the @OneToOne annotation should be added (see Listing 4-13).

Listing 4-13. The Customer Entity Dealing with Orphan Address Removal

```
@Entity
public class Customer {

    @Id @GeneratedValue
    private Long id;
    private String firstName;
    private String lastName;
    private String email;
    @OneToOne (fetch = FetchType.LAZY, orphanRemoval=true)
    private Address address;

    // Constructors, getters, setters
}
```

With this mapping, the code in Listing 4-12 will automatically remove the Address entity when the customer is removed, or when the relationship is broken (by setting to null the address attribute, or by removing the child entity from the collection in a one-to-many case). The remove operation is applied at the time of the flush operation (transaction committed).

Synchronizing with the Database

Until now, the synchronization with the database has been done at commit time. The entity manager is a first-level cache, waiting for the transaction to be committed to flush the data to the database, but what happens when a customer and an address need to be inserted?

```
tx.begin();
em.persist(customer);
em.persist(address);
tx.commit();
```

All pending changes require an SQL statement, with two `insert` statements produced and made permanent only when the database transaction commits. For most applications, this automatic data synchronization is sufficient. Although at exactly which point in time the provider actually flushes the changes to the database is not known, you can be sure it happens inside the commit of the transaction. The database is synchronized with the entities in the persistence context, but data to the database can be explicitly flushed (`flush`), or entities refreshed with data from the database (`refresh`). If the data is flushed to the database at one point, and if later in the code the application calls the `rollback()` method, the flushed data will be taken out of the database.

Flushing Data

With the `EntityManager.flush()` method, the persistence provider can be explicitly forced to flush the data, allowing a developer to manually trigger the same process used by the entity manager internally to flush the persistence context.

```
tx.begin();
em.persist(customer);
em.flush();
em.persist(address);
tx.commit();
```

Two interesting things happen in the preceding code. The first is that `em.flush()` will not wait for the transaction to commit and will force the provider to flush the persistence context. An `insert` statement will be generated and executed at the flush. The second is that this code will not work because of integrity constraint. Without an explicit flush, the entity manager caches all changes, and orders and executes them in a coherent way for the database. With an explicit flush, the `insert` statement to `CUSTOMER` will be executed, but the integrity constraint on the address foreign key will be violated (the `ADDRESS_FK` column in `CUSTOMER`). That will lead the transaction to roll back. Data that has been flushed will also get rolled back. Explicit flushes should be carefully used and only when needed.

Refreshing an Entity

The `refresh()` method is used for data synchronization in the opposite direction of the flush, meaning it overwrites the current state of a managed entity with data as it is present in the database. A typical case is where the `EntityManager.refresh()` method is used to undo changes that have been done to the entity in memory only. The test class snippet in Listing 4-14 finds a `Customer` by ID, changes its first name, and undoes this change using the `refresh()` method.

Listing 4-14. Refreshing the Customer Entity from the Database

```
Customer customer = em.find(Customer.class, 1234L)
assertEquals(customer.getFirstName(), "Antony");

customer.setFirstName("William");

em.refresh(customer);
assertEquals(customer.getFirstName(), "Antony");
```

Content of the Persistence Context

The persistence context holds the managed entities. With the `EntityManager` interface, you can check whether an entity is being managed, detach it, or clear all entities from the persistence context.

Contains

Entities are either managed or not by the entity manager. The `EntityManager.contains()` method returns a Boolean and allows checking of whether a particular entity instance is currently managed by the entity manager within the current persistence context. In the test case in Listing 4-15, a `Customer` is persisted, and you can immediately check whether the entity is managed (`em.contains(customer)`). The answer is `true`. Afterward, the `remove()` method is called, and the entity is removed from the database and from the persistence context (`em.contains(customer)` returns `false`).

Listing 4-15. Test Case for Whether the Customer Entity Is in the Persistence Context

```
Customer customer = new Customer("Antony", "Balla", "tballa@mail.com");

tx.begin();
em.persist(customer);
tx.commit();

assertTrue(em.contains(customer));

tx.begin();
em.remove(customer);
tx.commit();

assertFalse(em.contains(customer));
```

Clear and Detach

The `clear()` method is straightforward: it empties the persistence context, causing all managed entities to become detached. The `detach(Object entity)` method removes the given entity from the persistence context. Changes made to the entity will not be synchronized to the database after such eviction has taken place. Listing 4-16 creates an entity, checks that it is managed, detaches it from the persistence context, and checks that it is detached.

Listing 4-16. Checking Whether the Customer Entity Is in the Persistence Context

```
Customer customer = new Customer("Antony", "Balla", "tballa@mail.com");

tx.begin();
em.persist(customer);
tx.commit();

assertTrue(em.contains(customer));

em.detach(customer);

assertFalse(em.contains(customer));
```

Merging an Entity

A detached entity is no longer associated with a persistence context. If you want to manage it, you need to merge it. Let's take the example of an entity that needs to be displayed in a JSF page. The entity is first loaded from the database in the persistent layer (it is managed), it is returned from an invocation of a local EJB (it is detached because the transaction context ends), the presentation layer displays it (it is still detached), and then it returns to be updated to the database. However, at that moment, the entity is detached and needs to be attached again, or merged, to synchronize its state with the database.

Listing 4-17 simulates this case by clearing the persistence context (em.clear()), which detaches the entity.

Listing 4-17. Clearing the Persistence Context and Merging an Entity

```
Customer customer = new Customer("Antony", "Balla", "tballa@mail.com");

tx.begin();
em.persist(customer);
tx.commit();

em.clear();

// Sets a new value to a detached entity
customer.setFirstName("William");

tx.begin();
em.merge(customer);
tx.commit();
```

In Listing 4-17, a customer is created and persisted. The call to em.clear() forces the detachment of the customer entity, but detached entities continue to live outside of the persistence context in which they were, and their state is no longer guaranteed to be synchronized with the database state. That's what happens with customer.setFirstName("William"); set is executed on a detached entity, and the data is not updated in the database. To replicate this change to the database, you need to reattach the entity (i.e., merge it) with em.merge(customer).

Updating an Entity

Updating an entity is simple, yet at the same time it can be confusing to understand. As you've just seen, you can use the EntityManager.merge() to attach an entity and synchronize its state with the database. But, if an entity is currently managed, changes to it will be reflected in the database automatically. If not, you will need to explicitly call merge().

Listing 4-18 demonstrates persisting a customer with a first name set to Antony. When the em.persist() method is called, the entity is managed, so any changes made to the entity will be synchronized with the database. When the setFirstName() method is called, the entity changes its state. The entity manager caches any action starting at tx.begin() and synchronizes them when committed.

Listing 4-18. Updating the Customer's First Name

```
Customer customer = new Customer("Antony", "Balla", "tballa@mail.com");

tx.begin();
em.persist(customer);

customer.setFirstName("Williman");

tx.commit();
```

Cascading Events

By default, every entity manager operation applies only to the entity supplied as an argument to the operation. But sometimes, when an operation is carried out on an entity, you want to propagate it on its associations. This is known as *cascading an event*. The examples so far have relied on default cascade behavior and not customized behavior. In Listing 4-19, to create a customer, you instantiate a Customer and an Address entity, link them together (customer.setAddress(address)), and then persist the two.

Listing 4-19. Persisting a Customer with an Address

```
Customer customer = new Customer("Antony", "Balla", "tballa@mail.com");
Address address = new Address("Ritherdon Rd", "London", "8QE", "UK");
customer.setAddress(address);

tx.begin();
em.persist(customer);
em.persist(address);
tx.commit();
```

Because there's a relationship between Customer and Address, you could cascade the persist action from the customer to the address. That would mean that a call to em.persist(customer) would cascade the persist event to the Address entity if it allows this type of event to be propagated. You could then shrink the code and do away with the em.persist(address) as shown in Listing 4-20.

Listing 4-20. Cascading a Persist Event to Address

```
Customer customer = new Customer("Antony", "Balla", "tballa@mail.com");
Address address = new Address("Ritherdon Rd", "London", "8QE", "UK");
customer.setAddress(address);

tx.begin();
em.persist(customer);
tx.commit();
```

Without cascading, the customer would get persisted, but not the address. Cascading an event is possible if the mapping of the relationship is changed. The annotations @OneToOne, @OneToMany, @ManyToOne, and @ManyToMany have a cascade attribute that takes an array of events to be cascaded, and a PERSIST event can be cascaded as well as a REMOVE event (commonly used to perform delete cascades). To allow this, the mapping of the Customer entity (see Listing 4-21) must be changed, and a cascade attribute to the @OneToOne annotation on Address must be added.

Listing 4-21. Customer Entity Cascading Persist and Remove Events

```
@Entity
public class Customer {

    @Id @GeneratedValue
    private Long id;
    private String firstName;
    private String lastName;
    private String email;
    @OneToOne (fetch = FetchType.LAZY, ↪
            cascade = {CascadeType.PERSIST, CascadeType.REMOVE})
    @JoinColumn(name = "address_fk")
    private Address address;

    // Constructors, getters, setters
}
```

You can choose from several events to cascade to a target association, and these are listed in Table 4-2. You can even cascade them all using the CascadeType.ALL type.

Table 4-2. Possible Events to Be Cascaded

Cascade Type	Description
PERSIST	Cascades persist operations to the target of the association
REMOVE	Cascades remove operations to the target of the association
MERGE	Cascades merge operations to the target of the association
REFRESH	Cascades refresh operations to the target of the association
DETACH	Cascades detach operations to the target of the association
ALL	Declares that all the previous operations should be cascaded

Cache API

Most specifications (not just Java EE) focus heavily on functional requirements, leaving nonfunctional ones like performance, scalability, or clustering as implementation details. Implementations have to strictly follow the specification but may also add specific features. A perfect example for JPA would be caching.

Until JPA 2.0, caching wasn't mentioned in the specification. The entity manager is a first-level cache used to treat data in a comprehensive way for the database and to cache short, live entities. The first-level cache is used on a per-transaction basis to reduce the number of SQL queries within a given transaction. For example, if an object is modified several times within the same transaction, the entity manager will generate only one UPDATE statement at the end of the transaction. A first-level cache is not a performance cache.

Nevertheless, all JPA implementations use a performance cache (a.k.a. a second-level cache) to optimize database access, queries, joins, and so on. As seen in Figure 4-4, the second-level cache sits between the entity manager and the database to reduce database traffic by keeping objects loaded in memory and available to the whole application.

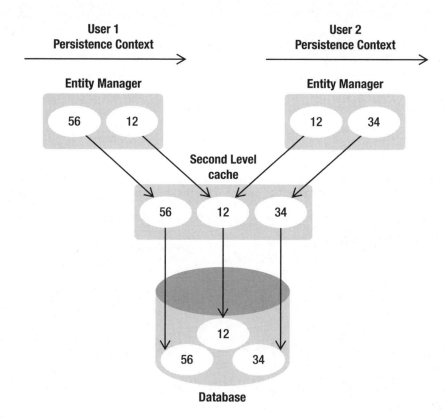

Figure 4-4. Second-level cache

Each implementation has its own way of caching objects, either by developing their own mechanism or by reusing open source ones. Caching can be distributed across a cluster or not—anything is possible when the specification ignores a topic. JPA 2.0 acknowledges that second-level cache is needed and has added caching operations to the standard API. The API, shown in Listing 4-22, is very minimalist (because the goal of JPA is not to standardize a fully functional cache), but it allows code to query and remove some entities from the second-level cache in a standard way. Like `EntityManager`, the `javax.persistence.Cache` is an interface implemented by the persistence provider caching system.

Listing 4-22. Cache API

```
public interface Cache {

    // Whether the cache contains data for the given entity.
    public boolean contains(Class cls, Object primaryKey);

    // Remove the data for the given entity from the cache.
    public void evict(Class cls, Object primaryKey);
```

```
// Remove the data for entities of the specified class
// (and its subclasses) from the cache.
public void evict(Class cls);

// Clear the cache.
public void evictAll();
}
```

Then you can use this API to check if a specific entity is in the second-level cache or not, remove it from the cache, or clear the entire cache. Combined with this API, you can explicitly inform the provider that an entity is cacheable or not by using the @Cacheable annotation as shown in Listing 4-23. If the entity has no @Cacheable annotation, it means that the entity and its state must not be cached by the provider.

Listing 4-23. The Customer Entity is Cacheable

```
@Entity
@Cacheable(true)
public class Customer {

    @Id @GeneratedValue
    private Long id;
    private String firstName;
    private String lastName;
    private String email;

    // Constructors, getters, setters
}
```

The @Cacheable annotation takes a boolean value. Once you've decided which entity should be cacheable or not, you need to inform the provider which caching mechanism to use. The way to do it with JPA is to set the shared-cache-mode attribute in the persistence.xml file. Here are the possible values:

- ALL: All entities and entity-related state and data are cached.

- DISABLE_SELECTIVE: Caching is enabled for all entities except those annotated with @Cacheable(false).

- ENABLE_SELECTIVE: Caching is enabled for all entities annotated with @Cacheable(true).

- NONE: Caching is disabled for the persistence unit.

- UNSPECIFIED: Caching behavior is undefined (the provider-specific defaults may apply).

Not setting one of these values leaves it up to the provider to decide which caching mechanism to use. The code in Listing 4-24 shows you how to use this caching mechanism. First, we create a Customer object and persist it. Because `Customer` is cacheable (see Listing 4-23), it should be in the second-level cache (by using the `EntityManagerFactory.getCache().contains()` method). Invoking the `cache.evict(Customer.class)` method removes the entity from the cache.

Listing 4-24. *The Customer Entity is Cacheable*

```
Customer customer = new Customer("Antony", "Balla", "tballa@mail.com");

tx.begin();
em.persist(customer);
tx.commit();

// Uses the EntityManagerFactory to get the Cache
Cache cache = emf.getCache();

// Customer should be in the cache
assertTrue(cache.contains(Customer.class, customer.getId()));

// Removes the Customer entity from the cache
cache.evict(Customer.class);

// Customer should not be in the cache anymore
assertFalse(cache.contains(Customer.class, customer.getId()));
```

JPQL

You just saw how to manipulate entities individually with the `EntityManager` API. You know how to find an entity by ID, remove it, update its attributes, and so on. But finding an entity by ID is quite limiting, as you only retrieve a single entity using its unique identifier. In practice, you may need to retrieve an entity by criteria other than the ID (by name, ISBN, etc.) or retrieve a set of entities based on different criteria (e.g., all customers living in the USA). This possibility is inherent to relational databases, and JPA has a language that allows this interaction: JPQL.

JPQL is used to define searches against persistent entities independent of the underlying database. JPQL is a query language that takes its roots in the syntax of Standard Query Language (SQL), which is the standard language for database interrogation. But the main difference is that in SQL the results obtained are in the form of rows and columns (tables), whereas JPQL uses an entity or a collection of entities. JPQL syntax is object oriented and therefore more easily understood by developers whose experience is limited to object-oriented languages. Developers manage their entity domain model, not a table structure, by using the dot notation (e.g., `myClass.myAttribute`).

Under the hood, JPQL uses the mechanism of mapping to transform a JPQL query into language comprehensible by an SQL database. The query is executed on the underlying database with SQL and JDBC calls, and then entity instances have their attributes set and are returned to the application—all in a very simple and powerful manner using a rich query syntax.

The simplest JPQL query selects all the instances of a single entity:

```
SELECT b
FROM Book b
```

If you know SQL, this should look familiar to you. Instead of selecting from a table, JPQL selects entities, here Book. The FROM clause is also used to give an alias to the entity: b is an alias for Book. The SELECT clause of the query indicates that the result type of the query is the b entity (the Book). Executing this statement will result in a list of zero or more Book instances.

To restrict the result, add search criteria where you can use the WHERE clause as follows:

```
SELECT b
FROM Book b
WHERE b.title = 'H2G2'
```

The alias is used to navigate across entity attributes through the dot operator. Since the Book entity has a persistent attribute named title of type String, b.title refers to the title attribute of the Book entity. Executing this statement will result in a list of zero or more Book instances that have a title equal to *H2G2*.

The simplest select query consists of two mandatory parts: the SELECT and the FROM clause. SELECT defines the format of the query results. The FROM clause defines the entity or entities from which the results will be obtained, and optional WHERE, ORDER BY, GROUP BY, and HAVING clauses can be used to restrict or order the result of a query. The select syntax is defined in Listing 4-25 in the next section.

There are also DELETE and UPDATE statements that can be used to perform delete and update operations across multiple instances of a specific entity class.

Select

The SELECT clause follows the path expressions syntax and results in one of the following forms: an entity, an entity attribute, a constructor expression, an aggregate function, or some sequence of these. Path expressions are the building blocks of queries and are used to navigate on entity attributes or across entity relationships (or a collection of entities) via the dot (.) navigation. Listing 4-25 defines the SELECT statement syntax.

Listing 4-25. SELECT Statement Syntax

```
SELECT <select expression>
FROM <from clause>
[WHERE <conditional expression>]
[ORDER BY <order by clause>]
[GROUP BY <group by clause>]
[HAVING <having clause>]
```

A simple SELECT returns an entity. For example, if a Customer entity has an alias called c, SELECT c will return an entity or a list of entities.

```
SELECT c
FROM Customer c
```

But a SELECT clause can also return attributes. If the Customer entity has a first name, SELECT c.firstName will return a String or a collection of Strings with the first names.

```
SELECT c.firstName
FROM Customer c
```

To retrieve the first name and the last name of a customer, you create a list containing the two attributes:

```
SELECT c.firstName, c.lastName
FROM Customer c
```

Since JPA 2.0, an attribute can be retrieved depending on a condition (using a CASE WHEN … THEN … ELSE … END expression). For example, instead of retrieving the price of a book, a statement can return a computation of the price (e.g., 50% discount) depending on the publisher (e.g., 50% discount on the Apress books, 20% discount for all the other books).

```
SELECT CASE b.editor WHEN 'Apress'
                     THEN b.price * 0.5
                     ELSE b.price * 0.8
       END
FROM Book b
```

If a Customer entity has a one-to-one relationship with Address, c.address refers to the address of the customer, and the result of the following query will return not a list of customers, but a list of addresses:

```
SELECT c.address
FROM Customer c
```

Navigation expressions can be chained together to traverse complex entity graphs. Using this technique, path expressions such as c.address.country.code can be constructed, referring to the country code of the customer's address.

```
SELECT c.address.country.code
FROM Customer c
```

A constructor may be used in the SELECT expression to return an instance of a Java class initialized with the result of the query. The class doesn't have to be an entity, but the constructor must be fully qualified and match the attributes.

```
SELECT NEW com.apress.javaee6.CustomerDTO(c.firstName, c.lastName, ↪
                              c.address.street1)
FROM Customer c
```

The result of this query is a list of CustomerDTO objects that have been instantiated with the new operator and initialized with the first name, last name, and street of the customers.

Executing these queries will return either a single value or a collection of zero or more entities (or attributes) including duplicates. To remove the duplicates, the DISTINCT operator must be used:

```
SELECT DISTINCT c
FROM Customer c
```

```
SELECT DISTINCT c.firstName
FROM Customer c
```

The result of a query may be the result of an aggregate function applied to a path expression. The following aggregate functions can be used in the SELECT clause: AVG, COUNT, MAX, MIN, SUM. The results may be grouped in the GROUP BY clause and filtered using the HAVING clause.

```
SELECT COUNT(c)
FROM Customer c
```

Scalar expressions also can be used in the SELECT clause of a query as well as in the WHERE and HAVING clauses. These expressions can be used on numeric (ABS, SQRT, MOD, SIZE, INDEX), string (CONCAT, SUBSTRING, TRIM, LOWER, UPPER, LENGTH, LOCATE), and date-time (CURRENT_DATE, CURRENT_TIME, CURRENT_TIMESTAMP) values.

From

The FROM clause of a query defines entities by declaring identification variables. An *identification variable*, or *alias*, is an identifier that can be used in the other clauses (SELECT, WHERE, etc.). The syntax of the FROM clause consists of an entity and an alias. In the following example, Customer is the entity and c the identification variable:

```
SELECT c
FROM Customer c
```

Where

The WHERE clause of a query consists of a conditional expression used to restrict the result of a SELECT, UPDATE, or DELETE statement. The WHERE clause can be a simple expression or set of conditional expressions to filter the query in a sophisticated way.

The simplest way to restrict the result of a query is to use the attribute of an entity. For example, the following query selects all customers named Vincent:

```
SELECT c
FROM Customer c
WHERE c.firstName = 'Vincent'
```

You can further restrict queries by using the logical operators AND and OR. The following example uses AND to select all customers named Vincent, living in France:

```
SELECT c
FROM Customer c
WHERE c.firstName = 'Vincent' AND c.address.country = 'France'
```

The WHERE clause also uses comparison operators: =, >, >=, <, <=, <>, [NOT] BETWEEN, [NOT] LIKE, [NOT] IN, IS [NOT] NULL, IS [NOT] EMPTY, [NOT] MEMBER [OF]. The following shows an example using two of these operators:

```
SELECT c
FROM Customer c
WHERE c.age > 18
```

```
SELECT c
FROM Customer c
WHERE c.age NOT BETWEEN 40 AND 50

SELECT c
FROM Customer c
WHERE c.address.country IN ('USA', 'Portugal')
```

The LIKE expression consists of a string and optional escape characters that define the match conditions: the underscore (_) for single-character wildcards and the percent sign (%) for multicharacter wildcards.

```
SELECT c
FROM Customer c
WHERE c.email LIKE '%mail.com'
```

Binding Parameters

Until now, the WHERE clauses shown herein only used fixed values. In an application, queries frequently depend on parameters. JPQL supports two types of parameter-binding syntax, allowing dynamic changes to the restriction clause of a query: positional and named parameters.

Positional parameters are designated by the question mark (?) followed by an integer (e.g., ?1). When the query is executed, the parameter numbers that should be replaced need to be specified.

```
SELECT c
FROM Customer c
WHERE c.firstName = ?1 AND c.address.country = ?2
```

Named parameters can also be used and are designated by a String identifier that is prefixed by the colon (:) symbol. When the query is executed, the parameter names that should be replaced need to be specified.

```
SELECT c
FROM Customer c
WHERE c.firstName = :fname AND c.address.country = :country
```

In the "Queries" section later in this chapter, you will see how an application binds parameters.

Subqueries

A subquery is a SELECT query that is embedded within a conditional expression of a WHERE or HAVING clause. The results of the subquery are evaluated and interpreted in the conditional expression of the main query. To retrieve the youngest customers from the database, a subquery with a MIN(age) is first executed and its result evaluated in the main query.

```
SELECT c
FROM Customer c
WHERE c.age = (SELECT MIN(cust. age) FROM Customer cust)
```

Order By

The ORDER BY clause allows the entities or values that are returned by a SELECT query to be ordered. The ordering applies to the entity attribute specified in this clause followed by the ASC or DESC keyword. The keyword ASC specifies that ascending ordering be used; DESC, the inverse, specifies that descending ordering be used. Ascending is the default and can be omitted.

```
SELECT c
FROM Customer c
WHERE c.age > 18
ORDER BY c.age DESC
```

Multiple expressions may also be used to refine the sort order.

```
SELECT c
FROM Customer c
WHERE c.age > 18
ORDER BY c.age DESC, c.address.country ASC
```

Group By and Having

The GROUP BY construct enables the aggregation of result values according to a set of properties. The entities are divided into groups based on the values of the entity field specified in the GROUP BY clause. To group customers by country and count them, use the following query:

```
SELECT c.address.country, count(c)
FROM Customer c
GROUP BY c.address.country
```

The GROUP BY defines the grouping expressions (c.address.country) over which the results will be aggregated and counted (count(c)). Note that expressions that appear in the GROUP BY clause must also appear in the SELECT clause.

The HAVING clause defines an applicable filter after the query results have been grouped, similar to a secondary WHERE clause filtering the result of the GROUP BY. Using the previous query, by adding a HAVING clause, a result of countries different to the UK can be achieved.

```
SELECT c.address.country, count(c)
FROM Customer c
GROUP BY c.address.country
HAVING c.address.country <> 'UK'
```

GROUP BY and HAVING can only be used within a SELECT clause (not a DELETE nor an UPDATE).

Bulk Delete

You know how to remove an entity with the EntityManager.remove() method and query a database to retrieve a list of entities that correspond to certain criteria. To remove a list of entities, you can execute a query, iterate through it, and remove each entity individually. Although this is a valid algorithm, it is terrible in terms of performance (too many database accesses). There is a better way to do it: bulk deletes.

JPQL performs bulk delete operations across multiple instances of a specific entity class. These are used to delete a large number of entities in a single operation. The DELETE statement looks like the SELECT statement, as it can have a restricting WHERE clause and take parameters. As a result, the number of entity instances affected by the operation is returned. The syntax of the DELETE statement is:

```
DELETE FROM <entity name> [[AS] <identification variable>]
[WHERE <conditional expression>]
```

As an example, to delete all customers younger than 18, you can use a bulk removal via a DELETE statement:

```
DELETE FROM Customer c
WHERE c.age < 18
```

Bulk Update

Bulk updates of entities are accomplished with the UPDATE statement, setting one or more attributes of the entity subject to conditions in the WHERE clause. The UPDATE statement syntax is:

```
UPDATE <entity name> [[AS] <identification variable>]
SET <update statement> {, <update statement>}*
[WHERE <conditional expression>]
```

Rather than deleting all the young customers, their first name can be changed to "too young" with the following statement:

```
UPDATE Customer c
SET c.firstName = 'TOO YOUNG'
WHERE c.age < 18
```

Queries

You've seen the JPQL syntax and how to describe statements using different clauses (SELECT, FROM, WHERE, etc.). But how do you integrate a JPQL statement to your application? The answer: through queries. JPA 2.0 has four different types of queries that can be used in code, each with a different purpose:

- *Dynamic queries*: This is the simplest form of queries, consisting of nothing more than a JPQL query string dynamically specified at runtime.

- *Named queries*: Named queries are static and unchangeable.

- *Native queries*: This type of query is useful to execute a native SQL statement instead of a JPQL statement.

- *Criteria API*: JPA 2.0 introduces this new concept of object-oriented query API.

The central point for choosing from these four types of queries is the `EntityManager` interface, which has several factory methods, listed in Table 4-3, returning either a `Query` or a `TypedQuery` interface (`TypedQuery` extends `Query`). The `Query` interface is used in cases when the result type is `Object`, and `TypedQuery` is used when a typed result is preferred.

Table 4-3. EntityManager Methods for Creating Queries

Method	Description
`Query createQuery(String jpqlString)`	Creates an instance of `Query` for executing a JPQL statement for dynamic queries
`Query createNamedQuery(String name)`	Creates an instance of `Query` for executing a named query (in JPQL or in native SQL)
`Query createNativeQuery(String sqlString)`	Creates an instance of `Query` for executing a native SQL statement
`Query createNativeQuery(String sqlString, Class resultClass)`	Creates an instance of `Query` for executing a native SQL statement passing the class of the expected results
`<T> TypedQuery<T> createNamedQuery(String name, Class<T> resultClass)`	Creates an instance of `TypedQuery` for executing a named query passing the class of the expected results
`<T> TypedQuery<T> createQuery(CriteriaQuery<T> criteriaQuery)`	Creates an instance of `TypedQuery` for executing a criteria query
`<T> TypedQuery<T> createQuery(String jpqlString, Class<T> resultClass)`	Creates an instance of `TypedQuery` for executing a query passing the class of the expected results

When an implementation of the `Query` or `TypedQuery` interface is obtained through one of the factory methods in the `EntityManager` interface, a rich API controls it. The `Query` API, shown in Listing 4-26, is used for static queries (i.e., named queries) and dynamic queries using JPQL, and native queries in SQL. The `Query` API also supports parameter binding and pagination control.

Listing 4-26. Query API

```
public interface Query {
    // Executes a query and returns a result
    List getResultList();
    Object getSingleResult();
    int executeUpdate();

    // Sets parameters to the query
    Query setParameter(String name, Object value);
    Query setParameter(String name, Date value, TemporalType temporalType);
```

```
Query setParameter(String name, Calendar value, TemporalType temporalType);
Query setParameter(int position, Object value);
Query setParameter(int position, Date value, TemporalType temporalType);
Query setParameter(int position, Calendar value, TemporalType temporalType);
<T> Query setParameter(Parameter<T> param, T value);
Query setParameter(Parameter<Date> param, Date value, TemporalType temporalType);
Query setParameter(Parameter<Calendar> param, Calendar value, ➥
                                        TemporalType temporalType);

// Gets parameters from the query
Set<Parameter<?>> getParameters();
Parameter<?> getParameter(String name);
Parameter<?> getParameter(int position);
<T> Parameter<T> getParameter(String name, Class<T> type);
<T> Parameter<T> getParameter(int position, Class<T> type);
boolean isBound(Parameter<?> param);
<T> T getParameterValue(Parameter<T> param);
Object getParameterValue(String name);
Object getParameterValue(int position);

// Constrains the number of results returned by a query
Query setMaxResults(int maxResult);
int getMaxResults();
Query setFirstResult(int startPosition);
int getFirstResult();

// Sets and gets query hints
Query setHint(String hintName, Object value);
Map<String, Object> getHints();

// Sets the flush mode type to be used for the query execution
Query setFlushMode(FlushModeType flushMode);
FlushModeType getFlushMode();

// Sets the lock mode type to be used for the query execution
Query setLockMode(LockModeType lockMode);
LockModeType getLockMode();

// Allows access to the provider-specific API
<T> T unwrap(Class<T> cls);
}
```

The methods that are mostly used in this API are ones that execute the query itself. To execute a SELECT query, you have to choose between two methods depending on the required result:

- The method getResultList() executes the query and returns a list of results (entities, attributes, expressions, etc.).

- The getSingleResult() method executes the query and returns a single result.

To execute an update or a delete, the `executeUpdate()` method executes the bulk query and returns the number of entities affected by the execution of the query.

As you saw in the "JPQL" section earlier, a query can take parameters that are either named (e.g., `:myParam`) or positional (e.g., `?1`). The `Query` API defines several `setParameter` methods to set parameters before executing a query.

When a query is executed, it can return a large number of results. Depending on the application, these can be processed together or in chunks (e.g., a web application only displays ten rows at one time). To control the pagination, the `Query` interface defines `setFirstResult()` and `setMaxResults()` methods to specify the first result to be received (numbered from zero) and the maximum number of results to return relative to that point.

The flush mode indicates to the persistence provider how to handle pending changes and queries. There are two possible flush mode settings: `AUTO` and `COMMIT`. `AUTO` (the default) means that the persistence provider is responsible for ensuring pending changes are visible to the processing of the query. `COMMIT` is when the effect of updates made to entities do not overlap with changed data in the persistence context.

Queries can be locked using the `setLockMode(LockModeType)` method. Locks are intended to provide a facility that enables the effect of repeatable read whether optimistically or pessimistically.

The following sections describe the four different types of queries using some of the methods just described.

Dynamic Queries

Dynamic queries are defined on the fly as needed by the application. To create a dynamic query, use the `EntityManager.createQuery()` method, which takes a `String` as a parameter that represents a JPQL query.

In the following code, the JPQL query selects all the customers from the database. As the result of this query is a list, the `getResultList()` method is used and returns a list of `Customer` entities (`List<Customer>`). However, if you know that your query only returns a single entity, use the `getSingleResult()` method. It returns a single entity and avoids the work of pulling it off a list.

```
Query query = em.createQuery("SELECT c FROM Customer c");
List<Customer> customers = query.getResultList();
```

This JPQL query returns a `Query` object. When the `query.getResultList()` method is invoked, a list of untyped object is returned. If you want the same query to return a list of type `Customer`, you need to use the `TypedQuery` as follows:

```
TypedQuery<Customer> query = em.createQuery("SELECT c FROM Customer c", Customer.class);
List<Customer> customers = query.getResultList();
```

This query string can also be dynamically created by the application, which can then specify a complex query at runtime not known ahead of time. String concatenation is used to construct the query dynamically depending on the criteria.

```
String jpqlQuery = "SELECT c FROM Customer c";
if (someCriteria)
    jpqlQuery += " WHERE c.firstName = 'Vincent'";
query = em.createQuery(jpqlQuery);
List<Customer> customers = query.getResultList();
```

The previous query retrieves customers named Vincent, but you might want to introduce a parameter for the first name. There are two possible choices for passing a parameter: using names or positions. In the following example, a named parameter called :fname (note the : symbol) is used in the query and bound with the setParameter method:

```
jpqlQuery = "SELECT c FROM Customer c";
if (someCriteria)
    jpqlQuery += " where c.firstName = :fname";
query = em.createQuery(jpqlQuery);
query.setParameter("fname", "Vincent");
List<Customer> customers = query.getResultList();
```

Note that the parameter name fname does not include the colon used in the query. The code using a position parameter would look like the following:

```
jpqlQuery = "SELECT c FROM Customer c";
if (someCriteria)
    jpqlQuery += " where c.firstName = ?1";
query = em.createQuery(jpqlQuery);
query.setParameter(1, "Vincent");
List<Customer> customers = query.getResultList();
```

If you need to use pagination to display the list of customers by chunks of ten, you can use the setMaxResults method as follows:

```
TypedQuery<Customer> query = em.createQuery("SELECT c FROM Customer c", Customer.class);
query.setMaxResults(10);
List<Customer> customers = query.getResultList();
```

An issue to consider with dynamic queries is the cost of translating the JPQL string into an SQL statement at runtime. Because the query is dynamically created and cannot be predicted, the persistence provider has to parse the JPQL string, get the ORM metadata, and generate the equivalent SQL. The performance cost of processing each of these dynamic queries can be an issue, and, if you have static queries that are unchangeable, use named queries instead.

Named Queries

Named queries are different from dynamic queries in that they are static and unchangeable. In addition to their static nature, which does not allow the flexibility of a dynamic query, named queries can be more efficient to execute because the persistence provider can translate the JPQL string to SQL once the application starts, rather than every time the query is executed.

Named queries are static queries expressed in metadata inside either a @NamedQuery annotation or the XML equivalent. To define these reusable queries, annotate an entity with the @NamedQuery annotation, which takes two elements: the name of the query and its content. So let's change the Customer entity and statically define three queries using annotations (see Listing 4-27).

Listing 4-27. The Customer Entity Defining Named Queries

```
@Entity
@NamedQueries({
    @NamedQuery(name = "findAll", query="select c from Customer c"),
    @NamedQuery(name = "findVincent", ↪
            query="select c from Customer c where c.firstName = 'Vincent'"),
    @NamedQuery(name = "findWithParam", ↪
            query="select c from Customer c where c.firstName = :fname")
})
public class Customer {

    @Id @GeneratedValue
    private Long id;
    private String firstName;
    private String lastName;
    private Integer age;
    private String email;
    @OneToOne
    @JoinColumn(name = "address_fk")
    private Address address;

    // Constructors, getters, setters
}
```

Because the `Customer` entity defines more than one named query, it uses the `@NamedQueries` annotation, which takes an array of @NamedQuery. The first query, called `findAll`, selects all customers from the database with no restriction (no `WHERE` clause). The `findWithParam` query takes the parameter `:fname` to restrict customers by their first name. Listing 4-27 shows an array of `@NamedQueries`, but, if the `Customer` only had one query, it would have been defined as follows:

```
@Entity
@NamedQuery(name = "findAll", query="select c from Customer c")
public class Customer {
    ...
}
```

The way to execute these named queries resembles the way dynamic queries are used. The `EntityManager.createNamedQuery()` method is invoked and passed to the query name defined by the annotations. This method returns a `Query` or a `TypedQuery` that can be used to set parameters, the max results, fetch modes, and so on. To execute the `findAll` query, write the following code:

```
Query query = em.createNamedQuery("findAll");
List<Customer> customers = query.getResultList();
```

Again, if you need to type the query to return a list of Customer objects, you'll need to use the TypedQuery as follows:

```
TypedQuery<Customer> query = em.createNamedQuery("findAll", Customer.class);
List<Customer> customers = query.getResultList();
```

Following is a fragment of code calling the findWithParam named query, passing the parameter
:fname, and setting the maximum result to 3:

```
Query query = em.createNamedQuery("findWithParam");
query.setParameter("fname", "Vincent");
query.setMaxResults(3);
List<Customer> customers = query.getResultList();
```

Because most of the methods of the Query API return a Query object, you can use the following
elegant shortcut to write queries. You call methods one after the other
(setParameter().setMaxResults(), etc.).

```
Query query = em.createNamedQuery("findWithParam").↪
     setParameter("fname", "Vincent").setMaxResults(3);
List<Customer> customers = query.getResultList();
```

Named queries are useful for organizing query definitions and powerful for improving application
performance. The organization comes from the fact that the named queries are defined statically on
entities and are typically placed on the entity class that directly corresponds to the query result (here the
findAll query returns customers, so it should be defined in the Customer entity).

There is a restriction in that the name of the query is scoped to the persistence unit and must be
unique within that scope, meaning that only one findAll method can exist. A findAll query for
customers and a findAll query for addresses should be named differently. A common practice is to
prefix the query name with the entity name. For example, the findAll query for the Customer entity
would be named Customer.findAll.

Another problem is that the name of the query, which is a string, is manipulated, and, if you make a
typo or refactor your code, you may get some exceptions indicating that the query doesn't exist. To limit
the risks, you can replace the name of a query with a constant. Listing 4-28 shows how to refactor the
Customer entity.

Listing 4-28. The Customer Entity Defining a Named Query with a Constant

```
@Entity
@NamedQuery(name = Customer.FIND_ALL, query="select c from Customer c"),
public class Customer {

    public static final String FIND_ALL = "Customer.findAll";

    // Attributes, constructors, getters, setters
}
```

The FIND_ALL constant identifies the findAll query in a nonambiguous way by prefixing the name of
the query with the name of the entity. The same constant is then used in the @NamedQuery annotation,
and you can use this constant to execute the query as follows:

```
TypedQuery<Customer> query = em.createNamedQuery(Customer.FIND_ALL, Customer.class);
List<Customer> customers = query.getResultList();
```

Native Queries

JPQL has a very rich syntax that allows you to handle entities in any form and in a portable way across databases. JPA enables you to use specific features of a database by using native queries. Native queries take a native SQL statement (`SELECT`, `UPDATE`, or `DELETE`) as the parameter and return a `Query` instance for executing that SQL statement. However, native queries are not expected to be portable across databases.

If the code is not portable, why not use JDBC calls? The main reason to use JPA native queries rather than JDBC calls is because the result of the query will get automatically converted back to entities. If you want to retrieve all the customer entities from the database using SQL, you need to use the `EntityManager.createNativeQuery()` method that takes in parameters the SQL query and the entity class that the result should be mapped to.

```
Query query = em.createNativeQuery("SELECT * FROM t_customer", Customer.class);
List<Customer> customers = query.getResultList();
```

As you can see in the preceding code fragment, the SQL query is a string that can be dynamically created at runtime (just like JPQL dynamic queries). Again, the query could be complex, and, because the persistence provider doesn't know in advance, it will interpret it each time. Like named queries, native queries can use annotations to define static SQL queries. Named, native queries are defined using the `@NamedNativeQuery` annotation, which must be placed on any entity (see Listing 4-29). Like JPQL named queries, the name of the query must be unique within the persistence unit.

Listing 4-29. The Customer Entity Defining a Native Named Query

```
@Entity
@NamedNativeQuery(name = "findAll", query="select * from t_customer")
@Table(name = "t_customer")
public class Customer {

    // Attributes, constructors, getters, setters
}
```

Criteria API (or Object-Oriented Queries)

Until now, I've been using strings to write JPQL (dynamic or named queries) and SQL (native queries) statements. This has the advantage of writing a database query in a very concise way, but has the inconvenience of being error prone: it is a String, so many typos can be made. For example, you could have typos on JPQL keywords (`SLECT` instead of `SELECT`), class names (`Custmer` instead of `Customer`) or attributes (`firstname` instead of `firstName`). You can also write a syntactically incorrect statement (`SELECT c WHERE c.firstName = 'John' FROM Customer`). Any of these mistakes will be discovered at runtime, and it may sometimes be difficult to find where the bug comes from.

JPA 2.0 comes with a new API, called Criteria API and defined in the package `javax.persistence.criteria`. It allows you to write any query in an object-oriented and syntactically correct way. Most of the mistakes that a developer could make writing a statement are found at compile time, not at runtime. The idea is that all the JPQL keywords (`SELECT`, `WHERE`, `LIKE`, `GROUP BY`...) are defined in this API. In other words, the Criteria API supports everything JPQL can do but with an object-based syntax. Let's have a first look at a query that retrieves all the customers named "Vincent". In JPQL, it would look like that:

```
SELECT c FROM Customer c WHERE c.firstName = 'Vincent'
```

This JPQL statement is rewritten in Listing 4-30 in an object-oriented way using the new Criteria API:

Listing 4-30. A Criteria Query Selecting All the Customers Named Vincent

```
CriteriaBuilder builder = em.getCriteriaBuilder();
CriteriaQuery<Customer> query = builder.createQuery(Customer.class);
Root<Customer> c = query.from(Customer.class);
query.select(c).where(builder.equal(c.get("firstName"), "Vincent"));
```

Without going into too much detail, you can see that the SELECT, FROM and WHERE keywords have an API representation through the methods select(), from() and where(). And this rule applies for every JPQL keyword. Criteria queries are constructed through the CriteriaBuilder interface that is obtained by the EntityManager (the em attribute in Listings 4-30 and 4-31). It contains methods to construct the query definition (this interface defines keywords such as desc(), asc(), avg(), sum(), max(), min(), count(), and(), or(), greaterThan(), lowerThan()…). The other role of the CriteriaBuilder is to create a CriteriaQuery. This interface defines methods such as select(), from(), where(), orderBy(), groupBy(), and having(), which have the equivalent meaning in JPQL. In Listing 4-30, the way you get the alias **c** (as in SELECT **c** FROM Customer) is through the Root interface (Root<Customer> c). Then you just have to use the builder, the query and the root to write any JPQL statement you want: from the simplest (select all the entities from the database) to the most complex (joins, subqueries, case expressions, functions…).

Let's take another example. Listing 4-31 shows a query that retrieves all the customers older than 40. The c.get("age") gets the attribute age from the Customer entity and checks if it's greater than 40.

Listing 4-31. A Criteria Query Selecting All the Customers Older than 40

```
CriteriaBuilder builder = em.getCriteriaBuilder();
CriteriaQuery<Customer> query = builder.createQuery(Customer.class);
Root<Customer> c = query.from(Customer.class);
query.select(c).where(builder.greaterThan(c.get("age").as(Integer.class), 40));
```

I started this section saying the Criteria API allows you to write error-prone statements. But it's not completely true yet. When you look at Listings 4-30 and 4-31, you can still see some strings ("firstName" and "age") that represent the attributes of the Customer entity. So typos can still be made. In Listing 4-31, we still need to cast the age into an Integer (c.get("age").as(Integer.class)) because there is no other way to discover that the age attribute is of type Integer. To solve these problems, the Criteria API comes with the idea of a static meta-model class for each entity bringing type safety to the API.

Type-Safe Criteria API

Listings 4-30 and 4-31 are almost type safe: each JPQL keyword can be represented by a method of the CriteriaBuilder and CriteriaQuery interface. The only missing part is the attributes of the entity that are string-based: the way to refer to the customer's firstName attribute is by calling c.get("firstName"). The get method takes a String as a parameter. Type-safe Criteria API solves this by overriding this method with a path expression from the meta-model API classes bringing type safety.

Listing 4-32 shows the Customer entity with several attributes of different type (Long, String, Integer, Address).

Listing 4-32. A Customer Entity with Several Attributes' Types

```
@Entity
public class Customer {

    @Id @GeneratedValue
    private Long id;
    private String firstName;
    private String lastName;
    private Integer age;
    private String email;
    private Address address;

    // Constructors, getters, setters
}
```

To bring type-safety, JPA 2.0 can generate a static meta-model class for each entity. The convention is that each entity X will have a meta-data class called X_ (with an underscore). So, the Customer entity will have its meta-model representation described in the Customer_ class shown in Listing 4-33.

Listing 4-33. The Customer_ Class Describing the Meta-model of Customer

```
@Generated("EclipseLink")
@StaticMetamodel(Customer.class)
public class Customer_ {

    public static volatile SingularAttribute<Customer, Long> id;
    public static volatile SingularAttribute<Customer, String> firstName;
    public static volatile SingularAttribute<Customer, String> lastName;
    public static volatile SingularAttribute<Customer, Integer> age;
    public static volatile SingularAttribute<Customer, String> email;
    public static volatile SingularAttribute<Customer, Address> address;
}
```

In the static meta-model class, each attribute of the Customer entity is defined by a subclass of javax.persistence.metamodel.Attribute (CollectionAttribute, ListAttribute, MapAttribute, SetAttribute or SingularAttribute). Each of these attributes uses generics and is strongly typed (e.g., SingularAttribute<Customer, Integer>, age). Listing 4-34 shows the exact same code as Listing 4-31 but revisited with the static meta-model class (the c.get("age") is turned into c.get(Customer_.age)). Another advantage of type safety is that the meta-model defines the age attribute as being an Integer, so there is no need to cast the attribute into an Integer using as(Integer.class):

Listing 4-34. A Type-Safe Criteria Query Selecting All the Customers Older than 40

```
CriteriaBuilder builder = em.getCriteriaBuilder();
CriteriaQuery<Customer> query = builder.createQuery(Customer.class);
Root<Customer> c = query.from(Customer.class);
query.select(c).where(builder.greaterThan(c.get(Customer_.age), 40));
```

Again, these are just examples of what you can do with the new Criteria API. It is a very rich API that is completely defined in chapter 6 of the JPA 2.0 specification.

■ **Note** The classes used in the static meta-model, such as `Attribute` or `SingularAttribute`, are standard and defined in the package `javax.persistence.metamodel`. But the generation of the static meta-model classes is implementation specific. EclipseLink uses an internal class called `CanonicalModelProcessor`. This processor can be invoked by your IDE while you develop, a java command, an Ant task or a Maven plug-in.

Concurrency

JPA can be used to change persistent data, and JPQL can be used to retrieve data following certain criteria. All this can happen within an application running in a cluster with multiple nodes, multiple threads, and one single database, so it is quite common for entities to be accessed concurrently. When this is the case, synchronization must be controlled by the application using a locking mechanism. Whether the application is simple or complex, chances are that you will make use of locking somewhere in your code.

To illustrate the problem of concurrent database access, let's see an example of an application with two methods, shown in Figure 4-5. One method finds a book by its identifier and raises the price of the book by $2. The other does the same thing but raises the price by $5. If these two methods are executed concurrently in separate transactions and manipulate the same book, you can't predict the final price of the book. In this example, the initial price of the book is $10. Depending on which transaction finishes last, the price can be $12 or $15.

```
tx1.begin();                                     tx2.begin();

// The price of the book is 10$                  // The price of the book is 10$
Book book = em.find(Book.class, 12);             Book book = em.find(Book.class, 12);

book.raisePriceByTwoDollars();                   book.raisePriceByFiveDollars();

tx1.commit();                                     tx2.commit();
// The price is now 12$                          // The price is now 15$

                          time
```

Figure 4-5. Transactions one (tx1) and two (tx2) updating the price of a book concurrently

This problem of concurrency, where the "winner" is the last one to commit, is not specific to JPA. Databases have had to deal with this for a long time and have found different solutions to isolate one transaction from others. One common mechanism that databases use is to lock the row on which the SQL statement is being executed.

There are two different locking mechanisms that JPA 2.0 uses (JPA 1.0 only had support for optimistic locking):

- *Optimistic locking* is based on the assumption that most database transactions don't conflict with other transactions, allowing concurrency to be as permissive as possible when allowing transactions to execute.

- *Pessimistic locking* is based on the opposite assumption, so a lock will be obtained on the resource before operating on it.

As an example from everyday life that reinforces these concepts, consider "optimistic and pessimistic street crossing." In an area with very light traffic, you might be able to cross the street without checking for approaching cars. But not in a busy city center!

JPA uses different locking mechanisms at different levels of the API. Both pessimistic and optimistic locks can be obtained via the `EntityManager.find` and `EntityManager.refresh` methods (in addition to the `lock` method), as well as through JPQL queries, meaning locking can be achieved at the `EntityManager` level and at the `Query` level with the methods listed in Tables 4-4 and 4-5.

Table 4-4. EntityManager Methods to Lock Entities

Method	Description
`<T> T find(Class<T> entityClass, Object primaryKey, LockModeType lockMode)`	Searches for an entity of the specified class and primary key and locks it with respect to the specified lock type
`void lock(Object entity, LockModeType lockMode)`	Locks an entity instance that is contained in the persistence context with the specified lock mode type
`void refresh(Object entity, LockModeType lockMode)`	Refreshes the state of the instance from the database, overwriting changes made to the entity, if any, and locks it with respect to the given lock mode type
`LockModeType getLockMode(Object entity)`	Get the current lock mode for the entity instance

Table 4-5. Query Method to Lock JPQL Queries

Method	Description
`LockModeType getLockMode()`	Get the current lock mode for the query
`Query setLockMode(LockModeType lockMode)`	Sets the lock mode type to be used for the query execution

Each of these methods takes a `LockModeType` as a parameter that can take different values:

- `OPTIMISTIC`: Uses optimistic locking

- `OPTIMISTIC_FORCE_INCREMENT`: Uses optimistic locking and forces an increment to the entity's version column (see the upcoming "Versioning" section)

- `PESSIMISTIC_READ`: Uses pessimistic locking without the need to reread the data at the end of the transaction to obtain a lock

- `PESSIMISTIC_WRITE`: Uses pessimistic locking and forces serialization among transactions attempting to update the entity

- `PESSIMISTIC_FORCE_INCREMENT`: Uses pessimistic locking and forces an increment to the entity's version column (see the upcoming "Versioning" section)

- `NONE`: Specifies no locking mechanism should be used

You can use these parameters on multiple places depending on how you need to specify locks. You can read *then* lock:

```
Book book = em.find(Book.class, 12);
// Lock to raise the price
em.lock(book, LockModeType.OPTIMISTIC_FORCE_INCREMENT);
book.raisePriceByTwoDollars();
```

Or you can read *and* lock:

```
Book book = em.find(Book.class, 12, LockModeType.OPTIMISTIC_FORCE_INCREMENT);
// The book is already locked, raise the price
book.raisePriceByTwoDollars();
```

Concurrency and locking are key motivators for versioning.

Versioning

Java specifications use versioning: Java SE 5.0, Java SE 6.0, EJB 3.1, JAX-RS 1.0, and so on. When a new version of JAX-RS is released, its version number is increased, and you upgrade to JAX-RS 1.1. JPA uses this exact mechanism when you need to version entities. So, when you persist an entity for the first time in the database, it will get the version number 1. Later, if you update an attribute and commit this change to the database, the entity version will get the number 2, and so on. This versioning will evolve each time a change is made to the entity.

In order for this to happen, the entity must have an attribute to store the version number, and it has to be annotated by `@Version`. This version number is then mapped to a column in the database. The attribute types supported for versioning can be `int`, `Integer`, `short`, `Short`, `long`, `Long`, or `Timestamp`. Listing 4-35 shows how to add a `version` attribute to the `Book` entity.

Listing 4-35. The Book Entity with a @Version Annotation on an Integer

```
@Entity
public class Book {

    @Id @GeneratedValue
    private Long id;
    @Version
    private Integer version;
    private String title;
    private Float price;
    private String description;
    private String isbn;
    private Integer nbOfPage;
    private Boolean illustrations;

    // Constructors, getters, setters
}
```

The entity can access the value of its **version** property but must not modify it. Only the persistence provider is permitted to set or update the value of the **version** attribute when the object is written or updated to the database. Let's look at an example to illustrate the behavior of this versioning. In Listing 4-36, a new **Book** entity is persisted to the database. Once the transaction is committed, the persistence provider sets the version to **1**. Later, the price of the book is updated, and, once the data is flushed to the database, the version number is incremented to **2**.

Listing 4-36. Transactions tx1 and tx2 Updating the Price of a Book Concurrently

```
Book book = new Book("H2G2", 21f, "Best IT book", "123-456", 321, false);

tx.begin();
em.persist(book);
tx.commit();
assertEquals(1, book.getVersion());

tx.begin();
book.raisePriceByTwoDollars();
tx.commit();
assertEquals(2, book.getVersion());
```

The **version** attribute is not required but is recommended when the entity can be concurrently modified by more than one process or thread. Versioning is the core of optimistic locking and provides protection for infrequent concurrent entity modification. In fact, an entity is automatically enabled for optimistic locking if it has a property mapped with a **@Version** annotation.

Optimistic Locking

As its name indicates, optimistic locking is based on the fact that database transactions don't conflict with one other. In other words, there is a good chance that the transaction updating an entity will be the only one that actually updates the entity during that interval. Therefore, the decision to acquire a lock on the entity is actually made at the end of the transaction. This ensures that updates to an entity are consistent with the current state of the database. Transactions that would cause this constraint to be violated result in an OptimisticLockException being thrown and the transaction marked for rollback.

How would you throw an OptimisticLockException? Either by explicitly locking the entity (with the lock or the find methods that you saw passing a LockModeType) or by letting the persistence provider check the attribute annotated with @Version. The use of a dedicated @Version annotation on an entity allows the EntityManager to perform optimistic locking simply by comparing the value of the version attribute in the entity instance with the value of the column in the database. Without an attribute annotated with @Version, the entity manager will not be able to do optimistic locking automatically (implicitly).

Transactions tx1 and tx2 both get an instance of the same Book entity. At that moment, the version of the Book entity is 1. The first transaction raises the price of the book by $2 and commits this change. When the data is flushed to the database, the persistence provider increases the version number and sets it to 2. At that moment, the second transaction raises the price by $5 and commits the change. The entity manager for tx2 realizes that the version number in the database is different from that of the entity. This means the version has been changed by a different transaction, so an OptimisticLockException is thrown, as shown in Figure 4-6.

```
tx1.begin();                                  tx2.begin();

// The price of the book is 10$               // The price of the book is 10$
Book book = em.find(Book.class, 12);          Book book = em.find(Book.class, 12);
// book.getVersion() == 1                      // book.getVersion() == 1

book.raisePriceByTwoDollars();
                                              book.raisePriceByFiveDollars();
tx1.commit();
// The price is now 12$
// book.getVersion() == 2                      tx2.commit();
                                              // version should be 1 but is 2
                                   time▼       // OptimisticLockException
```

Figure 4-6. OptimisticLockException thrown on transaction tx2

This is the default behavior when the @Version annotation is used: an OptimisticLockException is thrown when the data is flushed (at commit time or by explicitly calling the em.flush() method). You can also control where you want to add the optimistic lock using read then lock or read and lock. The code of read and lock, for example, would look like this:

```
Book book = em.find(Book.class, 12);
// Lock to raise the price
em.lock(book, LockModeType.OPTIMISTIC);
book.raisePriceByTwoDollars();
```

With optimistic locking, the LockModeType that you pass as a parameter can take two values: OPTIMISTIC and OPTIMISTIC_FORCE_INCREMENT (or READ and WRITE, respectively, but these values are deprecated). The only difference is that `OPTIMISTIC_FORCE_INCREMENT` will force an update (increment) to the entity's `version` column.

Applications are strongly encouraged to enable optimistic locking for all entities that may be concurrently accessed. Failure to use a locking mechanism may lead to inconsistent entity state, lost updates, and other state irregularities. Optimistic locking is a useful performance optimization that offloads work that would otherwise be required of the database and is an alternative to pessimistic locking, which requires low-level database locking.

Pessimistic Locking

Pessimistic locking is based on the opposite assumption to optimistic locking, because a lock is eagerly obtained on the entity before operating on it. This is very resource restrictive and results in significant performance degradation, as a database lock is held using a `SELECT ... FOR UPDATE` SQL statement to read data.

Databases typically offer a pessimistic locking service that allows the entity manager to lock a row in a table to prevent another thread from updating the same row. This is an effective mechanism to ensure that two clients do not modify the same row at the same time, but requires expensive, low-level checks inside the database. Transactions that would cause this constraint to be violated result in a `PessimisticLockException` being thrown and the transaction marked for rollback.

Optimistic locking is appropriate in dealing with moderate contention among concurrent transactions. But in some applications with a higher risk of contentions, pessimistic locking may be more appropriate, as the database lock is immediately obtained as opposed to the often late failure of optimistic transactions. For example, in times of economic crises, stock markets receive huge numbers of selling orders. If 100 million Americans need to sell their stock options at the same time, the system needs to use pessimistic locks to ensure data consistency. Note that at the moment the market is rather pessimistic instead of optimistic, and that has nothing to do with JPA.

Pessimistic locking may be applied to entities that do not contain the annotated `@Version` attribute.

Summary

In this chapter, you learned how to query entities. The entity manager is central to articulating entities with persistence. It can create, update, find by ID, remove, and synchronize entities with the database with the help of the persistence context, which acts as a level-one cache. JPA also comes with a very powerful query language, JPQL, which is database vendor-independent. You can retrieve entities with a rich syntax using `WHERE`, `ORDER BY`, or `GROUP BY` clauses, and, when concurrent access occurs to your entities, you know how to use versioning and when to use optimistic or pessimistic locking.

In the next chapter, you'll learn more about the life cycle of entities and will see how to hook some logic to this life cycle using callback annotations or listeners.

Callbacks and Listeners

In the previous chapter, you saw how to query mapped entities. Now you know how to persist, remove, update, and find an entity by its identifier. With JPQL, you can retrieve one or more entities according to certain search criteria with dynamic, static, and native queries. All these actions are carried out by the entity manager—the central piece that manipulates entities and manages their life cycle.

I described the entity life cycle by saying that entities are managed by the entity manager (meaning that they have a persistence identity and are synchronized with the database) or are detached from the database and used as normal POJOs. But the life cycle of an entity is slightly richer. Importantly, JPA allows you to hook in your own business logic when certain events occur on the entity. This business code is then automatically called by the persistence provider using callback methods.

You can think of life-cycle callback methods and listeners as triggers in a relational database. A trigger executes business logic for each row in a table. Life-cycle callback methods and listeners are invoked for each instance of an entity in response to a certain event or, more precisely, before or after the event occurs. You can use metadata annotations or XML descriptors to define "Pre" and "Post" callback methods.

Entity Life Cycle

By now, you know most of the mysteries of entities, so let's look at their life cycle. When an entity is instantiated (with the new operator), it is just seen as a regular POJO by the JVM (i.e., detached) and can be used as a regular object by the application. Then, when the entity is persisted by the entity manager, it is said to be managed. When an entity is managed, the entity manager will automatically synchronize the value of its attributes with the underlying database (e.g., if you change the value of an attribute by using a set method while the entity is managed, this new value will be automatically synchronized with the database).

To have a better understanding of this, take a look at Figure 5-1, a UML state diagram showing the transitions between each state of a Customer entity.

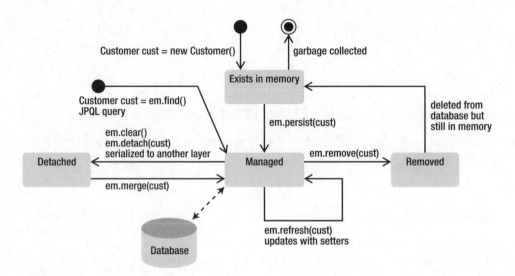

Figure 5-1. Entity life cycle

To create an instance of the Customer entity, you use the new operator. This object exists in memory, although JPA knows nothing about it. If you do nothing with this object, it will go out of scope and will end up being garbage collected, and that will be the end of its life cycle. What you can do next is persist an instance of Customer with the EntityManager.persist() method. At that moment, the entity becomes managed, and its state is synchronized with the database. During this managed state, you can update attributes using the setter methods (e.g., customer.setFirstName()) or refresh the content with an EntityManager.refresh() method. All these changes will be synchronized between the entity and the database. During this state, if you call the EntityManager.contains(customer) method, it will return true because customer is contained in the persistence context (i.e., managed).

Another way for an entity to be managed is when it is loaded from the database. When you use the EntityManager.find() method, or create a JPQL query to retrieve a list of entities, all are automatically managed, and you can start updating or removing their attributes.

In the managed state, you can call the EntityManager.remove() method, and the entity is deleted from the database and not managed anymore. But the Java object continues living in memory, and you can still use it until the garbage collector gets rid of it.

Now let's look at the detached state. You've seen in the previous chapter how explicitly calling the EntityManager.clear() or EntityManager.detach(customer) methods will clear the entity from the persistence context; it becomes detached. But there is also another, more subtle, way to detach an entity: when it's serialized. In many examples in this book, entities don't implement anything, but, if they need to cross a network to be invoked remotely or cross layers to be displayed in a presentation tier, they need to implement the java.io.Serializable interface. This is not a JPA restriction but a Java restriction. When a managed entity is serialized, crosses the network, and gets deserialized, it is seen as a detached object. To reattach an entity, you need to call the EntityManager.merge() method. A common-use case is when an entity is used in a JSF page. Let's say that a Customer entity is displayed in a form on a remote JSF page to be updated. Being remote, the entity needs to be serialized on the server side before being sent to the presentation layer. At that moment, the entity is automatically detached. Once displayed, if any data is changed and needs to be updated, the form is submitted, the entity is sent back to the server, deserialized, and needs to be merged to be attached again.

Callback methods and listeners allow you to add your own business logic when certain life-cycle events occur on an entity, or broadly whenever a life-cycle event occurs on any entity.

Callbacks

The life cycle of an entity falls into four categories: persisting, updating, removing, and loading, which correspond to the database operations of inserting, updating, deleting, and selecting, respectively. Each life cycle has a "Pre" and "Post" event that can be intercepted by the entity manager to invoke a business method. These business methods have to be annotated by one of the annotations described in Table 5-1.

Table 5-1. *Life-Cycle Callback Annotations*

Annotation	Description
@PrePersist	Marks a method to be invoked before `EntityManager.persist()` is executed.
@PostPersist	Marks a method to be invoked after the entity has been persisted. If the entity autogenerates its primary key (with `@GeneratedValue`), the value is available in the method.
@PreUpdate	Marks a method to be invoked before a database update operation is performed (calling the entity setters or the `EntityManager.merge()` method).
@PostUpdate	Marks a method to be invoked after a database update operation is performed.
@PreRemove	Marks a method to be invoked before `EntityManager.remove()` is executed.
@PostRemove	Marks a method to be invoked after the entity has been removed.
@PostLoad	Marks a method to be invoked after an entity is loaded (with a JPQL query or an `EntityManager.find()`) or refreshed from the underlying database. There is no `@PreLoad` annotation, as it doesn't make sense to preload data on an entity that is not built yet.

Adding the callback annotations to the UML state diagram shown previously in Figure 5-1 results in the diagram you see in Figure 5-2.

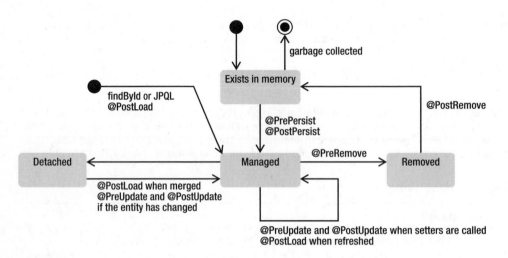

Figure 5-2. Entity life cycle with callback annotations

Before inserting an entity into the database, the entity manager calls the method annotated with `@PrePersist`. If the insert does not throw an exception, the entity is persisted, its identity is initialized, and the method annotated with `@PostPersist` is then invoked. This is the same behavior for updates (`@PreUpdate`, `@PostUpdate`) and deletes (`@PreRemove`, `@PostRemove`). A method annotated with `@PostLoad` is called when an entity is loaded from the database (via an `EntityManager.find()` or a JPQL query). When the entity is detached and needs to be merged, the entity manager first has to check whether there are any differences with the database (`@PostLoad`) and, if so, update the data (`@PreUpdate`, `@PostUpdate`).

How does it look in the code? Entities can have not only attributes, constructors, getters, and setters, but also business logic used to validate their state or compute some of their attributes. These can consist of normal Java methods that are invoked by other classes or callback annotations (also referred to as callback methods), as shown in Listing 5-1. The entity manager invokes them automatically depending on the event triggered.

Listing 5-1. The Customer Entity with Callback Annotations

```
@Entity
public class Customer {

    @Id @GeneratedValue
    private Long id;
    private String firstName;
    private String lastName;
    private String email;
    private String phoneNumber;
    @Temporal(TemporalType.DATE)
    private Date dateOfBirth;
    @Transient
    private Integer age;
    @Temporal(TemporalType.TIMESTAMP)
    private Date creationDate;
```

```
@PrePersist
@PreUpdate
private void validate() {
    if (firstName == null || "".equals(firstName))
        throw new IllegalArgumentException("Invalid first name");
    if (lastName == null || "".equals(lastName))
        throw new IllegalArgumentException("Invalid last name");
}

@PostLoad
@PostPersist
@PostUpdate
public void calculateAge() {
    if (dateOfBirth == null) {
        age = null;
        return;
    }

    Calendar birth = new GregorianCalendar();
    birth.setTime(dateOfBirth);
    Calendar now = new GregorianCalendar();
    now.setTime(new Date());
    int adjust = 0;
    if (now.get(DAY_OF_YEAR) - birth.get(DAY_OF_YEAR) < 0) {
        adjust = -1;
    }
    age = now.get(YEAR) - birth.get(YEAR) + adjust;
}

// Constructors, getters, setters
}
```

In Listing 5-1, the Customer entity has a method to validate its data (checks the firstName and lastName attributes). This method is annotated with @PrePersist and @PreUpdate and will get called before inserting data into or updating data in the database. If the data is not valid, a runtime exception is launched, and the insert or update will roll back to ensure that the data inserted or updated in the database is valid.

The method calculateAge() calculates the age of the customer. The age attribute is transient and doesn't get mapped into the database. After the entity gets loaded, persisted, or updated, the calculateAge() method takes the date of birth of the customer, calculates the age, and sets the attribute.

The following rules apply to life-cycle callback methods:

- Methods can have public, private, protected, or package-level access, but must not be static or final. Notice in Listing 5-1 that the validate() method is private.

- A method may be annotated with multiple life-cycle event annotations (the validateData() method is annotated with @PrePersist and @PreUpdate). However, only one life-cycle annotation of a given type may be present in an entity class (you can't have two @PrePersist annotations in the same entity, for example).

- A method can throw unchecked (runtime) exceptions but not checked exceptions. Throwing a runtime exception will roll back the transaction if one exists.

- A method can invoke JNDI, JDBC, JMS, and EJBs but cannot invoke any `EntityManager` or `Query` operations.

- With inheritance, if a method is specified on the superclass, it will get invoked before the method on the child class. For example, if in Listing 5-1 `Customer` was inheriting from a `Person` entity, the `Person @PrePersist` method would be invoked before the `Customer @PrePersist` method.

- If event cascading is used in the relationships, the callback method will also get called in a cascaded way. For example, let's say a `Customer` has a collection of addresses, and a cascade remove is set on the relation. When you delete the customer, the `Address @PreRemove` method would be invoked as well as the `Customer @PreRemove` method.

Listeners

Callback methods in an entity work well when you have business logic that is only related to that entity. Entity listeners are used to extract the business logic to a separate class and share it between other entities. An entity listener is just a POJO on which you can define one or more life-cycle callback methods. To register a listener, the entity needs to use the `@EntityListeners` annotation.

Using the customer example, extract the `calculateAge()` and `validate()` methods to separate listener classes, `AgeCalculationListener` (see Listing 5-2) and `DataValidationListener` (see Listing 5-3), respectively.

Listing 5-2. A Listener Calculating the Customer's Age

```
public class AgeCalculationListener {

    @PostLoad
    @PostPersist
    @PostUpdate
    public void calculateAge(Customer customer) {
        if (customer.getDateOfBirth() == null) {
            customer.setAge(null);
            return;
        }

        Calendar birth = new GregorianCalendar();
        birth.setTime(customer.getDateOfBirth());
        Calendar now = new GregorianCalendar();
        now.setTime(new Date());
        int adjust = 0;
```

```
        if (now.get(DAY_OF_YEAR) - birth.get(DAY_OF_YEAR) < 0) {
            adjust = -1;
        }
        customer.setAge(now.get(YEAR) - birth.get(YEAR) + adjust);
    }
}
```

Listing 5-3. A Listener Validating the Customer's Attributes

```
public class DataValidationListener {

    @PrePersist
    @PreUpdate
    private void validate(Customer customer) {
        if (customer.getFirstName() == null || "".equals(customer.getFirstName()))
            throw new IllegalArgumentException("Invalid first name");
        if (customer.getLastName() == null || "".equals(customer.getLastName()))
            throw new IllegalArgumentException("Invalid last name");
    }
}
```

Only simple rules apply to a listener class. The first is that the class must have a public no-arg constructor. Second, the signatures of the callback methods are slightly different from the ones in Listing 5-1. When the callback method is invoked on a listener, the method needs to have access to the entity state (e.g., the customer's first name and last name, which need to be validated). The methods must have a parameter of a type that is compatible with the entity type as the entity related to the event is being passed into the callback. A callback method defined on an entity has the following signature with no parameter:

```
void <METHOD>();
```

Callback methods defined on an entity listener can have two different types of signatures. If the method has to be used on several entities, it must have an `Object` argument:

```
void <METHOD>(Object anyEntity)
```

If it is only for one entity or its subclasses (when there's inheritance), the parameter can be of the entity type:

```
void <METHOD>(Customer customerOrSubclasses)
```

To designate that these two listeners are notified of life-cycle events on the `Customer` entity, you need to use the `@EntityListeners` annotation (see Listing 5-4). This annotation can take one entity listener as a parameter or an array of listeners. When several listeners are defined and the life-cycle event occurs, the persistence provider iterates through each listener in the order in which they are listed and will invoke the callback method, passing a reference of the entity to which the event applies. It will then invoke the callback methods on the entity itself (if there are any).

Listing 5-4. The Customer Entity Defining Two Listeners

```
@EntityListeners({DataValidationListener.class, AgeCalculationListener.class})
@Entity
public class Customer {

    @Id @GeneratedValue
    private Long id;
    private String firstName;
    private String lastName;
    private String email;
    private String phoneNumber;
    @Temporal(TemporalType.DATE)
    private Date dateOfBirth;
    @Transient
    private Integer age;
    @Temporal(TemporalType.TIMESTAMP)
    private Date creationDate;

    // Constructors, getters, setters
}
```

The result of this code is exactly the same as that of the previous example (shown earlier in Listing 5-1). The `Customer` entity validates its data before an insert or an update using the `DataValidationListener.validate()` method and calculates its age with the listener's `AgeCalculationListener.calculateAge()` method.

The rules that an entity listener's methods have to follow are similar to the entity callback methods except for a few details:

- Only unchecked exceptions can be thrown. This causes the remaining listeners and callback methods to not be invoked and the transaction to be roll backed if one exists.

- In an inheritance hierarchy, if multiple entities define listeners, the listeners defined on the superclass are invoked before the listeners defined on the subclasses. If an entity doesn't want to inherit the superclass listeners, it can explicitly exclude them by using the `@ExcludeSuperclassListeners` annotation (or its XML equivalent).

In Listing 5-4, you saw a `Customer` entity defining two listeners, but a listener can also be defined by more than one entity. This can be useful in cases where the listener provides more general logic that many entities can benefit from. For example, you could create a debug listener that displays the name of the triggered events, as shown in Listing 5-5.

Listing 5-5. A Debug Listener Usable by Any Entity

```java
public class DebugListener {

    @PrePersist
    void prePersist(Object object) {
        System.out.println("prePersist");
    }
    @PostPersist
    void postPersist(Object object) {
        System.out.println("postPersist");
    }

    @PreUpdate
    void preUpdate(Object object) {
        System.out.println("preUpdate");
    }
    @PostUpdate
    void postUpdate(Object object) {
        System.out.println("postUpdate");
    }

    @PreRemove
    void preRemove(Object object) {
        System.out.println("preRemove");
    }
    @PostRemove
    void postRemove(Object object) {
        System.out.println("postRemove");
    }

    @PostLoad
    void postLoad(Object object) {
        System.out.println("postLoad");
    }
}
```

Note that each method takes an `Object` as a parameter, meaning that any type of entity could use this listener by adding the `DebugListener` class to its `@EntityListeners` annotation. To have every single entity of your application use this listener, you would have to go through each one and add it manually to the annotation. For this case, JPA has a notion of default listeners that can cover all entities in a persistence unit. As there is no annotation targeted for the entire scope of the persistence unit, the default listeners can only be declared in an XML mapping file.

In Chapter 3, you saw how to use XML mapping files instead of annotations. The same steps have to be followed to define the `DebugListener` as a default listener. A mapping file with the XML defined in Listing 5-6 needs to be created and deployed with the application.

Listing 5-6. A Debug Listener Defined As the Default Listener

```xml
<?xml version="1.0" encoding="UTF-8"?>
<entity-mappings xmlns="http://java.sun.com/xml/ns/persistence/orm"
                 xmlns:xsi="http://www.w3.org/2001/XMLSchema-instance"
                 xsi:schemaLocation="http://java.sun.com/xml/ns/persistence/orm
                 http://java.sun.com/xml/ns/persistence/orm_2_0.xsd"
                 version="2.0">

    <persistence-unit-metadata>
        <persistence-unit-defaults>
            <entity-listeners>
                <entity-listener class="com.apress.javaee6.DebugListener"/>
            </entity-listeners>
        </persistence-unit-defaults>
    </persistence-unit-metadata>

</entity-mappings>
```

In this file, the `<persistence-unit-metadata>` tag is used to define all the metadata that doesn't have any annotation equivalent. The `<persistence-unit-defaults>` tag defines all the defaults of the persistence unit, and the `<entity-listener>` tag is where the default listener is defined. This file needs to be referred in the `persistence.xml` and deployed with the application. The `DebugListener` will then be automatically invoked for every single entity.

When a list of default entity listeners is declared, each listener gets called in the order in which it is listed in the XML mapping file. Default entity listeners always get invoked before any of the entity listeners listed in the `@EntityListeners` annotation. If an entity doesn't want to have the default entity listeners applied to it, it can use the `@ExcludeDefaultListeners` annotation, as shown in Listing 5-7.

Listing 5-7. The Customer Entity Excluding Default Listeners

```java
@ExcludeDefaultListeners
@Entity
public class Customer {

    @Id @GeneratedValue
    private Long id;
    private String firstName;
    private String lastName;
    private String email;
    private String phoneNumber;
    @Temporal(TemporalType.DATE)
    private Date dateOfBirth;
    @Transient
    private Integer age;
    @Temporal(TemporalType.TIMESTAMP)
    private Date creationDate;

    // Constructors, getters, setters
}
```

Summary

This chapter described the entity life cycle and how the entity manager catches events to invoke callback methods. Callback methods can be defined on a single entity and annotated by several annotations (@PrePersist, @PostPersist, etc.). The method can also be extracted to listener classes and used by several or all entities (using default entity listeners). With callback methods, you see that entities are not just anemic objects (objects with no business logic, just attributes, getters, and setters); entities can have business logic that can be invoked by other objects in the application, or invoked automatically by the entity manager, depending on the life cycle of the entity. Other Java EE 6 components, such as EJBs, also use these kinds of interceptors.

CHAPTER 6

■■■

Enterprise Java Beans

The previous chapter showed how to implement persistent objects using JPA and how to query them with JPQL. The persistence layer is developed using objects that encapsulate and map their attributes to a relational database, thanks to annotations. The idea is to keep the entities as transparent as possible and not intermingle them with business logic. Entities can have methods to validate their attributes, but they are not made to represent complex tasks, which often require an interaction with other components (other persistent objects, external services, etc.).

The persistence layer is not the appropriate layer for business processing. Similarly, the user interface should not perform business logic, especially when there are multiple interfaces (Web, Swing, portable devices, etc.). To separate the persistence layer from the presentation layer, to implement business logic, to add transaction management and security, applications need a business layer. In Java EE, this layer is implemented using Enterprise Java Beans (EJBs).

For most applications, layering is important. Following a bottom-up approach, the previous chapters on JPA modeled domain classes, usually defining nouns (`Artist`, `CD`, `Book`, `Customer`, and so on). On top of the domain layer, the business layer models the actions (or verbs) of the application (create a book, buy a book, print an order, deliver a book, etc.). Often, this business layer interacts with external web services (SOAP or RESTful web services), sends asynchronous messages to other systems (using JMS), or posts e-mails; it orchestrates several components from databases to external systems, and serves as the central place for transaction and security demarcation as well as the entry point to any kind of client such as web interfaces (servlets or JSF managed beans), batch processing, or external systems.

This chapter is an introduction to EJBs, and the three following chapters give you all the necessary information to build the business layer of an enterprise application. The different types of EJBs are explained; their life cycle and how to add Aspect-Oriented Programming (AOP) capabilities and deal with transactions and security are also described.

Understanding EJBs

EJBs are server-side components that encapsulate business logic and take care of transactions and security. They also have an integrated stack for messaging, scheduling, remote access, web service endpoints (SOAP and REST), dependency injection, component life cycle, AOP with interceptors, and so on. In addition, EJBs seamlessly integrate with other Java SE and Java EE technologies, such as JDBC, JavaMail, JPA, Java Transaction API (JTA), Java Messaging Service (JMS), Java Authentication and Authorization Service (JAAS), Java Naming and Directory Interface (JNDI), and Remote Method Invocation (RMI). This is why they are used to build business layers (see Figure 6-1) to sit on top of the persistence layer and as an entry point for presentation-tier technologies like JavaServer Faces (JSF).

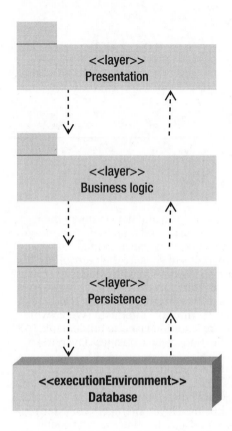

Figure 6-1. Architecture layering

EJBs use a very powerful programming model that combines ease of use and robustness. Today EJBs are a very simple Java server-side development model, reducing complexity while bringing reusability and scalability to mission-critical enterprise applications. All this comes from annotating a single Plain Old Java Object (POJO) that will be deployed into a container. An EJB container is a runtime environment that provides services, such as transaction management, concurrency control, pooling, and security authorization. Historically, application servers have added other features such as clustering, load balancing, and failover. EJB developers can then concentrate on implementing business logic while the container deals with all the technical plumbing.

Today more than ever, with version 3.1, EJBs can be written once and deployed on any container that supports the specification. Standard APIs, portable JNDI names, lightweight components, and configuration by exception allow easy deployment of EJBs on open source as well as commercial implementations. The underlying technology was created more than ten years ago, resulting in EJB applications that benefit from proven concepts such as transaction, security, multi-threading, and so on.

Types of EJBs

Because enterprise applications can be complex, the Java EE platform defines several types of EJBs. From Chapter 6 to Chapter 9, I will only focus on session beans and the timer service. Session beans are used to encapsulate high-level business logic, which makes them the most important part of the EJB technology. A session bean may have the following traits:

- *Stateless*: The session bean contains no conversational state between methods, and any instance can be used for any client.

- *Stateful*: The session bean contains conversational state, which must be retained across methods for a single user.

- *Singleton*: A single session bean is shared between clients and supports concurrent access.

The EJB timer service is the standard Java EE answer to scheduling tasks. Enterprise applications dependent on calendar-based notifications use this service to model workflow-type business processes.

Message-driven beans (MDBs) are used for integrating with external systems by receiving asynchronous messages using JMS. Even though MDBs are part of the EJB specification, I shall deal with them separately (in Chapter 13) because this component model is mainly used to integrate systems with message-oriented middleware (MOM). MDBs usually delegate the business logic to session beans.

EJBs can also be used as web service endpoints. Chapters 14 and 15 demonstrate SOAP and RESTful web services that can be either simple POJOs deployed in a web container or session beans deployed in an EJB container.

■ **Note** For compatibility reasons, the EJB 3.1 specification still mentions entity beans. This persistent component model has been pruned and may disappear in Java EE 7. JPA is the preferred technology for mapping and querying relational databases. This book does not cover entity beans.

Anatomy of an EJB

Session beans encapsulate business logic, are transactional, rely on a container that does pooling, multithreading, security, and so on. What artifacts are needed to create such a powerful component? One Java class and one annotation, that's all. The next chapter shows that session beans can be more complex; they can use different types of interfaces, annotations, XML configuration, and intercept calls. Listing 6-1 shows how simple it is for a container to recognize that a class is a session bean and apply all the enterprise services.

Listing 6-1. *A Simple Stateless EJB*

```
@Stateless
public class BookEJB {

    @PersistenceContext(unitName = "chapter06PU")
    private EntityManager em;

    public Book findBookById(Long id) {
        return em.find(Book.class, id);
    }

    public Book createBook(Book book) {
        em.persist(book);
        return book;
    }
}
```

Previous versions of J2EE required developers to create several artifacts in order to create a session bean: a local or remote interface (or both), a local home or a remote home interface (or both), and a deployment descriptor. Java EE 5 and EJB 3.0 drastically simplified the model to the point where only one class and one or more business interfaces are sufficient. EJB 3.1 goes further as it allows an annotated POJO to be a session bean. As the code in Listing 6-1 shows, the class doesn't implement any interface, and no XML configuration is needed. Only one annotation is used to turn a Java class into a transactional and secure component: `@Stateless`. Then, using the entity manager (as seen in the previous chapters), the `BookEJB` creates and retrieves books from the database in a simple yet powerful manner. The next chapter will demonstrate how easy it is to declare a stateful bean or a singleton.

Simplicity also is applied to the client side. Invoking a method on this `BookEJB` requires only one annotation to obtain a reference using dependency injection. Dependency injection allows a container (client, web, or EJB container) to automatically inject a reference on an EJB with the help of the `@EJB` annotation. In Listing 6-2, the `Main` class acquires a reference to the `BookEJBRemote` by annotating the private, static `bookEJB` attribute with `@EJB`. If the EJB is deployed in a container, the `Main` class needs to access that EJB remotely. Adding a simple remote interface to the EJB will give it remote access capabilities.

Listing 6-2. *A Client Class Invoking the Remote Stateless EJB*

```
public class Main {

    @EJB
    private static BookEJBRemote bookEJB;

    public static void main(String[] args) {

        Book book = new Book();
        book.setTitle("The Hitchhiker's Guide to the Galaxy");
        book.setPrice(12.5F);
        book.setDescription("Scifi book created by Douglas Adams");
```

```
        book.setIsbn("1-84023-742-2");
        book.setNbOfPage(354);

        bookEJB.createBook(book);
    }
}
```

One of the differences between a pure Java class and a session bean is shown in Listing 6-2; even if the code is similar, the `Main` class doesn't create an instance of the `BookEJB` using the `new` keyword; instead, the class needs to first obtain a reference to the EJB, either by injection or by JNDI lookup, before calling a method. This mechanism is used because the EJB runs in a managed environment. It needs to be deployed in a container (embedded or not).

Like most Java EE 6 components, EJBs need metadata to inform the container of required actions (transaction demarcation) or services to inject. Metadata can take the form of either annotations or XML. EJBs can be deployed with the optional `ejb-jar.xml` deployment descriptor, which will override annotations. With configuration by exception, a single annotation (`@Stateless` in this case) is enough to turn a POJO into an EJB because the container applies all the default behavior.

EJB Container

As mentioned, an EJB is a server-side component and needs to be executed in a container. This runtime environment provides core features common to many enterprise applications such as the following:

- *Remote client communication*: Without writing any complex code, an EJB client (another EJB, a user interface, a batch process, etc.) can invoke methods remotely via standard protocols.

- *Dependency injection*: The container can inject several resources into an EJB (JMS destinations and factories, datasources, other EJBs, environment variables, and so on).

- *State management*: For stateful session beans, the container manages their state transparently. You can maintain state for a particular client, as if you were developing a desktop application.

- *Pooling*: For stateless beans and MDBs, the container creates a pool of instances that can be shared by multiple clients. Once invoked, an EJB returns to the pool to be reused instead of being destroyed.

- *Component life cycle*: The container is responsible for managing the life cycle of each component.

- *Messaging*: The container allows MDBs to listen to destinations and consume messages without too much JMS plumbing.

- *Transaction management*: With declarative transaction management, an EJB can use annotations to inform the container about the transaction policy it should use. The container takes care of the commit or the rollback.

- *Security*: Class or method-level access control can be specified on EJBs to enforce user and role authentication.

- *Concurrency support*: Except for singletons, where some concurrency declaration is needed, all the other types of EJB are thread-safe by nature. You can develop high-performance applications without worrying about thread issues.

- *Interceptors*: Cross-cutting concerns can be put into interceptors, which will be invoked automatically by the container.

- *Asynchronous method invocation*: With EJB 3.1, it's now possible to have asynchronous calls without involving messaging.

Once the EJB is deployed, the container takes care of these features, leaving the developer to focus on business logic while benefiting from these services without adding any system-level code.

EJBs are managed objects. When a client invokes an EJB (as in Listing 6-2), it doesn't work directly with an instance of that EJB but rather with a proxy on an instance. Each time a client invokes a method on an EJB, the call is actually proxied through the container, which provides services on behalf of the bean instance. Of course, this is completely transparent to the client; from its creation to its destruction, an enterprise bean lives in a container.

In a Java EE application, the EJB container will usually interact with other containers: the servlet container (responsible for managing the execution of servlets and JSF pages), the application client container (ACC) (for managing stand-alone applications), the message broker (for sending, queuing, and receiving messages), the persistence provider, and so on. These containers will all run inside an application server (GlassFish, JBoss, Weblogic, etc.). Application servers are implementation specific, and most provide clustering capabilities, scalability, load balancing, transparent failover, administration, monitoring, caching, pools, and so forth.

Embedded Container

Right from the moment they were invented (EJB 1.0), EJBs had to be executed in a container that would run on top of a JVM. Think of GlassFish, JBoss, Weblogic, and so on, and you'll remember that the application server first needs to be started before deploying and using your EJB. This is appropriate in a production environment, where the server runs continuously, but it is time consuming in a development environment, where you frequently need to deploy it for debugging purposes, for example. Another issue with servers running in a different process is that unit-testing capabilities are limited, and unit tests cannot be easily run without deploying the EJB in a live server. To solve these problems, some application server implementations came with embedded containers, but these were implementation specific. Today EJB 3.1 has specified an embedded container that is portable across servers.

The idea of an embedded container is to be able to execute EJB applications within a Java SE environment allowing clients to run within the same JVM and class loader. This provides better support for testing, offline processing (e.g., batch processing), and the use of the EJB in desktop applications. The embeddable container API (defined in `javax.ejb.embeddable`) provides the same managed environment as the Java EE runtime container and includes the same services: injection, access to a component environment, container-managed transactions (CMTs), and so forth. You can now execute the embedded container on the same JVM as your IDE and debug your EJB without doing any deployment to a separate application server.

The following code snippet shows you how to create an instance of an embeddable container, get a JNDI context, get a lookup for an EJB, and invoke a method:

```
EJBContainer ec = EJBContainer.createEJBContainer();
Context ctx = ec.getContext();
BookEJB bookEJB = (BookEJB) ctx.lookup("java:global/classes/BookEJB");
bookEJB.createBook(book);
ec.close();
```

In the next chapter, you'll see how to use the bootstrapping API to start the container and execute EJBs.

Dependency Injection and JNDI

EJBs use dependency injection to access several kinds of resources (other EJBs, datasources, JMS destinations, environment resources, etc.). In this model, the container pushes data into the bean. As shown in Listing 6-2, a client gets injected with a reference of an EJB using the @EJB annotation:

```
@EJB
private static BookEJB bookEJB;
```

Injection is made at deployment time. If there is a chance that the data will not be used, the bean can avoid the cost of resource injection by performing a JNDI lookup. JNDI is an alternative to injection; through JNDI, the code pulls data only if it is needed, instead of accepting pushed data that may not be needed at all.

JNDI is an API for accessing different kinds of directory services, allowing clients to bind and look up objects via a name. JNDI is defined in Java SE and is independent of the underlying implementation, which means that objects can be looked up in a Lightweight Directory Access Protocol (LDAP) directory or a Domain Name System (DNS) using a standard API.

The alternative to the preceding code is to use the InitialContext of JNDI and look up a deployed EJB named java:global/chapter06/BookEJB as follows:

```
Context ctx = new InitialContext();
BookEJB bookEJB = (BookEJB) ctx.lookup("java:global/chapter06/BookEJB");
```

JNDI has been around for a long time. Its API is specified and is portable across application servers. But this wasn't the case with the JNDI name, which was implementation specific. When an EJB in GlassFish or JBoss was deployed, the name of the EJB in the directory service was different and thus not portable. A client would have to look up an EJB using one name for GlassFish, and another name for JBoss. With EJB 3.1, JNDI names have been specified so the code could be portable. In the preceding example, the java:global/chapter06/BookEJB name respects the new naming convention:

```
java:global[/<app-name>]/<module-name>/<bean-name>[!<fully-qualified-interface-name>]
```

So, if the EJB is in the com.apress.javaee6.chapter06 package, the JNDI name to look up will be as follows:

```
ctx.lookup("java:global/chapter06/BookEJB!com.apress.javaee6.chapter06.BookEJB");
```

The following chapter shows how to use this portable name to look up EJBs.

Callback Methods and Interceptors

Each EJB type (stateless, stateful, singleton, and MDB) has a life cycle managed by the container. EJBs allow annotated methods (@PostConstruct, @PreDestroy, etc.), similar to the callback methods used in entities in the previous chapter, that will automatically be invoked by the container during certain phases of its life. These methods may initialize state information on the bean, look up resources using JNDI, or release database connections.

For any cross-cutting concerns, developers can use interceptors, which are based on the AOP model, in which the invocation of a method is wrapped by extra functionality automatically.

EJBs' life cycles, callback methods, and interceptors will be explained in Chapter 8 (Chapter 5 focused on the life cycle of JPA entities).

Packaging

Like most Java EE components (servlets, JSF pages, web services, etc.), EJBs need to be packaged before they are deployed into a runtime container. In the same archive, you will usually find the enterprise bean class, its interfaces, interceptors, any needed superclasses or superinterfaces, exceptions, helper classes, and an optional deployment descriptor (ejb-jar.xml). Once these artifacts are packaged in a jar (Java archive) file, they can be deployed directly into a container. Another option is also to embed the jar file into an ear (enterprise archive) file and deploy the ear file.

An ear file is used to package one or more modules (EJBs or web applications) into a single archive so that deployment into an application server happens simultaneously and coherently. For example, as shown in Figure 6-2, if you need to deploy a web application, you might want to package your EJBs and entities into separate jar files, your servlets into a war file, and the whole thing into an ear file. Deploy the ear file into an application server, and you will be able to manipulate entities from the servlet using the EJB.

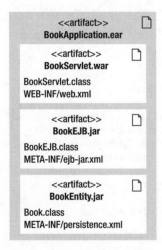

BookApplication.war contents:
```
<<artifact>>
BookApplication.war

WEB-INF/classes/BookEJB.class
WEB-INF/classes/Book.class
WEB-INF/classes/BookServlet.class
WEB-INF/ejb-jar.xml
WEB-INF/persistence.xml
WEB-INF/web.xml
```

Figure 6-2. Packaging EJBs

Since EJB 3.1, EJBs Lite (more on this later) can also be directly packaged within a web module (war file). On the right side of Figure 6-2, the servlet, the EJB, and the entity are all packaged within the same war file with all the deployment descriptors. Note that in the EJB module the deployment descriptor is stored under META-INF/ejb-jar.xml and under WEB-INF/ejb-jar.xml for the web module. EJBs Lite can be packaged directly in a war or in a jar file. If you need to use the full EJB specification (e.g., remote interface, JMS, asynchronous calls…), you have to package it into a jar, not in a war.

EJB Specification Overview

EJB 1.0 was created back in 1998, and EJB 3.1 was released in December 2009 with Java EE 6. During these eleven years, the EJB specification went through many changes, but it still retains its mature foundations. From heavyweight components, to annotated POJOs, to entity beans, back to JPA, EJBs have reinvented themselves to meet the needs of developers and modern architectures.

More than ever, the EJB 3.1 specification helps to avoid vendor lock-in by providing features that were previously nonstandard (such as nonstandard JNDI names or embedded containers, for example). Today, EJB 3.1 is much more portable than in the past.

History of the Specification

Soon after the creation of the Java language, the industry felt the need for a technology that could address the requirements of large-scale applications, embracing RMI and JTA. The idea of creating a distributed and transactional business component framework arose, and as a result IBM first started creating what eventually became known as EJBs.

EJB 1.0 supported stateful and stateless session beans, with optional support for entity beans. The programming model used home and remote interfaces in addition to the session bean itself. EJBs were made accessible through an interface that offered remote access with arguments passed by value.

EJB 1.1 mandated support for entity beans and introduced the XML deployment descriptor to store metadata (which was then serialized as binary in a file). This version provided better support for application assembly and deployment by introducing roles.

In 2001, EJB 2.0 was the first version to be standardized by the JCP (as JSR 19). It addressed the overhead of passing arguments by value by introducing local interfaces. Clients running inside the container would access EJBs through their local interface (using arguments passed by reference), and clients running in a different container would use the remote interface. This version introduced MDBs, and entity beans gained support for relationships and a query language (EJB QL).

Two years later, EJB 2.1 (JSR 153) added support for web services, allowing session beans to be invoked through SOAP/HTTP. A timer service was created to allow EJBs to be invoked at designated times or intervals.

Three years passed between EJB 2.1 and EJB 3.0, which allowed the expert group to remodel the entire design. In 2006, the EJB 3.0 specification (JSR 220) broke with previous versions as it focused on ease of use, with EJBs looking more like POJOs. The entity beans were replaced by a brand-new specification (JPA), and session beans no longer required home or EJB-specific component interfaces. Dependency injection, interceptors, and life-cycle callbacks were introduced.

In 2009, the EJB 3.1 specification (JSR 318) shipped with Java EE 6, following the path of the previous version by simplifying the programming model even further and bringing new features.

What's New in EJB 3.1

The EJB 3.1 specification (JSR 318) brings several changes: JPA is no longer part of the EJB specification and evolves in a separate JSR (JSR 317), and the specification itself is organized into two different documents:

- *"EJB Core Contracts and Requirements"*: The main document that specifies EJBs

- *"Interceptor Requirements"*: The document that specifies interceptors

It is necessary to be mindful that the specification must support the EJB 2.*x* component model, meaning that the 600 pages of the specification deal with home interfaces, entity beans, EJB QL, and so on. To simplify future adoption of the specification, the Java EE 6 expert group has compiled a list of features for possible future removal. None of the following features is actually removed from EJB 3.1, but the next version will have to either remove or retain some of them:

- Entity bean 2.*x*

- Client view of an entity bean 2.*x*

- EJB QL (query language for container-managed persistence)

- JAX-RPC-based web service endpoints

- Client view of a JAX-RPC web service

The EJB 3.1 specification includes the following new functionalities and simplifications:

- *No-interface view*: Session beans with a local view can be accessed without a separate local business interface.

- *War deployment*: Packaging and deployment of EJB components directly in a war file is now possible.

- *Embedded container*: A new embeddable API is available for executing EJB components within a Java SE environment (for unit testing, batch processing, etc.).

- *Singleton*: This new type of component provides easy access to shared state.

- *Richer timer service*: This feature allows automatic creation of EJB timers and calendar-based expressions.

- *Asynchrony*: Asynchronous invocations are now possible without MDBs.

- *EJB Lite*: This definition of a lightweight subset of functionalities can be provided within Java EE Profiles (such as the Java EE Web Profile).

- *Portable JNDI name*: The syntax for looking up EJB components is now specified.

EJB Lite

Enterprise Java Beans are the predominant component model in Java EE 6, being the simplest method for transactional and secure business processing. However, EJB 3.1 still defines the old entity beans, home interfaces, EJB QL, and so on, meaning that any new vendor implementing the EJB 3.1 specification has to implement entity beans. Developers getting started with EJBs would also be weighed down by many technologies that they would never use otherwise.

For these reasons, the specification defines a minimal subset of the full EJB API known as EJB Lite. It includes a small, powerful selection of EJB features suitable for writing portable transactional and secure business logic. Any EJB Lite application can be deployed on any Java EE product that implements EJB 3.1. EJB Lite is composed of the subset of the EJB API listed in Table 6-1.

Table 6-1. Comparison Between EJB Lite and Full EJB

Feature	EJB Lite	Full EJB 3.1
Session beans (stateless, stateful, singleton)	Yes	Yes
MDBs	No	Yes
Entity beans 1.*x*/2.*x*	No	Yes (proposed for pruning)
No-interface view	Yes	Yes
Local interface	Yes	Yes
Remote interface	No	Yes
2.*x* interfaces	No	Yes (proposed for pruning)
JAX-WS web services	No	Yes
JAX-RS web services	No	Yes
JAX-RPC web services	No	Yes (proposed for pruning)
Timer service	No	Yes
Asynchronous calls	No	Yes
Interceptors	Yes	Yes
RMI/IIOP interoperability	No	Yes
Transaction support	Yes	Yes
Security	Yes	Yes
Embeddable API	Yes	Yes

Reference Implementation

GlassFish is an open source application server project led by Sun Microsystems for the Java EE platform. The project was launched in 2005 and became the reference implementation of Java EE 5 in 2006. Today, GlassFish v3 includes the reference implementation for EJB 3.1. Internally, the product is built around modularity (based on the Apache Felix OSGi runtime), allowing a very fast startup time and use of a set of various application containers (Java EE 6, of course, but also Ruby, PHP, and so on).

GlassFish will be used throughout this book as the main application server to deploy and run EJBs, as well as JSF pages, SOAP and RESTful web services, and JMS MDBs.

Putting It All Together

In the "Putting It All Together" section in Chapter 2, I demonstrated development of a Book entity (shown in Listing 2-3) that is mapped to a Derby database. Then I showed you a Main class (shown in Listing 2-4) that uses the entity manager to persist a book and retrieve all the books from the database (using explicit transactional demarcation: tx.begin() and tx.commit()). This example employs the same use case, but replaces the Main class used in Chapter 2 with a stateless session bean (BookEJB).

EJBs are transactional by nature, so our stateless session bean (BookEJB) will handle Create, Read, Update, Delete (CRUD) operations on the Book entity with CMTs. The BookEJB and the Book entity will then be packaged and deployed into GlassFish. The EJB needs a remote interface, as an external client application (Main class) will invoke methods remotely on the EJB (see Figure 6-3) using the ACC.

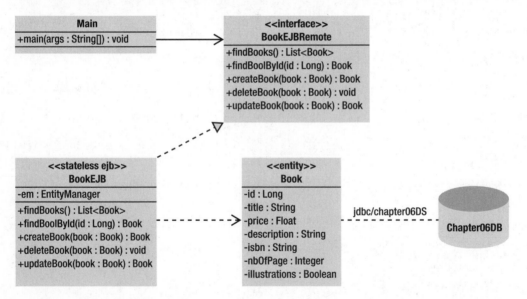

Figure 6-3. Putting it all together

To use transactions, the stateless session bean needs to access the database through a datasource (jdbc/chapter06DS) that will have to be created in GlassFish and linked to the chapter06DB database.

The directory structure for the project follows the Maven conventions, so classes and files have to be placed in the following directories:

- src/main/java: For the Book entity, the BookEJB, the BookEJBRemote interface, and the Main class

- src/main/resources: The persistence.xml file containing the persistence unit used for the Derby database server

- src/test/java: The BookTest class for unit testing

- src/test/resources: The persistence.xml file used by the test cases for an embedded Derby database

- pom.xml: The Maven Project Object Model (POM) describing the project, its dependencies on other external modules, and components

Writing the Book Entity

Listing 6-3 refers to the same Book entity described in Chapter 2 (Listing 2-3), so I will not explain it in much detail. Note that the entity has to be under the src/main/java directory.

Listing 6-3. A Book Entity with a Named Query

```
@Entity
@NamedQuery(name = "findAllBooks", query = "SELECT b FROM Book b")
public class Book implements Serializable {

    @Id @GeneratedValue
    private Long id;
    @Column(nullable = false)
    private String title;
    private Float price;
    @Column(length = 2000)
    private String description;
    private String isbn;
    private Integer nbOfPage;
    private Boolean illustrations;

    // Constructors, getters, setters
}
```

Writing the BookEJB Stateless Session Bean

The BookEJB is a stateless session bean that acts like a façade and handles CRUD operations on the Book entity. Listing 6-4 shows the Java class that needs to be annotated with @javax.ejb.Stateless and implements the BookEJBRemote interface (see Listing 6-5). The EJB obtains a reference of an entity manager using dependency injection, employed on each of the following methods:

- findBooks: This method uses the findAllBooks named query defined in the Book entity to retrieve all the book instances from the database.

- findBookById: Given an ID, this method uses the EntityManager.find() method to retrieve a book from the database.

- createBook: This method takes a Book as a parameter and persists it to the database.

- updateBook: This method takes a detached Book object as a parameter. By using the merge() method, the object is attached to the entity manager and synchronized with the database.

- deleteBook: Before removing a Book entity from the database, this method has to reattach the object to the entity manager and then remove it.

Listing 6-4. A Stateless Session Bean Acting Like a Façade for CRUD Operations

```java
@Stateless
@LocalBean
public class BookEJB implements BookEJBRemote {

    @PersistenceContext(unitName = "chapter06PU")
    private EntityManager em;

    public List<Book> findBooks() {
        TypedQuery<Book> query = em.createNamedQuery("findAllBooks", Book.class);
        return query.getResultList();
    }

    public Book findBookById(Long id) {
        return em.find(Book.class, id);
    }

    public Book createBook(Book book) {
        em.persist(book);
        return book;
    }

    public void deleteBook(Book book) {
        em.remove(em.merge(book));
    }

    public Book updateBook(Book book) {
        return em.merge(book);
    }
}
```

The main differences between the Main class defined in Chapter 2 (Listing 2-4) and the class in Listing 6-4 is that an instance of EntityManager is directly injected into the session bean instead of using the `EntityManagerFactory` to create it. The EJB container deals with the `EntityManager` life cycle, so it injects an instance of it and then closes it when the EJB is destroyed. Also, JPA calls are not wrapped between `tx.begin()` and `tx.commit()` anymore, as session bean methods are implicitly transactional. This default behavior is known as a CMT and is discussed in Chapter 9.

Because the `BookEJB` is invoked remotely by the `Main` class, it needs to implement a remote interface. The only difference between a normal Java interface and a remote interface is the presence of the `@Remote` annotation as shown in Listing 6-5.

Listing 6-5. A Remote Interface

```
@Remote
public interface BookEJBRemote {

    List<Book> findBooks();
    Book findBookById(Long id);
    Book createBook(Book book);
    void deleteBook(Book book);
    Book updateBook(Book book);
}
```

Persistence Unit for the BookEJB

In Chapter 2, the persistence unit (Listing 2-5) had to define the JDBC driver, the JDBC URL, the user, and the password to connect to the Derby database because the transactions were managed by the application (`transaction-type ="RESOURCE_LOCAL"`). In a container-managed environment, EJBs and transactions are managed by the container, not by the application, so `transaction-type` of the persistent unit (see Listing 6-6) is commonly set to JTA.

Listing 6-6. A Persistence Unit Using the chapter06DS Datasource

```
<?xml version="1.0" encoding="UTF-8"?>
<persistence xmlns="http://java.sun.com/xml/ns/persistence"
             xmlns:xsi="http://www.w3.org/2001/XMLSchema-instance"
             xsi:schemaLocation="http://java.sun.com/xml/ns/persistence
             http://java.sun.com/xml/ns/persistence/persistence_2_0.xsd"
             version="2.0">

  <persistence-unit name="chapter06PU" transaction-type="JTA">
    <provider>org.eclipse.persistence.jpa.PersistenceProvider</provider>
    <jta-data-source>jdbc/chapter06DS</jta-data-source>
    <class>com.apress.javaee6.chapter06.Book</class>
    <properties>
      <property name="eclipselink.ddl-generation" value="drop-and-create-tables"/>
      <property name="eclipselink.logging.level" value="INFO"/>
    </properties>
  </persistence-unit>
</persistence>
```

In Listing 6-4, the `BookEJB` gets injected with a reference of an `EntityManager` associated with the `chapter06PU` persistence unit. This persistence unit (defined in Listing 6-6) needs to define the name of the datasource to connect to (jdbc/chapter06DS) without specifying any access properties (URL, JDBC driver, etc.). This information is held by the datasource, to be created later in GlassFish.

Writing the Main Class

Frequently, Java EE applications consist of web applications acting as clients for EJBs, as described in Chapter 10, where JSF managed beans will invoke EJBs. For now, let's use a plain Java class.

The Main class (see Listing 6-7) declares an instance of the BookEJBRemote interface and decorates it with the @EJB annotation so a reference can be injected. Remember that this Main class is executed within the application client container (see the "Containers" section in Chapter 1), so injection is possible. The main() method starts by creating a new instance of the Book object, sets some values to the attributes, and uses the EJB createBook() method to persist the entity. It then changes the value of the book's title, updates the book, and removes it. Because the code of this Main class has no persistence context, the Book entity is seen as a detached object manipulated as a normal Java class by another Java class, with no JPA involved. The EJB is the one holding the persistence context and using the entity manager to access the database.

Listing 6-7. A Main Class Invoking the BookEJB

```
public class Main {

    @EJB
    private static BookEJBRemote bookEJB;

    public static void main(String[] args) {

        Book book = new Book();
        book.setTitle("The Hitchhiker's Guide to the Galaxy");
        book.setPrice(12.5F);
        book.setDescription("Scifi book created by Douglas Adams");
        book.setIsbn("1-84023-742-2");
        book.setNbOfPage(354);
        book.setIllustrations(false);

        bookEJB.createBook(book);

        book.setTitle("H2G2");
        bookEJB.updateBook(book);

        bookEJB.deleteBook(book);
    }
}
```

Compiling and Packaging with Maven

Now you can use Maven to compile the Book entity, the BookEJB, the BookEJBRemote interface, and the Main class, and package the lot in a jar file with the persistence unit. Maven needs a pom.xml file (see Listing 6-8) to describe the project and the external dependencies. This example needs the JPA API (javax.persistence) as well as the EJB API (javax.ejb). The classes will be compiled and packaged (<packaging>jar</packaging>) in a jar file named chapter06-2.0.jar, and Maven needs to be informed that you are using Java SE 6 by configuring the maven-compiler-plugin as shown in Listing 6-8.

Listing 6-8. The Maven pom.xml File Used to Build the Application

```xml
<?xml version="1.0" encoding="UTF-8"?>
<project xmlns="http://maven.apache.org/POM/4.0.0" ↪
        xmlns:xsi="http://www.w3.org/2001/XMLSchema-instance"↪
        xsi:schemaLocation="http://maven.apache.org/POM/4.0.0 ↪
        http://maven.apache.org/xsd/maven-4.0.0.xsd">

    <modelVersion>4.0.0</modelVersion>
    <groupId> com.apress.javaee6</groupId>
    <artifactId>chapter06</artifactId>
    <packaging>jar</packaging>
    <version>2.0</version>
    <name>chapter06</name>

    <dependencies>
        <dependency>
            <groupId>org.eclipse.persistence</groupId>
            <artifactId>javax.persistence</artifactId>
            <version>2.0.0</version>
        </dependency>
        <dependency>
            <groupId>org.glassfish</groupId>
            <artifactId>javax.ejb</artifactId>
            <version>3.0.1</version>
        </dependency>

        <dependency>
            <groupId>org.glassfish.extras</groupId>
            <artifactId>glassfish-embedded-all</artifactId>
            <version>3.0.1</version>
            <scope>test</scope>
        </dependency>
    </dependencies>

    <build>
        <plugins>
            <plugin>
                <groupId>org.apache.maven.plugins</groupId>
                <artifactId>maven-jar-plugin</artifactId>
                <version>2.2</version>
                <configuration>
                    <archive>
                        <manifest>
                            <mainClass>
                                com.apress.javaee6.chapter06.Main
                            </mainClass>
```

```
                            </manifest>
                        </archive>
                    </configuration>
                </plugin>
                <plugin>
                    <groupId>org.apache.maven.plugins</groupId>
                    <artifactId>maven-compiler-plugin</artifactId>
                    <inherited>true</inherited>
                    <configuration>
                        <source>1.6</source>
                        <target>1.6</target>
                    </configuration>
                </plugin>
            </plugins>
        </build>
</project>
```

The produced jar file has a special `META-INF\MANIFEST.MF` file that can be used to add metadata to the structure of the jar; that's the role of the `maven-jar-plugin`. You can add the `Main` class to the `Main-Class` element so that the jar becomes executable.

Notice this code includes the `glassfish-embedded-all` dependency, used by the `test` class (`<scope>test</scope>`), to invoke the embedded container and run the EJB (as you'll see in a later section).

To compile and package the classes, open a command-line interpreter and enter the following Maven command:

```
mvn package
```

The `BUILD SUCCESSFUL` message should appear, letting you know that compilation and packaging were successful. Further, if you check under the `target` subdirectory, you'll see that Maven has created the `chapter06-2.0.jar` file. Thanks to the `META-INF\MANIFEST.MF` file, you will be able to execute this jar file in the application client container.

Deploying on GlassFish

Now that the `BookEJB` session bean has been packaged into a jar archive, it can be deployed to the GlassFish application server. Before doing so, make sure GlassFish and Derby are up and running. The `jdbc/chapter06DS` datasource required by the persistence unit must be created using the GlassFish administration console or the command line. The command-line method is quick and easy to reproduce.

Before creating a datasource, you need a connection pool. GlassFish comes with a set of already-defined pools you can use, or you can create your own with the following command:

```
asadmin create-jdbc-connection-pool ↪
--datasourceclassname=org.apache.derby.jdbc.ClientDataSource ↪
--restype=javax.sql.DataSource ↪
--property portNumber=1527:password=APP:user=APP:serverName=localhost:↪
databaseName=chapter06DB:connectionAttributes=;create\=true Chapter06Pool
```

This command creates the `Chapter06Pool` using a Derby datasource and a set of properties to connect to the database: its name (`chapter06DB`), the server (`localhost`) and the port (`1527`) it listens to, a user (`APP`), and password (`APP`) to connect to. If you now ping this datasource, Derby will create the database automatically (because you set `connectionAttributes=;create\=true`). To ping the datasource, use the following command:

```
asadmin ping-connection-pool Chapter06Pool
```

After this command is successfully executed, you should see the directory `chapter06DB` on your hard drive where Derby stores the data. The database and the connection pool are created, and now you need to declare the `jdbc/chapter06DS` datasource and link it to the newly created pool as follows:

```
asadmin create-jdbc-resource --connectionpoolid Chapter06Pool jdbc/chapter06DS
```

To list all the datasources hosted by GlassFish, enter the following command:

```
asadmin list-jdbc-resources
```

Use the `asadmin` utility to deploy the application into GlassFish. After executing, this command gives a message informing you of the result of the deployment operation:

```
asadmin deploy --force=true target\chapter06-2.0.jar
```

Now that the EJB is deployed with the entity and the persistent unit in GlassFish, Derby is running, and the datasource is created, it's time to run the `Main` class.

Running the Main Class with the Application Client Container

The `Main` class (shown earlier in Listing 6-7) is a stand-alone application that runs outside the GlassFish container, yet it uses the `@EJB` annotation, which needs a container to inject a reference of the `BookEJBRemote` interface. The `Main` class has to be executed in an ACC. A JNDI lookup could have been used instead of the ACC, but the ACC can wrap a jar file and gives it access to the application server resources. To execute the ACC, use the `appclient` utility that comes with GlassFish and pass the jar file as a parameter as follows:

```
appclient -client target\chapter06-2.0.jar
```

Remember that the `chapter06-2.0.jar` file is executable, as we've added a `Main-Class` element to the `MANIFEST.MF` file. By executing the previous command line, the ACC executes the `Main` class and injects a reference of the `BookEJBRemote`, which in turns creates, updates, and removes the `Book` entity.

Writing the BookEJBTest Class

Running the `Main` class is not enough in modern development teams—you need to unit test your classes. In the previous version of EJB, to unit test our `BookEJB` wasn't easy; you had to use specific features of certain application servers or make some twists to the code. With the new embedded container, an EJB becomes a testable class like any other, as it can run in a normal Java SE environment. The only thing necessary is to add a specific jar file to your classpath, as done in the `pom.xml` file (shown earlier in Listing 6-8) with the `glassfish-embedded-all` dependency.

In Chapter 2, I explained all the required artifacts to unit test with an embedded database, so I will not go into too much detail here on the subject. To unit test the EJB, you use the embedded Derby database, a different persistence unit, and the EJB embedded container. Everything is embedded and runs in the same process, necessitating only a JUnit test class (see Listing 6-9) to initialize the EJBContainer (EJBContainer.createEJBContainer()), run some tests (shouldCreateABook()), and close the container (ec.close()).

Listing 6-9. JUnit Class Testing the EJB with the Embeddable Container

```java
public class BookEJBTest {

    private static EJBContainer ec;
    private static Context ctx;

    @BeforeClass
    public static void initContainer() throws Exception {
        ec = EJBContainer.createEJBContainer();
        ctx = ec.getContext();
    }

    @AfterClass
    public static void closeContainer() throws Exception {
        ec.close();
    }

    @Test
    public void shouldCreateABook() throws Exception {

        // Creates an instance of book
        Book book = new Book();
        book.setTitle("The Hitchhiker's Guide to the Galaxy");
        book.setPrice(12.5F);
        book.setDescription("Science fiction comedy book");
        book.setIsbn("1-84023-742-2");
        book.setNbOfPage(354);
        book.setIllustrations(false);

        // Looks up the EJB
        BookEJB bookEJB = (BookEJB) ctx.lookup("java:global/classes/BookEJB");

        // Persists the book to the database
        book = bookEJB.createBook(book);
        assertNotNull("ID should not be null", book.getId());

        // Retrieves all the books from the database
        List<Book> books = bookEJB.findBooks();
        assertNotNull(books);
    }
}
```

The `shouldCreateABook()` method creates an instance of a `Book`, looks up the EJB using JNDI to persist the `Book` to the database, checks whether the returned identifier is null or not, retrieves a collection of all books from the database, and checks whether the returned collection is not null. Ensure that the `BookEJBTest` class is under the `src/test/java` Maven directory and enter the following command:

```
mvn test
```

The `BookEJBTest` class is executed, and a Maven report should inform you that the test was successful.

```
Tests run: 1, Failures: 0, Errors: 0, Skipped: 0, Time elapsed: 12.691 sec
Results :
Tests run: 1, Failures: 0, Errors: 0, Skipped: 0

[INFO] ------------------------------------------------------------
[INFO] BUILD SUCCESSFUL
[INFO] ------------------------------------------------------------
[INFO] Total time: 26 seconds
[INFO] Finished
[INFO] Final Memory: 4M/14M
[INFO] ------------------------------------------------------------
```

Summary

This chapter provided an introduction to EJB 3.1. Starting with EJB 2.*x*, the EJB specification has evolved over the years since its creation from a heavyweight model where home and remote/local interfaces had to be packaged with tons of XML, to a simple Java class with no interface and one annotation. The underlying functionality is always the same: transactional and secure business logic.

EJB 3.1 brings many new features that simplify the programming model (no-interface view, war deployment), make it richer (embedded container, singletons, timer service, asynchronous calls), and make it more portable across application servers (standard global JNDI names). One major simplification is the creation of EJB Lite, which is a subset of the full EJB API, giving newcomers a simpler yet still powerful version of EJB that can be used in the Java EE Web Profile. The embedded EJB container also makes unit testing easier and portable across implementations. EJB 3.1 follows the trajectory of its predecessor EJB 3.0.

Looking forward to the next chapters, Chapter 7 will focus on describing stateless, stateful, and singleton session beans and the timer service. Chapter 8 will explain callback methods and interceptors, and Chapter 9 will look at transactions and security.

CHAPTER 7

■■■

Session Beans and the Timer Service

From Chapter 2 to Chapter 5, I focused on persistent objects using JPA entities. Entities encapsulate data, relational mapping, and sometimes validation logic. Chapter 6 gave you an introduction on how to develop a business layer that handles these persistent objects using session beans. Session beans handle complex tasks that require interaction with other components (entities, web services, messaging, etc.). This logical separation between entities and session beans follows the "separation of concerns" paradigm wherein an application is split into separate components whose functions overlap as little as possible.

In this chapter, you will learn about the three different types of session beans: stateless, stateful, and singleton. Stateless beans are the most scalable of the three, as they keep no state and complete business logic in a single method call. Stateful beans maintain a conversational state with one client. The singleton session bean (one instance per application) is the new model brought about by EJB 3.1.

The last section of the chapter will show you how to use the enhanced timer service to schedule tasks.

Message-driven beans, which are part of the EJB specification, are discussed in Chapter 13 along with Java Message Service (JMS). As you will see in Chapters 14 and 15, a stateless session bean can be turned into a SOAP web service or a RESTful web service. Or, more precisely, these web services can profit from some EJB features such as transactions, security, interceptors, and so on.

Session Beans

Session beans are great for implementing business logic, processes, and workflow. But before using them, you need to choose which type of session bean to use:

- *Stateless*: This type of session bean does not maintain any conversational state on behalf of a client application. It is used to handle tasks that can be concluded with a single method call.

- *Stateful*: This type of bean maintains state and is associated with a specific client. It is useful for tasks that have to be done in several steps.

- *Singleton*: This type of bean follows the singleton design pattern. The container will make sure that only one instance exists for the entire application.

The three types of session beans all have their specific features, of course, but they also have a lot in common. First of all, they have the same programming model. As you'll see later on, a session bean can have a local or remote interface, or no interface at all. Session beans are container-managed components, so they need to be packaged in an archive (jar, war, or ear file) and deployed in a container. The container is responsible for managing its session beans' life cycle (as you'll see in the next chapter), transactions, interceptors, and much more. Figure 7-1 shows a very high-level picture of session beans and the timer service in an EJB container.

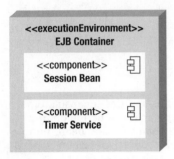

Figure 7-1. *Session beans and the timer service in an EJB container*

Stateless Beans

In Java EE applications, stateless beans are the most popular session bean components. They are simple, powerful, and efficient, and respond to the common task of doing stateless business processing. What does stateless mean? It means that a task has to be completed in a single method call.

As an example, we can go back to the roots of object-oriented programming where an object encapsulates its state and behavior. In object modeling, to persist a book to a database, you would do something like this: create an instance of a Book object (using the new keyword), set some values, and call a method so it could persist itself to a database (book.persistToDatabase()). In the following code, you can see that, from the very first line to the last one, the book object is called several times and keeps its state.

```
Book book = new Book();
book.setTitle("The Hitchhiker's Guide to the Galaxy");
book.setPrice(12.5F);
book.setDescription("Science fiction comedy series created by Douglas Adams.");
book.setIsbn("1-84023-742-2");
book.setNbOfPage(354);
book.setIllustrations(false);
book.persistToDatabase();
```

In a service architecture, you would delegate the business logic to an external service. Stateless services are ideal when you need to implement a task that can be concluded with a single method call. Stateless services are independent, self-contained and do not require information or state from one request to another. So, if you take the preceding code and introduce a stateless service, you need to create a Book object, set some values, and then use a stateless service to invoke a method that will persist the book on its behalf, in a single call. The state is maintained by Book, but not by the stateless service.

```
Book book = new Book();
book.setTitle("The Hitchhiker's Guide to the Galaxy");
book.setPrice(12.5F);
book.setDescription("Science fiction comedy series created by Douglas Adams.");
book.setIsbn("1-84023-742-2");
book.setNbOfPage(354);
book.setIllustrations(false);
statelessComponent.persistToDatabase(book);
```

Stateless session beans follow the stateless service architecture and are the most efficient component model because they can be pooled and shared by several clients. This means that, for each stateless EJB, the container keeps a certain number of instances in memory (i.e., a pool) and shares them between clients. Because stateless beans have no client state, all instances are equivalent. When a client invokes a method on a stateless bean, the container picks up an instance from the pool and assigns it to the client. When the client request finishes, the instance returns to the pool to be reused. This means only a small number of beans are needed to handle several clients, as shown in Figure 7-2. The container doesn't guarantee the same instance for the same client.

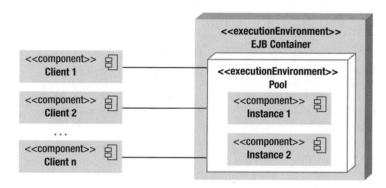

Figure 7-2. Clients accessing stateless beans in a pool

Listing 7-1 shows what a stateless EJB could look like: a standard Java class with just a single @Stateless annotation. Because it lives in a container, it can use any container-managed service, one of which is dependency injection. The @PersistenceContext annotation is used to inject a reference of an entity manager. For stateless session beans, the persistence context is transactional, which means that any method invoked in this EJB (createBook(), createCD(), etc.) is transactional. This will be explained in more detail in Chapter 9. Notice that all methods have the needed parameters to process business logic in one single call. For example, the createBook() method takes a Book as a parameter and persists it without relying on any other state.

Listing 7-1. Stateless Session Bean ItemEJB

```
@Stateless
public class ItemEJB {

    @PersistenceContext(unitName = "chapter07PU")
    private EntityManager em;
```

```
    public List<Book> findBooks() {
        TypedQuery<Book> query = em.createNamedQuery("findAllBooks", Book.class);
        return query.getResultList();
    }

    public List<CD> findCDs() {
        TypedQuery<CD> query = em.createNamedQuery("findAllCDs", CD.class);
        return query.getResultList();
    }

    public Book createBook(Book book) {
        em.persist(book);
        return book;
    }

    public CD createCD(CD cd) {
        em.persist(cd);
        return cd;
    }
}
```

Stateless session beans often contain several closely related business methods. For example, the ItemEJB bean in Listing 7-1 defines methods related to items sold by the CD-BookStore application. So you will find methods to create, update, or find books and CDs, as well as other related business logic.

The @Stateless annotation marks the ItemEJB POJO as a stateless session bean, thus turning a simple Java class into a container-aware component. The specification of the @javax.ejb.Stateless annotation is described in Listing 7-2.

Listing 7-2. @Stateless Annotation API

```
@Target({TYPE}) @Retention(RUNTIME)
public @interface Stateless {
    String name() default "";
    String mappedName() default "";
    String description() default "";
}
```

The name parameter specifies the name of the bean and by default is the name of the class (ItemEJB in the example in Listing 7-1). This parameter can be used to look up an EJB with JNDI, for example. The description parameter is a string that can be used to describe the EJB. The mappedName attribute is the global JNDI name assigned by the container. Note that this JNDI name is vendor specific and is therefore not portable. mappedName has no relationship with the *portable* global JNDI name, which I introduced in the previous chapter and I'll describe in detail later in the "Global JNDI Access" section.

Stateless session beans can support a large number of clients, minimizing any needed resources. Having stateless applications is one way to improve scalability (as the container doesn't have to store and manage state).

Stateful Beans

Stateless beans provide business methods to their clients but don't maintain a conversational state with them. Stateful session beans, on the other hand, preserve conversational state. They are useful for tasks that have to be done in several steps, each of which relies on the state maintained in a previous step. Let's take the example of a shopping cart in an e-commerce web site. A customer logs on (his session starts), chooses a first book, adds it to his shopping cart, chooses a second book, and adds it to his cart. At the end, the customer checks out the books, pays for them, and logs out (the session ends). The shopping cart keeps the state of how many books the customer has chosen throughout the interaction (which can take some time, specifically the time of the client's session).

```
Book book = new Book();
book.setTitle("The Hitchhiker's Guide to the Galaxy");
book.setPrice(12.5F);
book.setDescription("Science fiction comedy series created by Douglas Adams.");
book.setIsbn("1-84023-742-2");
book.setNbOfPage(354);
book.setIllustrations(false);
statefulComponent.addBookToShoppingCart(book);
book.setTitle("The Robots of Dawn");
book.setPrice(18.25F);
book.setDescription("Isaac Asimov's Robot Series");
book.setIsbn("0-553-29949-2");
book.setNbOfPage(276);
book.setIllustrations(false);
statefulComponent.addBookToShoppingCart(book);
statefulComponent.checkOutShoppingCart();
```

The preceding code shows exactly how a stateful session bean works. Two books are created and added to a shopping cart of a stateful component. At the end, the checkOutShoppingCart() method relies on the maintained state and can check out the two books.

When a client invokes a stateful session bean in the server, the EJB container needs to provide the same instance for each subsequent method invocation. Stateful beans cannot be reused by other clients. Figure 7-3 shows the one-to-one correlation between a bean instance and a client. As far as the developer is concerned, no extra code is needed, as this one-to-one correlation is managed automatically by the EJB container.

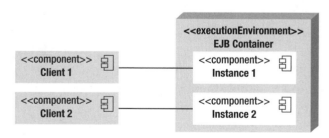

Figure 7-3. Clients accessing stateful beans

The one-to-one correlation comes at a price because, as you might have guessed, if you have one million clients, you will get one million stateful beans in memory. To avoid such a big memory footprint, the container temporarily clears stateful beans from memory before the next request from the client brings them back. This technique is called *passivation and activation.* Passivation is the process of removing an instance from memory and saving it to a persistent location (a file on a disk, a database, etc.). It helps you to free memory and release resources (a database or JMS connections, etc.). Activation is the inverse process of restoring the state and applying it to an instance. Passivation and activation are done automatically by the container; you shouldn't worry about doing it yourself, as it's a container service. What you should worry about is freeing any resource (e.g., database connection, JMS factories connection, etc.) before the bean is passivated, as you'll see in the next chapter.

Let's return to the shopping-cart example and apply it to a stateful bean (see Listing 7-3). A customer logs on to a web site, browses the catalog of items, and adds two books to the shopping cart (addItem() method). The cartItems attribute holds the content of the cart. Then the customer decides to get a coffee at a coffee machine. During this time, the container might passivate the instance to free some memory, which in turn saves the shopping content to permanent storage. A few minutes later, the customer comes back and wants to know the total price (getTotal() method) of his shopping cart before buying anything. The container activates the EJB and restores the data to the shopping cart. The customer can then check out (checkout() method) and buy the books. Once the customer logs off, the customer's session ends, and the container frees memory by permanently removing the instance of the stateful bean.

Listing 7-3. Stateful Session Bean ShoppingCartEJB

```java
@Stateful
@StatefulTimeout(value = 20, unit = TimeUnit.SECONDS)
public class ShoppingCartEJB {

    private List<Item> cartItems = new ArrayList<Item>();

    public void addItem(Item item) {
        if (!cartItems.contains(item))
            cartItems.add(item);
    }

    public void removeItem(Item item) {
        if (cartItems.contains(item))
            cartItems.remove(item);
    }

    public Integer getNumberOfItems() {
        if (cartItems == null || cartItems.isEmpty())
            return 0;

        return cartItems.size();
    }

    public Float getTotal() {
        if (cartItems == null || cartItems.isEmpty())
            return 0f;
```

```
        Float total = 0f;
        for (Item cartItem : cartItems) {
            total += (cartItem.getPrice());
        }
        return total;
    }

    public void empty() {
        cartItems.clear();
    }


    @Remove
    public void checkout() {
        // Do some business logic
        cartItems.clear();
    }
}
```

The shopping-cart situation is a standard way of using stateful beans in which the container automatically takes care of maintaining the conversational state. The only needed annotation is @javax.ejb.Stateful, which has the same parameters as @Stateless, described in Listing 7-2.

Notice the optional @javax.ejb.StatefulTimeout and @javax.ejb.Remove annotations. @Remove decorates the checkout()method. This causes the bean instance to be permanently removed from memory after the checkout() method is invoked. @StatefulTimeout assigns a timeout value, which is the duration the bean is permitted to remain idle (not receiving any client invocations) before being removed by the container. The time unit of this annotation is a java.util.concurrent.TimeUnit, so it can go from DAYS, HOURS… to NANOSECONDS (the default is MINUTES). Alternatively, you can avoid these annotations and rely on the container automatically removing an instance when the client's session ends or expires. However, making sure the stateful bean is removed at the appropriate moment might reduce memory consumption. This could be critical in highly concurrent applications.

Singletons

A singleton bean is a session bean that is instantiated once per application. It implements the widely used Singleton pattern from the famous book by the Gang of Four—*Design Patterns: Elements of Reusable Object-Oriented Software* by Erich Gamma, Richard Helm, Ralph Johnson, and John M. Vlissides (Addison-Wesley, 1995). A singleton ensures that only one instance of a class exists in the whole application and provides a global point of access to it. There are many situations where singleton objects are needed, that is, where your application only needs one instance of an object: a mouse, a window manager, a printer spooler, a file system, and so on.

Another common-use case is a caching system whereby the entire application shares a single cache (a Hashmap, for example) to store objects. In an application-managed environment, you need to tweak your code a little bit to turn a class into a singleton, as shown in Listing 7-4. First, you need to prevent the creation of a new instance by having a private constructor. The public static method getInstance() returns the single instance of the CacheSingleton class. If a client class wants to add an object to the cache using the singleton, it needs to call:

```
CacheSingleton.getInstance().addToCache(myObject);
```

If you want this code to be thread-safe, you will have to use the **synchronized** keyword to prevent thread interference and inconsistent data. Instead of a Map, you can also use a `java.util.concurrent.ConcurrentMap` which will result in much more concurrent and scalable behavior. This can be useful if those are critical considerations.

Listing 7-4. *A Java Class Following the Singleton Design Pattern*

```java
public class Cache {

    private static CacheSingleton instance = new CacheSingleton();
    private Map<Long, Object> cache = new HashMap<Long, Object>();

    private CacheSingleton() {
    }

    public static synchronized CacheSingleton getInstance() {
        return instance;
    }

    public void addToCache(Long id, Object object) {
        if (!cache.containsKey(id))
            cache.put(id, object);
    }

    public void removeFromCache(Long id) {
        if (cache.containsKey(id))
            cache.remove(id);
    }

    public Object getFromCache(Long id) {
        if (cache.containsKey(id))
            return cache.get(id);
        else
            return null;
    }
}
```

EJB 3.1 introduces the brand-new singleton session bean, which follows the singleton design pattern. Once instantiated, the container makes sure there is only one instance of a singleton for the duration of the application. An instance is shared between several clients, as shown in Figure 7-4. Singletons maintain their state between client invocations.

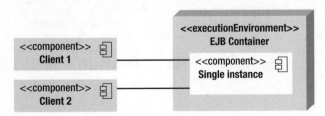

Figure 7-4. *Clients accessing a singleton bean*

■ **Note** Singletons are not cluster-aware. A cluster is a group of containers that work together closely (sharing the same resources, EJBs, and so on). So, in cases where there are several distributed containers clustered together over several machines, each container will have its own instance of the singleton.

To turn the code in Listing 7-4 from a singleton Java class to a singleton session bean (see Listing 7-5), there is not much to do. In fact, you just need to annotate a class with @Singleton and not worry about the private constructor or the static getInstance() method. The container will make sure only one instance is created. The @javax.ejb.Singleton annotation has the same API as the @Stateless annotation described earlier in Listing 7-2.

Listing 7-5. Singleton Session Bean

```
@Singleton
public class CacheEJB {

    private Map<Long, Object> cache = new HashMap<Long, Object>();

    public void addToCache(Long id, Object object) {
        if (!cache.containsKey(id))
            cache.put(id, object);
    }

    public void removeFromCache(Long id) {
        if (cache.containsKey(id))
            cache.remove(id);
    }

    public Object getFromCache(Long id) {
        if (cache.containsKey(id))
            return cache.get(id);
        else
            return null;
    }
}
```

As you can see, stateless, stateful, and singleton session beans are very easy to develop: you just need one annotation. Singletons, though, have a bit more to them. They can be initialized at startup, be chained together, and have their concurrency access customized.

Initialization

When a client class needs to access a method on a singleton session bean, the container makes sure to either instantiate it or use the one already living in the container. However, sometimes initializing a singleton can be time consuming. Imagine if CacheEJB (shown previously in Listing 7-5) needs to access a database to load its cache with thousands of objects. The first call to the bean will be expensive, and the first client will have to wait for initialization to be completed.

To avoid such latency, you can ask the container to initialize a singleton bean at startup. If the `@Startup` annotation appears on the bean class, the container initializes it during the application startup, not when a client invokes it. The following code shows you how to use the annotation:

```
@Singleton
@Startup
public class CacheEJB {
    // ...
}
```

Chaining Singletons

In some cases, when you have several singleton beans, explicit initialization ordering can be important. Imagine if the `CacheEJB` needs to store data that comes from another singleton bean (let's say a `CountryCodeEJB` that returns all the ISO country codes). The `CountryCodeEJB` then needs to be initialized before the `CacheEJB` . Dependencies can exist between multiple singletons, and the `@javax.ejb.DependsOn` annotation is there to express it. The following example illustrates the use of the annotation:

```
@Singleton
public class CountryCodeEJB {
    ...
}

@DependsOn("CountryCodeEJB")
@Singleton
public class CacheEJB {
    ...
}
```

`@DependsOn` holds one or more strings, where each specifies the name of the target singleton bean. The following code shows how `CacheEJB` depends on the initialization of `CountryCodeEJB` and `ZipCodeEJB`. `@DependsOn("CountryCodeEJB", "ZipCodeEJB")` tells the container to guarantee that singleton `CountryCodeEJB` and `ZipCodeEJB` are initialized before `CacheEJB`.

```
@Singleton
public class CountryCodeEJB {
    ...
}

@Singleton
public class ZipCodeEJB {
    ...
}
```

```
@DependsOn("CountryCodeEJB", "ZipCodeEJB")
@Startup
@Singleton
public class CacheEJB {
    ...
}
```

As you can see in this code, you can even combine dependencies with startup initialization. CacheEJB is eagerly initialized at startup (because it holds the @Startup annotation), and therefore CountryCodeEJB and ZipCodeEJB will also be initialized at startup before CacheEJB.

You can also use fully qualified names to refer to a Singleton packaged within a different module in the same application. Let's say that both CacheEJB and CountryCodeEJB are packaged in the same application (same ear file) but in different jar files (respectively, technical.jar and business.jar), this is how CacheEJB would depend on CountryCodeEJB:

```
@DependsOn("business.jar#CountryCodeEJB")
@Singleton
public class CacheEJB {
    ...
}
```

Note that this kind of reference introduces a code dependency on packaging details (in this case, the names of the module files).

Concurrency

As you understand by now, there is only one instance of a singleton session bean shared by multiple clients. So concurrent access by clients is allowed and can be controlled with the @ConcurrencyManagement annotation in two different ways:

- *Container-managed concurrency (CMC)*: The container controls concurrent access to the bean instance based on metadata (annotation or the XML equivalent).

- *Bean-managed concurrency (BMC)*: The container allows full concurrent access and defers the synchronization responsibility to the bean.

If no concurrency management is specified, the CMC demarcation is used by default. A singleton bean can be designed to use either CMC or BMC, but not both. As you'll see in the following sections, you can use the @AccessTimeout annotation to disallow concurrency (i.e., if a client invokes a business method that is being used by another client, the concurrent invocation will result in a ConcurrentAccessException).

Container-Managed Concurrency

With CMC, the default demarcation, the container is responsible for controlling concurrent access to the singleton bean instance. You can then use the @Lock annotation to specify how the container must manage concurrency when a client invokes a method. The annotation can take the values READ (shared) or WRITE (exclusive):

- @Lock(LockType.WRITE): A method associated with an exclusive lock will not allow concurrent invocations until the method's processing is completed. For example, if a client C1 invokes a method with an exclusive lock, client C2 will not be able to invoke the method until C1 has finished.

- @Lock(LockType.READ): A method associated with a shared lock will allow any number of other concurrent invocations to the bean's instance. For example, two clients, C1 and C2, can access simultaneously a method with a shared lock.

The @Lock annotation can be specified on the class, the methods, or both. Specifying on the class means that it applies to all methods. If the concurrency locking attribute is not specified, it is assumed to be @Lock(WRITE) by default. The code in Listing 7-6 shows CacheEJB with a READ lock in the bean class. This implies that all methods will have READ concurrency except getFromCache(), which is overridden by WRITE.

Listing 7-6. A Singleton Session Bean with CMC

```
@Singleton
@Lock(LockType.READ)
public class CacheEJB {

    private Map<Long, Object> cache = new HashMap<Long, Object>();

    public void addToCache(Long id, Object object) {
        if (!cache.containsKey(id))
            cache.put(id, object);
    }

    public void removeFromCache(Long id) {
        if (cache.containsKey(id))
            cache.remove(id);
    }

    @AccessTimeout(value = 20, unit = TimeUnit.SECONDS)
    @Lock(LockType.WRITE)
    public Object getFromCache(Long id) {
        if (cache.containsKey(id))
            return cache.get(id);
        else
            return null;
    }
}
```

In Listing 7-6, the getFromCache() method uses an @AccessTimeout annotation. When a concurrent access is blocked, a timeout can be specified to reject a request if the lock is not acquired within a certain time. If a getFromCache() invocation is locked for more than 20 seconds, the client will get a ConcurrentAccessTimeoutException.

Bean-Managed Concurrency

With BMC demarcation, the container allows full concurrent access to the singleton bean instance. You are then responsible for guarding its state against synchronization errors due to concurrent access. In this case, you are allowed to use Java synchronization primitives such as synchronized and volatile . The code in Listing 7-7 shows CacheEJB with BMC (@ConcurrencyManagement(BEAN)) using the synchronized keyword on the addToCache() method.

Listing 7-7. A Singleton Session Bean with BMC

```
@Singleton
@ConcurrencyManagement(ConcurrencyManagementType.BEAN)
public class CacheEJB {

    private Map<Long, Object> cache = new HashMap<Long, Object>();

    public synchronized void addToCache(Long id, Object object) {
        if (!cache.containsKey(id))
            cache.put(id, object);
    }

    public synchronized void removeFromCache(Long id) {
        if (cache.containsKey(id))
            cache.remove(id);
    }

    public Object getFromCache(Long id) {
        if (cache.containsKey(id))
            return cache.get(id);
        else
            return null;
    }
}
```

Concurrent Access Timeouts and Not Allowing Concurrency

A concurrent access attempt that cannot immediately acquire the appropriate lock is blocked until it can make forward progress. @AccessTimeout is used to specify the duration the access attempt should be blocked before timing out. An @AccessTimeout value of -1 indicates that the client request will block indefinitely until forward progress can be made. An @AccessTimeout value of 0 indicates that concurrent access is not allowed. This will result in throwing a ConcurrentAccessException if a client invokes a method that is currently being used. This can have performance implications, as clients might have to handle the exception, retry to access the bean, potentially receive another exception, try again, and so on. In Listing 7-8, CacheEJB disallows concurrency on the addToCache() method. This means that, if client A is adding an object to the cache and client B wants to do the same thing at the same time, client B will get an exception and will have to retry later (or manage the exception in another way). The other two methods are, by default, CMC with a @Lock(WRITE).

Listing 7-8. A Singleton Session Bean Not Allowing Concurrency

```
@Singleton
public class CacheEJB {

    private Map<Long, Object> cache = new HashMap<Long, Object>();

    @AccessTimeout(0)
    public void addToCache(Long id, Object object) {
        if (!cache.containsKey(id))
            cache.put(id, object);
    }

    public void removeFromCache(Long id) {
        if (cache.containsKey(id))
            cache.remove(id);
    }

    public Object getFromCache(Long id) {
        if (cache.containsKey(id))
            return cache.get(id);
        else
            return null;
    }
}
```

Session Bean Model

So far you've seen examples of code using the easiest programming model for session beans: an annotated POJO with no interface. But, depending on your needs, session beans can give you a much richer model, allowing you to perform remote calls, dependency injection, or asynchronous calls.

Interfaces and Bean Class

Until now you've seen session beans composed only of a bean class. In fact, they can be richer and made of the following elements:

- *Business interfaces*: These interfaces contain the declaration of business methods that are visible to the client and implemented by the bean class. A session bean can have local interfaces, remote interfaces, or no interface at all (a no-interface view with local access only).

- *A bean class*: The bean class contains the business method implementation and can implement zero or several business interfaces. The session bean must be annotated with @Stateless, @Stateful, or @Singleton depending on its type.

As shown in Figure 7-5, a client application can access a session bean by one of its interfaces (local or remote) or directly by invoking the bean class itself.

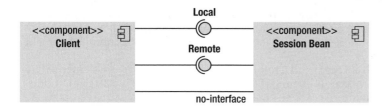

Figure 7-5. Session beans have several types of interfaces.

Remote, Local, and No-Interface Views

Depending from where a client invokes a session bean, the bean class will have to implement remote or local interfaces, or no interface at all. If your architecture has clients residing outside the EJB container's JVM instance, they must use a remote interface. As shown in Figure 7-6, this applies for clients running in a separate JVM (e.g., a rich client), in an application client container (ACC), or in an external web or EJB container. In this case, clients will have to invoke session bean methods through Remote Method Invocation (RMI). You can use local invocation when the bean and the client are running in the same JVM. That can be an EJB invoking another EJB or a web component (servlet, JSF) running in a web container in the same JVM. It is also possible for your application to use both remote and local calls on the same session bean.

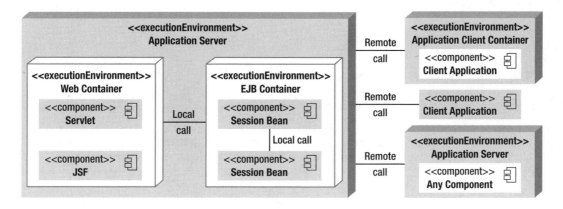

Figure 7-6. Session beans invoked by several clients

A session bean can implement several interfaces or none. A business interface is a standard Java interface that does not extend any EJB-specific interfaces. Like any Java interface, business interfaces define a list of methods that will be available for the client application. They can use the following annotations:

- @Remote: Denotes a remote business interface. Method parameters are passed by value and need to be serializable as part of the RMI protocol.

- @Local: Denotes a local business interface. Method parameters are passed by reference from the client to the bean.

You cannot mark the same interface with more than one annotation. The session beans that you have seen so far in this chapter have no interface. The no-interface view is a variation of the local view that exposes all public business methods of the bean class locally without the use of a separate business interface.

Listing 7-9 shows a local interface (ItemLocal) and a remote interface (ItemRemote) implemented by the ItemEJB stateless session bean. With this code, clients will be able to invoke the findCDs() method locally or remotely as it is defined in both interfaces. The createCd() will only be accessible remotely through RMI.

Listing 7-9. Stateless Session Bean Implementing a Remote and Local Interface

```
@Local
public interface ItemLocal {
    List<Book> findBooks();
    List<CD> findCDs();
}


@Remote
public interface ItemRemote {
    List<Book> findBooks();
    List<CD> findCDs();
    Book createBook(Book book);
    CD createCD(CD cd);
}


@Stateless
public class ItemEJB implements ItemLocal, ItemRemote {
    ...
}
```

Alternatively to the code in Listing 7-9, you might specify the interface in the bean's class. In this case, you would have to include the name of the interface in the @Local and @Remote annotations as shown in Listing 7-10. This is handy when you have legacy interfaces and need to use them in your session bean.

Listing 7-10. A Bean Class Defining a Remote and Local Interface

```
public interface ItemLocal {
    List<Book> findBooks();
    List<CD> findCDs();
}

public interface ItemRemote {
    List<Book> findBooks();
    List<CD> findCDs();
    Book createBook(Book book);
    CD createCD(CD cd);
}
```

```
@Stateless
@Remote (ItemRemote.class)
@Local (ItemLocal.class)
public class ItemEJB implements ItemLocal, ItemRemote {
    ...
}
```

Web Services Interface

In addition to remote invocation through RMI, stateless beans can also be invoked remotely as SOAP web services or RESTful web services. Chapters 14 and 15 are dedicated to web services, so I won't describe them here. I just want to show you how a stateless session bean can be accessed in various forms just by implementing different annotated interfaces. Listing 7-11 shows a stateless bean with a local interface, a SOAP web services endpoint (@WebService), and a RESTful web service endpoint (@Path). Note that these annotations come respectively from JAX-WS and JAX-RS and are not part of EJB.

Listing 7-11. A Stateless Session Bean Implementing Several Interfaces

```
@Local
public interface ItemLocal {
    List<Book> findBooks();
    List<CD> findCDs();
}

@WebService
public interface ItemSOAP {
    List<Book> findBooks();
    List<CD> findCDs();
    Book createBook(Book book);
    CD createCD(CD cd);
}

@Path(/items)
public interface ItemRest {
    List<Book> findBooks();
}

@Stateless
public class ItemEJB implements ItemLocal, ItemSOAP, ItemRest {
    ...
}
```

Bean Class

A session bean class is any standard Java class that implements business logic. The requirements to develop a session bean class are as follows:

- The class must be annotated with @Stateless, @Stateful, @Singleton, or the XML equivalent in a deployment descriptor.

- It must implement the methods of its interfaces, if any.

- The class must be defined as `public`, and must not be `final` or `abstract`.

- The class must have a public no-arg constructor that the container will use to create instances.

- The class must not define the `finalize()` method.

- Business method names must not start with `ejb`, and they cannot be `final` or `static`.

- The argument and return value of a remote method must be legal RMI types.

Client View

Now that you have seen examples of session beans and their different interfaces, you might want to take a look at how the client invokes these beans. The client of a session bean can be any kind of component: a POJO, a graphical interface (Swing), a managed bean (`@javax.annotation.ManagedBean` from the Common Annotations specification), a servlet, a JSF-managed bean, a web service (SOAP or REST), or another EJB (deployed in the same or a different container).

To invoke a method on a session bean, a client does not directly instantiate the bean (using the `new` operator). It needs a reference to the bean (or to its interfaces). It can obtain it via dependency injection (with the `@EJB` annotation) or via JNDI lookup. Unless specified, a client invokes a session bean synchronously. As you'll see later, EJB 3.1 now allows asynchronous method calls as well.

@EJB

Java EE uses several annotations to inject references of resources (`@Resource`), entity managers (`@PersistenceContext`), web services (`@WebServiceRef`), and so on. But the `@javax.ejb.EJB` annotation is specifically intended for injecting session bean references into client code. Dependency injection is only possible within managed environments such as EJB containers, web containers, and application-client containers.

Let's take our initial examples in which session beans had no interface. For a client to invoke a session bean's no-interface view, it needs to obtain a reference to the bean class itself. For example, in the following code, the client gets a reference to the `ItemEJB` class using the `@EJB` annotation:

```
@Stateless
public class ItemEJB {
    ...
}
// Client code
@EJB ItemEJB itemEJB;
```

If the session bean implements several interfaces, the client has to specify which one it wants a reference to. In the following code, the ItemEJB implements two interfaces. The client can invoke the EJB through either its local or remote interface, but not through the no-interface view anymore.

```
@Stateless
@Remote (ItemRemote.class)
@Local (ItemLocal.class)
public class ItemEJB implements ItemLocal, ItemRemote {

    ...

}
// Client code
@EJB ItemEJB itemEJB; // An exception is thrown at deployment time
@EJB ItemLocal itemEJBLocal;
@EJB ItemRemote itemEJBRemote;
```

If the bean exposes at least one interface, it needs to explicitly specify that it exposes a no-interface view by using the @LocalBean annotation on the bean class. As you can see in the following code, the client can now invoke the bean through its local, remote, and no-interface view.

```
@Stateless
@Remote (ItemRemote.class)
@Local (ItemLocal.class)
@LocalBean
public class ItemEJB implements ItemLocal, ItemRemote {
    ...
}
// Client code
@EJB ItemEJB itemEJB;
@EJB ItemLocal itemEJBLocal;
@EJB ItemRemote itemEJBRemote;
```

Depending on your client environment, you might not be able to use injection (if the component is not managed by the container). In this case, you can use JNDI to look up session beans through their portable JNDI name.

Portable JNDI Name

Session beans can also be looked up using JNDI. JNDI is mostly used for remote access when a client is not container managed and cannot use dependency injection. But JNDI can also be used by local clients, even if dependency injection results in simpler code. To look up session beans, a client application needs the JNDI API to communicate with a directory naming service.

Once a session bean is deployed to the container, it is automatically bound to a JNDI name. This name wasn't standardized before Java EE 6, so a session bean deployed in different containers (GlassFish, JBoss, WebLogic, etc.) would have a different name. The Java EE 6 specification defines portable JNDI names with the following syntax:

```
java:<scope>[/<app-name>]/<module-name>/<bean-name>[!<fully-qualified-interface-name>]
```

Each portion of the JNDI name has the following meaning:

- `<scope>` defines a series of standard namespaces that map to the various scopes of a Java EE application:

  - global: The `java:global` prefix allows a component executing outside a Java EE application to access a global namespace.

  - app: The `java:app` prefix allows a component executing within a Java EE application to access an application-specific namespace.

  - module: The `java:module` prefix allows a component executing within a Java EE application to access a module-specific namespace.

  - comp: The `java:comp` prefix is a private component-specific namespace and is not accessible by other components.

- `<app-name>` is only required if the session bean is packaged within an ear file. If this is the case, the `<app-name>` defaults to the name of the ear file (without the `.ear` file extension).

- `<module-name>` is the name of the module in which the session bean is packaged. It can be an EJB module in a stand-alone jar file or a web module in a war file. The `<module-name>` defaults to the base name of the archive with no file extension.

- `<bean-name>` is the name of the session bean.

- `<fully-qualified-interface-name>` is the fully qualified name of each defined business interface. For the no-interface view, the name is the fully qualified bean class name.

To illustrate this naming convention, let's take the example of ItemEJB. ItemEJB is the `<bean-name>` and is packaged in the `cdbookstore.jar` (the `<module-name>`). The EJB has a remote interface and a no-interface view (using the `@LocalBean` annotation).

```
package com.apress.javaee6;
@Stateless
@LocalBean
@Remote (ItemRemote.class)
public class ItemEJB implements ItemRemote {
    ...
}
```

Once deployed, an external component will be able to access the ItemEJB using the following global JNDI names:

```
java:global/cdbookstore/ItemEJB
java:global/cdbookstore/ItemEJB!com.apress.javaee6.ItemEJB
java:global/cdbookstore/ItemEJB!com.apress.javaee6.ItemRemote
```

Note that, if the ItemEJB was deployed within an ear file (e.g., myapplication.ear), you would have to use the <app-name> as follow:

```
java:global/myapplication/cdbookstore/ItemEJB
java:global/myapplication/cdbookstore/ItemEJB!com.apress.javaee6.ItemEJB
java:global/myapplication/cdbookstore/ItemEJB!com.apress.javaee6.ItemRemote
```

The container is also required to make JNDI names available through the java:app and java:module namespaces. So a component deployed in the same application as the ItemEJB will be able to look it up using the following JNDI names:

```
java:app/cdbookstore/ItemEJB
java:app/cdbookstore/ItemEJB!com.apress.javaee6.ItemEJB
java:app/cdbookstore/ItemEJB!com.apress.javaee6.ItemRemote
java:module/ItemEJB
java:module/ItemEJB!com.apress.javaee6.ItemEJB
java:module/ItemEJB!com.apress.javaee6.ItemRemote
```

Session Context

Session beans are business components that live in a container. Usually, they don't access the container or use the container services directly (transaction, security, dependency injection, and so forth). These services are meant to be handled transparently by the container on the bean's behalf. However, it is sometimes necessary for the bean to explicitly use container services in code (such as explicitly marking a transaction to be rolled back). And this can be done through the javax.ejb.SessionContext interface. The SessionContext allows programmatic access to the runtime context provided for a session bean instance. SessionContext extends the javax.ejb.EJBContext interface. Some methods of the SessionContext API are described in Table 7-1.

Table 7-1. Some Methods of the SessionContext Interface

Method	Description
getCallerPrincipal	Returns the java.security.Principal associated with the invocation.
getRollbackOnly	Tests whether the current transaction has been marked for rollback.
getTimerService	Returns the javax.ejb.TimerService interface. Only stateless beans and singletons can use this method. Stateful session beans cannot be timed objects.
getUserTransaction	Returns the javax.transaction.UserTransaction interface to demarcate transactions. Only session beans with bean-managed transaction (BMT) can use this method.
isCallerInRole	Tests whether the caller has a given security role.

Continued

Method	Description
lookup	Enables the session bean to look up its environment entries in the JNDI naming context.
setRollbackOnly	Allows the bean to mark the current transaction for rollback.
wasCancelCalled	Checks whether a client invoked the cancel() method on the client Future object corresponding to the currently executing asynchronous business method.

A session bean can have access to its environment context by injecting a reference of SessionContext with a @Resource annotation.

```
@Stateless
public class ItemEJB {
    @Resource
    private SessionContext context;
    ...
    public Book createBook(Book book) {
        ...
        if (cantFindAuthor())
            context.setRollbackOnly();
    }
}
```

Deployment Descriptor

Java EE 6 components use configuration by exception, which means that the container, the persistence provider, or the message broker will apply a set of default services to that component. Configuring these default services is the exception. If nondefault behavior is desired, an annotation, or its counterpart in XML, needs to be explicitly specified. That's what you've already seen with JPA entities, where a set of annotations allows you to customize the default mapping. The same principal applies for session beans. A single annotation (@Stateless, @Stateful, etc.) is enough to inform the container to apply certain services (transaction, life cycle, security, interceptors, concurrency, asynchrony, etc.), but, if you need to change them, you use annotations or XML. Annotations attach additional information to a class, an interface, a method, or a variable, and so does an XML deployment descriptor.

An XML deployment descriptor is an alternative to annotations, which means that any annotation has an equivalent XML tag. If both annotations and deployment descriptors are used, the settings in the deployment descriptor will override the annotations during deployment process. I will not go into too much detail describing the structure of the XML deployment descriptor (called ejb-jar.xml), as it is optional and can end up being very verbose. As an example, Listing 7-12 shows what the ejb-jar.xml file of ItemEJB (shown previously in Listing 7-9) could look like. It defines the bean class, the remote and local interface, its type (Stateless), and that it uses container-managed transaction (CMT) (Container). The <env-entry> defines the environment entries of the session bean. I will explain these soon in the "Environment Naming Context" section.

Listing 7-12. The ejb-jar.xml File

```xml
<ejb-jar xmlns="http://java.sun.com/xml/ns/javaee"
        xmlns:xsi="http://www.w3.org/2001/XMLSchema-instance"
        xsi:schemaLocation="http://java.sun.com/xml/ns/javaee
        http://java.sun.com/xml/ns/javaee/ejb-jar_3_1.xsd"
        version="3.1">
    <enterprise-beans>
        <session>
            <ejb-name>ItemEJB</ejb-name>
            <ejb-class>com.apress.javaee6.ItemEJB</ejb-class>
            <local>com.apress.javaee6.ItemLocal</local>
            <local-bean/>
            <remote>com.apress.javaee6.ItemRemote</remote>
            <session-type>Stateless</session-type>
            <transaction-type>Container</transaction-type>
            <env-entry>
                <env-entry-name>aBookTitle</env-entry-name>
                <env-entry-type>java.lang.String</env-entry-type>
                <env-entry-value>Beginning Java EE 6</env-entry-value>
            </env-entry>
        </session>
    </enterprise-beans>
</ejb-jar>
```

If the session bean is deployed in a jar file, the deployment descriptor needs to be stored in the `META-INF/ejb-jar.xml` file. If it's deployed in a war file, it needs to be stored in the `WEB-INF/ejb-jar.xml` file. XML configuration is useful for details that are environment-specific and shouldn't be specified in the code through annotations (e.g., if an EJB needs to be run one way in development and another in test/production environments).

Dependency Injection

I've already talked about dependency injection in this book, and you will come across this mechanism several times in the next chapters. It is a simple yet powerful mechanism used by Java EE 6 to inject references of resources into attributes. Instead of the application looking up resources in JNDI, they are injected by the container.

The containers can inject various types of resources into session beans using different annotations (or deployment descriptors):

- `@EJB`: Injects a reference of the local, remote, or no-interface view of an EJB into the annotated variable.

- `@PersistenceContext` and `@PersistenceUnit`: Expresses a dependency on an `EntityManager` and on an `EntityManagerFactory`, respectively (see the discussion "Obtaining an Entity Manager" in Chapter 4).

- @WebServiceRef: Injects a reference to a web service.

- @Resource: Injects several resources such as JDBC datasources, session context, user transactions, JMS connection factories and destinations, environment entries, the timer service, and so on.

Listing 7-13 shows a snippet of a stateless session bean using various annotations to inject different resources into attributes. Note that these annotations can be set on instance variables as well as on setter methods.

Listing 7-13. A Stateless Bean Using Injection

```
@Stateless
public class ItemEJB {

    @PersistenceContext(unitName = "chapter07PU")
    private EntityManager em;

    @EJB
    private CustomerEJB customerEJB;

    @WebServiceRef
    private ArtistWebService artistWebService;

    private SessionContext ctx;

    @Resource
    public void setCtx(SessionContext ctx) {
        this.ctx = ctx;
    }

    ...
}
```

Environment Naming Context

When you work with enterprise applications, there are some situations where parameters of your application change from one deployment to another (depending on the country you are deploying in, the version of the application, etc.). For example, in the CD-BookStore application, ItemEJB (see Listing 7-14) converts the price of an item to the currency of the country where the application is deployed (applying a change rate based on the dollar). If you deploy this stateless bean somewhere in Europe, you need to multiply the price of the item by 0.80 and change the currency to euros.

Listing 7-14. A Stateless Session Bean Converting Prices to Euros

```
@Stateless
public class ItemEJB {

    public Item convertPrice(Item item) {
        item.setPrice(item.getPrice() * 0.80);
        item.setCurrency("Euros");
        return item;
    }
}
```

As you can understand, the problem of hard-coding these parameters is that you have to change your code, recompile it, and redeploy the component for each country where the currency changes. The other option is to access a database each time you invoke the `convertPrice()` method. That's wasting resources. What you really want is to store these parameters somewhere you can change them at deployment time. The deployment descriptor is the perfect place to set these parameters.

The deployment descriptor (`ejb-jar.xml`) might be optional in EJB 3.1, but its use is legitimate with environment entries. Environment entries are specified in the deployment descriptor and are accessible via dependency injection (or via JNDI). They support the following Java types: `String`, `Character`, `Byte`, `Short`, `Integer`, `Long`, `Boolean`, `Double`, and `Float`. Listing 7-15 shows the `ejb-jar.xml` file of `ItemEJB` defining two entries: `currencyEntry` of type `String` with the value `Euros` and a `changeRateEntry` of type `Float` with the value `0.80`.

Listing 7-15. ItemEJB Environment Entries in ejb-jar.xml

```
<ejb-jar xmlns="http://java.sun.com/xml/ns/javaee"
        xmlns:xsi="http://www.w3.org/2001/XMLSchema-instance"
        xsi:schemaLocation="http://java.sun.com/xml/ns/javaee
        http://java.sun.com/xml/ns/javaee/ejb-jar_3_1.xsd"
        version="3.1">
    <enterprise-beans>
        <session>
            <ejb-name>ItemEJB</ejb-name>
            <ejb-class>com.apress.javaee6.ItemEJB</ejb-class>
            <env-entry>
                <env-entry-name>currencyEntry</env-entry-name>
                <env-entry-type>java.lang.String</env-entry-type>
                <env-entry-value>Euros</env-entry-value>
            </env-entry>
            <env-entry>
                <env-entry-name>changeRateEntry</env-entry-name>
                <env-entry-type>java.lang.Float</env-entry-type>
                <env-entry-value>0.80</env-entry-value>
            </env-entry>
        </session>
    </enterprise-beans>
</ejb-jar>
```

Now that the parameters of the application are externalized in the deployment descriptor, `ItemEJB` can use dependency injection to get the value of each environment entry. In Listing 7-16, `@Resource(name = "currencyEntry")` injects the value of the `currencyEntry` into the `currency` attribute. Note that the data types of the environment entry and the injected variable must be compatible; otherwise, the container throws an exception.

Listing 7-16. An ItemEJB Using Environment Entries

```
@Stateless
public class ItemEJB {

    @Resource(name = "currencyEntry")
    private String currency;
    @Resource(name = "changeRateEntry")
    private Float changeRate;

    public Item convertPrice(Item item) {
        item.setPrice(item.getPrice() * changeRate);
        item.setCurrency(currency);
        return item;
    }
}
```

Asynchronous Calls

By default, session bean invocations through remote, local, and no-interface views are synchronous: a client invokes a method, and it gets blocked for the duration of the invocation until the processing has completed, the result is returned, and the client can carry on its work. But asynchronous processing is a common requirement in many applications handling long-running tasks. For example, printing an order can be a very long task depending on whether the printer is online, there is enough paper, or dozens of documents are already waiting to be printed in the printer's spool. When a client calls a method to print a document, it wants to trigger a fire-and-forget process that will print the document so the client can carry on its processing.

Before EJB 3.1, asynchronous processing could only be handled by JMS and MDBs (see Chapter 13). You had to create administrated objects (JMS factories and destinations), deal with the low-level JMS API to send a message to a destination, and then develop an MDB that would consume and process the message. JMS comes with good reliability mechanisms (persistent message storage, delivery guarantees, integration with other systems, etc.) but it could be heavyweight for some use cases when you just want to call a method asynchronously.

Since EJB 3.1, you can call methods asynchronously simply by annotating a session bean method with `@javax.ejb.Asynchronous`. Listing 7-17 shows `OrderEJB`, which has one method for sending an e-mail to a customer and another for printing the order. Since these two methods are time consuming, they are both annotated with `@Asynchronous`.

Listing 7-17. An OrderEJB That Declares Two Asynchronous Methods

```
@Stateless
public class OrderEJB {

    @Asynchronous
    public void sendEmailOrderComplete(Order order, Customer customer) {
        // Send e-mail
    }

    @Asynchronous
    public void printOrder(Order order) {
        // Print order
    }
}
```

When a client invokes either the `printOrder()` or `sendEmailOrderComplete()` method, the container returns control to the client immediately and continues processing the invocation on a separate thread of execution. As you can see in Listing 7-17, the return type of the two asynchronous methods is `void`. This might be suitable in a vast majority of use cases, but sometimes you need a method to return a value. An asynchronous method can return `void` as well as a `java.util.concurrent.Future<V>` object, where V represents the result value. `Future` objects allow you to obtain a return value from a method executed in a separate thread. The client can then use the `Future` API to get the result or even cancel the call.

Listing 7-18 shows an example of a method that returns a `Future<Integer>`. The `sendOrderToWorkflow()` method uses a workflow to process an `Order` object. Let's imagine that it calls several enterprise components (messages, web services, etc.), and each step returns a status (an integer). When the client invokes the `sendOrderToWorkflow()` method asynchronously, it expects to receive the status of the workflow. The client can retrieve the result using the `Future.get()` method, or, if for any reason it wants to cancel the call, it can use `Future.cancel()`. If a client invokes `Future.cancel()`, the container will attempt to cancel the asynchronous call only if that call has not already started. Notice that the `sendOrderToWorkflow()` method uses the `SessionContext.wasCancelCalled()` method to check whether the client has requested to cancel the call or not. As a result, the method returns `javax.ejb.AsyncResult<V>`, which is a convenient implementation of `Future<V>`. Bear in mind that `AsyncResult` is used as a way to pass the result value to the container, not directly to the caller.

Listing 7-18. An OrderEJB Declares Two Asynchronous Methods

```
@Stateless
@Asynchronous
public class OrderEJB {

    @Resource
    SessionContext ctx;

    public void sendEmailOrderComplete(Order order, Customer customer) {
        // Send e-mail
    }
```

```
    public void printOrder(Order order) {
        // Print order
    }

    public Future<Integer> sendOrderToWorkflow(Order order) {
        Integer status = 0;
        // processing
        status = 1;
        if (ctx.wasCancelCalled()) {
            return new AsyncResult<Integer>(2);
        }
        // processing
        return new AsyncResult<Integer>(status);
    }
}
```

Notice in Listing 7-18 that the @Asynchronous annotation can also be applied at the class level. This defines all methods as being asynchronous. When the client invokes the sendOrderToWorkflow() method, it needs to call Future.get() in order to retrieve the result value.

```
Future<Integer> status = orderEJB.sendOrderToWorkflow (order);
Integer statusValue = status.get();
```

Embeddable Usage

Session beans are container-managed components, and that's their advantage. The container deals with all sorts of services (transaction, life cycle, asynchrony, interceptors, etc.), which leaves you to concentrate on business code. The downside is that you always need to execute your EJBs in a container, even if you just want to test them. To solve this problem, you end up having to tweak your business code to be able to test it: adding remote interfaces when your EJB only needs local access, creating a remote TestEJB façade that delegates the calls to your real EJBs, or using a vendor's specific features—but one way or another, you need to have a container running with your deployed EJBs.

This problem has been solved in EJB 3.1 with the creation of an embeddable EJB container. EJB 3.1 brings a standard API to execute EJBs in a Java SE environment. The embeddable API (package javax.ejb.embeddable) allows a client to instantiate an EJB container that runs within its own JVM. The embeddable container provides a managed environment with support for the same basic services that exist within a Java EE container: injection, transactions, life cycle, and so forth. Embeddable EJB containers only work with the EJB Lite subset API (no MDBs, no Entity Beans 2.x, etc.), meaning it has the same capabilities as an EJB Lite container (but not a full EJB container).

Listing 7-19 shows a JUnit test class that uses the bootstrapping API to start the container (the javax.ejb.embeddable.EJBContainer abstract class), look up an EJB, and invoke methods on it.

Listing 7-19. A Test Class Using the Embeddable Container

```java
public class ItemEJBTest {

    private static EJBContainer ec;
    private static Context ctx;

    @BeforeClass
    public static void initContainer() throws Exception {
        ec = EJBContainer.createEJBContainer();
        ctx = ec.getContext();
    }

    @AfterClass
    public static void closeContainer() throws Exception {
        if (ec != null)
            ec.close();
    }

    @Test
    public void shouldCreateABook() throws Exception {

        // Creates an instance of book
        Book book = new Book();
        book.setTitle("The Hitchhiker's Guide to the Galaxy");
        book.setPrice(12.5F);
        book.setDescription("Science fiction comedy book");
        book.setIsbn("1-84023-742-2");
        book.setNbOfPage(354);
        book.setIllustrations(false);

        // Looks up for the EJB
        ItemEJB bookEJB = (ItemEJB) ctx.lookup("java:global/classes/ItemEJB");

        // Persists the book to the database
        book = itemEJB.createBook(book);
        assertNotNull("ID should not be null", book.getId());

        // Retrieves all the books from the database
        List<Book> books = itemEJB.findBooks();
        assertNotNull(books);
    }
}
```

As you can see in the `initContainer()` method in Listing 7-19, `EJBContainer` contains a factory method (`createEJBContainer()`) for creating a container instance. By default, the embeddable container searches the client's classpath to find the set of EJBs for initialization. Once the container has been initialized, the method gets the container context (`EJBContainer.getContext()`, which returns a `javax.naming.Context`) to look up the `ItemEJB` (using the portable global JNDI name syntax).

Note that `ItemEJB` (shown earlier in Listing 7-1) is a stateless session bean exposing business methods through a no-interface view. It uses injection, container-managed transactions, and a JPA `Book` entity. The embeddable container takes care of injecting an entity manager and committing or rolling back any transaction. The `closeContainer()` method invokes the `EJBContainer.close()` method to shut down the embeddable container instance.

I've used a test class in this example to show you how to use an embeddable EJB container. But bear in mind that EJBs can now be used in any kind of Java SE environment: from test classes to Swing applications, or even just a `Main` class with a `public static void main()`.

The Timer Service

Some Java EE applications need to schedule tasks in order to get notified at certain times. For example, the CD-BookStore application needs to send a birthday e-mail to its customers every year, print monthly statistics about the items sold, generate nightly reports about inventory levels, and refresh a technical cache every 30 seconds.

As a result, EJB 2.1 introduced a scheduling facility called the timer service because clients couldn't use the `Thread` API directly. Compared with other proprietary tools or frameworks (the Unix cron utility, Quartz, etc.), the timer service was less feature-rich. The EJB specification had to wait until the 3.1 version to see a drastic improvement of the timer service. It took inspiration from Unix cron and other successful tools, and today competes with the other products as it responds to most scheduling use cases.

The EJB timer service is a container service that allows EJBs to be registered for callback invocation. EJB notifications may be scheduled to occur according to a calendar-based schedule, at a specific time, after a specific elapsed duration, or at specific recurring intervals. The container keeps a record of all the timers, and invokes the appropriate bean instance method when a timer has expired. Figure 7-7 shows the two steps involving the timer service. First, the EJB needs to create a timer (automatically or programmatically) and get registered for callback invocation, and then the timer service triggers the registered method on the EJB instance.

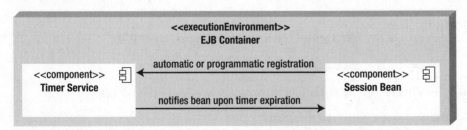

Figure 7-7. Interaction between the timer service and the session bean

Timers are intended for long-lived business processes and are by default persistent. This means they survive server shutdowns, and, once the server starts again, the timers are executed as if no shutdown had happened. Optionally, you can specify timers to be nonpersistent.

■ **Note** Stateless beans, singletons, and MDBs can be registered by the timer service, but stateful beans can't and shouldn't use the scheduling API.

Timers can be created automatically by the container at deployment time if the bean has methods annotated with the @Schedule annotation. But timers can also be created programmatically and must provide one callback method annotated with the @Timeout annotation.

Calendar-Based Expression

The timer service uses a calendar-based syntax that takes its roots from the Unix cron utility. This syntax is used for programmatic timer creation (using the ScheduleExpression class) and for automatic timer creation (via the @Schedule annotation or the deployment descriptor). The attributes creating calendar-based expressions are defined in Table 7-2.

Table 7-2. Attributes of a Calendar-Based Expression

Attribute	Description	Possible Values	Default Value
second	One or more seconds within a minute	[0,59]	0
minute	One or more minutes within an hour	[0,59]	0
hour	One or more hours within a day	[0,23]	0
dayOfMonth	One or more days within a month	[1,31] or {"1st", "2nd", "3rd",..., 0th", "31st"} or {"Sun", "Mon", "Tue", "Wed", "Thu", "Fri", "Sat"} or "Last" (the last day of the month) or -x (means x day(s) before the last day of the month)	*
month	One or more months within a year	[1,12] or {"Jan", "Feb", "Mar", "Apr", "May", "Jun", "Jul", "Aug", "Sep", "Oct", "Nov", "Dec"}	
dayOfWeek	One or more days within a week	[0,7] or {"Sun", "Mon", "Tue", "Wed", Thu", "Fri", "Sat"}—"0" and "7" both refer to Sunday	*
year	A particular calendar year	A four-digit calendar year	*
timezone	A specific time zone	List of time zones as provided by the zoneinfo (or tz) database	

Each attribute of a calendar-based expression (second, minute, hour, etc.) supports values expressed in different forms. For example, you can have a list of days or a range of years. Table 7-3 defines the different forms that an attribute can take.

Table 7-3. Forms of Expression

Form	Description	Example
Single value	The attribute has only one possible value.	`year = "2010" month= "May"`
Wildcard	This form represents all possible values for a given attribute.	`second = "*" dayOfWeek = "*"`
List	The attribute has two or more values separated by a comma.	`year = "2008,2012,2016" dayOfWeek = "Sat,Sun" minute = "0-10,30,40"`
Range	The attribute has a range of values separated by a dash.	`second = "1-10". dayOfWeek = "Mon-Fri"`
Increments	The attribute has a starting point and an interval separated by a forward slash.	`minute = "*/15" second = "30/10"`

If you have used Unix cron syntax before, this might sound familiar and much simpler. With this rich syntax, you can express nearly any kind of calendar expression, as shown in Table 7-4.

Table 7-4. Examples of Expressions

Example	Expression
Every Wednesday at midnight	`dayOfWeek="Wed"`
Every Wednesday at midnight	`second="0", minute="0", hour="0", dayOfMonth="*", month="*", dayOfWeek="Wed", year="*"`
Every weekday at 6:55	`minute="55", hour="6", dayOfWeek="Mon-Fri"`
Every weekday at 6:55 Paris time	`minute="55", hour="6", dayOfWeek="Mon-Fri", timezone="Europe/Paris"`
Every minute of every hour of every day	`minute="*", hour="*"`
Every second of every minute of every hour of every day	`second="*", minute="*", hour="*"`
Every Monday and Friday at 30 seconds past noon	`second="30", hour="12",`

Example	Expression
	dayOfWeek="Mon, Fri"
Every five minutes within the hour	minute="*/5", hour="*"
Every five minutes within the hour	minute="0,5,10,15,20,25,30,35, 40,45,50,55", hour="*"
The last Monday of December at 3 p.m.	hour="15", dayOfMonth="Last Mon", month="Dec"
Three days before the last day of each month at 1 p.m.	hour="13", dayOfMonth="-3"
Every other hour within the day starting at noon on the second Tuesday of every month	hour="12/2", dayOfMonth="2nd Tue"
Every 14 minutes within the hour, for the hours of 1 and 2 a.m.	minute = "*/14", hour="1,2"
Every 14 minutes within the hour, for the hours of 1 and 2 a.m.	minute = "0,14,28,42,56", our = "1,2"
Every 10 seconds within the minute, starting at second 30	second = "30/10"
Every 10 seconds within the minute, starting at second 30	second = "30,40,50"

Automatic Timer Creation

Timers can be created automatically by the container at deployment time based on metadata. The container creates a timer for each method annotated with @javax.ejb.Schedule or @Schedules (or the XML equivalent in the ejb-jar.xml deployment descriptor). By default, each @Schedule annotation corresponds to a single persistent timer, but you can also define nonpersistent timers.

Listing 7-20 shows the StatisticsEJB bean that defines several methods. statisticsItemsSold() creates a timer that will call the method every first day of the month at 5:30 a.m. The generateReport() method creates two timers (using @Schedules): one every day at 2 a.m., and another one every Wednesday at 2 p.m. refreshCache() creates a nonpersistent timer that will refresh the cache every 10 minutes.

Listing 7-20. A StatisticsEJB Registering Four Timers

```
@Stateless
public class StatisticsEJB {

    @Schedule(dayOfMonth = "1", hour = "5", minute = "30")
    public void statisticsItemsSold() {
        // ...
    }
```

```
@Schedules({
        @Schedule(hour = "2"),
        @Schedule(hour = "14", dayOfWeek = "Wed")
})
public void generateReport() {
    // ...
}

@Schedule(minute = "*/10", hour = "*", persistent = false)
public void refreshCache() {
    // ...
}
}
```

Programmatic Timer Creation

To create a timer programmatically, the EJB needs to access the `javax.ejb.TimerService` interface using either dependency injection or the `EJBContext` (`EJBContext.getTimerService()`), or through JNDI lookup. The `TimerService` API has several methods that allow you to create different kinds of timers divided into four categories:

- `createTimer`: Creates a timer based on dates, intervals, or durations. These methods do not use calendar-based expressions.

- `createSingleActionTimer`: Creates a single-action timer that expires at a given point in time or after a specified duration. The container removes the timer after the timeout callback method has been successfully invoked.

- `createIntervalTimer`: Creates an interval timer whose first expiration occurs at a given point in time and whose subsequent expirations occur after specified intervals.

- `createCalendarTimer`: Creates a timer using a calendar-based expression with the `ScheduleExpression` helper class.

The `ScheduleExpression` helper class allows you to create calendar-based expressions programmatically. You will find methods related to the attributes defined in Table 7-2, and you will be able to program all the examples that you saw in Table 7-4. Here are some examples to give you an idea:

```
new ScheduleExpression().dayOfMonth("Mon").month("Jan");
new ScheduleExpression().second("10,30,50").minute("*/5").hour("10-14");
new ScheduleExpression().dayOfWeek("1,5").timezone("Europe/Lisbon");
new ScheduleExpression().dayOfMonth(customer.getBirthDay())
```

All the methods of `TimerService` (`createSingleActionTimer`, `createCalendarTimer`, etc.) return a `javax.ejb.Timer` object that contains information about the created timer (what time was it created, whether it is persistent, etc.). `Timer` also allows the EJB to cancel the timer prior to its expiration. When the timer expires, the container calls the associated @javax.ejb.Timeout method of the bean, passing the Timer object. A bean can have at most one @Timeout method.

When CustomerEJB (see Listing 7-21) creates a new customer in the system (createCustomer() method), it creates a calendar timer based on the date of birth of the customer. Thus, every year the container will trigger a bean to create and send a birthday e-mail to the customer. To do that, the stateless bean first needs to inject a reference of the timer service (using @Resource). The createCustomer() persists the customer in the database and uses the day and the month of her birth to create a ScheduleExpression. A calendar timer is created given this ScheduleExpression and the customer object using a TimerConfig. new TimerConfig(customer, true) configures a persistent timer (as indicated by the true parameter) that passes the customer object.

Listing 7-21. A CustomerEJB Creating a Timer Programmatically

```
@Stateless
public class CustomerEJB {

    @Resource
    TimerService timerService;

    @PersistenceContext(unitName = "chapter07PU")
    private EntityManager em;

    public void createCustomer(Customer customer) {
        em.persist(customer);

        ScheduleExpression birthDay = new ScheduleExpression().↪
                dayOfMonth(customer.getBirthDay()).month(customer.getBirthMonth());
        timerService.createCalendarTimer(birthDay, new TimerConfig(customer, true));
    }

    @Timeout
    public void sendBirthdayEmail(Timer timer) {
        Customer customer = (Customer) timer.getInfo();
        // ...
    }
}
```

Once the timer is created, the container will invoke the @Timeout method (sendBirthdayEmail()) every year, which passes the Timer object. Because the timer had been serialized with the customer object, the method can access it by calling the getInfo() method.

Summary

This chapter focused on session beans and the timer service (you will find MDBs in Chapter 13, SOAP web services in Chapter 14, and RESTful web services in Chapter 15). Session beans are container-managed components that are used to develop business layers. There are three different types of session beans: stateless, stateful, and singleton. Stateless beans are easily scalable because they keep no state, live in a pool, and process tasks that can be completed in a single method call. Stateful beans have a one-to-one correlation with a client and can be temporarily cleared from memory using passivation and activation. Singletons have a unique instance shared among several clients and can be initialized at startup time, chained together, and customized in their concurrency access.

Despite these differences, session beans share a common programming model. They can have a local, remote, or no-interface view, use annotations, or be deployed with a deployment descriptor. Session beans can use dependency injection to get references to several resources (JDBC datasources, persistence context, environment entries, etc.), as well as their runtime environment context (the `SessionContext` object). Since EJB 3.1, you can invoke methods asynchronously, look up EJBs with a portable JNDI name, or use the embeddable EJB container in the Java SE environment. EJB 3.1 has also enhanced the timer service, which can now effectively compete with other scheduling tools.

The next chapter will explain the life cycle of the different session beans and how you can interact with callback annotations. Interceptors, which provide a way of doing Aspect-Oriented Programming (AOP) with session beans, will also be discussed.

CHAPTER 8

■■■

Callbacks and Interceptors

In the previous chapter, you learned that session beans are container-managed components. They live in an EJB container, which wraps business code behind the scenes with several services (dependency injection, transaction management, security, and so on). Two of these services are life-cycle management and interception.

Life cycle means that a session bean goes through a predefined set of state transitions. Depending on the type of your bean (stateless, stateful, singleton), the life cycle will consist of different states. Each time the container changes the life-cycle state, it can invoke methods that are annotated with callback annotations. As an example, you can use these annotations to initialize any resources on your session beans or release them before they get destroyed.

Interceptors allow you to add cross-cutting concerns to your beans. When a client invokes a method on your session bean, the container is able to intercept the call and process business logic before the bean's method is invoked.

This chapter shows you the different life cycles used by session beans and the callback annotations you can apply to process business logic during certain phases. You will also learn how to intercept method invocations and wrap them with your own code.

Session Beans Life Cycle

As you've seen in the previous chapter, a client doesn't create an instance of a session bean using the new operator. It gets a reference to a session bean either through dependency injection or JNDI lookup. The container is the one creating the instance and destroying it. This means that neither the client nor the bean is responsible for determining when the bean instance is created, when dependencies are injected, or when the instance is destroyed. The container is responsible for managing the life cycle of the bean.

All session beans have two obvious phases in their life cycle: creation and destruction. In addition, stateful session beans go through the passivation and activation phases that I mentioned in the previous chapter.

Stateless and Singleton

Stateless and singleton beans have in common the fact that they don't maintain conversational state with a dedicated client. Both bean types allow access by any client—stateless does this serially on a per-instance basis, while singleton provides concurrent access to a single instance. Both share the same life cycle shown in Figure 8-1 and described as follows:

1. The life cycle of a stateless or singleton session bean starts when a client requests a reference to the bean (using either dependency injection or JNDI lookup). In the case of a singleton, it can also start when the container is bootstrapped (using the `@Startup` annotation). The container creates a new session bean instance.

2. If the newly created instance uses dependency injection through annotations (`@Resource`, `@EJB`, `@PersistenceContext`, etc.) or deployment descriptors, the container injects all the needed resources.

3. If the instance has a method annotated with `@PostContruct`, the container invokes it.

4. The bean instance processes the call invoked by the client and stays in ready mode to process future calls. Stateless beans stay in ready mode until the container frees some space in the pool. Singletons stay in ready mode until the container is shut down.

5. The container does not need the instance any more. It invokes the method annotated with `@PreDestroy`, if any, and ends the life of the bean instance.

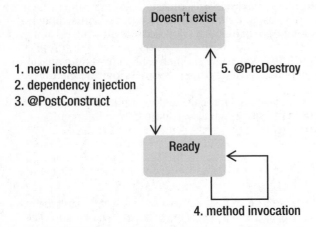

Figure 8-1. Stateless and singleton bean life cycle

Stateless and singleton beans share the same life cycle, but there are some differences in the way they are created and destroyed.

When a stateless session bean is deployed, the container creates several instances and adds them into a pool. When a client calls a method on a stateless session bean, the container selects one instance from the pool, delegates the method invocation to that instance, and returns it to the pool. When the container no longer needs the instance (usually when the container wants to reduce the number of instances in the pool), it destroys it.

■ **Note** GlassFish allows you to customize several EJB pool parameters. You can set a pool size (initial, minimum, and maximum number of beans in the pool), the number of beans to be removed when the pool idle timeout expires, and the number of milliseconds for the pool to time out. These options are implementation specific and may not be available on other EJB containers.

For singleton session beans, creation depends on whether they are instantiated eagerly (@Startup) or not, or whether they depend (@DependsOn) on another singleton that had been eagerly created. If the answer is yes, an instance will be created at deployment time. If not, the container will create an instance when a business method is invoked by a client. Because singletons last for the duration of the application, the instance is destroyed when the container shuts down.

Stateful

Stateful session beans are programmatically not very different from stateless or singleton session beans: only the metadata changes (@Stateful instead of @Stateless or @Singleton). But the real difference is that stateful beans maintain conversational state with their client, and therefore have a slightly different life cycle. The container generates an instance and assigns it only to one client. Then, each request from that client is passed to the same instance. Following this principle and depending on your application, you might end up with a one-to-one relationship between a client and a stateful bean (e.g., a thousand simultaneous users might produce a thousand stateful beans). If one client doesn't invoke its bean's instance for a long enough time, the container has to clear it before the JVM runs out of memory, preserve the instance state to a permanent storage, and then bring back the instance with its state when it's needed. The container employs the technique of passivation and activation.

As discussed in Chapter 7, passivation is when the container serializes the bean instance to a permanent storage medium (file on a disk, database, etc.) instead of holding it in memory. Activation, which is the opposite, is done when the bean instance is needed again by the client. The container deserializes the bean from permanent storage and activates it back into memory. This means the bean's attributes have to be serializable (it must either be a Java primitive or implement the java.io.Serializable interface). The stateful bean life cycle is shown in Figure 8-2 and described as follows:

1. The life cycle of a stateful bean starts when a client requests a reference to the bean (either using dependency injection or JNDI lookup). The container creates a new session bean instance and stores it in memory.

2. If the newly created instance uses dependency injection through annotations (@Resource, @EJB, @PersistenceContext, etc.) or deployment descriptors, the container injects all the needed resources.

3. If the instance has a method annotated with @PostContruct, the container invokes it.

4. The bean executes the requested call and stays in memory, waiting for subsequent client requests.

5.   If the client remains idle for a period of time, the container invokes the method annotated with `@PrePassivate`, if any, and passivates the bean instance into a permanent storage.

6.   If the client invokes a passivated bean, the container activates it back to memory and invokes the method annotated with `@PostActivate`, if any.

7.   If the client does not invoke a passivated bean instance for the session timeout period, it is destroyed by the container.

8.   Alternatively to step 7, if the client calls a method annotated by `@Remove`, the container then invokes the method annotated with `@PreDestroy`, if any, and ends the life of the bean instance.

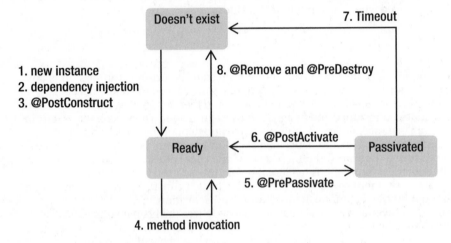

Figure 8-2. Stateful bean life cycle

In some cases, a stateful bean contains open resources such as network sockets or database connections. Because a container cannot keep these resources open for each bean, you will have to close and reopen the resources before and after passivation. That's when life-cycle callback methods can be used.

Callbacks

As you just saw, each session bean has its own container-managed life cycle. The container lets you optionally provide your own business code when the state of the bean changes. The change from one state to another can be intercepted by the container to invoke methods annotated by one of the annotations listed in Table 8-1.

Table 8-1. Life-Cycle Callback Annotations

Annotation	Description
@PostConstruct	Marks a method to be invoked immediately after a bean instance is created and dependency injection is done by the container. This annotation is often used to perform any initialization.
@PreDestroy	Marks a method to be invoked immediately before the bean instance is destroyed by the container. The method annotated with @PreDestroy is often used to release resources that had been previously initialized. With stateful beans, this happens after a method annotated with @Remove has been completed.
@PrePassivate	Marks a method to be invoked before the container passivates the instance. It usually gives the bean the time to prepare for serialization and to release resources that cannot be serialized (e.g., it closes connections to a database, a message broker, a network socket, etc.).
@PostActivate	Marks a method to be invoked immediately after the container reactivates the instance. Gives the bean a chance to reinitialize resources that had been closed during passivation.

■ **Note** @PrePassivate and @PostActivate annotations are defined in the `javax.ejb` package and the EJB 3.1 specification (JSR 318). They are related to the EJB life cycle and can happen many times during the EJB lifetime. @PostConstruct and @PreDestroy are part of the Common Annotations 1.1 specification (JSR 250) and come from the `javax.annotation` package (like @Resource or other security annotations that you'll see in the next chapter). They are related to Java classes' life cycle and happen only once during the class lifetime (at creation and at destruction).

A callback method is required to have the following signature:

```
void <METHOD>();
```

The following rules apply to a callback method:

- The method must not have any parameters and must return void.

- The method must not throw a checked exception but can throw runtime exceptions. Throwing a runtime exception will roll back the transaction if one exists (as explained in the next chapter).

- The method can have public, private, protected, or package-level access, but must not be static or final.

- A method may be annotated with multiple annotations (the init() method shown later in Listing 8-2 is annotated with @PostConstruct and @PostActivate). However, only one annotation of a given type may be present on a bean (you can't have two @PostConstruct annotations in the same session bean, for example).

- A callback method can access the beans' environment entries (see the "Environment Naming Context" section in Chapter 7).

These callbacks are typically used to allocate and/or release the bean's resources. As an example, Listing 8-1 shows the singleton bean CacheEJB using a @PostConstruct annotation to initialize its cache. Straight after creating the single instance of the CacheEJB, the container invokes the initCache() method.

Listing 8-1. A Singleton Initializing Its Cache with the @PostConstruct Annotation

```
@Singleton
public class CacheEJB {

    private Map<Long, Object> cache = new HashMap<Long, Object>();

    @PostConstruct
    private void initCache() {
        // Initializes the cache
    }

    public Object getFromCache(Long id) {
        if (cache.containsKey(id))
            return cache.get(id);
        else
            return null;
    }
}
```

Listing 8-2 shows a snippet of code for a stateful bean. The container maintains conversational state, which can include heavy-duty resources such as a database connection. Because it is expensive to open a database connection, it should be shared across calls but released when the bean is idle (or passivated).

After creating an instance of a stateful bean, the container injects the reference of a datasource to the ds attribute. Once the injection is done, the container will call the designated @PostConstruct method (init()), which creates a database connection. If the container happens to passivate the instance, the close() method will be invoked (@PrePassivate). The purpose of this is to close the JDBC connection, which holds native resources and is no longer needed during passivation. When the client invokes a business method on the bean, the container activates it and calls the init() method again (@PostActivate). When the client invokes the checkout() method (annotated with the @Remove annotation), the container removes the instance but first will call the close() method again (@PreDestroy).

Listing 8-2. A Stateful Bean Initializing and Releasing Resources

```
@Stateful
public class ShoppingCartEJB {

    @Resource
    private DataSource ds;

    private Connection connection;
    private List<Item> cartItems = new ArrayList<Item>();

    @PostConstruct
    @PostActivate
    private void init() {
        connection = ds.getConnection();
    }

    @PreDestroy
    @PrePassivate
    private void close() {
        connection.close();
    }

    // ...

    @Remove
    public void checkout() {
        cartItems.clear();
    }
}
```

For better readability, I've omitted the SQL exception handling in the callback methods.

Interceptors

Before talking about interceptors, I want to briefly discuss Aspect-Oriented Programming (AOP). AOP is a programming paradigm that separates cross-cutting concerns (concerns that cut across the application) from your business code. Most applications have common code that is repeated across components. These could be technical concerns (log the entry and exit from each method, log the duration of a method invocation, store statistics of method usage, etc.) or business concerns (perform additional checks if a customer buys more than $10,000 of items, send a refill order when the inventory level is too low, etc.). These concerns can be applied automatically through AOP to your entire application or to a subset of it.

EJBs support AOP-like functionality by providing the ability to intercept method invocation through interceptors. Interceptors are automatically triggered by the container when an EJB method is invoked. As shown in Figure 8-3, interceptors can be chained and are called before and/or after the execution of a method.

■ **Note** Since Java EE 6, interceptors have evolved into a separate specification (they used to be bundled with the EJB specification). They can be applied to session beans and message-driven beans as well as SOAP and RESTful web services, as you will see in Chapters 14 and 15. So now, the EJB 3.1 specification (JSR 318) is composed of two documents: the core EJB specification and the interceptor requirements document. The interceptors specification might be undertaken independently of EJBs in future revisions.

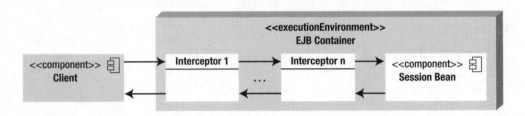

Figure 8-3. A container intercepting a call and invoking interceptors

Figure 8-3 shows you a number of interceptors that are called between the client and the EJB. You could think of an EJB container as a chain of interceptors itself. When you develop a session bean, you just concentrate on your business code. But behind the scenes, when a client invokes a method on your EJB, the container intercepts the invocation and applies different services (life-cycle management, transaction, security, etc.). With interceptors, you add your own cross-cutting mechanisms and apply them transparently to your business code. Interceptors fall into three types (which I explain in the next section):

- Around-invoke interceptors
- Business method interceptors
- Life-cycle callback interceptors

Around-Invoke Interceptors

There are several ways of defining a business method interceptor. The simplest is to add a `@javax.interceptor.AroundInvoke` annotation (or `<around-invoke>` deployment descriptor element) in the bean itself as shown in Listing 8-3. `CustomerEJB` annotates `logMethod()` with `@AroundInvoke`. `logMethod()` is used to log a message when a method is entered, and to log another message when a method is exited. Once this EJB is deployed, any client invocation to `createCustomer()` or `findCustomerById()` methods will be intercepted, and the `logMethod()` will be applied. Note that the scope of this interceptor is limited to this bean. Around-invoke methods occur within the same transaction and security context as the method on which they are interposing.

Listing 8-3. CustomerEJB Uses an Interceptor

```
@Stateless
public class CustomerEJB {

  @PersistenceContext(unitName = "chapter08PU")
  private EntityManager em;
  private Logger logger = Logger.getLogger("com.apress.javaee6");

  public void createCustomer(Customer customer) {
    em.persist(customer);
  }

  public Customer findCustomerById(Long id) {
    return em.find(Customer.class, id);
  }

  @AroundInvoke
  private Object logMethod(InvocationContext ic) throws Exception {
    logger.entering(ic.getTarget().toString(), ic.getMethod().getName());
    try {
      return ic.proceed();
    } finally {
      logger.exiting(ic.getTarget().toString(), ic.getMethod().getName());
    }
  }
}
```

Despite being annotated with @AroundInvoke, the logMethod() has to follow a certain signature:

```
@AroundInvoke
Object <METHOD>(InvocationContext ic) throws Exception;
```

The following rules apply to an around-invoke method:

- The method can have public, private, protected, or package-level access, but must not be static or final.

- The method must have a javax.interceptor.InvocationContext parameter and must return Object, which is the result of the invoked target method (if the method returns void, it returns null).

- The method can throw a checked exception.

The InvocationContext object allows interceptors to control the behavior of the invocation chain. If several interceptors are chained, the same InvocationContext instance is passed to each interceptor, which can add contextual data to be processed by other interceptors. The InvocationContext API is described in Table 8-2.

Table 8-2. Definition of the InvocationContext Interface

Method	Description
getContextData	Allows values to be passed between interceptor methods in the same InvocationContext instance using a Map.
getMethod	Returns the method of the bean class for which the interceptor was invoked.
getParameters	Returns the parameters that will be used to invoke the business method.
getTarget	Returns the bean instance that the intercepted method belongs to.
getTimer	Returns the timer associated with a @Timeout method.
Proceed	Causes the invocation of the next interceptor method in the chain. It returns the result of the next method invoked. If a method is of type void, proceed returns null.
setParameters	Modifies the value of the parameters used for the target class method invocation. The types and the number of parameters must match the bean's method signature, or IllegalArgumentException is thrown.

To explain how the code works in Listing 8-3, let's take a look at the sequence diagram shown in Figure 8-4 to see what happens when a client invokes the createCustomer() method. First of all, the container intercepts the call and, instead of directly processing createCustomer(), first invokes the logMethod() method. logMethod() uses the InvocationContext interface to get the name of the invoked bean (ic.getTarget()) and invoked method (ic.getMethod()) to log an entry message (logger.entering()). Then, the proceed() method is called. Calling InvocationContext.proceed() is extremely important as it tells the container that it should proceed to the next interceptor or call the bean's business method. Not calling proceed() would stop the interceptors chain and would avoid calling the business method. The createCustomer() is finally invoked, and, once it returns, the interceptor finishes its execution by logging an exit message (logger.exiting()). The same sequence would happen if a client invokes the findCustomerById() method.

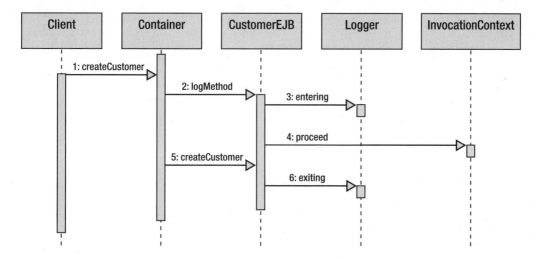

Figure 8-4. A call to a business method being intercepted

Method Interceptors

Listing 8-3 defines an interceptor that is only available for `CustomerEJB`. But most of the time you want to isolate a cross-cutting concern into a separate class and tell the container to intercept the calls on several session beans. Logging is a typical example of a situation when you want all the methods of all your EJBs to log entering and exiting messages. To specify an interceptor, you need to develop a separate class and instruct the container to apply it on a specific bean or bean's method.

To share some code among multiple beans, let's take the `logMethod()` from Listing 8-3 and isolate it in a separate class as shown in Listing 8-4. As you can see, `LoggingInterceptor` is a simple POJO that has a method annotated with `@AroundInvoke`.

Listing 8-4. An Interceptor Class Logging a Method on Entering and Exiting

```
public class LoggingInterceptor {

  private Logger logger = Logger.getLogger("com.apress.javaee6");

  @AroundInvoke
  public Object logMethod(InvocationContext ic) throws Exception {
    logger.entering(ic.getTarget().toString(), ic.getMethod().getName());
    try {
      return ic.proceed();
    } finally {
      logger.exiting(ic.getTarget().toString(), ic.getMethod().getName());
    }
  }
}
```

247

The LoggingInterceptor can now be wrapped transparently by any EJB interested in this interceptor. To do this, the bean needs to inform the container with a @javax.interceptor.Interceptors annotation. In Listing 8-5, the annotation is set on the createCustomer() method. This means that any invocation of this method will be intercepted by the container, and the LoggingInterceptor class will be invoked (logging a message on entry and exit of the method).

Listing 8-5. CustomerEJB Uses an Interceptor on One Method

```
@Stateless
public class CustomerEJB {

    @PersistenceContext(unitName = "chapter08PU")
    private EntityManager em;

    @Interceptors(LoggingInterceptor.class)
    public void createCustomer(Customer customer) {
        em.persist(customer);
    }

    public Customer findCustomerById(Long id) {
        return em.find(Customer.class, id);
    }
}
```

In Listing 8-5, @Interceptors is only attached to the createCustomer() method. This means that, if a client invokes findCustomerById(), the container will not intercept the call. If you want the calls to both methods to be intercepted, you can add the @Interceptors annotation either on both methods or on the bean itself. When you do so, the interceptor is triggered if either method is invoked:

```
@Stateless
@Interceptors(LoggingInterceptor.class)
public class CustomerEJB {
    public void createCustomer(Customer customer) { ... }
    public Customer findCustomerById(Long id) { ... }
}
```

If your bean has several methods, and you want to apply an interceptor to the entire bean except for a specific method, you can use the javax.interceptor.ExcludeClassInterceptors annotation to exclude a call from being intercepted. In the following code, the call to updateCustomer() will not be intercepted, but all others will:

```
@Stateless
@Interceptors(LoggingInterceptor.class)
public class CustomerEJB {
    public void createCustomer(Customer customer) { ... }
    public Customer findCustomerById(Long id) { ... }
    public void removeCustomer(Customer customer) { ... }

    @ExcludeClassInterceptors
    public Customer updateCustomer(Customer customer) { ... }
}
```

Life-Cycle Interceptor

In the first part of this chapter, you learned how to handle callback events in your EJB. With a callback annotation, you can inform the container to invoke a method at a certain life-cycle phase (@PostConstruct, @PrePassivate, @PostActivate, and @PreDestroy). For example, if you want to log an entry each time a bean instance is created, you just need to add a @PostConstruct annotation on one method of your bean and add some logging mechanisms to it. But what if you need to capture life-cycle events across many types of beans? Life-cycle interceptors allow you to isolate some code into a class and invoke it when a life-cycle event is triggered.

Life-cycle interceptors really look like what you've just seen in Listing 8-4. Instead of @AroundInvoke, methods can be annotated with callback annotations. Listing 8-6 shows the ProfileInterceptor class with two methods: logMethod(), used for postconstruction, and profile(), used for predestruction.

Listing 8-6. A Life-Cycle Interceptor Defining Two Methods

```java
public class ProfileInterceptor {

  private Logger logger = Logger.getLogger("com.apress.javaee6");

  @PostConstruct
  public void logMethod(InvocationContext ic) {
    logger.entering(ic.getTarget().toString(), ic.getMethod().getName());
    try {
      return ic.proceed();
    } finally {
      logger.exiting(ic.getTarget().toString(), ic.getMethod().getName());
    }
  }

  @PreDestroy
  public void profile(InvocationContext ic) {
    long initTime = System.currentTimeMillis();
    try {
      return ic.proceed();
    } finally {
      long diffTime = System.currentTimeMillis() - initTime;
      logger.fine(ic.getMethod() + " took " + diffTime + " millis");
    }
  }
}
```

As you can see in Listing 8-6, life-cycle interceptor methods take an InvocationContext parameter, return void instead of Object (because life-cycle callback methods return void, as explained earlier in the "Callbacks" section), and cannot throw checked exceptions.

To apply the interceptor defined in Listing 8-6, the session bean needs to use the @Interceptors annotation. As you can see in Listing 8-7, CustomerEJB defines the ProfileInterceptor. When the EJB is instantiated by the container, the logMethod() of the interceptor will be invoked prior to the init() method. Then, if a client calls createCustomer() or findCustomerById(), no interception will happen. But, before CustomerEJB is destroyed by the container, the profile() method will be invoked.

Listing 8-7. CustomerEJB Using a Callback Interceptor

```
@Stateless
@Interceptors(ProfileInterceptor.class)
public class CustomerEJB {

    @PersistenceContext(unitName = "chapter08PU")
    private EntityManager em;

    @PostConstruct
    public void init() {
        // ...
    }

    public void createCustomer(Customer customer) {
        em.persist(customer);
    }

    public Customer findCustomerById(Long id) {
        return em.find(Customer.class, id);
    }
}
```

Life-cycle callback methods and `@AroundInvoke` methods may be defined in the same interceptor class.

Chaining and Excluding Interceptors

You've seen how to intercept calls within a single bean (with `@AroundInvoke`) and across multiple beans (using `@Interceptors`). Interceptors 1.1 lets you chain several interceptors, as well as have default interceptors that can apply to all your session beans.

In fact, the `@Interceptors` annotation is capable of attaching more than one interceptor, as it takes a comma-separated list of interceptors as a parameter. When multiple interceptors are defined, the order in which they are invoked is determined by the order in which they are specified in the `@Interceptors` annotation. For example, the code in Listing 8-8 uses `@Interceptors` at the bean and method level.

Listing 8-8. CustomerEJB Using a Callback Interceptor

```
@Stateless
@Interceptors(I1.class, I2.class)
public class CustomerEJB {
    public void createCustomer(Customer customer) { ... }
    @Interceptors(I3.class, I4.class)
    public Customer findCustomerById(Long id) { ... }
    public void removeCustomer(Customer customer) { ... }
    @ExcludeClassInterceptors
    public Customer updateCustomer(Customer customer) { ... }
}
```

When a client calls the updateCustomer() method, no interceptor is invoked (the method is annotated with @ExcludeClassInterceptors). When the createCustomer() method is called, interceptor I1 is executed followed by interceptor I2. When the findCustomerById() method is invoked, interceptors I1, I2, I3, and I4 get executed in this order.

Besides specifying method and class-level interceptors, Interceptors 1.1 allows you to create default interceptors that are used for all methods of all the EJBs defined in the application. There is no annotation that has an application scope. If you want to apply default interceptors in your application, you need to define them in the deployment descriptor (ejb-jar.xml). If you want to apply the default interceptor ProfileInterceptor to all your EJBs, this is the portion of XML you need to add to the deployment descriptor:

```
<assembly-descriptor>
    <interceptor-binding>
        <ejb-name>*</ejb-name>
        <interceptor-class>
            com.apress.javaee6.ProfileInterceptor
        </interceptor-class>
    </interceptor-binding>
</assembly-descriptor>
```

As you can see, the wildcard * in <ejb-name> means that every EJB should apply the interceptor defined in the <interceptor-class> element. If you deploy CustomerEJB in Listing 8-7 with this default interceptor, the ProfileInterceptor will be invoked before any other interceptor.

If multiple types of interceptor are defined for a session bean, the container applies them from the largest scope (default interceptor) to the smallest (method interceptor). The rules governing their invocation order are shown in Figure 8-5.

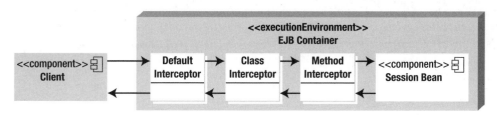

Figure 8-5. *Chaining different types of interceptors*

If you want to disable default interceptors for a specific EJB, you can apply the @javax.interceptor.ExcludeDefaultInterceptors annotation either at the class or at the method level as shown in Listing 8-9.

Listing 8-9. EJB Excluding Default Interceptors

```
@Stateless
@ExcludeDefaultInterceptors
@Interceptors(LoggingInterceptor.class)
public class CustomerEJB {
    public void createCustomer(Customer customer) { ... }
    public Customer findCustomerById(Long id) { ... }
    public void removeCustomer(Customer customer) { ... }
    @ExcludeClassInterceptors
    public Customer updateCustomer(Customer customer) { ... }
}
```

Summary

In this chapter, you learned that stateless and singleton session beans share the same life cycle and that stateful beans have a slightly different one. That's because stateful beans keep a conversational state with the client and need to temporarily serialize their state to a permanent storage (passivation). Callback annotations allow you to add business logic to your bean before or after an event occurs (@PostConstruct, @PreDestroy, etc.).

Interceptors are the AOP-like mechanism of Java EE, allowing the container to invoke cross-cutting concerns on your application. Interceptors are easy to use, powerful, and can be chained together to apply several concerns to your beans. You can also specify default interceptors that are applied to every method of every bean of your application.

An EJB container can be seen as a chain of interceptors. Method invocations are intercepted by the container, which then applies several services such as transaction and security management. The next chapter will focus on these two container-managed services.

■ ■ ■

Transactions and Security

Transaction and security management are important matters for enterprises. They allow applications to have consistent data and secure the access to it. Both services are low-level concerns that a business developer shouldn't have to code himself. EJBs provide these services in a very simple way: either programmatically with a high level of abstraction or declaratively using metadata.

Most of an enterprise application's work is about managing data: storing it (typically in a database), retrieving it, processing it, and so on. Often this is done simultaneously by several applications attempting to access the same data. A database has low-level mechanisms to preserve concurrent access, such as pessimistic locking, and uses transactions to ensure that data stays in a consistent state. EJBs make use of these mechanisms.

Securing data is also important. You want your business tier to act like a firewall and authorize some actions to certain groups of users and deny access to others (e.g., only employees are allowed to persist data, but users and employees are authorized to read data).

The first part of this chapter is devoted to exploring transaction management in EJB 3.1. I'll introduce transactions as a whole, and then discuss the different types of transaction demarcation supported by EJBs. In the second part of the chapter, I'll focus on security.

Transactions

Data is crucial for business, and it must be accurate regardless of the operations you perform and the number of applications concurrently accessing it. A *transaction* is used to ensure that the data is kept in a consistent state. It represents a logical group of operations that must be performed as a single unit, also known as a *unit of work*. These operations can involve persisting data in one or several databases, sending messages, or invoking web services. Companies rely on transactions every day for their banking and e-commerce applications or business-to-business interactions with partners

These indivisible business operations are performed either sequentially or in parallel over a relatively short period of time. Every operation must succeed in order for the transaction to succeed (we say that the transaction is committed). If one of the operations fails, the transaction fails as well (the transaction is rolled back). Transactions must guarantee a degree of reliability and robustness and follow the ACID properties.

ACID

ACID refers to the four properties that define a reliable transaction: Atomicity, Consistency, Isolation, and Durability (described in Table 9-1). To explain these properties, I'll take the classical example of a banking transfer: you need to debit your savings account to credit your current account.

Table 9-1. *ACID Properties*

Property	Description
Atomicity	A transaction is composed of one or more operations grouped in a unit of work. At the conclusion of the transaction, these operations are either all performed successfully (commit), or none of them is performed at all (rollback) if something unexpected or irrecoverable happens.
Consistency	At the conclusion of the transaction, the data is left in a consistent state.
Isolation	The intermediate state of a transaction is not visible to external applications.
Durability	Once the transaction is committed, the changes made to the data are visible to other applications.

When you transfer money from one account to the other, you can imagine a sequence of database accesses: the savings account is debited using a SQL update statement, the current account is credited using a different update statement, and a log is created in a different table to keep track of the transfer. These operations have to be done in the same unit of work (Atomicity) because you don't want the debit to occur but not the credit. From the perspective of an external application querying the accounts, only when both operations have been successfully performed are they visible (Isolation). With isolation, the external application cannot see the interim state when one account has been debited and the other is still not credited (if it could, it would think the user has less money than he really does). Consistency is when transaction operations (either with a commit or a rollback) are done within the constraints of the database (such as primary keys, relationships, or fields). Once the transfer is completed, the data can be accessed from other applications (Durability).

Local Transactions

Several components have to be in place for transactions to work and follow the ACID properties. Let's first take the simplest example of an application performing several changes to a single resource (e.g., a database). When there is only one transactional resource, all that is needed is a local transaction. Distributed transactions (à la JTA) can still be used, but are not strictly necessary. Figure 9-1 shows the application interacting with a resource through a transaction manager and a resource manager.

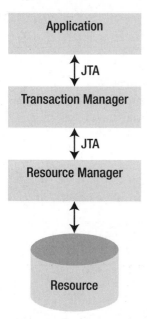

Figure 9-1. *A transaction involving one resource*

The components shown in Figure 9-1 abstract most of the transaction-specific processing from the application:

- The *transaction manager* is the core component responsible for managing the transactional operations. It creates the transactions on behalf of the application, informs the resource manager that it is participating in a transaction (an operation known as *enlistment*), and conducts the commit or rollback on the resource manager.

- The *resource manager* is responsible for managing resources and registering them with the transaction manager. An example of a resource manager is a driver for a relational database, a JMS resource, or a Java connector.

- The *resource* is persistent storage from which you read or write (a database, a message destination, etc.).

It is not the application's responsibility to preserve ACID properties. The application just decides to either commit or roll back the transaction, and the transaction manager prepares all the resources to successfully make it happen.

In Java EE, these components handle transactions through the Java Transaction API (JTA) specified by JSR 907. JTA defines a set of interfaces for the application to demarcate transactions' boundaries, and it also defines APIs to deal with the transaction manager. These interfaces are defined in the `javax.transaction` package, and some of them are described in Table 9-2.

Table 9-2. Main JTA Interfaces

Interface	Description
UserTransaction	Defines the methods that an application can use to control transaction boundaries programmatically. It is used by EJBs with bean-managed transaction (BMT) to begin, commit, or roll back a transaction (as discussed in the "Bean-Managed Transaction" section).
TransactionManager	Allows the EJB container to demarcate transaction boundaries on behalf of the EJB.
Transaction	Allows operations to be performed against the transaction in the target Transaction object.
XAResource	Serves as Java mapping of the industry standard X/Open XA interface (as discussed in the following section).

Distributed Transactions and XA

As you've just seen, a transaction using a single resource (shown previously in Figure 9-1) is called a local transaction. However, many enterprise applications use more than one resource. Returning to the example of the fund transfer, the savings account and the current account could be in separate databases. You would then need transaction management across several resources, or resources that are distributed across the network. Such enterprise-wide transactions require special coordination involving XA and Java Transaction Service (JTS).

Figure 9-2 shows an application that uses transaction demarcation across several resources. This means that, in the same unit of work, the application can persist data in a database and send a JMS message, for example.

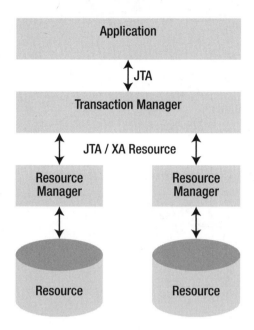

Figure 9-2. An XA transaction involving two resources

To have a reliable transaction across several resources, the transaction manager needs to use an XA resource manager interface. XA is a standard specified by the Open Group (`http://www.opengroup.org`) for distributed transaction processing (DTP) that preserves the ACID properties. It is supported by JTA and allows heterogeneous resource managers from different vendors to interoperate through a common interface. XA uses a two-phase commit (2pc) to ensure that all resources either commit or roll back any particular transaction simultaneously.

In our fund transfer example, suppose that the savings account is debited on a first database, and the transaction commits successfully. Then the current account is credited on a second database, but the transaction fails. We would have to go back to the first database and undo the committed changes. To avoid this data inconsistency problem, the two-phase commit performs an additional preparatory step before the final commit as shown in Figure 9-3. During phase 1, each resource manager is notified through a "prepare" command that a commit is about to be issued. This allows the resource managers to declare whether they can apply their changes or not. If they all indicate that they are prepared, the transaction is allowed to proceed, and all resource managers are asked to commit in the second phase.

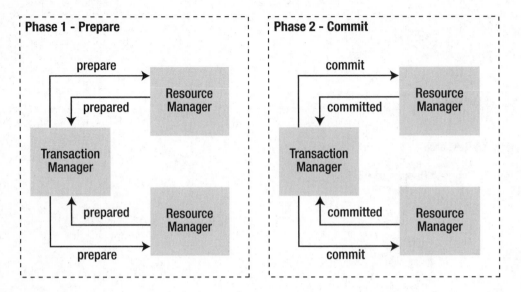

Figure 9-3. *Two-phase commit*

Most of the time, the resources are distributed across the network (see Figure 9-4). Such a system relies on JTS. JTS implements the Object Management Group (OMG) Object Transaction Service (OTS) specification, allowing transaction managers to participate in distributed transactions through Internet Inter-ORB Protocol (IIOP). Compared to Figure 9-2, where there is only one transaction manager, Figure 9-4 allows the propagation of distributed transactions using IIOP. This allows transactions to be distributed across different computers and different databases from different vendors. JTS is intended for vendors who provide the transaction system infrastructure. As an EJB developer, you don't have to worry about it; just use JTA, which interfaces with JTS at a higher level.

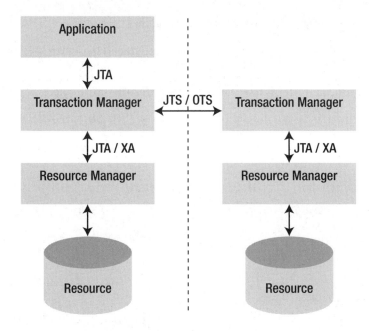

Figure 9-4. A distributed XA transaction

Transaction Support in EJB

When you develop business logic with EJBs, you don't have to worry about the internal structure of transaction managers or resource managers because JTA abstracts most of the underlying complexity. With EJBs, you can develop a transactional application very easily, leaving the container to implement the low-level transaction protocols, such as the two-phase commit or the transaction context propagation. An EJB container is a transaction manager that supports JTA as well as JTS to participate in distributed transactions involving other EJB containers and/or other transactional resources. In a typical Java EE application, session beans establish the boundaries of a transaction, call entities to interact with the database, or send JMS messages in a transaction context.

From its creation, the EJB model was designed to manage transactions. In fact, transactions are natural to EJBs, and by default each method is automatically wrapped in a transaction. This default behavior is known as a container-managed transaction (CMT), because transactions are managed by the EJB container (a.k.a. declarative transaction demarcation). You can also choose to manage transactions yourself using bean-managed transactions (BMTs), also called programmatic transaction demarcation. Transaction demarcation determines where transactions begin and end.

Container-Managed Transactions

When managing transactions declaratively, you delegate the demarcation policy to the container. You don't have to explicitly use JTA in your code (even if JTA is used underneath); you can leave the container to demarcate transaction boundaries by automatically beginning and committing transactions based on metadata. The EJB container provides transaction management services to session beans and MDBs (see Chapter 13 for more on MDBs).

In Chapter 7, you saw several examples of session beans, annotations, and interfaces, but never anything specific to transactions. Listing 9-1 shows the code of a stateless session bean using CMT. As you can see, there is no extra annotation added nor special interface to implement. EJBs are by nature transactional. With configuration by exception, all the transaction management defaults are applied (REQUIRED is the default transaction attribute as explained later in this section).

Listing 9-1. A Stateless Bean with CMT

```
@Stateless
public class ItemEJB {

    @PersistenceContext(unitName = "chapter09PU")
    private EntityManager em;
    @EJB
    private InventoryEJB inventory;

    public List<Book> findBooks() {
        Query query = em.createNamedQuery("findAllBooks");
        return query.getResultList();
    }

    public Book createBook(Book book) {
        em.persist(book);
        inventory.addItem(book);
        return book;
    }
}
```

You might ask what makes the code in Listing 9-1 transactional. The answer is the container. Figure 9-5 shows what happens when a client invokes the createBook() method. The client call is intercepted by the container, which checks immediately before invoking the method whether a transaction context is associated with the call. By default, if no transaction context is available, the container begins a new transaction before entering the method and then invokes the createBook() method. Once the method exits, the container automatically commits the transaction or rolls it back (if a particular type of exception is thrown, as you'll see later in the "Exception Handling" section).

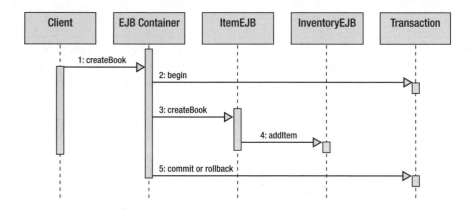

Figure 9-5. *The container handles the transaction.*

It's interesting to note in Listing 9-1 and Figure 9-5 that a business method of a bean (`ItemEJB.createBook()`) can be a client of a business method of another bean (`InventoryEJB.addItem()`).The default behavior is that whatever transaction context is used for `createBook()` (from the client or created by the container) is applied to `addItem()`. The final commit happens if both methods have returned successfully. This behavior can be changed using metadata (annotation or XML deployment descriptor). Depending on the transaction attribute you choose (`REQUIRED`, `REQUIRES_NEW`, `SUPPORTS`, `MANDATORY`, `NOT_SUPPORTED`, or `NEVER`), you can affect the way the container demarcates transactions: on a client invocation of a transactional method, the container uses the client's transaction, runs the method in a new transaction, runs the method with no transaction, or throws an exception. Table 9-3 defines the transaction attributes.

Table 9-3. *CMT Attributes*

Attribute	Description
REQUIRED	This attribute, the default value, means that a method must always be invoked within a transaction. The container creates a new transaction if the method is invoked from a nontransactional client. If the client has a transaction context, the business method runs within the client's transaction. You should use REQUIRED if you are making calls that should be managed in a transaction, but can't assume that the client is calling the method from a transaction context.
REQUIRES_NEW	The container always creates a new transaction before executing a method, regardless of whether the client is executed within a transaction. If the client is running within a transaction, the container suspends that transaction temporarily, creates a second one, commits it, and then resumes the first transaction. This means that the success or failure of the second transaction has no effect on the existing client transaction. You should use REQUIRES_NEW when you don't want a rollback to affect the client.

Continued

Attribute	Description
SUPPORTS	The EJB method inherits the client's transaction context. If a transaction context is available, it is used by the method; if not, the container invokes the method with no transaction context. You should use SUPPORTS when you have read-only access to the database table.
MANDATORY	The container requires a transaction before invoking the business method but should not create a new one. If the client has a transaction context, it is propagated; if not, a javax.ejb.EJBTransactionRequiredException is thrown.
NOT_SUPPORTED	The EJB method cannot be invoked in a transaction context. If the client has no transaction context, nothing happens; if it does, the container suspends the client's transaction, invokes the method, and then resumes the transaction when the method returns.
NEVER	The EJB method must not be invoked from a transactional client. If the client is running within a transaction context, the container throws a javax.ejb.EJBException.

Figure 9-6 illustrates all the possible behaviors that an EJB can have depending on the presence or not of a client's transaction context. For example, if the createBook() method doesn't have a transaction context (top part of the figure) and invokes addItem() with a MANDATORY attribute, an exception is thrown. The bottom part of Figure 9-6 shows the same combinations but with a client that has a transaction context.

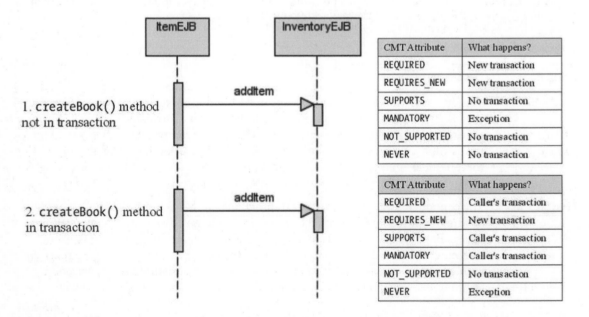

Figure 9-6. *Two calls made to InventoryEJB with different transaction policies*

To apply one of these six demarcation attributes to your session bean, you have to use the `@javax.ejb.TransactionAttribute` annotation or the deployment descriptor (setting the `<trans-attribute>` element in the `ejb-jar.xml`). This metadata can be applied either to individual methods or to the entire bean. If applied at the bean level, all business methods will inherit the bean's transaction attribute value. Listing 9-2 shows how the `ItemEJB` uses a `SUPPORT` transaction demarcation policy and overrides the `createBook()` method with `REQUIRED`.

Listing 9-2. A Stateless Bean with CMT

```
@Stateless
@TransactionAttribute(TransactionAttributeType.SUPPORTS)
public class ItemEJB {

    @PersistenceContext(unitName = "chapter09PU")
    private EntityManager em;
    @EJB
    private InventoryEJB inventory;

    public List<Book> findBooks() {
        Query query = em.createNamedQuery("findAllBooks");
        return query.getResultList();
    }

    @TransactionAttribute(TransactionAttributeType.REQUIRED)
    public Book createBook(Book book) {
        em.persist(book);
        inventory.addItem(book);
        return book;
    }
}
```

■ **Note** Client transaction context does not propagate with asynchronous method invocation. MDBs support only the `REQUIRED` and `NOT_SUPPORTED` attributes as explained in Chapter 13.

Marking a CMT for Rollback

You've seen that the EJB container demarcates transactions automatically and invokes begin, commit, and rollback operations on your behalf. But, as a developer, you might want to prevent the transaction from being committed if some error or business condition is encountered. It is important to stress that a CMT bean is not allowed to roll back the transaction explicitly. Instead, you need to use the EJB context (see the "Session Context" section in Chapter 7) to inform the container to roll back.

As you can see in Listing 9-3, the `InventoryEJB` has a `oneItemSold()` method that accesses the database through the persistence manager, and sends a JMS message to inform the shipping company that an item has been sold and should be delivered. If the inventory level is equal to zero (which means no more items are available), the method needs to explicitly roll back the transaction. To do so, the stateless bean first needs to obtain the `SessionContext` through dependency injection and then call its `setRollbackOnly()` method. Calling this method doesn't roll back the transaction immediately; instead, a flag is set for the container to do the actual rollback when it is time to end the transaction. Only session beans with container-managed transaction demarcation can use this method (BMT session beans roll back transactions directly, as shown in the "Bean-Managed Transactions" section).

Listing 9-3. *A Stateless Bean CMT Marks the Transaction for Rollback*

```
@Stateless
public class InventoryEJB {

    @PersistenceContext(unitName = "chapter09PU")
    private EntityManager em;
    @Resource
    private SessionContext ctx;

    public void oneItemSold(Item item) {
        item.decreaseAvailableStock();
        sendShippingMessage();

        if (inventoryLevel(item) == 0)
            ctx.setRollbackOnly();
    }
}
```

Similarly, a bean can call the `SessionContext.getRollbackOnly()` method, which returns a `boolean`, to determine whether the current transaction has been marked for rollback.

Another way to programmatically inform the container to roll back is through throwing specific types of exceptions.

Exception Handling

Exception handling in Java has been confusing since the creation of the language (as it involves both checked exceptions and unchecked exceptions). Associating transactions and exceptions in EJBs is also quite intricate. Before going any further, I just want to say that throwing an exception in a business method will not always mark the transaction for rollback. It depends on the type of exception or the metadata defining the exception. In fact, the EJB 3.1 specification outlines two types of exceptions:

- *Application exceptions*: Exceptions related to business logic handled by the EJB. For example, an application exception might be raised if invalid arguments are passed to a method, the inventory level is too low, or the credit card number is invalid. Throwing an application exception does not automatically result in marking the transaction for rollback. As detailed later in this section in Table 9-4, the container doesn't roll back when checked exceptions (which extend `java.lang.Exception`) are thrown, but it does for unchecked exceptions (which extend `RuntimeException`).

- *System exceptions*: Exceptions caused by system-level faults, such as JNDI errors, JVM errors, failure to acquire a database connection, and so on. A system exception must be a subclass of a `RuntimeException` or `java.rmi.RemoteException` (and therefore a subclass of `javax.ejb.EJBException`). Throwing a system exception results in marking the transaction for rollback.

With this definition, we know now that, if the container detects a system exception, such as an `ArithmeticException`, `ClassCastException`, `IllegalArgumentException`, or `NullPointerException`, it will roll back the transaction. Application exceptions depend on various factors. As an example, let's change the code from Listing 9-3 and use an application exception as shown in Listing 9-4.

Listing 9-4. A Stateless Bean Throwing an Application Exception

```
@Stateless
public class InventoryEJB {

  @PersistenceContext(unitName = "chapter09PU")
  private EntityManager em;

  public void oneItemSold(Item item) throws InventoryLevelTooLowException{
    item.decreaseAvailableStock();
    sendShippingMessage();

    if (inventoryLevel(item) == 0)
      throw new InventoryLevelTooLowException();
  }
}
```

`InventoryLevelTooLowException` is an application exception because it's related to the business logic of the `oneItemSold()` method. It is then a business concern to know whether you want to roll back the transaction or not. An application exception is one that extends from a checked or unchecked exception, and is annotated with `@javax.ejb.ApplicationException` (or the XML equivalent in the deployment descriptor). This annotation has a `rollback` element that can be set to `true` to explicitly roll back the transaction. Listing 9-5 shows the `InventoryLevelTooLowException` as an annotated checked exception.

Listing 9-5. An Application Exception with rollback = true

```
@ApplicationException(rollback = true)
public class InventoryLevelTooLowException extends Exception {

    public InventoryLevelTooLowException() {
    }

    public InventoryLevelTooLowException(String message) {
        super(message);
    }
}
```

If the `InventoryEJB` in Listing 9-4 throws the exception defined in Listing 9-5, it will mark the transaction for rollback, and the container will do the actual rollback when it is time to end the transaction. That's because the `InventoryLevelTooLowException` is annotated with `@ApplicationException(rollback = true)`. Table 9-4 shows all the possible combinations with application exceptions. The first line of the table could be interpreted as "If the application exception extends from `Exception` and has no `@ApplicationException` annotation, throwing it will not mark the transaction for rollback."

Table 9-4. *Combination of Application Exceptions*

Extends from	@ApplicationException	The transaction is marked for rollback
Exception	No annotation	No
Exception	rollback = true	Yes
Exception	rollback = false	No
RuntimeException	No annotation	Yes
RuntimeException	rollback = true	Yes
RuntimeException	rollback = false	No

Bean-Managed Transactions

With CMT, you leave the container to do the transaction demarcation just by specifying a transaction attribute and using the session context or exceptions to mark a transaction for rollback. In some cases, the declarative CMT may not provide the demarcation granularity that you require (for example, a method cannot generate more than one transaction). To address this, EJBs offer a programmatic way to manage transaction demarcations with BMT. BMT allows you to explicitly manage transaction boundaries (begin, commit, rollback) using JTA.

To turn off the default CMT demarcation and switch to BMT mode, a bean simply has to use the `@javax.ejb.TransactionManagement` annotation (or the XML equivalent in the `ejb-jar.xml` file) as follows:

```
@Stateless
@TransactionManagement(TransactionManagementType.BEAN)
public class ItemEJB {
    ...
}
```

With BMT demarcation, the application requests the transaction, and the EJB container creates the physical transaction and takes care of a few low-level details. Also, it does not propagate transactions from one BMT to another.

The main interface used to carry out BMT is `javax.transaction.UserTransaction`. It allows the bean to demarcate a transaction, get its status, set a timeout, and so on. The `UserTransaction` is instantiated by the EJB container and made available through dependency injection, JNDI lookup, or the `SessionContext` (with the `SessionContext.getUserTransaction()` method). The API is described in Table 9-5.

Table 9-5. Methods of the javax.transaction.UserTransaction Interface

Interface	Description
Begin	Begins a new transaction and associates it with the current thread
Commit	Commits the transaction attached to the current thread
Rollback	Rolls back the transaction attached to the current thread
setRollbackOnly	Marks the current transaction for rollback
getStatus	Obtains the status of the current transaction
setTransactionTimeout	Modifies the timeout for the current transactions

Listing 9-6 shows how to develop a BMT bean. First of all, we get a reference of the UserTransaction using injection through the @Resource annotation. The oneItemSold() method begins the transaction, does some business processing, and then, depending on some business logic, commits or rolls back the transaction. Notice also that the transaction is marked for rollback in the catch block (I've simplified exception handling for better readability).

Listing 9-6. A Stateless Bean with BMT

```
@Stateless
@TransactionManagement(TransactionManagementType.BEAN)
public class InventoryEJB {

    @PersistenceContext(unitName = "chapter09PU")
    private EntityManager em;
    @Resource
    private UserTransaction ut;

    public void oneItemSold(Item item) {
        try {
            ut.begin();

            item.decreaseAvailableStock();
            sendShippingMessage();

            if (inventoryLevel(item) == 0)
                ut.rollback();
            else
                ut.commit();

        } catch (Exception e) {
            ut.rollback();
        }
        sendInventoryAlert();
    }
}
```

The difference with the CMT code shown in Listing 9-3 is that with CMT the container starts the transaction before the method execution and commits it immediately after. With the BMT code shown in Listing 9-6, you manually define transaction boundaries inside the method itself.

Security

Securing applications is (or should be) a primary concern for companies. It can go from securing a network, to encrypting data transfer, to granting users certain permissions on a system. In our day-to-day Internet browsing, we cross many web sites where we need to enter a username and a password to have access to certain parts of an application. Security has become a common necessity in the Web, and, consequently, Java EE has defined several mechanisms to secure applications.

Various concepts have to be understood when securing a Java EE application. One of them is the way users are bound to a principal and can have several roles. Each of these roles will give permission to a set of resources. But to have an identity in the security domain, a user needs to be authenticated. Then the platform will control the access by authorizing resources depending on the user's role.

Principals and Roles

Principals and roles are an important notion in software security. A *principal* represents a user who has been authenticated by an authentication system (e.g., by verifying a username and password in the database). You can then organize principals into groups, known as *roles*, allowing principals to share a common set of permissions (e.g., having access to the billing system or being able to send messages to a workflow).

Figure 9-7 shows you how users can be represented in a secure system. As you can see, a user, once authenticated, is bound to a principal. The principal has a unique identifier and can be linked to several roles. For example, the user Frank has a principal (identified by a user ID, for example) bound to the `employee` and `admin` roles.

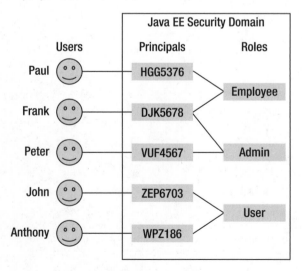

Figure 9-7. Principals and roles

Authentication and Authorization

Securing an application involves two functions: authentication and authorization. Authentication is the process of verifying the user's identity (user ID and password, OpenID, fingerprint check, and so on) against an authentication system, and assigning a principal to the user. Authorization is the process of determining whether a principal (an authenticated user) has access to a particular resource (e.g., a book) or a function (e.g., removing a book). Depending on his role, the user can have access to all resources, none, or a subset.

Figure 9-8 shows a common security scenario. A user is asked to enter her username and password through a client interface (web or Swing). Her credentials are checked using Java Authentication and Authorization Service (JAAS) against an underlying authentication system. If the authentication succeeds, the user is given a principal. At this point, the principal is associated with one or more roles. When the user accesses a secured EJB, the principal is passed transparently to the EJB, which uses it to determine whether the caller's role is allowed to access the method she is trying to execute.

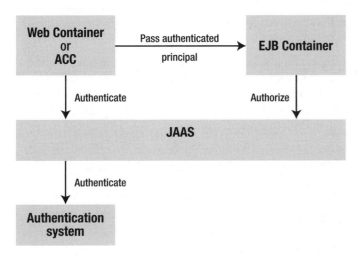

Figure 9-8. Common security scenario using JAAS

As shown in Figure 9-8, Java EE security is largely based on the JAAS API. In fact, JAAS is the API used internally by the web and EJB tier to perform authorization and authentication. It also accesses the underlying authentication systems such as the Lightweight Directory Access Protocol (LDAP), Microsoft Active Directory, and so on.

Security Support in EJB

The primary purpose of the EJB security model is to control access to business code. As you've just seen, authentication is handled by the web tier (or a client application); the principal and its roles are then passed to the EJB tier, and the EJB checks whether the authenticated user is allowed to access a method based on its role. Like transaction management, authorization can be done either in a declarative or a programmatic way.

With declarative authorization, access control is made by the EJB container. With programmatic authorization, access control is made in the code using the JAAS API.

Declarative Security

The declarative security policy can be defined in the bean using annotations or in the XML deployment descriptor. Declarative authorization involves declaring roles, assigning permission to methods (or to the entire bean), or changing temporarily a security identity. These controls are made by the annotations described in Table 9-6. Each annotation can be used on the bean and/or on the method.

Table 9-6. Security Annotations

Annotation	Bean	Method	Description
@PermitAll	X	X	Indicates that the given method (or the entire bean) is accessible by everyone (all roles are permitted)
@DenyAll	X	X	Indicates that no role is permitted to execute the specified method or all methods of the bean (all roles are denied). This can be useful if you want to deny access to a method in a certain environment (e.g., the method launchNuclearWar() should only be allowed in production but not in a test environment)
@RolesAllowed	X	X	Indicates that a list of roles is allowed to execute the given method (or the entire bean)
@DeclareRoles	X		Defines roles for security checking
@RunAs	X		Temporarily assigns a new role to a principal

■ **Note** The @TransactionManagement and @TransactionAttribute annotations that you saw at the beginning of this chapter are defined in the javax.ejb package in the EJB 3.1 specification (JSR 318). Security annotations (@RolesAllowed, @DenyAll, etc.) are part of the Common Annotations 1.1 specification (JSR 250) and come from the javax.annotation.security package.

The @RolesAllowed annotation is used to authorize a list of roles to access a method. It can be applied to a particular method or to the entire bean (then all business methods will inherit the bean's role access). This annotation can take either a single String (only one role can access the method) or an array of String (any of the roles can access the method). The @DeclareRoles annotation that you'll see later in this section can be used to declare other roles.

Listing 9-7 shows the ItemEJB using the @RolesAllowed annotation at the bean and method levels. This code indicates that any method is accessible by a principal associated with one of the following roles: user, employee, or admin. The deleteBook() method overrides the class-level settings and is only allowing access to the admin role.

Listing 9-7. A Stateless Bean Allowing Certain Roles

```
@Stateless
@RolesAllowed({"user", "employee", "admin"})
public class ItemEJB {

    @PersistenceContext(unitName = "chapter09PU")
    private EntityManager em;

    public Book findBookById(Long id) {
        return em.find(Book.class, id);
    }

    public Book createBook(Book book) {
        em.persist(book);
        return book;
    }

    @RolesAllowed("admin")
    public void deleteBook(Book book) {
        em.remove(em.merge(book));
    }
}
```

@RolesAllowed defines a list of roles that are allowed to access a method. The @PermitAll and @DenyAll annotations are applied for any role. So, you can use the @PermitAll annotation to mark an EJB, or a method, to be invoked by any role. Conversely, the @DenyAll forbids any role to have access to a method.

As you can see in Listing 9-8, because the findBookById() method is annotated with @PermitAll, it can now be accessible to any role, not just user, employee, and admin. On the other hand, the findConfidentialBook() method is not accessible at all (@DenyAll).

Listing 9-8. A Stateless Bean Using @PermitAll and @DenyAll

```
@Stateless
@RolesAllowed({"user", "employee", "admin"})
public class ItemEJB {

    @PersistenceContext(unitName = "chapter09PU")
    private EntityManager em;

    @PermitAll
    public Book findBookById(Long id) {
        return em.find(Book.class, id);
    }
```

```
    public Book createBook(Book book) {
        em.persist(book);
        return book;
    }

    @RolesAllowed("admin")
    public void deleteBook(Book book) {
        em.remove(em.merge(book));
    }

    @DenyAll
    public Book findConfidentialBook(Long secureId){
        return em.find(ConfidentialBook.class, secureId);
    }
}
```

The `@DeclareRoles` annotation is slightly different as it doesn't permit or deny any access. It declares roles for the entire application. When the EJB in Listing 9-8 is deployed, the container will automatically declare the `user`, `employee`, and `admin` roles by inspecting the `@RolesAllowed` annotation. But you might want to declare other roles in the security domain for the entire application (not just for a single EJB) through the `@DeclareRoles` annotation. This annotation, which only applies at the class level, takes an array of roles and declares them in the security domain. In fact, you declare security roles using either of these two annotations or a combination of both. If both annotations are used, the aggregation of the roles in `@DeclareRoles` and `@RolesAllowed` are declared. We usually declare roles for the entire enterprise application, so in this case it makes more sense to declare roles in the deployment descriptor than with the `@DeclareRoles` annotation.

When the `ItemEJB` in Listing 9-9 is deployed, the five roles `HR`, `salesDpt`, `user`, `employee`, and `admin` are declared. Then, with the `@RolesAllowed` annotation, certain of these roles are given access to certain methods (as previously explained).

Listing 9-9. A Stateless Bean Declaring Roles

```
@Stateless
@DeclareRoles({"HR", "salesDpt"})
@RolesAllowed({"user", "employee", "admin"})
public class ItemEJB {

    @PersistenceContext(unitName = "chapter09PU")
    private EntityManager em;

    public Book findBookById(Long id) {
        return em.find(Book.class, id);
    }

    public Book createBook(Book book) {
        em.persist(book);
        return book;
    }
```

```
@RolesAllowed("admin")
public void deleteBook(Book book) {
    em.remove(em.merge(book));
}
}
```

The last annotation, @RunAs, is handy if you need to temporarily assign a new role to the existing principal. You might need to do this, for example, if you're invoking another EJB within your method, but the other EJB requires a different role.

For example, the ItemEJB in Listing 9-10 authorizes access to the user, employee, and admin role. When one of these roles accesses a method, the method is run with the temporary inventoryDpt role (@RunAs("inventoryDpt")). This means that, when the createBook() method is executed, the InventoryEJB.addItem() method will be invoked with an inventoryDpt role.

Listing 9-10. A Stateless Bean Running as a Different Role

```
@Stateless
@RolesAllowed({"user", "employee", "admin"})
@RunAs("inventoryDpt")
public class ItemEJB {

    @PersistenceContext(unitName = "chapter09PU")
    private EntityManager em;
    @EJB
    private InventoryEJB inventory;

    public List<Book> findBooks() {
        Query query = em.createNamedQuery("findAllBooks");
        return query.getResultList();
    }

    public Book createBook(Book book) {
        em.persist(book);
        inventory.addItem(book);
        return book;
    }
}
```

As you can see, declarative security gives you easy access to a powerful authentication policy. But what if you need to provide security settings to an individual, or apply some business logic based on the current principal's role? This is where programmatic security comes into play.

Programmatic Security

Declarative security covers most security cases needed by an application. But sometimes you need means of a finer grain for authorizing access (allowing a block of code instead of the entire method, permitting or denying access to an individual, etc.). You can use programmatic authorization to selectively permit or block access to a role or a principal. That's because you have direct access to the

JAAS `java.security.Principal` interface, as well as the EJB context to check the principal's role in the code.

The following methods related to security are defined in the `SessionContext` interface:

- `isCallerInRole()`: This method returns a `boolean` and tests whether the caller has a given security role.

- `getCallerPrincipal()`: This method returns the `java.security.Principal` that identifies the caller.

To show how to use these methods, let's take a look at an example. The `ItemEJB` in Listing 9-11 doesn't use any declarative security but still needs to do some kind of checking programmatically. First of all, the bean needs to get a reference to its context (using the `@Resource` annotation). With this context, the `deleteBook()` method can check whether the caller has an `admin` role or not. If it doesn't, it throws a `java.lang.SecurityException` to notify the user about the authorization violation. The `createBook()` method does some business logic using the roles and the principal. Notice that the `getCallerPrincipal()` method returns a `Principal` object, which has a name. The method checks whether the principal's name is `paul`, and then sets the `special user` value to the book entity.

Listing 9-11. A Bean Using Programmatic Security

```
@Stateless
public class ItemEJB {

  @PersistenceContext(unitName = "chapter09PU")
  private EntityManager em;
  @Resource
  private SessionContext ctx;

  public Book findBookById(Long id) {
    return em.find(Book.class, id);
  }

  public void deleteBook(Book book) {
    if (!ctx.isCallerInRole("admin"))
      throw new SecurityException("Only admins are allowed");

    em.remove(em.merge(book));
  }

  public Book createBook(Book book) {
    if (ctx.isCallerInRole("employee") && !ctx.isCallerInRole("admin")){
      book.setCreatedBy("employee only");
    } else if (ctx.getCallerPrincipal().getName().equals("paul")){
      book.setCreatedBy("special user");
    }
    em.persist(book);
    return book;
  }
}
```

Summary

In this last chapter related to EJBs, I have shown you how to handle transaction and security management. These two very important services can be defined either declaratively or programmatically.

Transactions allow the business tier to keep the data in an accurate state even when accessed concurrently by several applications. They follow the ACID properties and can be distributed across several resources (databases, JMS destinations, web services, etc.). CMT allows you to easily customize the EJB container behavior in terms of transaction demarcation. You can influence this behavior by marking a transaction for rollback through the EJB context or exceptions. You can always use BMT if you need finer control of the transaction demarcation directly using JTA.

For security, you have to bear in mind that the business tier doesn't authenticate users, it authorizes roles to access methods. Declarative security is done through a relatively small number of annotations and allows you to cover most cases an enterprise application is likely to need. Again, you can switch to programmatic security and manipulate the JAAS API.

The next three chapters will explain how to develop a presentation layer using JSF. JSF pages use managed beans to invoke business methods on EJB.

CHAPTER 10

■■■

JavaServer Faces

If information coming from the back end is to be displayed graphically, a user interface has to be added. These can be of various types: desktop applications, web applications running in a browser, or mobile applications running in a portable device that displays a graphical interface and interacts with the end user. Chapter 10 through Chapter 12 will focus on web user interfaces.

The World Wide Web (WWW) started as a mechanism for sharing documents written in Hypertext Markup Language (HTML). Hypertext Transfer Protocol (HTTP) was used to serve these documents, which were mostly static (in that their content didn't change much over time). Static pages are composed of pure HTML, optionally with some static graphics (e.g., JPG, PNG). Dynamic pages are, to some extent, assembled in real time with data computed from user input.

Today we live in an Internet world where static pages are not enough. With our transactional back end processing thousands of requests, and communicating with heterogeneous systems through web services, we need a presentation layer to interact with end users, preferably one that runs in a browser. Browsers are everywhere, and user interfaces are richer, more dynamic, and easier to use. Rich Internet Applications (RIAs) are gaining in popularity as users expect more from their browsing experience. They need to consult catalogs of books and CDs online, but they also want to access e-mail and documents, receive e-mail notification, or have parts of their browser page selectively refreshed when a server event occurs. Add to that the Web 2.0 philosophy whereby people can share any kind of information with groups of friends and interact with each other, and the result is web interfaces that are getting more and more complex to develop.

To create dynamic content, you need to parse HTTP requests, understand what they mean, and create responses in an appropriate format for the browser to display. That's what the servlet API simplified by providing an object-oriented view of the HTTP world (`HttpRequest`, `HttpResponse`, etc.). The servlet model was too low level, however; JavaServer Pages (JSP) simplified the creation of dynamic pages. Behind the scenes, a JSP is a servlet, except that it's mostly written using HTML—but still with a bit of Java for processing.

In response to some limitations of JSP, JavaServer Faces (JSF, or simply Faces) was created with a new model in mind: bringing graphical components to the Web. Inspired by the Swing component model, and other GUI frameworks, JSF allows developers to think in terms of components, events, managed beans, and their interactions, instead of requests, responses, and markup language. Its goal is to make web development faster and easier by supporting user interface components (such as text boxes, list boxes, tabbed panes, and data grids) in a rapid application development (RAD) approach.

This chapter introduces JSF, and Chapters 11 and 12 show different technologies bundled with Java EE 6 to create web interfaces (JSP, EL, and JSTL) and will mostly focus on JSF 2.0, which is more powerful and the preferred technology to create modern web applications.

Understanding JSF

JSF's architecture is easy to understand (see Figure 10-1), if you are familiar with web frameworks. JSF applications are standard web applications that intercept HTTP via the Faces servlet and produce HTML. Under the hood, the architecture allows you to plug in any page declaration language (PDL) or view declaration language (VDL), render it for different devices (web browser, portable devices, etc.), and create pages using events, listeners, and components, à la Swing. Swing is a Java widget toolkit that has been part of Java SE since release 1.2. It is a GUI framework to create desktop applications (not web applications) using graphical components and the event-listener model to process user inputs. JSF also brings a standard set of UI widgets (buttons, hyperlinks, check boxes, text fields, etc.) and allows easy plug-in of third-party components. On a very high level, the JSF architecture is represented in Figure 10-1.

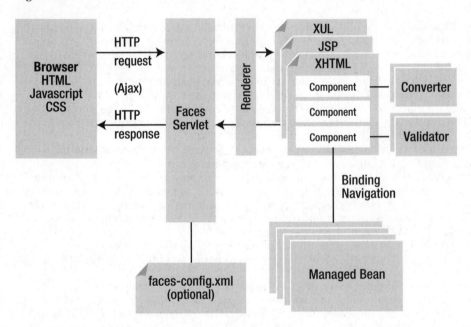

Figure 10-1. *JSF architecture*

This figure represents several important pieces of JSF that make its architecture rich and flexible:

- `FacesServlet` *and* `faces-config.xml`: `FacesServlet` is the main servlet for the application and can optionally be configured by a `faces-config.xml` descriptor file.

- *Pages and components*: JSF allows multiple PDLs such as JSP or Facelets (which is the default and recommended PDL as of JSF 2.0).

- *Renderers*: These are responsible for displaying a component and translating a user's input into the component property values.

- *Converters*: These convert a component's value (Date, Boolean, etc.) to and from markup values (String).

- *Validators*: These are responsible for ensuring that the value entered by a user is valid.

- *Managed bean and navigation*: The business logic is made in managed beans, which also control the navigation between pages.

- *Ajax support*: JSF 2.0 comes with built-in support for Ajax as explained in Chapter 12.

FacesServlet and faces-config.xml

Most of the web frameworks use the Model-View-Controller (MVC) design pattern, as does JSF. The MVC pattern is used to decouple the view (the page) and the model (the data to be displayed in the view). The controller handles user actions that might result in changes in the model and updates to the views. In JSF, this controller is a servlet called FacesServlet. All user requests go through the FacesServlet, which examines the request and calls various actions on the model using managed beans.

This servlet is internal and part of JSF. The only way it can be configured is by using external metadata. Up to JSF 1.2, the only source of configuration was the faces-config.xml file. Today, with JSF 2.0, this file is optional, and most metadata can be defined through annotations (on managed beans, converters, components, renderers, and validators).

Pages and Components

The JSF framework has to send a page to the client's output device (a browser, for example) and requires some sort of display technology. This display technology is the PDL (aka VDL). A JSF application is free to use several technologies for its PDL such as JSP or Facelets. A JSF 2.0 implementation that claims compliance with the specification must include a complete JSP implementation. JSP was the default PDL in JSF 1.1 and JSF 1.2, but Facelets is preferred for JSF 2.0.

Both JSP and Facelets pages are made up of a tree of components (also called widgets or controls) that provide specific functionality for interacting with an end user (text field, button, list box, etc.). JSF has a standard set of components and allows you to easily create your own. The page goes through a complex life cycle to manage this tree of components (initialization, events, rendering, etc.).

The code in Listing 10-1 is a Facelets XHTML page that uses JSF tags (xmlns:h="http://java.sun.com/jsf/html") to display a form with two input fields (the ISBN and the title of a book) and a button. This page is composed of several JSF components. Some of them have no visual appearance, like the ones used to declare the header (<h:head>), the body (<h:body>), or the form (<h:form>). Others are visual and represent a label (<h:outputLabel>), a text field (<h:inputText>), or a button (<h:commandButton>). Notice that pure HTML tags can also be mixed in the page (<table>, <tr>, <hr/>, etc.).

Listing 10-1. Snippet of an XHTML Page

```
<!DOCTYPE html PUBLIC "-//W3C//DTD XHTML 1.0 Transitional//EN"
         "http://www.w3.org/TR/xhtml1/DTD/xhtml1-transitional.dtd">
<html xmlns="http://www.w3.org/1999/xhtml"
      xmlns:h="http://java.sun.com/jsf/html">
<h:head>
    <title>Creates a new book</title>
</h:head>
<h:body>
<h1>Create a new book</h1>
<hr/>
<h:form>
  <table border="0">

    <tr>
        <td><h:outputLabel value="ISBN : "/></td>
        <td><h:inputText value="#{bookController.book.isbn}"/></td>
    <tr>

    </tr>
        <td><h:outputLabel value="Title :"/> </td>
        <td><h:inputText value="#{bookController.book.title}"/></td>
    </tr>

  </table>
  <h:commandButton value="Create a book" ↪
        action="#{bookController.doCreateBook}" styleClass="submit"/>

</h:form>
<hr/>
<i>APress - Beginning Java EE 6</i>
</h:body>
</html>
```

Renderer

JSF supports two programming models for displaying components: the direct implementation and the delegated implementation. When the direct model is used, components must decode themselves from, and encode themselves to, a graphical representation. When the delegated model is used, these operations are delegated to a renderer. This allows a component to be independent of a rendering technology (browser, portable device, etc.) and to have several graphical representations.

A renderer is responsible for displaying a component and translating user input into the component's value. Think of it as a translator between the client and the server: it decodes the user request to set values to the component, and encodes the response to create a representation of a component that the client understands and can display.

Renderers are organized into render kits, which focus on a specific type of output. To ensure application portability, JSF includes support for a standard render kit and associated renderers for HTML 4.01. JSF implementations can then create their own render kit to generate Wireless Markup Language (WML), Scalable Vector Graphics (SVGs), and so on.

Converters and Validators

Once the page is rendered, the user can interact with it to enter data. As there are no type constraints, a renderer cannot know beforehand how to display the object. This is where converters come in: they translate an object (`Integer`, `Date`, `Enum`, `Boolean`, etc.) to a string for display, and from an input string back into an object. JSF comes with a set of converters for common types (in the `javax.faces.convert` package), but you can develop your own or incorporate third-party types.

Sometimes this data also has to be validated before being processed in the back end. Validators are responsible for ensuring that the value entered by a user is acceptable. One or more validators can be associated with a single component. JSF comes with a few validators (`LengthValidator`, `RegexValidator`, etc.) and allows you to create your own using annotated classes. When there's a conversion or validation error, a message is sent back to the response to be displayed.

Managed Beans and Navigation

All of the concepts so far have been related to a single page: what is a page, what is a component, how are they rendered, converted, and validated. Web applications are made up of multiple pages and need to perform business logic (by calling an EJB layer, for example). Going from one page to another, invoking EJBs, and synchronizing data with components is handled by managed beans.

A managed bean is a specialized Java class that synchronizes values with components, processes business logic, and handles navigation between pages. You associate a component with a specific managed bean property or action using the Expression Language (EL). Using some snippets of code from the previous example:

```
<h:inputText value="#{bookController.book.isbn}"/>
<h:commandButton value="Create" action="#{bookController.doCreateBook}"/>
```

The first line of code hooks up the input text's value directly to the `book.isbn` property of a managed bean called `bookController`. The value of the input text is synchronized with the `book.isbn` property of the managed bean.

A managed bean also handles events. The second line of code shows a submit button associated with an action. When the submit button is clicked, it triggers an event to the managed bean where an event listener method is executed (here the `doCreateBook()` method).

Listing 10-2 shows the `BookController` managed bean. This Java class is annotated with `@ManagedBean`, and it has a property, `book`, that is synchronized with the component's value of the page. The `doCreateBook()` method invokes a stateless EJB and then returns a string that allows navigation between pages.

Listing 10-2. BookController Managed Bean

```
@ManagedBean
public class BookController {

    @EJB
    private BookEJB bookEJB;

    private Book book = new Book();

    public String doCreateBook() {
        book = bookEJB.createBook(book);
        return "listBooks.xhtml";
    }

    // Getters, setters
}
```

■ **Note** A managed bean is the class that acts as a controller, navigates from one page to another, calls EJBs, and so on. Backing beans are the objects that hold properties bound to components. In this example, we could say that BookController is a managed bean and the book attribute the backing bean.

Ajax Support

A web application must provide a rich and responsive interface. This reactivity can be obtained by updating only small portions of the page in an asynchronous manner, which is what Ajax is all about. Previous versions of JSF didn't offer any out-of-the-box solution, so third-party libraries such as a4jsf filled this gap. With JSF 2.0, Ajax support has been added in the form of a JavaScript library (jsf.js) defined in the specification and a <f:ajax> tag. For example, you can use the <f:ajax> tag to submit a form in an asynchronous way as shown in the following code:

```
<h:commandButton value="Create a book" action="#{bookController.doCreateBook}">
    <f:ajax execute="@form" render=":booklist"/>
</h:commandButton>
```

Don't worry if you don't understand this code; an entire section is dedicated to Ajax in Chapter 12.

Web Interface Specifications Overview

Web development in Java started in 1996 with the servlet API, a very rudimentary way to create dynamic web content. You had to manipulate a low-level HTTP API (HttpServletRequest, HttpServletResponse, HttpSession, etc.) to display HTML tags inside your Java code. JSPs arrived in 1999 and provided a higher level of abstraction than servlets. In 2004, the first version of JSF arrived, with version 1.2 becoming part of Java EE 5 in 2006. JSF 2.0 is now bundled with Java EE 6.

A Brief History of Web Interfaces

At first, web pages were static. A user would request a resource (a web page, an image, a video, etc.), and the server would return it; simple, but very limited. With the growth of commercial activity on the Web, companies had to deliver dynamic content to their customers. The first solution for creating dynamic content was the Common Gateway Interface (CGI). By using HTML pages and CGI scripts written in any number of languages (from Perl to Visual Basic), an application could access databases and serve dynamic content, but it was clear that CGI was too low level (you had to handle HTTP headers, call HTTP commands, etc.) and needed to be improved.

In 1995, a new language called Java was released with a platform-independent user interface API called Abstract Window Toolkit (AWT). Later on, in Java SE 1.2, AWT, which relies on the operating system's user interface module, was superseded by the Swing API (which draws its own widgets by using Java 2D). During these early days of Java, Netscape's Navigator browser offered support for this new language, which opened the era of applets. *Applets* are applications that run on the client side, inside a browser. This allowed developers to write applications in AWT or Swing and embed them on a web page. However, applets never really took off. Netscape also created a scripting language called JavaScript that executes directly in the browser. Despite some incompatibilities between browsers, JavaScript is still heavily used today and is a powerful way to create dynamic web applications.

After the failure of applets to become widely adopted, Sun introduced servlets as a way to have thin, dynamic web clients. Servlets were an alternative to CGI scripts because they would offer a higher-level library for handling HTTP, had full access to the Java API (allowing database access, remote invocation, etc.), and could create HTML as a response to be displayed for the user.

Sun released JSP in 1999 as an enhancement of the servlet model. But, because JSPs were mixing Java and HTML code, in 2001 an open source framework arrived and opened doors to a new approach: Struts. This extended the servlet API and encouraged developers to adopt an MVC architecture. Recent history is full of other web frameworks, each trying to fill the gaps of the last (Tapestry, Wicket, WebWork, DWR, Spring MVC, etc.). Today, JSF 2.0 is the standard web framework in Java EE 6. It competes with Struts and Tapestry within the Java space. Rails and Grails compete with JSF overall, in the sense that Java competes with Ruby or Groovy. Google Web Toolkit (GWT), Flex, and JavaFX can be complementary to JSF.

JSP 2.2, EL 2.2, and JSTL 1.2

Architecturally, JSPs are a high-level abstraction of servlets and were implemented as an extension of Servlet 2.1. JSP 1.2 and Servlet 2.3 were specified together in JSR 53. At the same time, the JSP Standard Tag Library (JSTL) was specified in JSR 52.

Since 2002, the JSP 2.0 specification has evolved separately from servlets in JSR 152. In 2006, JSP 2.1 was part of Java EE 5 and facilitated the integration between JSF and JSP by introducing a unified EL. With Java EE 6, both JSP and EL specifications have been updated to a 2.2 version. One of the major changes is the possibility of invoking a method with EL (instead of just properties).

JSF 2.0

JSF is a specification published by the Java Community Process (JCP) and was created in 2001 as JSR 127. In 2004, a 1.1 maintenance version was released. Only in 2006 was JSF 1.2 introduced into Java EE as

JSR 252 (with Java EE 5). The biggest challenge in this version was to preserve backward compatibility as well as integrate JSP with a unified EL. Despite these efforts, JSF and JSP didn't fit well, so other frameworks such as Facelets were introduced as alternatives to JSPs.

JSF 2.0 is a major release evolving in JSR 314 and is the preferred choice for web development in Java EE 6 (JSP is still maintained in Java EE 6, but no major improvements have been made). JSF 2.0 was inspired by many open source web frameworks and today brings many new features.

What's New in JSF 2.0

With many new features, JSF 2.0 is an evolution from 1.2, but it's also a step forward—for example, in terms of PDL, where Facelets is preferred to JSP. New features of JSF 2.0 include the following:

- An alternative viewing technology to JSP based on Facelets

- Easier navigation between pages with implicit and conditional navigation

- JSF has been using POST HTTP requests intensively; this new release brings back GET requests as a first-class citizen (allowing users to bookmark pages)

- A new resource-handling mechanism (for images, CSS, JavaScript files, and so on)

- Additional scopes (view scope, flash and component scope)

- Easy development with annotations for managed beans, renderers, converters, validators, and so on

- Reducing XML configuration by exploiting annotations and configuration by exception (`faces-config.xml` is optional)

- Ajax support

- Better error handling (provides information such as line numbers and not just a stack trace)

- Easy component development

Reference Implementation

Mojarra, named after a fish that is found on the South American and Caribbean coast, is the open source reference implementation of JSF 2.0. Mojarra, available in the GlassFish V3 update center, allows development of JSF 2.0 web applications invoking an EJB 3.1 business tier and a JPA 2.0 persistence tier. It is used in the example presented next.

Putting It All Together

Using this information, you can write a small web application consisting of two web pages: one that displays a form, letting you create a book (`newBook.xhtml`), and the other listing all books available in the database (`listBooks.xhtml`). These two pages use the `BookController` managed bean to store the necessary properties and for navigation. Using persistence with JPA and business logic with EJB, everything can be plugged together. The managed bean delegates all the business logic to the BookEJB, which contains two methods: one to persist a book into a database (createBook()) and another to retrieve the books (findBooks()). This stateless session bean uses the EntityManager API to manipulate a Book entity. The navigation is quite simple: once a book is created, the list is shown. A link on the list page allows you to go back to the newBook.xhtml page and create another book.

Figure 10-2 shows the interacting components in this web application. They are packaged in a war file, deployed in a running instance of GlassFish and a live Derby database.

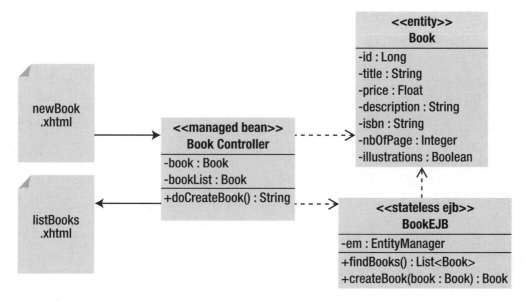

Figure 10-2. Pages and classes involved in the web application

This web application follows the Maven directory structure, so classes, files, and web pages have to be placed in the following directories:

- src/main/java: Contains the Book entity, the BookEJB, and the BookController managed bean

- src/main/resources: Contains the persistence.xml file used to map the entity in the database

- src/main/webapp: Contains the two web pages newBook.xhtml and listBooks.xhtml

- src/main/webapp/WEB-INF: Contains the web.xml file used to declare the FacesServlet

- pom.xml: Represents the Maven Project Object Model (POM) describing the project, its dependencies, and plug-ins

Writing the Book Entity

I will not go into too much detail about Listing 10-3, as you should by now understand the code of the Book entity. Despite the mapping annotations, notice the named query, findAllBooks, that retrieves books from the database.

Listing 10-3. A Book Entity with a Named Query

```
@Entity
@NamedQuery(name = "findAllBooks", query = "SELECT b FROM Book b")
public class Book {

    @Id @GeneratedValue
    private Long id;
    @Column(nullable = false)
    private String title;
    private Float price;
    @Column(length = 2000)
    private String description;
    private String isbn;
    private Integer nbOfPage;
    private Boolean illustrations;

    // Constructors, getters, setters
}
```

As you know, this entity also has to be packaged with a persistence.xml file, but in the interests of simplicity I won't show it here.

Writing the BookEJB

Listing 10-4 represents a stateless session bean that exposes a no-interface view. This means that the client (i.e., the managed bean) doesn't need an interface (local or remote) and can directly invoke the EJB. This EJB gets injected with a reference to an entity manager, with which it persists a Book entity (createBook() method), and retrieves all the books from the database (using the findAllBooks named query). No deployment descriptor is needed for this EJB.

Listing 10-4. A Stateless EJB That Creates and Retrieves Books

```
@Stateless
public class BookEJB {

    @PersistenceContext(unitName = "chapter10PU")
    private EntityManager em;

    public List<Book> findBooks() {
        TypedQuery<Book> query = em.createNamedQuery("findAllBooks", Book.class);
        return query.getResultList();
    }
}
```

```
    public Book createBook(Book book) {
        em.persist(book);
        return book;
    }
}
```

Writing the BookController Managed Bean

One of the roles of a managed bean is to interact with other layers of the application (the EJB layer, for example) or perform validation. The BookController in Listing 10-5 is a managed bean because it is annotated with @ManagedBean. The second annotation, @RequestScoped, defines the life duration of the bean; it lasts for the duration of the request (note that there are other scopes related to other durations such as application, session and view scope). This managed bean contains two attributes that will be used by the pages:

- bookList is the list of books retrieved from the database to be displayed in the listBooks.xhtml page.

- book is the object that will get mapped to the form (newBook.xhtml page) and persisted to the database.

All the business processing (creating and retrieving books) is done through the BookEJB. The managed bean gets injected with a reference to the EJB using the @EJB annotation and has one method that will get invoked by the pages:

- doCreateBook(): This method allows book creation by invoking the stateless EJB and passing the book attribute. It then invokes the EJB again to get all the books from the database. This list is stored in the bookList attribute of the managed bean. Then the method returns the name of the page it needs to navigate to.

Listing 10-5 shows the BookController managed bean. All the getters and setters in this snippet of code have been omitted for better readability but are required for each attribute (book and booklist).

Listing 10-5. *The BookController Managed Bean Invoking the EJB*

```
@ManagedBean
@RequestScoped
public class BookController {

    @EJB
    private BookEJB bookEJB;

    private Book book = new Book();
    private List<Book> bookList = new ArrayList<Book>();
```

```
    public String doCreateBook() {
        book = bookEJB.createBook(book);
        bookList = bookEJB.findBooks();
        return "listBooks.xhtml";
    }

    // Getters, setters
}
```

Writing the newBook.xhtml Page

The newBook.xhtml page in Listing 10-6 is a form that allows the user to enter the data needed to create a book (ISBN, title, price, description, number of pages, and illustrations).

Listing 10-6. The newBook.xhtml Page

```
<!DOCTYPE html PUBLIC "-//W3C//DTD XHTML 1.0 Transitional//EN"
        "http://www.w3.org/TR/xhtml1/DTD/xhtml1-transitional.dtd">
<html xmlns="http://www.w3.org/1999/xhtml"
      xmlns:h="http://java.sun.com/jsf/html">
<h:head>
    <title>Creates a new book</title>
</h:head>
<h:body>
    <h1>Create a new book</h1>
    <hr/>
    <h:form>
        <h:panelGrid columns="2" >
            <h:outputLabel value="ISBN : "/>
            <h:inputText value="#{bookController.book.isbn}"/>

            <h:outputLabel value="Title :"/>
            <h:inputText value="#{bookController.book.title}"/>

            <h:outputLabel value="Price : "/>
            <h:inputText value="#{bookController.book.price}"/>

            <h:outputLabel value="Description   : "/>
            <h:inputTextarea value="#{bookController.book.description}" cols="20" rows="5"/>

            <h:outputLabel value="Number of pages : "/>
            <h:inputText value="#{bookController.book.nbOfPage}"/>

            <h:outputLabel value="Illustrations : "/>
            <h:selectBooleanCheckbox value="#{bookController.book.illustrations}"/>

        </h:panelGrid>
        <h:commandButton value="Create a book" action="#{bookController.doCreateBook}"/>
```

```
  </h:form>
  <hr/>
  <i>APress - Beginning Java EE 6</i>

</h:body>
</html>
```

As shown in Figure 10-3, most of the data is entered in text fields except for the description, which uses a text area, and the Illustrations check box option.

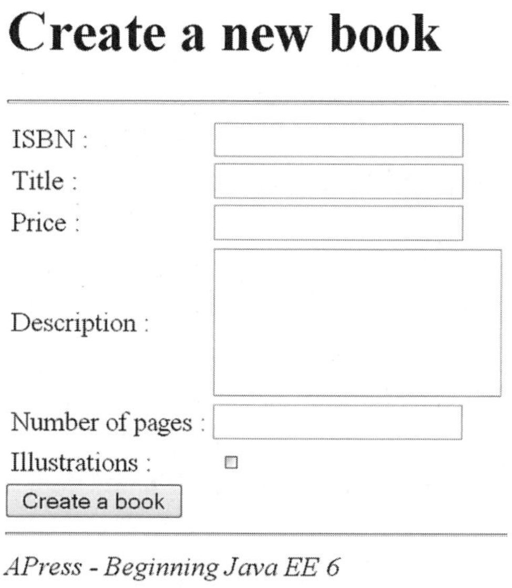

Create a new book

ISBN : [   ]

Title : [   ]

Price : [   ]

Description : [   ]

Number of pages : [   ]

Illustrations : ☐

[Create a book]

APress - Beginning Java EE 6

Figure 10-3. *The* newBook.xhtml *page*

When the *Create a book* button is pressed, the doCreateBook() method of the managed bean is invoked, and the EJB persists the book to the database.

The code has been simplified but contains the essentials. First you need to declare the HTML components with the h namespace, so you can use components for displaying text (<h:outputText>) or buttons (<h:commandButton>). The EL allows you to dynamically bind the value of a component to the corresponding property in the managed bean. So the following code:

```
<h:inputText value="#{bookController.book.isbn}"/>
```

will set the value of the isbn attribute of the book with the content of the input text component. bookController is the default name for our managed bean, so the code above is identical to:

```
bookController.getBook().setISBN("the value of the input text component")
```

The page uses different graphical components. Here is a quick overview of those used in the newBook.xhtml page:

- `<h:form>` allows you to create a form, the values of the components of which will be sent to the server on submission.

- `<h:panelGrid>` is used to create a table with two columns (one with all the `<h:outputLabel` tags and the other one with all the different input components).

- `<h:outputLabel>` is used to display a label, either by using a fixed string (like `value="ISBN : ")` or by binding to a property of the bean.

- `<h:inputTextarea>` displays a text area and binds its value to the book's `description` attribute.

- `<h:selectBooleanCheckbox>` displays a check box and binds it to the `Boolean` `illustrations` attribute.

- `<h:commandButton>` shows a submit button. When clicked, it invokes the `doCreateBook()` method on the managed bean (`action="#{bookController.doCreateBook}"`).

Writing the listBooks.xhtml Page

When the submit button is clicked in the `newBook.xhtml` page (see Figure 10-3), the `doCreateBook()` method of the managed bean is invoked, a book is persisted, the list of all books is retrieved into `booklist`, and, if no exception is thrown, the name of the page to navigate to is returned: `listBooks.xhtml`. You've just created a book, and the `listBooks.xhtml` page displays all the books from the `booklist` property of the managed bean (see Figure 10-4). A link allows you to go back to the `newBook.xhtml` page to create another book.

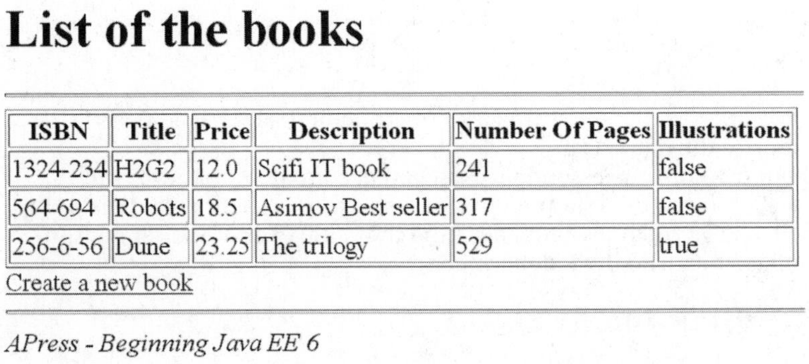

List of the books

ISBN	Title	Price	Description	Number Of Pages	Illustrations
1324-234	H2G2	12.0	Scifi IT book	241	false
564-694	Robots	18.5	Asimov Best seller	317	false
256-6-56	Dune	23.25	The trilogy	529	true

Create a new book

APress - Beginning Java EE 6

Figure 10-4. *The* `listBooks.xhtml` *page*

The code of the `listBooks.xhtml` page (see Listing 10-7) uses different components but has the same underlying ideas as the previous page. The most important component is the one that displays the data in a table:

```
<h:dataTable value="#{bookController.bookList}" var="bk">
```

The <h:dataTable> tag binds to the bookList attribute of the managed bean (an ArrayList of books) and declares the variable bk to iterate through the list. Then, inside the <h:dataTable> tag, you can use expressions such as #{bk.isbn} to get the isbn attribute of a book. Each column of the table is defined with an <h:column> tag. At the bottom of the page, the <h:link> tag creates an HTML link that, when clicked, navigates back to the newBook.xhtml page).

Listing 10-7. The listBooks.xhtml Page

```
<!DOCTYPE html PUBLIC "-//W3C//DTD XHTML 1.0 Transitional//EN"
        "http://www.w3.org/TR/xhtml1/DTD/xhtml1-transitional.dtd">
<html xmlns="http://www.w3.org/1999/xhtml"
     xmlns:h="http://java.sun.com/jsf/html"
     xmlns:f="http://java.sun.com/jsf/core">
<h:head>
    <title>List of the books</title>
</h:head>
<h:body>
<h1>List of the books</h1>
<hr/>

<h:dataTable value="#{bookController.bookList}" var="bk">

  <h:column>
    <f:facet name="header">
      <h:outputText value="ISBN"/>
    </f:facet>
    <h:outputText value="#{bk.isbn}"/>
  </h:column>

  <h:column>
    <f:facet name="header">

      <h:outputText value="Title"/>

    </f:facet>
    <h:outputText value="#{bk.title}"/>
  </h:column>

  <h:column>
    <f:facet name="header">
      <h:outputText value="Price"/>
    </f:facet>
    <h:outputText value="#{bk.price}"/>
  </h:column>

  <h:column>
    <f:facet name="header">
      <h:outputText value="Description"/>
    </f:facet>
    <h:outputText value="#{bk.description}"/>
  </h:column>
```

```
<h:column>
  <f:facet name="header">
    <h:outputText value="Number Of Pages"/>
  </f:facet>
  <h:outputText value="#{bk.nbOfPage}"/>
</h:column>

<h:column>
  <f:facet name="header">
    <h:outputText value="Illustrations"/>
  </f:facet>
  <h:outputText value="#{bk.illustrations}"/>
</h:column>

</h:dataTable>

<h:form>
  <h:link outcome="newBook.xhtml" value="Create a new book"/>
</h:form>

<hr/>
<i>APress - Beginning Java EE 6</i>
</h:body>
</html>
```

Configuration with web.xml

Web applications are usually configured with a web.xml deployment descriptor. I say "usually" because, with the new Servlet 3.0 specification, the web.xml file has become optional (as most of the XML descriptor elements have an annotation as a replacement). But, because JSF 2.0 is based on Servlet 2.5 (and not Servlet 3.0), you still need to deploy your web application with a descriptor.

JSF applications require a servlet, called FacesServlet, which acts as a front controller for the entire application. This servlet must be defined in the web.xml file with mapping added, as shown in Listing 10-8.

Listing 10-8. The web.xml File Declaring the FacesServlet

```
<?xml version='1.0' encoding='UTF-8'?>
<web-app version="2.5"
        xmlns="http://java.sun.com/xml/ns/javaee"
        xmlns:xsi="http://www.w3.org/2001/XMLSchema-instance"
        xsi:schemaLocation="http://java.sun.com/xml/ns/javaee
        http://java.sun.com/xml/ns/javaee/web-app_2_5.xsd">

    <servlet>
        <servlet-name>Faces Servlet</servlet-name>
        <servlet-class>javax.faces.webapp.FacesServlet</servlet-class>
        <load-on-startup>1</load-on-startup>
    </servlet>
```

```
<servlet-mapping>
    <servlet-name>Faces Servlet</servlet-name>
    <url-pattern>*.faces</url-pattern>
</servlet-mapping>
</web-app>
```

The deployment descriptor maps the requests to a URL finished with `.faces` to the servlet, meaning that any page requested with the extension `.faces` will be handled by the `FacesServlet`.

Compiling and Packaging with Maven

The web application needs to be compiled and packaged in a war file (`<packaging>war</packaging>`). The `pom.xml` shown in Listing 10-9 declares all the dependencies necessary for compiling code (`jsf-api`, `javax.ejb`, and `javax.persistence`) and uses version 1.6 of the JDK. The `faces-config.xml` file has become optional in JSF 2.0.

Listing 10-9. Maven `pom.xml` File for Compiling and Packaging the Web Application

```xml
<?xml version="1.0" encoding="UTF-8"?>
<project xmlns="http://maven.apache.org/POM/4.0.0" ➥
        xmlns:xsi="http://www.w3.org/2001/XMLSchema-instance"➥
        xsi:schemaLocation="http://maven.apache.org/POM/4.0.0 ➥
        http://maven.apache.org/xsd/maven-4.0.0.xsd">

    <modelVersion>4.0.0</modelVersion>
    <groupId>com.apress.javaee6</groupId>
    <artifactId>chapter10</artifactId>
    <packaging>war</packaging>
    <version>2.0</version>

    <dependencies>
        <dependency>
            <groupId>javax.faces</groupId>
            <artifactId>jsf-api</artifactId>
            <version>2.0.0</version>
            <scope>provided</scope>
        </dependency>
        <dependency>
            <groupId>org.glassfish</groupId>
            <artifactId>javax.ejb</artifactId>
            <version>3.0.1</version>
            <scope>provided</scope>
        </dependency>
        <dependency>
            <groupId>org.eclipse.persistence</groupId>
            <artifactId>javax.persistence</artifactId>
             <version>2.0.0</version>
             <scope>provided</scope>
        </dependency>
    </dependencies>
```

```
    <build>
        <plugins>
            <plugin>
                <groupId>org.apache.maven.plugins</groupId>
                <artifactId>maven-compiler-plugin</artifactId>
                <inherited>true</inherited>
                <configuration>
                    <source>1.6</source>
                    <target>1.6</target>
                </configuration>
            </plugin>
        </plugins>
    </build>
</project>
```

To compile and package the classes, open a command-line interpreter in the directory that contains the `pom.xml` file and enter the following Maven command:

```
mvn package
```

Go to the `target` directory to find the `chapter10-2.0.war` file. Open it, and you will see that it contains the `Book` entity, the `BookEJB`, the `BookController` managed bean, the two deployment descriptors (`persistence.xml` and `web.xml`), and the two web pages (`newBook.xhtml` and `listBooks.xhtml`).

Deploying on GlassFish

Once the web application has been packaged, it needs to be deployed into GlassFish. Ensure GlassFish is up and running, and, because the application stores data in the database, check that Derby is running and listening on its default port. Open a DOS console, go to the `target` directory where the `chapter10-2.0.war` file is located, and enter the following:

```
asadmin deploy chapter10-2.0.war
```

If the deployment is successful, the following command should return the name of the deployed application and its type. There are two types: `web`, because it's a web application, and `ejb`, because the application contains an EJB:

```
asadmin list-components
chapter10-2.0 <ejb, web>
```

Running the Example

Now that the application is deployed, open your browser and go to the following URL:

```
http://localhost:8080/chapter10-2.0/newBook.faces
```

The browser is pointing to `newBook.faces`, not `newBook.xhtml`, because of the mapping you used for the `FacesServlet`. With the `.faces` extension, JSF knows it has to process the page before rendering it. Once the `newBook` page shows up, enter some data, and click the submit button to be redirected to the `listBooks` page.

Summary

Today, the race between user interfaces continues, with the proliferation of Rich Desktop Applications (RDAs), Rich Internet Applications (RIAs), mobile device applications, and so forth. A few years ago, JSF entered this race, and today, with the new features of JSF 2.0, it is holding its own.

JSF has an architecture based on components and a rich API for developing renderers, converters, validators, and more. It can render and convert several languages, and the preferred presentation declaration language (PDL) of JSF 2.0 is Facelets.

Annotations have been introduced in JSF 2.0 and are now used in most Java EE 6 specifications. Chapter 11 focuses on the presentation part of Java EE 6. It covers specifications like JSP 2.2, EL 2.2, and JSTL 1.2, introduces Facelets, and concentrates mostly on JSF. Chapter 12 deals with all the dynamic aspects of the specification. You will learn how navigation works, about managed beans, and also how to write your own converter and validator.

CHAPTER 11

■ ■ ■

Pages and Components

In the early days of Java, developers dealt with HTML directly, by emitting HTML from servlets. We then moved from servlets to Java Server Pages (JSP) to custom tags. Today, Java EE 6 brings a new version of JSF, simplifying web interface development.

In this chapter, you will see different technologies used in Java EE 6 to create web pages. First, the text covers some basic concepts such as HTML, CSS, and JavaScript, and then moves on to JSP, EL, and JSTL. I then introduce you to Facelets, the preferred page declaration language (PDL) in JSF. The remainder of the chapter focuses on how to create web interfaces using JSF or custom components. The next chapter will focus on how to navigate between pages and how to interact with a back end so that dynamic data can be displayed.

Web Pages

When we create a web application, we are really interested in displaying dynamic content: a list of items from a catalog (CDs and books, for instance), the customer details for a given identifier, a shopping cart containing the items the customer wants to buy, and so on. Conversely, static content, such as the address of a book company and FAQs with information on how to buy or ship items, rarely or never changes. Static content can also be the images, videos, or artwork that make up a page.

The final goal of creating a page is to display it in a browser. The page has to use languages that the browser can understand, of which there are several: HTML, XHTML, CSS, and JavaScript.

HTML

Hypertext Markup Language (HTML) is the predominant language for web pages. It is based on Standard Generalized Markup Language (SGML), which is a standard metalanguage to define markup languages. HTML uses *markups*, or *tags*, to structure text into paragraphs, lists, links, buttons, text areas, and so on.

An HTML page is a text document used by browsers to present text and graphics. These documents are text files that often have an `.html` or `.htm` extension. A web page is made of content, tags to change some aspects of the content, and external objects such as images, videos, JavaScript, or CSS files.

In Chapter 10, the "Putting It All Together" section showed a couple of JSF pages, with one displaying a form to create a new book. In pure HTML, without using any JSF tags, this page could look like the code in Listing 11-1.

Listing 11-1. The newBook.html Page with Invalid HTML Structure

```
<H1>Creates a new book</h1>
<hr>
<TABLE border=0>
    <TR>
            <TD>ISBN : </TD>
            <TD><input type=text/></td>
    </tr>
    <tr>
            <td>Title : </td>
            <TD><input type=text/></td>
    </tr>
    <tr>
            <td>Price :
            <TD><input type=text/>
    </tr>
    <tr>
            <td>Description :
            <td><textarea name=textarea cols=20 rows=5></textarea>
    </tr>
    <TR>
            <TD>Number of pages :
            <td><input type=text/>
    </tr>
    <tr>
            <td>Illustrations :
            <td><input type=checkbox/>
    </tr>
    </table>
<input type=submit value=Create>
<hr>
<i>APress - Beginning Java EE 6</i>
```

Normally, a valid HTML page starts with an `<html>` tag that acts like a container for the document. It is followed by a `<head>` and `<body>` tag. `<body>` contains the visible content such as the HTML code displaying a table, labels, input fields, and a button. As you can see in Listing 11-1, the `newBook.html` markup doesn't follow these rules, but browsers will display nonvalid HTML pages to a certain extent. So the visible result would look like Figure 11-1.

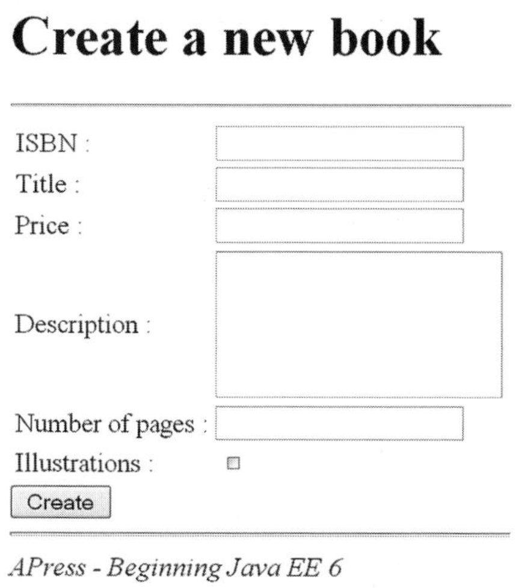

Create a new book

ISBN : [   ]

Title : [   ]

Price : [   ]

Description : [   ]

Number of pages : [   ]

Illustrations : ☐

[Create]

APress - Beginning Java EE 6

***Figure 11-1.** Graphical representation of the newBook.html page*

The graphical representation shown in Figure 11-1 is the one expected despite the fact that Listing 11-1 is not well formatted in terms of XML:

- The page does not have any `<html>`, `<head>`, or `<body>` tags.

- The `<input type=submit value=Create>` tag is not closed.

- Uppercase and lowercase are mixed in tags (e.g., `<TR>`and `</tr>` both appear in the listing).

Most browsers will permit such mistakes and display this form. However, if you want to process this document with XML parsers, for example, it would fail. To uncover why this is, let's look at a web page that uses a strict XML structure with Extensible Hypertext Markup Language (XHTML).

XHTML

XHTML was created shortly after HTML 4.01. It has its roots in HTML but is reformulated in strict XML. This means an XHTML document is an XML document that follows a certain schema and has a graphical representation on browsers. An XHTML file (which has the extension `.xhtml`) can be used as XML right away or displayed in a browser. In contrast to HTML, this has the advantage of providing document validation using standard XML tools (XSL, or Extensible Stylesheet Language; XSLT, or XSL Transformations; etc.). Hence, XHTML is much more flexible and powerful than HTML, because it allows you to define any set of tags you wish.

Listing 11-2 shows how the XHTML version of the web page to create a book would look.

Listing 11-2. The newBook.xhtml Page with a Valid XML Structure

```
<?xml version="1.0" encoding="UTF-8"?>
<!DOCTYPE html
        PUBLIC "-//W3C//DTD XHTML 1.0 Transitional//EN"
        "http://www.w3.org/TR/xhtml1/DTD/xhtml1-transitional.dtd">
<html xmlns="http://www.w3.org/1999/xhtml" xml:lang="en" lang="en">
<head>
    <title>Creates a new book</title>
</head>
<body>
<h1>Creates a new book</h1>
<hr/>
<table border="0">
    <tr>
            <td>ISBN :</td>
            <td><input type="text"/></td>
    </tr>
    <tr>
            <td>Title :</td>
            <td><input type="text"/></td>
    </tr>
    <tr>
            <td>Price :</td>
            <td><input type="text"/></td>
    </tr>
    <tr>
            <td>Description :</td>
            <td><textarea name="textarea" cols="20" rows="5"></textarea></td>
    </tr>
    <tr>
            <td>Number of pages :</td>
            <td><input type="text"/></td>
    </tr>
    <tr>
            <td>Illustrations :</td>
            <td><input type="checkbox"/></td>
    </tr>
    </table>
<input name="" type="submit" value="Create"/>
<hr/>
<i>APress - Beginning Java EE 6</i>
</body>
</html>
```

Some differences exist between Listing 11-1 and Listing 11-2: the document in Listing 11-2 follows a strict structure and has `<html>`, `<head>`, and `<body>` tags; all the tags are closed, even ones with empty elements (each `<td>` is closed, and `<hr/>` is used instead of `<hr>`); attributes appear between single or double quotes (`<table border="0">` or `<table border='0'>`, but not `<table border=0>`); and tags are all lowercase (`<tr>` instead of `<TR>`). Compare this to Listing 11-1, which as mentioned previously shows invalid HTML that browsers will be able to display anyway.

The strict validation of XML syntax rules and schema constraints makes XHTML easier to maintain and to parse than HTML, and as a result it is now the preferred language for web pages. A conforming XHTML document is an XML document that follows the HTML 4.01 specification. There are three different validation formats a document can use:

- XHTML 1.0 Transitional: most conciliatory variant of XHTML that lets you use presentational elements (such as center, font, and strike) that are excluded from the strict version.

- XHTML 1.0 Frameset: transitional variant that also allows the definition of frameset documents (a common Web feature in the late 1990s).

- XHTML 1.0 Strict: most restrictive variant of XHTML that strictly follows the HTML 4.01 specification.

CSS

Browsers live in a world of client-side languages such as HTML, XHTML, CSS, and JavaScript. Cascading Style Sheets (CSS) is a styling language used to describe the presentation of a document written in HTML or XHTML. CSS is used to define colors, fonts, layouts, and other aspects of document presentation. It allows separation of a document's content (written in XHTML) from its presentation (written in CSS). Like HTTP, HTML, and XHTML, the CSS specifications are maintained by the World Wide Web Consortium (W3C).

For example, say you want to alter the labels on the `newBook.xhtml` page by making them italic (`font-style: italic;`), changing the color to blue (`color: #000099;`), and increasing the font size (`font-size: 22px;`); you do not have to repeat these changes for each tag. You can define a CSS style (in a `<style type="text/css">` tag) and give it an alias (e.g., `.title` and `.row`), and the page (see Listing 11-3) will use this alias on all elements to be changed in the presentation (`<h1 class="title">`).

Listing 11-3. ThenewBook.xhtml Page with Some CSS Styles

```
<?xml version="1.0" encoding="UTF-8"?>
<!DOCTYPE html
        PUBLIC "-//W3C//DTD XHTML 1.0 Transitional//EN"
        "http://www.w3.org/TR/xhtml1/DTD/xhtml1-transitional.dtd">
<html xmlns="http://www.w3.org/1999/xhtml" xml:lang="en" lang="en">
<head>
    <title>Creates a new book</title>
    <style type="text/css">
        .title {
            font-family: Arial, Helvetica, sans-serif;
            font-size: 22px;
```

```
            color: blue;
            font-style: italic;
        }

        .row {
            font-family: Arial, Helvetica, sans-serif;
            color: #000000;
            font-style: italic;
        }
    </style>
</head>
<body>
<h1 class="title">Creates a new book</h1>
<hr/>
<table border="0">
    <tr>
            <td class="row">ISBN :</td>
            <td><input type="text"/></td>
    </tr>
    <tr>
            <td class="row">Title :</td>
            <td><input type="text"/></td>
    </tr>
    <tr>
            <td class="row">Price :</td>
            <td><input type="text"/></td>
    </tr>
    <tr>
            <td class="row">Description :</td>
            <td><textarea name="textarea" cols="20" rows="5"></textarea></td>
    </tr>
    <tr>
            <td class="row">Number of pages :</td>
            <td><input type="text"/></td>
    </tr>
    <tr>
            <td class="row">Illustrations :</td>
            <td><input type="checkbox"/></td>
    </tr>
    </table>
<input name="" type="submit" value="Create"/>
<hr/>
<i>APress - Beginning Java EE 6</i>
</body>
</html>
```

In this example, the CSS code is embedded in the XHTML page. In a real application, all the styles would be written in a separate file and this file imported into the web page. The webmaster can draw up one or more sets of CSS for various groups of pages, and then content contributors can write or change pages without needing to be concerned about the look and feel.

Compared with Figure 11-1, the end result is that all the labels are in italic and the title is blue (see Figure 11-2).

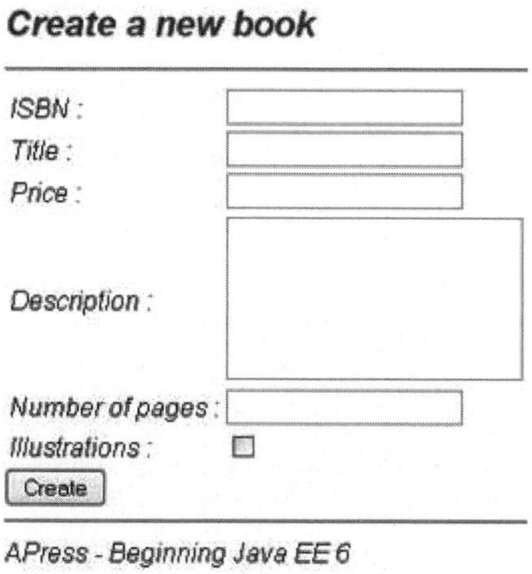

Create a new book

ISBN :

Title :

Price :

Description :

Number of pages :

Illustrations :

Create

APress - Beginning Java EE 6

Figure 11-2. Graphical representation of the newBook.xhtml page with CSS

DOM

An XHTML page is an XML document and thus has a Document Object Model (DOM) representation. DOM is a W3C specification for accessing and modifying the content and structure of XML documents as well as an abstract API for querying, traversing, and manipulating such documents. DOM can be thought of as a tree representation of the structure of a document. Figure 11-3 shows how the newBook.xhtml page might look as a DOM representation; at the root there's the `html` tag, at the same level, `head` and `body`, and under `body` a `table` with a list of `tr` tags.

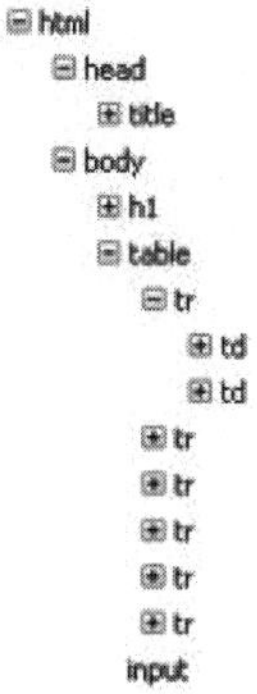

```
⊟ html
    ⊟ head
        ⊞ title
    ⊟ body
        ⊞ h1
        ⊟ table
            ⊟ tr
                ⊞ td
                ⊞ td
            ⊞ tr
            ⊞ tr
            ⊞ tr
            ⊞ tr
            ⊞ tr
            input
```

Figure 11-3. Tree representation of the newBook.xhtml page

DOM provides a standard way to interact with XML documents. You can traverse the tree and edit the content of a node (a leaf of the tree). With some JavaScript, you can introduce dynamism into your web pages. As you will see in the next chapter, Ajax is based on JavaScript interacting with the DOM representation of a web page.

JavaScript

Until now, you've seen different languages used to represent static content and graphical aspects of a web page. But, often, a web page needs to interact with the end user by showing dynamic content. As you'll see, dynamic content can be handled with server-side technologies such as JSP or JSF, but browsers can also do so by executing JavaScript.

JavaScript is a scripting language used for client-side web development. Despite its name, it is unrelated to the Java programming language, as it is an interpreted, weakly typed language. JavaScript is a powerful way to create dynamic web applications by writing functions that interact with the DOM of a page. W3C standardized DOM, whereas the European Computer Manufacturers Association (ECMA) standardized JavaScript as the ECMAScript specification. Any page written with these standards (XHTML, CSS, and JavaScript) should look and behave mostly identically in any browser that adheres to these guidelines.

An example of JavaScript interacting with DOM is the newBook.xhtml page in Listing 11-4. This page displays a form where you can enter information about a book. The price of the book needs to be completed by the user on the client side before hitting the server. To do such a validation, you can create a JavaScript function (priceRequired()) that checks whether the price text field is empty or not.

Listing 11-4. The newBook.xhtml Page with Some JavaScript

```
<?xml version="1.0" encoding="UTF-8"?>
<!DOCTYPE html
        PUBLIC "-//W3C//DTD XHTML 1.0 Transitional//EN"
        "http://www.w3.org/TR/xhtml1/DTD/xhtml1-transitional.dtd">
<html xmlns="http://www.w3.org/1999/xhtml" xml:lang="en" lang="en">
<head>
    <title>Creates a new book</title>

    <script type="text/javascript">
        function priceRequired() {
            if (document.getElementById("price").value == "") {
                document.getElementById("priceError").innerHTML = ↦
                                        "Please, fill the price !";
            }
        }
    </script>

</head>
<body>
<h1>Creates a new book</h1>
<hr/>
```

```
<table border="0">

    <tr>
            <td>ISBN :</td>
            <td><input type="text"/></td>
    </tr>
    <tr>
            <td>Title :</td>
            <td><input type="text"/></td>
    </tr>
    <tr>
            <td>Price :</td>
            <td><input id="price" type="text" onblur="javascript:priceRequired()"/>
                <span id="priceError"/>
            </td>
    </tr>
    <tr>
            <td>Description :</td>
            <td><textarea name="textarea" cols="20" rows="5"></textarea></td>
    </tr>
    <tr>
            <td>Number of pages :</td>
            <td><input type="text"/></td>
    </tr>
    <tr>
            <td>Illustrations :</td>
            <td><input type="checkbox"/></td>
    </tr>
    </table>
<input name="" type="submit" value="Create"/>
<hr/>
<i>APress - Beginning Java EE 6</i>
</body>
</html>
```

In Listing 11-4, the priceRequired() JavaScript function is embedded in the page within a <script> tag. This function is called when the price text field loses the focus (that's what the onblur event does). The priceRequired() function uses the implicit document object that represents the DOM of the XHTML document. The getElementById("price") method looks for an element that has an identifier called price (<input id="price">) and checks whether it's empty. If so, the function looks for another element called priceError (getElementById("priceError")) and sets the value to Please, fill the price !. If the price is not completed, the client validation will display the message shown in Figure 11-4.

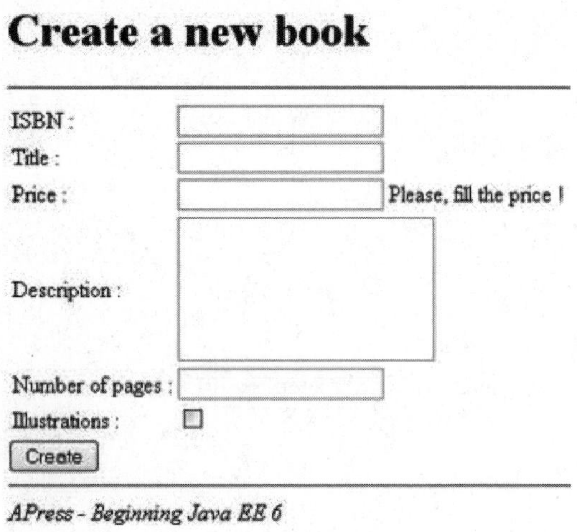

Create a new book

ISBN :

Title :

Price :   Please, fill the price !

Description :

Number of pages :

Illustrations : ☐

[Create]

APress - Beginning Java EE 6

Figure 11-4. *The newBook.html page with an error message*

JavaScript is a rich language. The preceding covers only a small part that demonstrates the interaction between JavaScript and DOM. It is important to understand that a JavaScript function can get to a node in the page (either by name or by ID such as the `getElementById()` method) and change its content dynamically on the client side. For details, see the "Ajax" section in the next chapter.

Java Server Pages

You've just seen technologies and languages, such as XHTML or CSS, that represent the content and the visual aspect of a static web page. To add some interaction and to change dynamically parts of the web page, you can use JavaScript functions that run on the browser. But, most of the time, you need to invoke a business layer of EJBs to display data from the database. This dynamic content can be obtained using JSP or JSF (with JSP or Facelets as the PDL, as you'll see later).

JSP, introduced in 1999 as part of J2EE 1.2, allows developers to create dynamically generated web pages in response to a client request. Pages are processed on the server side and compiled as servlets. JSPs look like HTML or XHTML pages, but have special tags to perform server-side processing, display values, and invoke server-side Java code.

Much of what a JSP does is based on the servlet API. Servlets were developed to extend the server's capabilities to accept HTTP requests from clients and create dynamic responses to those requests. Servlets can use any server-side resources such as EJBs, databases, web services, and other components, as can JSPs. JSPs are dynamic because they execute Java code to tailor a response based on the request.

JSPs run on the server side within a servlet container and respond to requests from clients who are users, accessing a web application through a web browser via HTTP, the same protocol used by browsers to get XHTML pages from a web server. The servlet container manages the life cycle of a JSP by:

- Compiling the JSP code into a servlet.

- Loading and initializing the servlet generated from the JSP.

- Processing clients' requests and dispatching them to the JSP's servlet.

- Returning responses to clients (responses consist solely of HTML or XHTML tags to be displayed in a browser).

- Unloading the JSP's servlet and stopping sending requests to the JSP (when the server shuts down, for example).

The difference between an HTML and XHTML page is that the latter complies strictly with XML rules. Similarly, JSPs can generate HTML or strict XHTML at runtime (as an example, you can use different file extensions, `.jsp` and `.jspx`, for strict XML format). So, now that you've seen how JSPs work, let's look at some code.

```
<html>
<head><title>Lists all the books</title></head>
<body>
    <h1>Lists all the books</h1>
    <hr/>
</body>
</html>
```

As you can see, a valid JSP can be formed of only HTML tags. You could save this code into a `listBooks.jsp` page and deploy it into a servlet container that would return a simple HTML page. The point is that a JSP looks like HTML, but with some extra tags allowing you to add dynamic content, so the response to the client changes depending on the request. The JSP specification defines the following elements:

- Directive elements

- Scripting elements

- Action elements

As you'll see, for all these elements the JSP specification defines two syntaxes: the XML syntax to use in XHTML pages (e.g., `<jsp:directive attributes/>`) and the JSP syntax, which is not XML compliant (e.g., `<%@ attributes %>`).

Directive Elements

Directive elements provide information about the JSP and do not produce any output. There are three directives: `page`, `include`, and `taglib`. Directives have two syntactic forms:

```
<%@ directive attributes %>
// or
<jsp:directive attributes />
```

The `page` directive is used to specify page attributes such as the programming language used in the page (Java in this case), the MIME type, and the character encoding for the response of the JSP, whether the current JSP is intended to be an error page, and so on.

```
<%@ page contentType="text/html; ISO-8859-1" language="java" %>
// or
<jsp:directive.page contentType="text/html; ISO-8859-1" language="java"/>
```

The include directive is used to include another page (HTML, XHTML, or JSP) within the current page. You use this directive when you have a standard page (such as a header or a footer) you want included in multiple JSPs.

```
<%@ include file="header.jsp"%>
// or
<jsp:directive.include file="header.jsp" />
```

The "JSP Standard Tag Library" section shows that JSPs can be extended through a tag library. The taglib directive in a JSP declares the page uses a certain tag library, uniquely identified by a URI and a prefix. In XML, it translates into a unique namespace (xmlns) at a given URI. In the following example, the http://java.sun.com/jstl/core tag library is made available to a page using the prefix c:

```
<%@ taglib uri="http://java.sun.com/jstl/core" prefix="c" %>
// or
<jsp:root xmlns:c="http://java.sun.com/jstl/core">
```

Scripting Elements

Scripting elements are used to manipulate objects and to perform computation that affects the content by including Java code. There are three categories of scripting elements: declarations, scriptlets, and expressions. These can be defined following two different syntaxes.

```
<%! this is a declaration %>
// or
<jsp:declaration>this is a declaration</jsp:declaration>
```

```
<% this is a scriptlet %>
// or
<jsp:scriptlet>this is a scriptlet</jsp:scriptlet>
```

```
<%= this is an expression %>
// or
<jsp:expression>this is an expression</jsp:expression>
```

Declarations are used to declare Java variables or methods that are available to all other scripting elements of the page. The declaration appears only within the translated JSP (i.e., the servlet) but not in the output to the client. Any variable or method declared within a declaration element becomes an instance method of the JSP and is global to the entire page. For example, you declare an ArrayList as follows:

```
<%! List books = new ArrayList(); %>
// or
<jsp:declaration>List books = new ArrayList();</jsp:declaration>
```

Scriptlets contain Java code used to describe actions to be performed in response to requests. They can be employed to do things like iterations and conditional execution of other elements in the JSP. Like declarations, the code in the scriptlet appears in the translated JSP (the servlet), but not in the output to the client. For example, you add a **Book** object to an **ArrayList** as follows:

```
<%
books.add(new Book("H2G2", 12f, "Scifi IT book", "1234-234", 241, true));
%>
// or
<jsp:scriptlet>
books.add(new Book("H2G2", 12f, "Scifi IT book", "1234-234", 241, true));
</jsp:scriptlet>
```

Expressions are used to output the value of a Java expression to the client. They get evaluated at response time, and the result is converted into a string and inserted into the output stream to be displayed in the browser. For example, the following code fragment would result in displaying the ISBN of a book:

```
<%= book.getIsbn()%>
// or
<jsp:expression>book.getIsbn()</jsp:expression>
```

Declarations, scriptlets, and expressions must contain valid Java code. And, when you choose to use the XML syntax, the content must be valid XML. For example, to declare an **ArrayList** of books using generics, you would do the following:

```
<%! List<Book> books = new ArrayList<Book>(); %>
```

If you declare this array list in a strict XML format, it will not be valid because you include the < and > symbols, which already have the meaning of opening and closing a tag in XML. To allow such a declaration, you must use **CDATA**. The term **CDATA** (which stands for character data) is used to indicate something that should not be parsed by the XML parser.

```
<jsp:declaration><![CDATA[
    List<Book> books = new ArrayList<Book>();
]]></jsp:declaration>
```

Action Elements

Standard actions are defined by the JSP specification and cause the page to perform some actions (include external resources, forward a request to another page, or use Java objects' properties). They look similar to HTML tags, as they are represented using XML elements with a prefix of **jsp** (e.g., `<jsp:useBean>`, `<jsp:include>`, etc.). Table 11-1 lists all the available action elements.

Table 11-1. JSP Action Elements

Action	Description
useBean	Associates an instance of an object within a given scope and available with a given ID.
setProperty	Sets the value of a property in a bean.
getProperty	Displays the value of a bean property.
include	Allows the inclusion of static and dynamic resources in the same context as the current page.
forward	Dispatches the current request to a static resource, a JSP, or a servlet in the same context as the current page.
param	Is used in the include, forward, and params elements. The included or forwarded page will see the original request object with the original parameters augmented with the new parameters.
plugin	Enables a JSP to generate HTML that contains the appropriate browser-dependent constructs (OBJECT or EMBED) that will result in the download of a plugin.
params	Passes parameters. This is part of the plugin action.
element	Dynamically defines the value of the tag of an XML element.
attribute	Defines an XML attribute. This is part of the element action.
body	Defines the body of an XML element. This is part of the element action.

Putting It All Together

These elements allow you to invoke Java code and any kind of component (EJBs, databases, web services, etc.). As an example, let's write some Java code. The web page that you want to create has to display a list of books stored in an ArrayList. There is no database access, just an ArrayList initialized with a fixed number of Book objects through which the JSP iterates and displays the attributes (ISBN, title of the book, description, and so on). The result should look like Figure 11-5.

Lists all the books

ISBN	Title	Price	Description	Number of pages	Illustrations
1234-234	H2G2	12.0	Scifi IT book	241	true
564-694	Robots	18.5	Best seller	317	true
256-6-56	Dune	23.25	The trilogy	529	true

APress - Beginning Java EE 6

Figure 11-5. The listBooks.jsp page displays a list of books

To construct this page, you need several elements. As shown in Listing 11-5, you need to import the `java.util.List` and `ArrayList` class as well as `Book` using a directive element (`<%@ page import="java.util.List" %>`). Once imported, you need to declare the `books` attribute of type `List` so it is accessible in the entire page. For this, you need a scripting element of type declaration (`<%! List<Book> books = new ArrayList<Book>(); %>`). One scriptlet adds book objects into a `List`, and another scriptlet loops through the list with a `for` statement. To display the attributes of each book, expression elements are used (`<%= book.getTitle()%>`). The full code of the page is shown in Listing 11-5.

Listing 11-5. The listBooks.jsp Page

```jsp
<%@ page import="com.apress.javaee6.chapter11.Book" %>
<%@ page import="java.util.ArrayList" %>
<%@ page import="java.util.List" %>
<%!
    List<Book> books = new ArrayList<Book>();
%>
<html>
<head>
    <title>Lists all the books</title>
</head>
<body>
<h1>Lists all the books</h1>
<hr/>
<%
books.add(new Book("H2G2", 12f, "Scifi IT book", "1234-234", 241, true));
books.add(new Book("Robots", 18.5f, "Best seller", "564-694", 317, true));
books.add(new Book("Dune", 23.25f, "The trilogy", "256-6-56", 529, true));
%>
<table border="1">
    <tr>
        <th>ISBN</td>
        <th>Title</th>
```

```
        <th>Price</th>
        <th>Description</th>
        <th>Number of pages</th>
        <th>Illustrations</th>
    <tr>
    <%

        for (Book book : books) {

    %>
    <tr>
        <td><%= book.getIsbn()%></td>
        <td><%= book.getTitle()%></td>
        <td><%= book.getPrice()%></td>
        <td><%= book.getDescription()%></td>
        <td><%= book.getNbOfPage()%></td>
        <td><%= book.getIllustrations()%></td>
    </tr>
    <%

        } // End of the for statement

    %>

</table>
<hr/>
<i>APress - Beginning Java EE 6</i>
</body>
</html>
```

You can freely interleave Java code, HTML tags, and text. Everything between the scriptlet tags (<% and %>) is Java code, which will be executed on the server, and everything outside is template data, which will be written to the response page. Notice in Listing 11-5 that the **for** statement block begins and ends in different scriptlets. A JSP can quickly get difficult to read if you start mixing a lot of HTML tags and Java code. Also, there is no separation between the business logic and the presentation, which makes the page difficult to maintain. And you are mixing two languages made for two different categories of people: Java for the business developer and XHTML/CSS for the web designer.

JSPs can use tag libraries and expression language (EL) to solve this problem. The JSP Standard Tag Library (JSTL) standardizes a number of common actions using a markup language familiar to web developers, while EL uses a simpler syntax for performing some of the same actions of JSP scripting elements.

Expression Language

You have just seen how to use scripting elements that embed Java code in the JSP. EL statements provide a simpler syntax to perform similar actions and are easier for non-Java programmers to use. You can use EL statements to print the value of variables or access objects' attributes in a page. It also has a rich set of mathematical, logical, and relational operators. The basic syntax for an EL statement is:

${expr}

where `expr` is a valid expression that is parsed and interpreted. As of JSP 2.1, you can also use the following syntax:

`#{expr}`

The `${expr}` and `#{expr}` statements will be parsed and evaluated in exactly the same manner for JSPs. However, for JSF, it is a different matter because, as you'll see, JSF pages have a life cycle different from that of JSPs. You can use `${expr}` for expressions that are evaluated immediately (the expression is compiled when the JSP is compiled and is evaluated once, when the JSP executes) and `#{expr}` for expressions with a deferred evaluation (the expression is not evaluated until its value is needed). These two ELs have been unified, so a JSP and a JSF page can use both, but with the life-cycle difference.

EL expressions can use most of the usual Java operators:

- *Arithmetic*: `+`, `-`, `*`, `/` (`div`), `%` (`mod`)

- *Relational*: `==` (`eq`), `!=` (`ne`), `<` (`lt`), `>` (`gt`), `<=` (`le`), `>=` (`ge`)

- *Logical*: `&&` (`and`), `||` (`or`), `!` (`not`)

- *Other*: `()`, `empty`, `[]`, `.`

Note that some operators have both symbolic and word variants (`>` can be `gt`, `/` can be `div`, and so on). These equivalents allow you to make your JSP XML compliant while avoiding using entity references (such as `&lt;` for `<`). A "less than" could be coded `#{2 lt 3}` rather than `#{2 < 3}`.

The `empty` operator tests whether an object is null or whether it references an empty `String`, `List`, `Map`, or array. It returns `true` if empty; otherwise, it returns `false`. For example, if a JSP uses a declaration element to define a `Book` object (`<%! Book book = new Book(); %>`), you could check whether the object or one of its attributes is null.

```
#{empty book}
#{empty book.isbn}
```

The dot operator is used to access the attribute `isbn` of the `book` object. Another syntax is possible by using the `[]` operator; the `isbn` attribute can be accessed using either notation, like this:

```
#{book.isbn}
#{book[isbn]}
```

An enhancement in EL 2.2 is its ability to invoke methods. The following code fragment shows how to buy a book by calling the `book.buy()` method and how to pass a parameter (the currency used).

```
#{book.buy()}
#{book.buy('EURO')}
```

EL statements can be used in conjunction with JSP and JSF pages, `faces-config.xml`, scriptlets, or JSTL.

JSP Standard Tag Library

There's a useful set of standard tags called JSTL that allow you to avoid mixing Java code and XHTML tags. The dynamic data within a JSP can be manipulated using XML tags instead of Java code. These actions range from setting the value of an object easily to catching exceptions, controlling the flow structure with conditions and iterators, and accessing databases.

A tag library is a collection of functions that can be used in a JSP or JSF page. Table 11-2 lists these functions along with the URIs used to reference the libraries and associated prefixes (which are commonly used but can also be changed).

Table 11-2. JSTL Tag Libraries

Functional Area	URI	Commonly Used Prefix
Core	http://java.sun.com/jsp/jstl/core	c
XML processing	http://java.sun.com/jsp/jstl/xml	x
I18N and formatting	http://java.sun.com/jsp/jstl/fmt	fmt
Database access	http://java.sun.com/jsp/jstl/sql	sql
Functions	http://java.sun.com/jsp/jstl/functions	fn

Before using any of these actions, the JSP needs to import the tag library URI and set a prefix. This can be done with a JSP directive element with either the JSP markup scheme or the XML-compliant syntax.

```
<%@ taglib uri="http://java.sun.com/jsp/jstl/core" prefix="c" %>
// or
<jsp:root xmlns:jsp="http://java.sun.com/JSP/Page"
          xmlns:c="http://java.sun.com/jstl/core" version="1.2">
```

With such a declaration, you can use all the actions of the core tag library by prefixing with the letter c as follows:

```
<c:set var="upperLimit" value="20"/>
```

This code sets the value 20 for a variable called upperLimit. Each tag library has a set of actions that can be used in a JSP or JSF page.

Core Actions

The core actions provide tags for manipulating variables, dealing with errors, performing tests, and executing loops and iterations. Table 11-3 shows the actions contained in the core library.

Table 11-3. Core Actions

Action	Description
<c:out>	Evaluates an expression and outputs the result of the evaluation.
<c:set>	Sets a value for a variable within a scope.
<c:remove>	Removes a variable from a given scope.
<c:catch>	Catches a `java.lang.Throwable` thrown by any of its nested actions.
<c:if>	Evaluates whether the expression is true.
<c:choose>	Provides mutually exclusive conditions.
<c:when>	Represents an alternative within a `<c:choose>` action.
<c:otherwise>	Represents the last alternative within a `<c:choose>` action.
<c:forEach>	Repeats the nested body over a collection of objects, or repeats it a fixed number of times.
<c:forTokens>	Iterates over tokens, separated by the supplied delimiters.
<c:import>	Imports a resource.
<c:url>	Encodes a URL.
<c:param>	Adds request parameters to a URL.
<c:redirect>	Redirects to a specific URL.

To see some of these tags in action, let's write a JSP that loops from number 3 to number 15, tests whether the number is odd or even, and displays this information in front of each number (see Listing 11-6).

Listing 11-6. A JSP Displaying a List of Odd and Even Numbers

```
<jsp:root xmlns:jsp="http://java.sun.com/JSP/Page"
    xmlns:c="http://java.sun.com/jstl/core" version="1.2">
<html>
<body>

<c:set var="upperLimit" value="20"/>
<c:forEach var="i" begin="3" end="${upperLimit - 5}">

    <c:choose>
        <c:when test="${i%2 == 0}">
            <c:out value="${i} is even"/><br/>
        </c:when>
        <c:otherwise>
```

315

```
            <c:out value="${i} is odd"/><br/>
        </c:otherwise>
    </c:choose>

</c:forEach>

</body>
</html>
```

To use the core tag library, the page needs to import its URI with a prefix (i.e., XML namespace), assign the value 20 to the upperLimit variable with the <c:set> tag, and then iterate from the number 3 to number 15. You can see the usage of the EL with the arithmetic expression ${upperLimit - 5}. Inside the loop, the value of the index (variable i) is tested to see whether its value is odd or even (<c:when test="${i%2 == 0}">). The <c:out> tag displays the value of the index with the text ("${i} is even").

The logic is only done via tags, and this page is totally XML compliant, using a markup language easy for non-Java programmers to read and understand.

Formatting Actions

Formatting actions provide support for formatting dates, numbers, currencies, and percentages, and also support internationalization (i18n). You can get or set locales and time zones, or get the encoding of the web page. Table 11-4 shows the actions contained in the format library.

Table 11-4. Formatting Actions

Action	Description
<fmt:message>	Internationalizes a JSP by pulling a message from a message bundle.
<fmt:param>	Supplies a parameter for <fmt:message>.
<fmt:bundle>	Determines the resource bundle.
<fmt:setLocale>	Sets the locale.
<fmt:requestEncoding>	Sets the request's character encoding.
<fmt:timeZone>	Specifies the time zone in which time information is to be formatted.
<fmt:setTimeZone>	Stores the specified time zone on a variable.
<fmt:formatNumber>	Formats a numeric value (number, currency, percentage) in a locale-sensitive manner.
<fmt:parseNumber>	Parses the string representation of numbers, currencies, and percentages.
<fmt:formatDate>	Formats dates and times in a locale-sensitive manner.
<fmt:parseDate>	Parses the string representation of dates and times.

For an understanding of these tags, take a look at the JSP shown in Listing 11-7, which uses some of these actions to format dates and numbers, and internationalize currencies.

Listing 11-7. A JSP Formatting Dates and Numbers

```
<%@ page contentType="text/html;charset=UTF-8" language="java" %>
<%@ taglib uri="http://java.sun.com/jsp/jstl/core" prefix="c" %>
<%@ taglib uri="http://java.sun.com/jsp/jstl/fmt" prefix="fmt" %>
<html>
<body>

Dates<br/>
<c:set var="now" value="<%=new java.util.Date()%>"/>
<fmt:formatDate type="time" value="${now}"/><br/>
<fmt:formatDate type="date" value="${now}"/><br/>
<fmt:formatDate type="both" dateStyle="short" timeStyle="short" value="${now}"/><br/>
<fmt:formatDate type="both" dateStyle="long" timeStyle="long" value="${now}"/><br/>

Currency<br/>
<fmt:setLocale value="en_us"/>
<fmt:formatNumber value="20.50" type="currency"/><br/>
<fmt:setLocale value="en_gb"/>
<fmt:formatNumber value="20.50" type="currency"/><br/>

</body>
</html>
```

The page imports the `core` and `format` tag libraries using the `<%@ taglib>` directive element. The `<c:set var="now" value="<%=new java.util.Date()%>"/>` line sets the current date to a variable named `now`. The `<fmt:formatDate>` tag formats this date using different patterns: shows only the time, only the date, both time and date. The `<fmt:setLocale value="en_us"/>` line sets the locale to USA and formats currency so the result is $20.50. Then, the locale is changed to Great Britain and the result is changed to pounds sterling. This JSP produces the following result:

```
Dates
11:31:12
14 may 2010
14/05/10 11:31
14 may 2010 11:31:12 CET

Currency
$20.50
£20.50
```

SQL Actions

The JSTL SQL actions allow database queries (inserts, updates, and deletes), access query results, and even establish a transaction context. You have seen how to access a database using EJBs and JPA entities. Sometimes, for specific applications, you need to access the database from the web page (for example, for a noncritical administrative web application used once in a while by a single user). For this kind of use case, the SQL library and its rich set of tags can be useful (see Table 11-5).

Table 11-5. SQL Actions

Action	Description
`<sql:query>`	Queries a database.
`<sql:update>`	Executes a SQL `INSERT`, `UPDATE`, or `DELETE` statement.
`<sql:transaction>`	Establishes a transaction context for `<sql:query>` and `<sql:update>` subtags.
`<sql:setDataSource>`	Sets the datasource.
`<sql:param>`	Sets the values of parameter markers (?) in a SQL statement.
`<sql:dateParam>`	Sets the values of parameter markers (?) in a SQL statement for values of type `java.util.Date`.

The JSP shown in Listing 11-8 accesses a database, retrieves all the book rows contained in the BOOK table, and displays them.

Listing 11-8. A JSP Accessing a Database and Retrieving All the Books

```
<%@ page contentType="text/html;charset=UTF-8" language="java" %>
<%@ taglib uri="http://java.sun.com/jsp/jstl/core" prefix="c" %>
<%@ taglib uri="http://java.sun.com/jsp/jstl/sql" prefix="sql" %>
<html>
<head>
    <title>Lists all the books</title>
</head>
<body>
<h1>Lists all the books</h1>
<hr/>

<sql:setDataSource dataSource="jdbc/__default"/>
<sql:query var="books">
    select * from book
</sql:query>

<table border="1">
    <tr>
        <th>ISBN</th>
        <th>Title</th>
        <th>Price</th>
        <th>Description</th>
        <th>Number of pages</th>
        <th>Illustrations</th>
    </tr>
```

```
        <c:forEach var="row" items="${books.rows}">
            <tr>
                <td><c:out value="${row.isbn}"/></td>
                <td><c:out value="${row.title}"/></td>
                <td><c:out value="${row.price}"/></td>
                <td><c:out value="${row.description}"/></td>
                <td><c:out value="${row.nbOfPage}"/></td>
                <td><c:out value="${row.illustrations}"/></td>
            </tr>
        </c:forEach>
</table>
<hr/>
<i>APress - Beginning Java EE 6</i>
</body>
</html>
```

This JSP first needs to import the **sql** taglib with the **<%@ taglib>** directive element and set the datasource (in this example, the default datasource **jdbc/__default** bundled with GlassFish). The query **select * from book** is executed, and the result is set in the **books** variable. The results can be accessed by **books.rows**, and the **<c:forEach>** tag iterates over this collection of rows. The result is the same one shown previously in Figure 11-5.

XML Actions

In certain aspects, the XML tag library is similar to the core library; it has core tags to perform XML parsing, flow control tags to iterate over element collections, operations based on XPath expressions, and XML transformation using XSLT documents. Table 11-6 shows the actions contained in the XML library.

Table 11-6. XML Actions

Action	Description
<x:parse>	Parses an XML document.
<x:out>	Evaluates an XPath expression and outputs the result.
<x:set>	Evaluates an XPath expression and stores the result into a variable.
<x:if>	Evaluates the XPath expression if the expression evaluates to **true**.
<x:choose>	Provides mutually exclusive conditions.
<x:when>	Represents an alternative within an <x:choose> action.
<x:otherwise>	Represents the last alternative within an <x:choose> action.
<x:forEach>	Evaluates an XPath expression and repeats its content over the result.
<x:transform>	Applies an XSLT style sheet transformation to an XML document.
<x:param>	Sets transformation parameters. Nested action of <x:transform>.

319

To perform some XML manipulation with these tags, first create an XML document. The `books.xml` file in Listing 11-9 contains a list of books where the data is stored in XML elements and XML attributes.

Listing 11-9. The books.xml File

```
<?xml version='1.0' encoding='UTF-8'?>

<books>
    <book isbn='1234-234' price='12' nbOfPage='241' illustrations='true'>
        <title>H2G2</title>
        <description>Scifi IT book</description>
    </book>
    <book isbn='564-694' price='18.5' nbOfPage='317' illustrations='true'>
        <title>Robots</title>
        <description>Best seller</description>
    </book>
    <book isbn='256-6-56' price='23.25' nbOfPage='529' illustrations='false'>
        <title>Dune</title>
        <description>The trilogy</description>
    </book>
</books>
```

To function, this `books.xml` file has to be deployed with the JSP or be imported by a URL. The JSP in Listing 11-10 parses the file and displays all the books on the page.

Listing 11-10. The JSP Parses the books.xml File and Displays Its Content

```
<%@ page contentType="text/html;charset=UTF-8" language="java" %>
<%@ taglib uri="http://java.sun.com/jsp/jstl/core" prefix="c" %>
<%@ taglib uri="http://java.sun.com/jsp/jstl/xml" prefix="x" %>
<html>
<body>

<table border="1">
    <tr>
        <th>ISBN</th>
        <th>Title</th>
        <th>Price</th>
        <th>Description</th>
        <th>Number of pages</th>
        <th>Illustrations</th>
    </tr>

    <c:import url="books.xml" var="bookUrl"/>
    <x:parse xml="${bookUrl}" var="doc"/>

    <x:forEach var="b" select="$doc/books/book">
```

```
        <tr>
            <td><x:out select="$b/@isbn"/></td>
            <td><x:out select="$b/title"/></td>
            <td><x:out select="$b/@price"/></td>
            <td><x:out select="$b/description"/></td>
            <td><x:out select="$b/@nbOfPage"/></td>
            <td><x:out select="$b/@illustrations"/></td>
        </tr>
    </x:forEach>
</table>
</body>
</html>
```

To commence, this JSP needs to import the XML taglib (with the directive `<%@ taglib>`) and then access the `books.xml` file, which is loaded into the variable `bookUrl` using the `<c:import>` tag. `bookUrl` contains the raw text that needs to be parsed using the `<x:parse>` tag, and the resulting DOM is stored in the variable `doc`. Now that the document is parsed, you iterate through it and display the values by using XPath expressions with `<x:out>` (`/@isbn` represents an XML attribute and `/title` an XML element). The result is the same as that in Figure 11-5.

Functions

Functions are not tags but are defined in the JSTL specification. They can be used with EL and are mostly employed to deal with string manipulation. For example:

```
${fn:contains("H2G2", "H2")}
```

This code checks whether a string contains a substring. In this example, it will return `true` because `H2G2` contains `H2`. The following function returns the length of a string or a collection. The result will be `4`.

```
${fn:length("H2G2")}
```

These functions can display their result in a JSP (within a `<c:out>` tag) and can be used in a test or in a loop.

```
<%@ page contentType="text/html;charset=UTF-8" language="java" %>
<%@ taglib uri="http://java.sun.com/jsp/jstl/core" prefix="c" %>
<%@ taglib uri="http://java.sun.com/jsp/jstl/functions" prefix="fn" %>
<html>
<body>
    <c:set var="sentence" value="Hitchhiker's Guide to the Galaxy"/>
    <c:out value="${fn:toLowerCase(sentence)}" />
    <c:if test="${fn:length('H2G2') == 4}">
        H2G2 is four characters long
    </c:if>
</body>
</html>
```

Table 11-7 shows all the functions contained in the library.

321

Table 11-7. Functions

Function	Description
fn:contains	Tests whether a string contains the specified substring.
fn:containsIgnoreCase	Tests whether a string contains the specified substring in a case-insensitive way.
fn:endsWith	Tests whether a string ends with the specified suffix.
fn:escapeXml	Escapes characters that could be interpreted as XML markup.
fn:indexOf	Returns the index within a string of the first occurrence of a specified substring.
fn:join	Joins all elements of an array into a string.
fn:length	Returns the number of items in a collection or the number of characters in a string.
fn:replace	Returns a string resulting from replacing an input string with all occurrences of a substring.
fn:split	Splits a string into an array of substrings.
fn:startsWith	Tests whether a string starts with the specified prefix.
fn:substring	Returns a subset of a string.
fn:substringAfter	Returns a subset of a string following a specific substring.
fn:substringBefore	Returns a subset of a string before a specific substring.
fn:toLowerCase	Converts all of the characters of a string to lowercase.
fn:toUpperCase	Converts all of the characters of a string to uppercase.
fn:trim	Removes white space from both ends of a string.

Facelets

When JSF was created, the intention was to reuse JSP as the main PDL, as it was already part of Java EE. JSP was using EL and JSTL, so the idea was to make use of all these technologies within JSF. JSP is a page language, and JSF is a component layer on top of it. However, JSP and JSF life cycles don't fit together well. Tags in JSPs are processed once from top to bottom in order to produce a response. JSF has a more complex life cycle where the component tree generation and the rendering occur at different phases. This is where Facelets comes into play: to fit the JSF life cycle.

Facelets began life as an open source alternative to JSP. Unlike JSP, EL, and JSTL, it didn't have a JSR and was not part of Java EE. Facelets was a replacement for JSP and provided an XML-based alternative (XHTML) for pages in a JSF-based application. Facelets was designed with JSF in mind, and this is why it provided a simpler programming model than JSP's. Because of that, today Facelets is specified by the JSF specification and comes with Java EE 6 as the preferred PDL for JSF.

Facelets comes with a tag library for writing the user interface and provides partial support for JSTL tags. While the function tag library is fully supported, only a few core tags are (`c:if`, `c:forEach`, `c:catch`, and `c:set`). But the key feature of Facelets is its page templating, which is more flexible than the JSP one. It also allows you to create custom components to be used in the JSF component tree model.

The Facelets tag library is defined by the http://java.sun.com/jsf/facelets URI and usually uses the `ui` prefix. Table 11-8 lists all the available tags.

Table 11-8. Facelets Tags

Tag	Description
`<ui:composition>`	Defines a composition that optionally uses a template. Multiple compositions can use the same template.
`<ui:component>`	Creates a component.
`<ui:debug>`	Captures debugging information.
`<ui:define>`	Defines content that is inserted into a page by a template.
`<ui:decorate>`	Allows you to decorate some content in a page.
`<ui:fragment>`	Adds a fragment of a page.
`<ui:include>`	Encapsulates and reuses content among multiple XHTML pages, similar to JSP's `<jsp:include>`.
`<ui:insert>`	Inserts content into a template.
`<ui:param>`	Passes parameters to an included file (using `<ui:include>`) or a template.
`<ui:repeat>`	Serves as an alternative to `<c:forEach>`.
`<ui:remove>`	Removes content from a page.

Facelets pages are written in XHTML and look like what you saw earlier in Listing 11-2. In the "Templating" section of this chapter, you will see how to use templating with Facelets.

JavaServer Faces

I began this chapter by introducing JSP, JSTL, and Facelets, as they are essential for an understanding of JSF 2.0. You need to choose a PDL to use when writing JSF. JSP was the preferred PDL until JSF 1.2. JSP and JSF have different page life cycles; with JSF 2.0, the preferred PDL is Facelets (XHTML formatted pages). This does not mean that you cannot use JSP, but it does mean that you will be limited in terms of tags and features.

JSPs have a relatively simple life cycle. A JSP source is compiled into a servlet, and, when a web container receives an HTTP request, it passes it to the servlet. The servlet processes the request, and then writes the response back to the client.

JSF has a more complex life cycle, and this is why, in the "Expression Language" section, I showed you two different syntaxes: one using the dollar symbol (${expression}) and the other using the hash (#{expression}). $ is for expressions that can be executed immediately (when you know that the objects in the expression are available), and # is for deferred expressions (which have to be evaluated later in the life cycle).

With JSF 1.2, both syntaxes were unified, but this led to much confusion and many errors. For example, if you use JSP as the PDL, you won't have access to some JSF tags (such as the Facelets tags for example). In this section, I will use Facelets as the PDL.

Table 11-9 lists all the tag libraries that a Facelets PDL page can use. There are the functions and core libraries that were in the JSTL sections, the Facelets tags (with the ui prefix), and new tags such as JSF's core and html, and composite, which allows you to create custom components. Other JSTL tags (formatting, SQL, and XML actions) are not supported by Facelets.

Table 11-9. Tag Libraries Allowed with Facelets PDL

URI	Common Prefix	Description
http://java.sun.com/jsf/html	h	This tag library contains components and their HTML renderers (h:commandButton, h:commandLink, h:inputText, etc.).
http://java.sun.com/jsf/core	f	This library contains custom actions that are independent of any particular rendering (f:selectItem, f:validateLength, f:convertNumber, etc.).
http://java.sun.com/jsf/facelets	ui	Tags in this library add templating support.
http://java.sun.com/jsf/composite	composite	This tag library is used for declaring and defining composite components.
http://java.sun.com/jsp/jstl/core	c	Facelets pages can use some of the core JSP tag libraries (<c:if/>, <c:forEach/>, and <c:catch/>).
http://java.sun.com/jsp/jstl/functions	fn	Facelets pages can use all the function JSP tag libraries.

Let's focus on the JSF HTML components that will allow you to create rich web interfaces. Chapter 12 shows most of the JSF core library with converters and validators. But first let's take a look at the JSF page life cycle.

Life Cycle

A JSF page is a component tree with a specific life cycle. You should understand it so you know when components are validated or the model is updated. Clicking a button causes a request to be sent from your web browser to the server. This request is translated into an event that can be processed by your application logic on the server. All data entered by the user enters a phase of validation before the model is updated and any business logic invoked. JSF is then responsible for making sure that every graphical component (child and parent components) is properly rendered to the browser. Figure 11-6 shows the different phases of a JSF page life cycle.

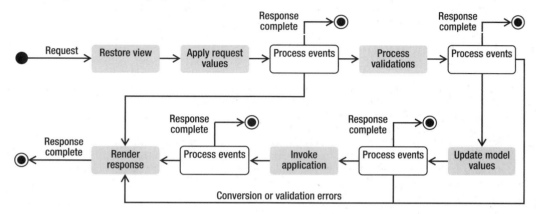

Figure 11-6. *The JSF life cyle*

The JSF life cycle is divided into six distinct phases:

1. *Restore view*: JSF finds the target view and applies the user's input to it. If this is the client's first visit to the page, JSF creates the view as a `UIViewRoot` component (root of the component tree that makes up a particular page). If this is a subsequent request, the previously saved `UIViewRoot` is retrieved for processing the current HTTP request.

2. *Apply request values*: Values that have come from the request (from input fields in a web form, from cookies, or from request headers) are applied to the various components of the page. Note that only UI components update their state—not the business objects that compose the model.

3. *Process validations*: After the preceding steps, the UI components have a value set. In the validation processing, JSF traverses the component tree and asks each component to ensure its submitted value is acceptable. If both conversion and validation are successful for all components, the life cycle continues to its next phase. Otherwise, the life cycle goes to the *Render response* phase with the appropriate validation and conversion error messages.

4. *Update model values*: With all values of the components set and validated, you can update the managed beans associated with them.

5. *Invoke application*: Now you can perform some business logic. Whatever action has been triggered will be executed on the managed bean, and this is where the navigation comes into effect, as its return will determine the render response.

6. *Render response*: To achieve the primary goal of this phase, send the response back to the user. The secondary goal is to save the state of the view so that it can be restored in the restore view phase if the user requests it again.

The thread of execution for a request/response cycle can flow through each phase or not, depending on the request and what happens during the processing; if an error occurs, the flow of execution transfers immediately to the render response phase. Note that four of these phases can generate messages: apply request values, process validations, update model values, and invoke application. With or without messages, it is the render response phase that sends output back to the user.

Standard HTML Components

JSF's architecture is designed to be independent of any particular protocol or markup language, and it is also made to write applications for HTML clients that communicate via HTTP. A user interface for a particular web page is created by assembling components. Components provide specific functionality for interacting with an end user (labels, tables, check boxes, etc.). JSF provides a number of component classes that cover most of the common requirements.

A page is a tree of classes that extend `javax.faces.component.UIComponent` and has properties, methods, and events. The components in the tree have parent-child relationships with other components, starting at the root element of the tree, which is an instance of `UIViewRoot`. Let's focus on using these components on web pages.

Commands

Commands are controls that a user can click to trigger an action. Such a component is typically rendered as a button or a hyperlink. Table 11-10 lists the two command tags that can be used.

Table 11-10. Command Tags

Tag	Description
`<h:commandButton>`	Represents an HTML input element for a button of type submit or reset.
`<h:commandLink>`	Represents an HTML element for a hyperlink that acts like a submit button. This component must be placed inside a form.

If on your page you need to add submit buttons, reset buttons, images that you can click, or hyperlinks that trigger an event, do so as follows:

```
<h:commandButton value="A submit button"/>
<h:commandButton type="reset" value="A reset button"/>
<h:commandButton image="javaee6.gif" title="A button with an image"/>
<h:commandLink>A hyperlink</h:commandLink>
```

By default, a `commandButton` is of type submit, but it can be changed to type reset (`type="reset"`). If you want to turn a button into an image, don't use the `value` attribute (that's the name of the button), instead use the `image` attribute to specify the path of the image you want to display. Following is the graphical result of the previous code:

A hyperlink

Both buttons and links have an `action` attribute to invoke a method on a managed bean. To call the `doNew()` method of the `bookController`, use the expression language to specify it in the `action` attribute as follows:

```
<h:commandLink action="#{bookController.doNew}">
    Create a new book
</h:commandLink>
```

Inputs

Inputs are components that display their current value to the user and allow the user to enter different kinds of textual information. These can be text fields, text areas, or components to enter a password or hidden data. The input tags are listed in Table 11-11.

Table 11-11. Input Tags

Tag	Description
`<h:inputHidden>`	Represents an HTML input element of type hidden (which is useful to propagate values outside of the session from page to page).
`<h:inputSecret>`	Represents an HTML input element of type password. On a redisplay, any previously entered value will not be rendered (for security reasons) unless the redisplay property is set to `true`.
`<h:inputText>`	Represents an HTML input element of type text.
`<h:inputTextarea>`	Represents an HTML text area element.

Many web pages contain forms in which a user has to enter some data or log on using a password. Input components have several attributes that allow you to change their length, content, or look and feel, as follows:

```
<h:inputHidden value="Hidden data"/>
<h:inputSecret maxlength="8"/>
<h:inputText value="An input text"/>
<h:inputText size="40" value="A longer input text"/>
<h:inputTextarea rows="4" cols="20" value="A text area"/>
```

All the components have a `value` attribute to set their default value. You can use the `maxLength` attribute to check that text entered doesn't go over a certain length or the `size` attribute to change the default size of the component. The previous code will have the following graphical representation:

Outputs

Output components display a value, optionally retrieved from a managed bean, a value expression, or fixed text. The user cannot directly modify the value because it is for display purposes only. Table 11-12 lists the output tags available.

Table 11-12. Output Tags

Tag	Description
`<h:outputLabel>`	Renders an HTML `<label>` element.
`<h:outputLink>`	Renders an HTML `<a>` anchor element.
`<h:outputText>`	Outputs text.
`<h:outputFormat>`	Renders parameterized text.
`<h:button>`	Renders an HTML input element for a button (produces a HTTP GET when clicked).
`<h:link>`	Renders an HTML `<a>` anchor element (produces a HTTP GET when clicked).

Most of the web pages have to display some text. You can do this with normal HTML elements, but JSF output tags allow you to display the content of a variable bound to a managed bean using EL. You can display text with `<h:outputText>` and hypertext links with `<h:outputLink>`. Notice that the difference between `<h:commandLink>` and `<h:outputLink>` is that the latter displays the link but doesn't invoke any method when clicked. It just creates an external link or anchor.

```
<h:outputLabel value="#{bookController.book.title}"/>
<h:outputText value="A text"/>
<h:outputLink value="http://www.apress.com/">A link</h:outputLink>
<h:outputFormat value="Welcome {0}. You have bought {1} items">
    <f:param value="#{user.firstName}" />
    <f:param value="#{user.itemsBought}" />
</h:outputFormat>
```

The preceding code doesn't have any special graphical representation. Following is the HTML rendering:

```
<label>The title of the book</label>
A text
<a href="http://www.apress.com/">A link</a>
Welcome Paul. You have bought 5 items
```

Selections

Selection components (see Table 11-13), which are used to select one or more values out of a list, are represented by check boxes, radio buttons, lists, or combo boxes. They allow the user to choose between a definite set of available options.

Table 11-13. Select Tags

Tag	Description
`<h:selectBooleanCheckbox>`	Renders one check box representing a single Boolean value. The check box will be rendered as checked or not based on the value of the property.
`<h:selectManyCheckbox>`	Renders a list of check boxes.
`<h:selectManyListbox>`	Renders a multiple-selection component where one or more options can be selected.
`<h:selectManyMenu>`	Renders an HTML `<select>` element.
`<h:selectOneListbox>`	Renders a single-selection component where only one available option can be selected.
`<h:selectOneMenu>`	Renders a single-selection component where only one available option can be selected. It only shows a single available option at a time.
`<h:selectOneRadio>`	Renders a list of radio buttons.

The tags listed in this table have a graphical representation but require different tags to hold available options: `<f:selectItem>` or `<f:selectItems>`. These tags are nested inside the graphical components and create additional available options. To represent a combo box with a list of book genres, you should nest a set of `<f:selectItem>` tags in an `<h:selectOneMenu>` tag.

```
<h:selectOneMenu>
    <f:selectItem itemLabel="History"/>
    <f:selectItem itemLabel="Biography"/>
    <f:selectItem itemLabel="Literature"/>
    <f:selectItem itemLabel="Comics"/>
    <f:selectItem itemLabel="Child"/>
    <f:selectItem itemLabel="Scifi"/>
</h:selectOneMenu>
```

Figure 11-7 shows all the possible representations. Some lists have multiple choices, others single choices, and, like all the other components, you can bind the value of a managed bean (List, Set, etc.) directly to one of the lists.

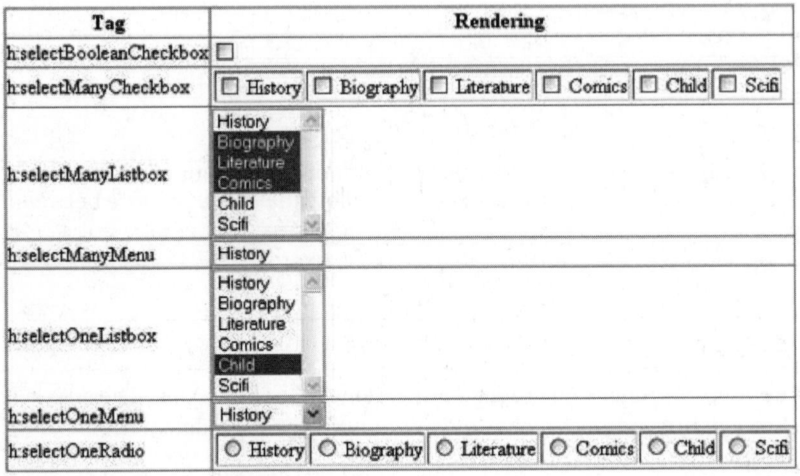

Tag	Rendering
h:selectBooleanCheckbox	☐
h:selectManyCheckbox	☐ History ☐ Biography ☐ Literature ☐ Comics ☐ Child ☐ Scifi
h:selectManyListbox	History / Biography / Literature / Comics / Child / Scifi
h:selectManyMenu	History
h:selectOneListbox	History / Biography / Literature / Comics / Child / Scifi
h:selectOneMenu	History
h:selectOneRadio	○ History ○ Biography ○ Literature ○ Comics ○ Child ○ Scifi

Figure 11-7. *Multiple representations of lists*

Graphics

There is only one component for displaying images: `<h:graphicImage>`. It displays a graphical image to users that they cannot click on (such as a button or a link). This tag is rendered as an HTML `<img>` element. It has several attributes that allow you to resize the image, use a graphic as an image map, and so on. You can display an image that is bound to a property in a managed bean and comes from a file system or a database. The following code displays an image and resizes it:

```
<h:graphicImage value="book.gif" height="200" width="320"/>
```

Grid and Tables

Very often data needs to be displayed in a table format (see Table 11-14). JSF has the very powerful `<h:dataTable>` tag that iterates through a list of elements and creates a table (refer back to the code of the `listBooks.xhtml` page that appears in Listing 10-7 in Chapter 10). Tables can also be used to create a layout for a grid-based user interface. In this case, you can employ the `<h:panelGrid>` and `<h:panelGroup>` tags to lay out your components.

Table 11-14. Grid and Table Tags

Tag	Description
`<h:dataTable>`	Represents a set of repeating data that will be rendered in an HTML `<table>` element.
`<h:column>`	Renders a single column of data within an `<h:dataTable>` component.
`<h:panelGrid>`	Renders an HTML `<table>` element.
`<h:panelGroup>`	Is a container of components that can be embedded in an `<h:panelGrid>`.

Unlike `<h:dataTable>`, the `<h:panelGrid>` tag does not use an underlying data model to render rows of data. Rather, this component is a layout container that renders other JSF components in a grid of rows and columns. You can specify how many columns are used to display the components, and the `<h:panelGrid>` will determine how many rows are needed. The `columns` attribute is the number of columns to render before starting a new row. For example, in the following code, the rendering will be three columns and two rows (displaying rows first and then columns):

```
<h:panelGrid columns="3" border="1">
    <h:outputLabel value="One"/>
    <h:outputLabel value="Two"/>
    <h:outputLabel value="Three"/>
    <h:outputLabel value="Four"/>
    <h:outputLabel value="Five"/>
    <h:outputLabel value="Six"/>
</h:panelGrid>
```

If you want to combine several components into a single column, you can use an `<h:panelGroup>` that will render its children as only one component. You can also define a header and a footer using the special `<f:facet>` tag.

```
<h:panelGrid columns="3" border="1">
    <f:facet name="header">
        <h:outputText value="Header"/>
    </f:facet>
    <h:outputLabel value="One"/>
    <h:outputLabel value="Two"/>
    <h:outputLabel value="Three"/>
    <h:outputLabel value="Four"/>
    <h:outputLabel value="Five"/>
    <h:outputLabel value="Six"/>
    <f:facet name="footer">
        <h:outputText value="Footer"/>
    </f:facet>
</h:panelGrid>
```

The two tables previously described will have the following graphical representation, one with a header and a footer, and the other with neither:

Error Messages

Applications can sometimes throw exceptions due to incorrectly formatted data or technical reasons. But, as far as users are concerned, enough information should be displayed on the interface to draw their attention to correct the problem (not the entire exception stack trace). The mechanism for managing error messages is to include <h:message> and <h:messages> tags in a page (see Table 11-15). <h:message> is tied to a particular component, while <h:messages> can provide global messaging for all components on the page.

Table 11-15. Message Tags

Tag	Description
<h:message>	Renders one error message.
<h:messages>	Renders all the enqueued error messages.

Messages can have different severities (INFO, WARN, ERROR, and FATAL), each of which corresponds to a CSS style (infoStyle, warnStyle, errorStyle, and fatalStyle). In this way, each type of message can have a different rendering style. For example, the following code will display all messages in red:

```
<h:messages style="color:red"/>
<h:form>
    Enter a title:
    <h:inputText value="#{bookController.title}" required="true"/>
    <h:commandButton action="#{bookController.save}" value="Save"/>
</h:form>
```

This will display an input field bound to a managed bean property. This property is required, so, if the user clicks the save button without filling it, an error message will be displayed.

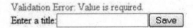

Miscellaneous

There are other tags that don't have any graphical representation but do have an HTML equivalent. The native HTML tag can be used and will work. With JSF tags, extra attributes are available to make development easier. For example, you can add a JavaScript library to a page using the standard HTML `<script type="text/javascript">` tag. But, with the JSF `<h:outputScript>` tag, you can use new resource management, as you'll see later in the "Resource Management" section. These miscellaneous tags are shown in Table 11-16.

Table 11-16. Miscellaneous Tags

Tag	Description
`<h:body>`	Renders an HTML `<body>` element.
`<h:head>`	Renders an HTML `<head>` element.
`<h:form>`	Renders an HTML `<form>` element.
`<h:outputScript>`	Renders the markup for a `<script>`.
`<h:outputStylesheet>`	Renders the markup for a `<link>` element.

Templating

A typical web application contains several pages that share a look and feel, a header, a footer, a menu, and so forth. Facelets allows you to define a layout in a template file that can be used for all the pages in the web application. A template defines areas (with the `<ui:insert>` tag) where the content can be replaced. The client page then uses the tags `<ui:component>`, `<ui:composition>`, `<ui:fragment>`, or `<ui:decorate>` to embed fragments into the template. Table 11-17 lists the various templating tags (see the full list of `ui` tags in Table 11-8).

Table 11-17. Templating Tags

Tag	Description
`<ui:composition>`	Defines a composition that optionally uses a template. Multiple compositions can use the same template.
`<ui:define>`	Defines a set of content to be inserted into a corresponding `<ui:insert>` element in a template.
`<ui:decorate>`	Allows you to decorate some content in a page.
`<ui:fragment>`	Adds a fragment of a page.
`<ui:insert>`	Defines an insertion point in a template where content can be inserted using `<ui:define>` tags around the actual content.
`<ui:param>`	Passes parameters to an included file (using `<ui:include>`) or a template.

As an example, let's reuse the page representing a form to create a new book (refer back to Figure 11-1). You could say that the title is the header of the page, and the footer would be the underlying text *Apress - Beginning Java EE 6*. So, the template called `layout.xml` would look like the code in Listing 11-11.

Listing 11-11. The layout.xml File as a Facelets Template

```
<html xmlns="http://www.w3.org/1999/xhtml"
      xmlns:ui="http://java.sun.com/jsf/facelets"
      xml:lang="en" lang="en">

<head>
    <title><ui:insert name="title">Default title</ui:insert></title>
</head>
<body>
    <h1><ui:insert name="title">Default title</ui:insert></h1>
    <hr/>

    <ui:insert name="content">Default content</ui:insert>

    <hr/>
    <i>APress - Beginning Java EE 6</i>

</body>
</html>
```

Our template must first define the needed tag library (`xmlns:ui="http://java.sun.com/jsf/facelets"`). Then, it uses the `<ui:insert>` tag to insert a `title` attribute into the `<title>` and `<h1>` tags. The body of the page will be inserted into the attribute called `content`.

To use this template, our `newBook.xhtml` page, shown in Listing 11-12, needs to declare which template it needs (`<ui:composition template="layout.xhtml">`). Then, the idea is to bind the attributes defined in the `<ui:define>` tag with the `<ui:insert>` tag in the template. For example, the title of the page is "Create a new book." This text is stored in the `title` variable (with `<ui:define name="title">`), which is bound to the matching `<ui:insert name="title">`. It is the same for the rest of the page, which is inserted into the `content` variable (`<ui:define name="content">`).

Listing 11-12. The newBook. xhtml Page Using the Template

```
<html xmlns="http://www.w3.org/1999/xhtml"
      xmlns:ui="http://java.sun.com/jsf/facelets"
      xml:lang="en" lang="en">

<ui:composition template="layout.xhtml">

    <ui:define name="title">Create a new book</ui:define>

    <ui:define name="content">

        <table border="0">
            <tr>
                <td>ISBN :</td>
                <td><input type="text"/></td>
            </tr>
            <tr>
                <td>Title : </td>
                <td><input type="text"/></td>
            </tr>
            <tr>
                <td>Price :</td>
                <td><input type="text"/></td>
            </tr>
            <tr>
                <td>Description :</td>
                <td><textarea name="textarea" cols="20" rows="5">
                    </textarea>
                </td>
            </tr>
            <tr>
                <td>Number of pages :</td>
                <td><input type="text"/></td>
            </tr>
            <tr>
                <td>Illustrations :</td>
                <td><input type="checkbox"/></td>
            </tr>
        </table>
        <input name="" type="submit" value="Create"/>

    </ui:define>

</ui:composition>
</html>
```

Figure 11-8 shows the result of the `newBook.xhtml` page being bound to the `layout.xhtml` template, which is the same as that shown previously in Figure 11-1.

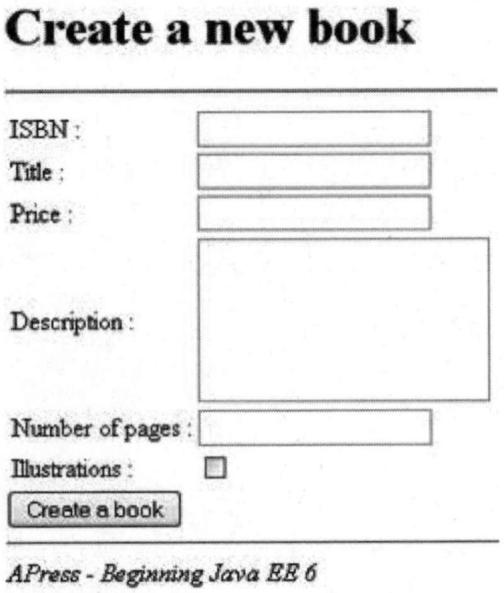

Create a new book

ISBN :

Title :

Price :

Description :

Number of pages :

Illustrations :

[Create a book]

APress - Beginning Java EE 6

Figure 11-8. *The newBook.html page with the layout.xhtml template*

Resource Management

Most of the components may need external resources in order to be rendered properly. `<h:graphicImage>` needs an external image to display, `<h:commandButton>` can also display an image as a button, `<h:outputScript>` references an external JavaScript file, and components can apply CSS styles (with `<h:outputStylesheet>`). In JSF, a resource is a static element that can be transmitted to components so they can be displayed (images) or processed (JavaScript, CSS) by the browser.

Previous versions of JSF had no facility for serving resources. When you wanted to provide a resource, you had to put it in the `WEB-INF` directory so that the client's browser could access it. The problem was that, if you wanted to update it, you had to replace the file in the directory and have different directories to render localized resources (for example, an image with English or Portuguese text). JSF 2.0 has support for this functionality, so you can now put your resources directly under the `resources` directory or package them into a separate jar (with an optional version and/or locale). The resource can be placed in the web application root under the path:

resources/`<resourceIdentifier>`

or under a jar file in the `WEB-INF/lib` directory:

`WEB-INF/lib/{*.jar}/META-INF/`**resources**`/<resourceIdentifier>`

`<resourceIdentifier>` consists of several subfolders, specified as follows:

`[localePrefix/][libraryName/][libVersion/]resourceName[/resourceVersion]`

Items in this resource identifier in [ ] are optional. The local prefix consists of the language code followed by an optional country code (en, en_US, pt, pt_BR). As this line indicates, you can add versioning to the library or the resource itself. Following are resource structures you might end up with:

```
book.gif
en/book.gif
en_us/book.gif
en/myLibrary/book.gif
myLibrary/book.gif
myLibrary/1_0/book.gif
myLibrary/1_0/book.gif/2_3.gif
```

You can then use a resource, such as this book.gif image, directly in the <h:graphicImage> component or by specifying the library name (library="myLibrary"). The resource with the right locale for your client will get pulled automatically.

```
<h:graphicImage value="book.gif" />
<h:graphicImage value="book.gif" library="myLibrary" />
<h:graphicImage value="#{resource['book.gif']}" />
<h:graphicImage value="#{resource['myLibrary:book.gif']}" />
```

Composite Components

All the previously discussed components are part of JSF and come with any implementation that follows the specification. Because JSF is based on reusable components, it provides a design that allows you to easily create and integrate your own components or third-party components into your applications.

Earlier, I mentioned that all components you've seen extend, directly or indirectly, the javax.faces.component.UIComponent class. Before JSF 2.0, if you wanted to create your own component, you had to extend the component class that most closely represented your component (UICommand, UIGraphic, UIOutput, etc.), declare it in the faces-config.xml file, and provide a tag handler and a renderer. These steps were complex, and other web frameworks such as Facelets showed that it was possible to create powerful components with less complexity. This is the point of composite components: to enable developers to write real, reusable, JSF UI components without any Java code or configuration XML.

This new approach involves creating an XHTML page that contains components, and then using this page as a component in other pages. This XHTML page is then seen as a real component that can support validators, converters, and listeners. Any valid markup can be used inside of a composite component, including the templating features. Composite components are handled as resources and therefore must reside within the new standard resource directories. Table 11-18 lists all the tags involved in the creation and definition of a composite component.

Table 11-18. Tags Used for Declaring and Defining Composite Components

Tag	Description
`<composite:interface>`	Declares the contract for a component.
`<composite:implementation>`	Defines the implementation of a component.
`<composite:attribute>`	Declares an attribute that may be given to an instance of the component. There may be zero or many of these inside of the `<composite:interface>` section.
`<composite:facet>`	Declares that this component supports a facet.
`<composite:insertFacet>`	Is used in the `<composite:implementation>` section. The inserted facet will be rendered in the component.
`<composite:insertChildren>`	Is used in the `<composite:implementation>` section. Any child components or template within the component will be inserted into the rendered output.
`<composite:valueHolder>`	Declares that the component whose contract is declared by the `<composite:interface>` in which this element is nested exposes an implementation of `ValueHolder`.
`<composite:renderFacet>`	Is used in the `<composite:implementation>` section to render a facet.
`<composite:extension>`	Is used within a `<composite:interface>` section to include XML content not defined by the JSF specification.
`<composite:editableValueHolder>`	Declares that the component whose contract is declared by the `<composite:interface>` in which this element is nested exposes an implementation of `EditableValueHolder`.
`<composite:actionSource>`	Declares that the component whose contract is declared by the `<composite:interface>` in which this element is nested exposes an implementation of `ActionSource`.

Let's explore an example that shows how easy it is to create a graphical component and use it in other pages. You might remember from previous chapters that the CD-BookStore application sells two different items: books and CDs. In Chapter 3, I represented them as three different objects: Book and CD extending Item. Item contains the common attributes (a title, a price, and a description), and then the Book and the CD have specialized ones (isbn, publisher, nbOfPage, and illustrations for Book; musicCompany, numberOfCDs, totalDuration, and gender for CD). If you want your web application to be able to create new books and CDs, you need two different forms. But the common attributes of Item could be in a separate page that would act as a component. Figure 11-9 shows these two pages.

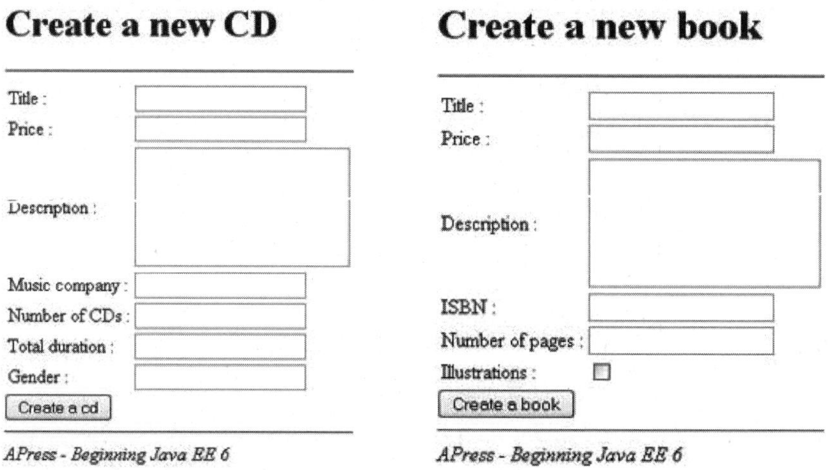

Create a new CD

Title :	
Price :	
Description :	
Music company :	
Number of CDs :	
Total duration :	
Gender :	

Create a cd

APress - Beginning Java EE 6

Create a new book

Title :	
Price :	
Description :	
ISBN :	
Number of pages :	
Illustrations :	☐

Create a book

APress - Beginning Java EE 6

Figure 11-9. Two forms, one to create a CD, another one to create a book

So let's create a composite component with two input texts (for the title and the price) and one text area (for the description). The approach to writing a component with JSF 2.0 is relatively close to what you are used to in Java. You must first write an interface, `<composite:interface>` (see Listing 11-13), that acts as an entry point for the component. It describes the names and the parameters used by the component. Then comes the implementation, `<composite:implementation>`. It is the body of the component written in XHTML and using any JSF tags or templates. Interface and implementation are in the same XHTML page. The implementation uses `<tr>` and `<td>` markups because I'm assuming it will be placed within a preexisting `<table>` with two columns.

Listing 11-13. The newItem. xhtml Contains a Composite Component

```
<!DOCTYPE html PUBLIC "-//W3C//DTD XHTML 1.0 Transitional//EN"
        "http://www.w3.org/TR/xhtml1/DTD/xhtml1-transitional.dtd">
<html xmlns="http://www.w3.org/1999/xhtml"
     xmlns:h="http://java.sun.com/jsf/html"
     xmlns:composite="http://java.sun.com/jsf/composite">

<composite:interface>
    <composite:attribute name="item" required="true"/>
    <composite:attribute name="style" required="false"/>
</composite:interface>

<composite:implementation>
    <tr style="#{cc.attrs.style}">
        <td>Title :</td>
        <td>
            <h:inputText value="#{cc.attrs.item.title}"/>
        </td>
```

```
        </tr>
        <tr style="#{cc.attrs.style}">
            <td>Price :</td>
            <td>
                <h:inputText value="#{cc.attrs.item.price}"/>
            </td>
        </tr>
        <tr style="#{cc.attrs.style}">
            <td>Description :</td>
            <td>
                <h:inputTextarea
                    value="#{cc.attrs.item.description}"
                    cols="20" rows="5"/>
            </td>
        </tr>
</composite:implementation>
</html>
```

This component declares an interface with two attributes: `item` represents the `Item` entity (and the subclasses `Book` and `CD`), and `style` is a CSS style used for rendering. These attributes are then employed in the implementation of the composite component using the following syntax:

```
#{cc.attrs.[attributeName]}
```

This code indicates the `getAttributes()` method will be called in the current composite component; within the returned `Map`, the code will look for the value under the key `attributeName`. This is how a component uses attributes that are defined in the interface.

Before I explain how to use this component, recall the discussion on resource management earlier in the chapter and the notion of configuration by exception. The component has to be saved in a file that resides inside a resource library. For example, the file for this example is called `newItem.xhtml` and is saved under `/resources/apress`. If you leave all the defaults, to use this component you need to declare a library called `apress` and give it an XML namespace (`ago` in the following code):

```
<html xmlns:ago="http://java.sun.com/jsf/composite/apress">
```

Then, call the component `newItem` (the name of the page), passing any required parameters: `item` is the parameter that refers to the `Item` entity, and `style` is the optional parameter that refers to a CSS style.

```
<ago:newItem item="#{itemController.book}" style="myCssStyle"/>
<ago:newItem item="#{itemController.cd}"/>
```

To give you an overall picture of how to incorporate a component, Listing 11-14 shows the `newBook.xhtml` page representing the form to enter the book data. It includes the `newItem` composite component and adds input fields for the ISBN, the number of pages, and a check box to indicate whether the book has illustrations or not.

Listing 11-14. The newBook. xhtml Page Uses the newItem Component

```
<!DOCTYPE html PUBLIC "-//W3C//DTD XHTML 1.0 Transitional//EN"
        "http://www.w3.org/TR/xhtml1/DTD/xhtml1-transitional.dtd">
<html xmlns="http://www.w3.org/1999/xhtml"
      xmlns:h="http://java.sun.com/jsf/html"
      xmlns:ago="http://java.sun.com/jsf/composite/apress">
<h:head>
    <title>Creates a new book</title>
</h:head>
<h:body>
<h1>Create a new book</h1>
<hr/>
<h:form>
  <table border="0">

    <ago:newItem item="#{itemController.book}"/>

    <tr>
      <td><h:outputLabel value="ISBN : "/></td>
      <td><h:inputText value="#{itemController.book.isbn}"/></td>
    </tr>

    <tr>
      <td><h:outputLabel value="Number of pages : "/></td>
      <td><h:inputText value="#{itemController.book.nbOfPage}"/></td>
    </tr>

    <tr>
        <td><h:outputLabel value="Illustrations : "/></td>
      <td><h:selectBooleanCheckbox
                value="#{itemController.book.illustrations}"/></td>
    </tr>

  </table>

  <h:commandButton value="Create a book"
                action="#{itemController.doCreateBook}"/>

  </h:form>
  <hr/>
  <i>APress - Beginning Java EE 6</i>

</h:body>
</html>
```

Implicit Objects

When you created your composite component, in the implementation you used a cc object. You didn't declare it anywhere; it was simply available so you could get the attributes of the component. These kinds of objects are called *implicit objects* (or *implicit variables*). Implicit objects are special identifiers that map to specific commonly used objects. They are implicit because a page has access to them and can use them without needing to explicitly declare or initialize them. Implicit objects are used within EL expressions. Table 11-19 lists all the implicit objects that a page can have access to.

Table 11-19. Implicit Objects

Implicit Object	Description	Returns
application	Represents the web application environment. Used to get application-level configuration parameters.	Object
applicationScope	Maps application-scoped attribute names to their values.	Map
component	Indicates the current component.	UIComponent
cc	Indicates the current composite component.	UIComponent
cookie	Specifies a Map containing cookie names (the key) and Cookie objects.	Map
facesContext	Indicates the FacesContext instance of this request.	FacesContext
flash	Represents the flash object (more on scopes in the next chapter).	Object
header	Maps HTTP header names to a single String header value.	Map
headerValues	Maps HTTP header names to a String[] of all values for that header.	Map
initParam	Maps context initialization parameter names to their String parameter values.	Map
param	Maps request parameter names to a single String parameter value.	Map
paramValues	Maps request parameter names to a String[] of all values for that parameter.	Map
request	Represents the HTTP request object.	Object
requestScope	Maps request-scoped attribute names to their values.	Map
resource	Specifies the resource object.	Object
session	Represents the HTTP session object.	Object
sessionScope	Maps session-scoped attribute names to their values.	Map
view	Represents the current view.	UIViewRoot
viewScope	Maps view-scoped attribute names to their values.	Map

All these implicit objects are actual objects with interfaces, and, once you know what they are (refer to the specification), you can access their attributes with EL. For example, `#{view.locale}` will get the locale of the current view (`en_US`, `pt_PT`, etc.). If you store a `book` object in the session scope, you could access it like this: `#{sessionScope.book}`. You can even use a richer algorithm to display all the HTTP headers and their values as follows:

Listing 11-15. A Page Displaying the HTTP Headers Using the headerValues Implicit Object

```
<h3>headerValues</h3>
<c:forEach var="parameter" items="#{headerValues}">
    <h:outputText value="#{parameter.key}"/> =
    <c:forEach var="value" items="#{parameter.value}">
        <h:outputText value="#{value}" escape="false"/><br/>
    </c:forEach>
</c:forEach>
```

If you execute this page, you will get a page that shows all the HTTP headers.

headerValues

host =localhost:8080
user-agent =Mozilla/5.0 (Windows; U; Windows NT 5.1; fr; rv:1.9.0.6) Gecko/2009011913 Firefox/3.0.6
accept =text/html,application/xhtml+xml,application/xml;q=0.9,*/*;q=0.8
accept-language =fr,fr-fr;q=0.8,en-us;q=0.5,en;q=0.3
accept-encoding =gzip,deflate
accept-charset =ISO-8859-1,utf-8;q=0.7,*;q=0.7
keep-alive =300
connection =keep-alive
referer =http://localhost:8080/chapter11-1.0/
cookie =com.sun.faces.extensions.flash.PostbackRequest=1; JSESSIONID=0a5ac1217660ad44e45d7956ec6e;
com.sun.faces.extensions.flash.PostbackRequest=123; JSESSIONID=eedf80c16a1382991d11cd67460a
cache-control =max-age=0

Summary

This chapter explained the different ways of creating web pages using static languages such as HTML, XHTML, or CSS and dynamic ones such as JavaScript or server-side technologies. To create dynamic web interfaces with Java EE 6, you can choose from several specifications. JSP 2.2, EL 2.2, and JSTL 1.2 are specifications that were created with servlets in mind. Pages consist of HTML data and Java code compiled into servlets that send back a response to a given request.

Even though JSP can serve as a JSF PDL, it is better to use Facelets to achieve the power of the JSF component-based architecture and rich life cycle. JSF provides a set of standard widgets (buttons, hyperlinks, check boxes, etc.) and a new model for creating your own widgets (composite components). JSF 2.0 also provides a new resource-handling mechanism, allowing you to easily version and localize your external resources.

JSF 2.0 uses a rich UI component architecture, and its components can be converted and validated, and can interact with managed beans. This will be the topic of the next chapter.

CHAPTER 12

Processing and Navigation

In the previous chapter, I showed you how to create web pages using different technologies (HTML, JSP, JSTL, etc.), knowing that JSF is the preferred Java EE specification for writing modern web applications. However, drawing pages with graphical components is not enough; these pages need to interact with a back-end system, navigate through pages, and validate and convert data. JSF is a rich specification: managed beans allow you to invoke the business tier and to navigate in your application, and a set of classes allow you to convert component values to and from a corresponding type or validate them to conform to business rules. With the use of annotations, it is now easy to develop custom converters and validators.

JSF 2.0 brings simplicity and richness in terms of dynamic user interfaces. It natively supports Ajax calls in a simple manner. The specification comes with a JavaScript library, allowing asynchronous calls to the server and refreshing small portions of the page.

Creating user interfaces, controlling navigation in the entire application, and calling business logic synchronously or asynchronously are possible because JSF is built on the Model-View-Controller (MVC) design pattern. Each part is separate from the other, allowing the UI to change without impacting the business logic and vice versa.

This chapter will present all these concepts, complementing the previous chapters.

The MVC Pattern

JSF, and most web frameworks, encourage separation of concerns by using variations of the MVC design pattern. MVC is an architectural pattern used to isolate business logic from user interface. Business logic doesn't mix well with user interface code. When the two are mixed, applications are much harder to maintain and less scalable. In the "JavaServer Pages" section in Chapter 11, I showed you a JSP with Java code and SQL statements. Though technically correct, you can imagine how difficult it would get to maintain with time. The page mixes two developer roles (graphic designer and business logic developer), and it could end up using many more APIs (database access, EJB invocation, and so on), handling exceptions, or processing complex business logic. All that would result in a very complex web page. When MVC is applied, it results in a loosely coupled application; with this type of application, it is easier to modify either the visual appearance of the application or the underlying business rules without one affecting the other.

In MVC, the model represents the data of the application, the view corresponds to the user interface, and the controller manages the communication between both (see Figure 12-1).

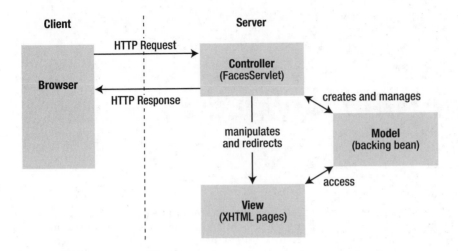

Figure 12-1. The MVC design pattern

The model is represented by the content, which is often stored in a database and displayed in the view. The model is built without concern for its look and feel when presented to the user. In JSF, it can consist of backing beans, EJB calls, JPA entities, and so forth.

The view in JSF is the actual XHTML page (XHTML is for web interfaces, but this could be something different, such as WML for wireless devices). As in the previous chapter, a view provides a graphical representation for a model. A model can also have several views, showing a book as a form or as a list, for example.

When a user manipulates a view, the view informs a controller of the desired changes. The controller then gathers, converts, and validates the data, invokes business logic, and generates the content in XHTML. In JSF, the controller is the `FacesServlet`.

FacesServlet

The `FacesServlet` is an implementation of `javax.servlet.Servlet` and acts as the central controller element, through which all user requests pass. As shown in Figure 12-2, when an event occurs (e.g., when the user clicks a button), the event notification is sent via HTTP to the server and is intercepted by `javax.faces.webapp.FacesServlet`. It examines the request and calls various actions on the model using managed beans.

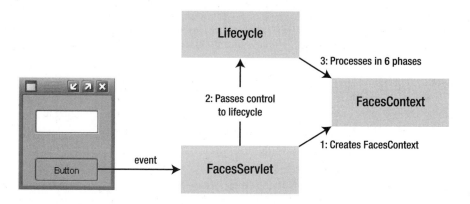

Figure 12-2. The FacesServlet interactions

Behind the scenes, the `FacesServlet` accepts incoming requests and hands control over to the `javax.faces.lifecycle.Lifecycle` object. Using a factory, it creates an object of type `javax.faces.context.FacesContext`, which contains and processes all the per-request state information. The `Lifecycle` object uses the `FacesContext` object in six phases (described in the previous chapter) before rendering the response.

For requests to be processed by the `FacesServlet`, they must be redirected using a servlet mapping in the deployment descriptor. The web pages, managed beans, converters, and so on have to be packaged with the `web.xml` file shown in Listing 12-1.

Listing 12-1. web.xml Defining the FacesServlet

```xml
<?xml version='1.0' encoding='UTF-8'?>
<web-app version="2.5"
         xmlns="http://java.sun.com/xml/ns/javaee"
         xmlns:xsi="http://www.w3.org/2001/XMLSchema-instance"
         xsi:schemaLocation="http://java.sun.com/xml/ns/javaee
         http://java.sun.com/xml/ns/javaee/web-app_2_5.xsd">

    <servlet>
        <servlet-name>Faces Servlet</servlet-name>
        <servlet-class>javax.faces.webapp.FacesServlet</servlet-class>
        <load-on-startup>1</load-on-startup>
    </servlet>
    <servlet-mapping>
        <servlet-name>Faces Servlet</servlet-name>
        <url-pattern>*.faces</url-pattern>
    </servlet-mapping>

    <context-param>
        <param-name>javax.faces.PROJECT_STAGE</param-name>
        <param-value>Development</param-value>
    </context-param>
</web-app>
```

This `web.xml` file defines the `javax.faces.webapp.FacesServlet` by giving it a name (e.g., `Faces Servlet`) and a mapping. In this example, all requests that have the `.faces` extension are mapped to be managed by the servlet, and any request such as `http://localhost:8080/chapter10-2.0/newBook.faces` will be handled by JSF.

■ **Note** The default extension for JSF pages is `.xhtml`. In Listing 12-1, this default value has been changed to `.faces` but, if `.xhtml` suits you, you can omit the servlet mapping configuration.

You can also configure a few JSF-specific parameters in the `<context-param>` element. Table 12-1 lists some of these parameters.

Table 12-1. Some JSF-Specific Configuration Parameters

Parameter	Description
`javax.faces.CONFIG_FILES`	Defines a comma-delimited list of context-relative resource paths under which the JSF implementation will look for resources.
`javax.faces.DEFAULT_SUFFIX`	Allows the web application to define a list of alternative suffixes for pages containing JSF content (e.g., `.xhtml`).
`javax.faces.FACELETS_BUFFER_SIZE`	The buffer size to set on the response. By default, the value is -1, which will not assign a buffer size on the response.
`javax.faces.FACELETS_REFRESH_PERIOD`	When a page is requested, the interval in seconds that the compiler should check for changes. A value of -1 disables the compiler check.
`javax.faces.FACELETS_SKIP_COMMENTS`	If set to true, the runtime ensures that XML comments in the Facelets page are not delivered to the client.
`javax.faces.LIFECYCLE_ID`	Identifies the `Lifecycle` instance to be used when processing JSF requests.
`javax.faces.STATE_SAVING_METHOD`	Defines the location where state is saved. Valid values are `server`, which is the default (typically saved in `HttpSession`) and `client` (saved as a hidden field in the subsequent form submit).

Parameter	Description
javax.faces.PROJECT_STAGE	Describes where this particular JSF application is in the software development life cycle (Development, UnitTest, SystemTest, or Production). This could be used by a JSF implementation to cache resources in order to improve performance in production, for example.
javax.faces.DISABLE_FACELET_JSF_VIEWHANDLER	Disables Facelets as the default page declaration language (PDL) if set to true.
javax.faces.LIBRARIES	Interprets each file found in the semicolon-separated list of paths as a Facelets tag library.

FacesContext

JSF defines the javax.faces.context.FacesContext abstract class for representing the contextual information associated with processing an incoming request and creating the corresponding response. This is the class that allows interaction with the UI and the rest of the JSF environment.

To gain access, you can either use the implicit facesContext object in your pages (see the previous chapter for discussion of implicit objects) or obtain a reference in your managed beans using the static method getCurrentInstance(). This will return the FacesContext instance for the current thread, and then you can invoke the methods listed in Table 12-2.

Table 12-2. Some Methods of the FacesContext

Method	Description
addMessage	Appends a message (information, warning, error or fatal).
getApplication	Returns the Application instance associated with this web application.
getAttributes	Returns a Map representing the attributes associated with the FacesContext instance.
getCurrentInstance	Returns the FacesContext instance for the request that is being processed by the current thread.
getELContext	Returns the ELContext instance for the current FacesContext instance.
getMaximumSeverity	Returns the maximum severity level recorded on any FacesMessage that has been queued.
getMessages	Returns a collection of FacesMessage.

Continued

Method	Description
getPartialViewContext	Returns the PartialViewContext object for this request. It is used to inject logic into the processing/rendering loop control (such as Ajax processing).
getViewRoot	Returns the root component that is associated with the request.
release	Releases any resources associated with this FacesContext instance.
renderResponse	Signals the JSF implementation that, as soon as the current phase of the request-processing life cycle has been completed, control should be passed to the *Render response* phase, bypassing any phases that have not been executed yet.
responseComplete	Signals the JSF implementation that the HTTP response for this request has already been generated (such as an HTTP redirect), and that the request-processing life cycle should be terminated as soon as the current phase is completed.

Faces Config

The FacesServlet is internal to JSF implementations, and, though you don't have access to its code, you do require metadata to configure it. By now, you may be accustomed to the two possible choices of metadata in Java EE 6: annotations and XML deployment descriptors (/WEB-INF/faces-config.xml). Before JSF 2.0, the only choice was XML; today, managed beans, converters, event listeners, renderers, and validators can have annotations, as using XML configuration files has become optional.

I mostly recommended annotations, but to show an extract of what a faces-config.xml file looks like, the example in Listing 12-2 defines a locale and a message bundle for internationalization and some navigation rules. Soon you will see how to navigate with and without faces-config.xml.

Listing 12-2. Snippet of a faces-config.xml File

```xml
<?xml version='1.0' encoding='UTF-8'?>
<faces-config xmlns="http://java.sun.com/xml/ns/javaee"
              xmlns:xsi="http://www.w3.org/2001/XMLSchema-instance"
              xsi:schemaLocation="http://java.sun.com/xml/ns/javaee
              http://java.sun.com/xml/ns/javaee/web-facesconfig_2_0.xsd"
              version="2.0">

    <application>
        <locale-config>
            <default-locale>fr</default-locale>
        </locale-config>
        <resource-bundle>
            <base-name>messages</base-name>
            <var>msg</var>
        </resource-bundle>
    </application>
```

```
<navigation-rule>
    <from-view-id>*</from-view-id>
    <navigation-case>
        <from-outcome>doCreateBook-success</from-outcome>
        <to-view-id>/listBooks.htm</to-view-id>
    </navigation-case>
</navigation-rule>
```

```
</faces-config>
```

Managed Beans

As noted earlier in this chapter, the MVC pattern encourages separation between the model, the view, and the controller: JSF pages form the view and the `FacesServlet` the controller. Managed beans are the gateway to the model.

Managed beans are annotated Java classes and are central to web applications. They can perform business logic (or delegate to EJBs, for example), handle navigation between pages, and hold data. A typical JSF application includes one or more managed beans that can be shared by several pages.

The data is held within attributes of the managed bean, also called a backing bean. A backing bean defines the data that a UI component is bound to (the target of a form, for example). To bind components to a backing bean, you need to use the expression language.

How to Write a Managed Bean

Writing a managed bean is as easy as writing an EJB or a JPA entity; it's simply a Java class annotated with @ManagedBean (see Listing 12-3). There are no `faces-config.xml` entries, no helper classes, nor inheritance. While these things aren't required, they are available if you want/need to use them. JSF 2.0 also uses the configuration-by-exception mechanism, whereby, with only one annotation, you can use all defaults and deploy your web application with such a managed bean.

Listing 12-3. A Simple Managed Bean

```
@ManagedBean
public class BookController {

    private Book book = new Book();

    public String doCreateBook() {
        createBook(book);
        return "listBooks.xhtml";
    }

    // Constructors, getters, setters
}
```

Listing 12-3 shows the programming model of a managed bean: it holds state (the book attribute), defines action methods (doCreateBook()) that are referenced in a page, and handles navigation (return "listBooks.xhtml").

Managed Bean Model

Managed beans are Java classes that are managed by the `FacesServlet`. The UI components are bound to the managed bean's properties (or backing bean) and can invoke action methods. A managed bean needs to follow these requirements:

- The class must be annotated with `@javax.faces.bean.ManagedBean` or the XML equivalent in the `faces-config.xml` deployment descriptor.

- It has a default scope (@RequestScoped) that you can configure.

- The class must be defined as public; it must not be final or abstract.

- The class must have a public no-arg constructor that the container will use to create instances.

- The class must not define the `finalize()` method.

- Attributes must have public getters and setters to be bound to a component.

Following the ease-of-use model of Java EE 6, a managed bean can simply be an annotated POJO, eliminating most of the configuration. However, if you still need customization, you can use the elements of the `@ManagedBean` and `@ManagedProperty` scope annotations (or XML equivalent).

@ManagedBean

The presence of the `@javax.faces.bean.ManagedBean` annotation on a class automatically registers it as a managed bean. The API of this annotation is simple, and all elements are optional (see Listing 12-4).

Listing 12-4. The Managed Bean Annotation API

```
@Target(TYPE) @Retention(RUNTIME)
public @interface ManagedBean {
    String name() default "";
    boolean eager() default false;
}
```

The `name` element specifies the name of the managed bean (which by default is the name of the class starting with a lowercase letter). If the value of the `eager` element is `true`, the managed bean is instantiated when the web application starts (only true if the bean is application-scoped, otherwise it is ignored for any other scope).

UI components are bound to managed bean properties; changing the default name of a managed bean has an impact on how you invoke a property or a method. The code in Listing 12-5 renames the managed bean to `myManagedBean`.

Listing 12-5. A Renamed Managed Bean

```
@ManagedBean(name = "myManagedBean")
public class BookController {

    private Book book = new Book();

    public String doCreateBook() {
        createBook(book);
        return "listBooks.xhtml";
    }

    // Constructors, getters, setters
}
```

To invoke attributes or methods of this managed bean in your pages, you must use the overridden name as follows:

```
<h:outputText value="#{myManagedBean.book.isbn}"/>
<h:form>
    <h:commandLink action="#{myManagedBean.doCreateBook}">
        Create a new book
    </h:commandLink>
</h:form>
```

Scopes

Objects that are created as part of a managed bean have a certain lifetime and may or may not be accessible to UI components or objects in the web application. The lifetime and accessibility of an object is known as *scope*. In your web application (managed beans and pages), you can specify the scope of an object using six different durations:

- Application: This is the least restrictive duration (use the `@ApplicationScoped` annotation in your managed bean), with the longest life span. Objects that are created are available in all request/response cycles for all clients using the web application, for as long as the application is active. These objects can be called concurrently and need to be thread-safe (using the `synchronized` keyword). Objects with this scope can use other objects with no scope or application scope.

- Session: Objects are available for any request/response cycles that belong to the client's session (`@SessionScoped`). These objects have their state persisted between requests and last until the session is invalidated. Objects with this scope can use other objects with no scope, session scope, or application scope.

- View: Objects are available within a given view until the view is changed, and have their state persisted until the user navigates to a new view, at which point they will be cleared out. Objects with this scope can use other objects with no scope, view scope, session scope, or application scope. Managed beans can be annotated with @ViewScoped.

- Request: If not specified, this is the default scope (in your managed bean, you can use the @RequestScoped annotation). Objects are available from the beginning of a request until the response has been sent to the client. A client can execute several requests but stay on the same view. That's why the @ViewScoped duration lasts longer than that of the @RequestScoped. Objects with this scope can use other objects with no scope, request scope, view scope, session scope, or application scope.

- Flash: Introduced in JSF 2.0, the new flash scope provides a short-lived conversation. It is a way to pass temporary objects that are propagated across a single view transition and cleaned up before moving on to another view. The flash scope can only be used programmatically as there is no annotation.

- None: Objects in this scope are not visible in any JSF page and define objects that are used by other managed beans in the application (with the @NoneScoped annotation). Objects with this scope can use other objects with the same scope.

You need to be careful when you choose a scope for your managed beans. You should give them only as much scope as needed. Excessively scoped beans (e.g., @ApplicationScoped) will increase memory usage, and the potential need to persist them could cause increased disk usage. It makes no sense to give application scope to an object that is used only within a single component. Likewise, an object with too much restriction will be unavailable to different parts of your application. You should also be concerned with concurrent access. Multiple sessions accessing the same application scoped bean might create thread-safety issues.

The code in Listing 12-6 defines a managed bean with application scope. It is eagerly instantiated (eager = true) and initializes the defaultBook attributes as soon as it's constructed (@PostConstruct). This could be a perfect bean to initialize parts of your web application or to be referenced by other managed beans' properties.

Listing 12-6. A Managed Bean with an Application Scope Eagerly Instantiated

```
@ManagedBean(eager = true)
@ApplicationScoped
public class InitController {

    private Book defaultBook;
```

```
@PostConstruct
private void init() {
    defaultBook=new Book("default title", 0, "default descritpion",↵
                         "0000-000", 100, true);
}

  // Constructors, getters, setters
}
```

@ManagedProperty

In a managed bean, you can instruct the system to inject a value into a property (an attribute with getters and/or setters) by using either the `faces-config.xml` file or the `@javax.faces.bean.ManagedProperty` annotation, which has a `value` attribute that can take a literal string or an EL expression. Listing 12-7 gives some examples of property initialization.

Listing 12-7. Managed Bean Properties Being Initialized

```
@ManagedBean
public class BookController {

    @ManagedProperty(value = "#{initController.defaultBook}")
    private Book book;

    @ManagedProperty(value = "this is a title")
    private String aTitle;

    @ManagedProperty(value = "999")
    private Integer aPrice;

    // Constructors, getters, setters & methods
}
```

In Listing 12-7, the properties `aTitle` and `aPrice` are initialized with a `String` value. The `aTitle` attribute, of type `String`, will be initialized to `this is a title` and the attribute `aPrice`, of type `Integer`, will be initialized with the number 999 (despite being a string, `"999"` will be converted to an `Integer`); as properties are evaluated at runtime (usually when a view is rendered), properties referencing other managed beans can be initialized. The value of `book` is initialized with an expression referencing the `defaultBook` property of the `initController` managed bean that you've seen before (`#{initController.defaultBook}`). Listing 12-6 shows that `defaultBook` is an attribute of type `Book` initialized by the `InitController` managed bean, and, as a result, when the `BookController` is initialized, the JSF implementation will inject the `defaultBook` attribute from the `InitController`. It is a good practice to initialize literals in the `faces-config.xml` and use the annotation for cross-managed bean references (with expression language).

Life Cycle and Callback Annotations

The previous chapter explained the life cycle of a page (with six phases from receiving the request to rendering the response). Managed beans also have a life cycle (see Figure 12-3), which is completely different from that of the page. In fact, managed beans have a similar life cycle to stateless session beans; if they do exist, it is for the lifetime of the defined scope.

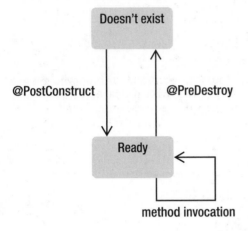

Figure 12-3. *The managed bean life cycle*

Managed beans running in a servlet container can use the @PostConstruct and @PreDestroy annotations. After the container creates an instance of a managed bean, it calls the @PostConstruct callback method, if any. After this stage, the managed bean is bound to a scope and responds to any user's request. Before removing the managed bean, the container calls the @PreDestroy method. These methods can be used to initialize attributes, or to create and release any external resource.

Navigation

Web applications are made of multiple pages that you need to navigate through. Depending on the application, you can have various levels of navigation with page flows that are more or less sophisticated. You can think of wizards, where you can go back to the previous or initial page, business cases where you go to a particular page depending on a certain rule, and so on. JSF has multiple options for navigation and allows you to control the flow, based on single pages or globally for the entire application.

When you just want to go from page to page by clicking a link or a button without doing any processing, you can use the UI components <h:button>, <h:link> and <h:outputLink>:

```
<h:link outcome="newBook.xhtml" value="Create a new book"/>
```

But most of the time this is not enough because you need to access a business tier or a database to retrieve or process data. In this case, you would use <h:commandButton> and <h:commandLink> with their action attribute that allows you to target managed bean methods, as opposed to targeting a page with <h:link> or <h:button>:

```
<h:commandButton value="Create" action="listBooks.xhtml"/>
```

In the "Putting It All Together" section of Chapter 10, we had a first page (newBook.xhtml) displaying a form to create a book. Once you click the Create button, the book is created and the managed bean navigates to the listBooks.xhtml page, which will list all the books. Once the page is loaded into the browser, the Create a new book link at the bottom of the page allows you to go back to the previous page (as shown in Figure 12-4).

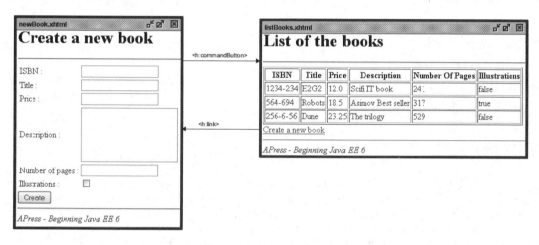

Figure 12-4. *Navigating between newBook.xhtml and listBooks.xhtml*

The page flow is simple but it still needs a managed bean (BookController) to do some business logic and navigation. Both pages use buttons and links components for navigating and interacting with the managed bean. The newBook.xhtml page uses a button to call the doCreateBook() method of the managed bean:

```
<h:commandButton value="Create" action="#{bookController.doCreateBook}"/>
```

The doCreateBook() method will then invoke an EJB to persist a Book entity in the database. The listBooks.xhtml page uses a link to just go back to the newBook.xhtml page without doing any processing:

```
<h:link outcome="newBook.xhtml" value="Create a new book"/>
```

The button does not directly call the page it needs to go to. It invokes a method on the managed bean that is responsible for navigation and decides which page to load next. The navigation operates on a set of rules that define all the application's possible navigation paths. The code of the managed bean in Listing 12-8 uses the simplest form of navigation rules: each method defines the page it needs to go to.

Listing 12-8. A Managed Bean Explicitly Defining Navigation

```java
@ManagedBean
public class BookController {

    @EJB
    private BookEJB bookEJB;

    private Book book = new Book();
    private List<Book> bookList = new ArrayList<Book>();

    public String doCreateBook() {
        book = bookEJB.createBook(book);
        bookList = bookEJB.findBooks();
        return "listBooks.xhtml";
    }

    // Constructors, getters, setters
}
```

When the `<h:commandButton>` invokes the `doCreateBook()` method, this method creates a book (using a stateless session bean) and returns the name of the page to navigate to: `listBooks.xhtml`. The `FacesServlet` will then redirect the page flow to the desired page.

The returned `String` can take several forms. Here is the simplest: it returns the page name. By default, the page file extension is `.xhtml`; the code could be simplified and the extension removed:

```java
public String doCreateBook() {
    book = bookEJB.createBook(book);
    bookList = bookEJB.findBooks();
    return "listBooks";
}
```

The `FacesServlet` understands that the target page is in fact `listBooks.xhtml` (and not `listBooks`).

With JSF, the page flow navigation can be defined externally via `faces-config.xml`. In `faces-config.xml`, navigation is specified in `<navigation-rule>` elements. A `<navigation-rule>` element identifies the start page, a condition, and the target page to navigate to when the condition occurs. The condition is based on a logical name rather than the name of the page. The code of the previous managed bean could have used the logical name `success` as shown in Listing 12-9.

Listing 12-9. Snippet of the Managed Bean Using Logical Names

```
@ManagedBean
public class BookController {
    // ...

    public String doCreateBook() {
        book = bookEJB.createBook(book);
        bookList = bookEJB.findBooks();
        return "success";
    }

    // Constructors, getters, setters
}
```

Listing 12-10 shows the structure of the `faces-config.xml` file. The `<from-view-id>` tag defines the page where the action request is initially made. In this case, you start on `newBook.xhtml` before making the call to the managed bean. If the returned logical name is `success` (`<from-outcome>`), the `FacesServlet` will forward the call to the `listBooks.xhtml` page (`<to-view-id>`).

Listing 12-10. A faces-config.xml File Defining Navigation

```xml
<?xml version='1.0' encoding='UTF-8'?>
<faces-config xmlns="http://java.sun.com/xml/ns/javaee"
              xmlns:xsi="http://www.w3.org/2001/XMLSchema-instance"
              xsi:schemaLocation="http://java.sun.com/xml/ns/javaee
              http://java.sun.com/xml/ns/javaee/web-facesconfig_2_0.xsd"
              version="2.0">

    <navigation-rule>
        <from-view-id>newBook.xhtml</from-view-id>
        <navigation-case>
            <from-outcome>success</from-outcome>
            <to-view-id>listBooks.xhtml</to-view-id>
        </navigation-case>
    </navigation-rule>

</faces-config>
```

Navigation can be done directly in the managed beans or by `faces-config.xml`, but when should you use one over the other? The first reason to directly return the page name in managed beans is simplicity; the Java code is explicit, and there is no external XML file to work with. If the web application has an extensive page flow, you might want to keep it in a single place, so that any changes can be made in a central location instead of across several pages; and again, using a mix of both can result in having part of your navigation in your beans and another in the `faces-config.xml` file.

There is one case where using XML configuration is very useful; when there are global links on several pages (for example, login or logout that can be done in an entire application), as you do not want to define them for every single page. Global navigation rules can be used in XML (but the same feature is not possible within managed beans):

```
<navigation-rule>
    <from-view-id>*</from-view-id>
    <navigation-case>
        <from-outcome>logout</from-outcome>
        <to-view-id>logout.xhtml</to-view-id>
    </navigation-case>
</navigation-rule>
```

If you have an action that applies to every page in the application, you can use a `navigation-rule` element without a `<from-view-id>` or using a wildcard (*). The preceding code indicates that, for any page the user is on, if the method of the managed bean returns the logical name `logout`, forward the user to the `logout.xhtml` page.

The previous examples showed simple navigation where one page has only one navigation rule and only one page to go to. This is not often the case, and, depending on certain rules or exceptions, users can be redirected to different pages. This is also possible with managed beans and with the `faces-config.xml` file. The following code shows a switch case that redirects to three different pages. Note that when the `null` value is returned, the user goes back to the page he is already on.

```
public String doCreateBook() {
    book = bookEJB.createBook(book);
    bookList = bookEJB.findBooks();
    switch (value) {
        case 1: return "page1.xhtml"; break;
        case 2: return "page2.xhtml"; break;
        case 3: return "page3.xhtml"; break;
        default: return null; break;
    }
}
```

An enhancement in JSF 2.0 is the addition of conditional navigation cases. It allows navigation cases to specify a pre-condition that must be met in order for the navigation case to be accepted. This precondition is specified as an EL expression using the new `<if>` configuration element. In the example below, if the user is in the admin role, the logout is specific and redirects the user to the `logout_admin.xhtml` page:

```
<navigation-rule>
    <from-view-id>*</from-view-id>
    <navigation-case>
        <from-outcome>logout</from-outcome>
        <to-view-id>logout_admin.xhtml</to-view-id>
        <if>#{userController.isAdmin}</if>
    </navigation-case>
</navigation-rule>
```

Message Handling

Managed beans process business logic, call EJBs and databases, and so on, and sometimes things can go wrong. In this case, the user has to be informed through a message to take action. Messages can be split into two categories: application errors (involving business logic or database or network connection) and user input errors (invalid ISBN or empty fields). Application errors can generate a completely different page asking the user to retry in a few moments, for example. Input errors can be displayed in the same page, with text describing the error, and messages can also be informational, such as one indicating that a book was successfully added to the database.

In Chapter 11, you saw tags that are used to display messages on pages (`<h:message>` and `<h:messages>`). To produce these messages, JSF allows you to queue messages by calling the `FacesContext.addMessage()` method in your managed beans. The signature of the method is as follows:

```
void addMessage(String clientId, FacesMessage message)
```

This method appends a `FacesMessage` to the set of messages to be displayed. The first parameter of this method specifies a client identifier. This parameter refers to the DOM location of the UI component that the message is registered to (e.g., `bookForm:isbn` refers to the UI component that has the `isbn` identifier within the `bookForm` form). If `clientId` is `null`, the message doesn't refer to any special component and is said to be global to all pages. A message consists of a summary text, a detailed text, and a severity level (fatal, error, warning, and info). Messages can also be internationalized using message bundles.

```
FacesMessage(Severity severity, String summary, String detail)
```

The following code is a snippet of a managed bean that creates a book. If the creation succeeds, an informational message is queued (the `FacesMessage` with a `SEVERITY_INFO`). If an exception is caught, an error message is added to the messages queue to be displayed. Note that both messages are global because the `clientId` is `null`. On the other hand, when we validate the ISBN and book title entered by the user, we want to display the warning messages (`SEVERITY_WARN`) related to the UI component (e.g., `bookForm:title` is the DOM identifier of the text field `title` located under the `bookForm` form).

Listing 12-11. Adding Different Severity Messages

```
public String doCreateBook() {
    FacesContext ctx = FacesContext.getCurrentInstance();

    if (book.getIsbn() == null || "".equals(book.getIsbn())) {
        ctx.addMessage(bookForm:isbn, new FacesMessage(FacesMessage.SEVERITY_WARN, ↪
                                     "Wrong isbn", "You should enter an ISBN number"));
    }
    if (book.getTitle() == null || "".equals(book.getTitle())) {
        ctx.addMessage(bookForm:title, new FacesMessage(FacesMessage.SEVERITY_WARN, ↪
                                     "Wrong title", "You should enter a title for the book"));
    }

    if (ctx.getMessageList().size() != 0)
        return null;
```

```
try {
    book = bookEJB.createBook(book);
    ctx.addMessage(null, new FacesMessage(FacesMessage.SEVERITY_INFO, "Book created", ↵
            "The book" + book.getTitle() + " has been created with id=" + book.getId()));
} catch (Exception e) {
    ctx.addMessage(null, new FacesMessage(FacesMessage.SEVERITY_ERROR, ↵
                                        "Book hasn't been created", e.getMessage()));
}
return null;
}
```

The FacesContext is available to the page and so is the FacesMessage. The page can then display the global messages (with clientId equals to null) using a single <h:messages> tag. When we want to display a message at a specific place on the page for a specific component (as is usually the case with validation or conversion errors), we use <h:message>. Figure 12-5 shows a page with messages specifically aimed at the ISBN and title input fields.

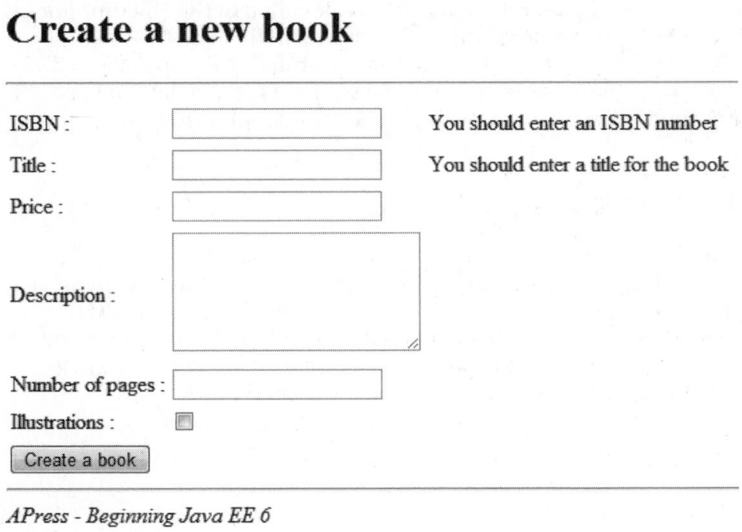

Create a new book

ISBN :	[ ]	You should enter an ISBN number
Title :	[ ]	You should enter a title for the book
Price :	[ ]	
Description :	[ ]	
Number of pages :	[ ]	
Illustrations :	☐	

[Create a book]

APress - Beginning Java EE 6

Figure 12-5. A page displaying a message per UI component

The page will have an input text field with an identifier (id="isbn"), and the <h:message> tag will refer to that component (for="isbn"). The result will be that this specific message will only be displayed for this component:

```
<h:inputText id="isbn" value="#{bookController.book.isbn}"/>
<h:message for="isbn"/>
```

If the ISBN field has not been filled, a message appears next to the ISBN input text field. JSF uses this messaging mechanism for converters and validators.

Conversion and Validation

You've just seen how to handle messages to inform the end user about actions to be taken. One possible action is to correct an invalid input value (e.g., invalid ISBN). JSF provides a standard conversion and validation mechanism that can process user inputs to ensure data integrity. In this way, when you invoke business methods to process, you can safely rely on valid data. Conversion and validation allow the developer to focus on business logic rather than checking whether the input data is not null, fits a range of values, and so on.

Conversion takes place when data input by the end user has to be converted from a `String` to an object and vice versa. It ensures that data is of the right type—for example, in converting a `String` to a `java.util.Date`, a `String` to an `Integer`, or a price in dollars to euros. As for validation, it ensures data contains the expected content (a date following the dd/MM/yyyy format, a float between 3.14 and 3.15, etc.).

Conversion and validation occur during different phases of the page life cycle (which you saw in the previous chapter) as shown in Figure 12-6.

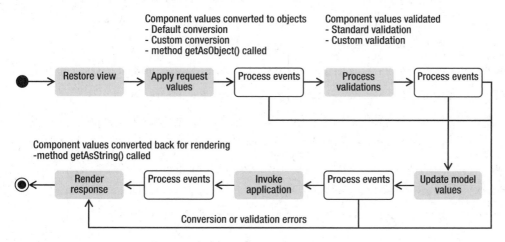

Figure 12-6. Conversion and validation during page life cycle

During the *Apply request values* phase in Figure 12-6, the UI component value is converted to the targeted object (e.g., from a string to a date) and then validated during the *Process validation* phase. It makes sense that conversion and validation occur before component data is bound to the backing bean (which happens during the *Update model values* phase). If any error is found, it will result in adding error messages and shortening the life cycle, so it goes straight to *Render response* (and messages will be displayed on the user interface with `<h:messages/>`). During this phase, the backing bean properties are converted back to a string to be displayed.

JSF has a set of standard converters and validators and allows you to create your own in a very easy way.

Converters

When a form is displayed on a browser, the end user fills the input fields and hits a button, resulting in transporting the data to the server in an HTTP request using string formats. Before updating the model on the managed bean, this data has to be converted from strings to the target objects (`Float`, `Integer`, `BigDecimal`, etc.). The reverse action will take place when the data has to be sent back to the client in the response and be rendered in the browser.

JSF ships with converters for common types like dates and numbers. In cases where the managed bean property is a primitive type (`Integer`, `int`, `Float`, `float`, and so on), JSF will automatically convert the UI component value to the correct type and back. When the property is some other data type, you need to provide your own converter. Table 12-3 lists all the standard converters that are in the `javax.faces.convert` package.

Table 12-3. Standard Converters

Converter	Description
BigDecimalConverter	Converts a `String` to a `java.math.BigDecimal` and vice versa.
BigIntegerConverter	Converts a `String` to a `java.math.BigInteger` and vice versa.
BooleanConverter	Converts a `String` to a `Boolean` (and `boolean` primitive) and vice versa.
ByteConverter	Converts a `String` to a `Byte` (and `byte` primitive) and vice versa.
CharacterConverter	Converts a `String` to a `Character` (and `char` primitive) and vice versa.
DateTimeConverter	Converts a `String` to a `java.util.Date` and vice versa.
DoubleConverter	Converts a `String` to a `Double` (and `double` primitive) and vice versa.
EnumConverter	Converts a `String` to an `Enum` (and `enum` primitive) and vice versa.
FloatConverter	Converts a `String` to a `Float` (and `float` primitive) and vice versa.
IntegerConverter	Converts a `String` to an `Integer` (and `int` primitive) and vice versa.
LongConverter	Converts a `String` to a `Long` (and `long` primitive) and vice versa.
NumberConverter	Converts a `String` to an abstract `java.lang.Number` class and vice versa.
ShortConverter	Converts a `String` to a `Short` (and `short` primitive) and vice versa.

JSF will automatically convert input values to numbers when the managed bean property is some primitive numeric type and to date or time when the property is some date type. If automatic conversion doesn't suit, you can explicitly control it through the standard `convertNumber` and `convertDateTime` tags. To use these tags, you need to nest the converter inside any of the input or output tags. The converter will be called by JSF during the life cycle.

The `convertNumber` tag has attributes that allow conversion of the input value to a number (default), a currency, or a percentage. You can specify a currency symbol or a number of fraction digits, as well as a formatting pattern determining how the number should be formatted and parsed.

```
<h:inputText value="#{bookController.book.price}">
    <f:convertNumber currencySymbol="$" type="currency"/>
</h:inputText>
```

The convertDateTime tag can convert dates in various formats (date, time, or both). It has several attributes that control the date conversion and time zones. A **pattern** attribute allows identification of the pattern of the date string that will be converted.

```
<h:inputText value="#{bookController.book.publishedDate}">
    <f:convertDateTime pattern="MM/dd/yy"/>
</h:inputText>
```

Custom Converters

Sometimes converting numbers, dates, enums, and so on is insufficient, and you may require custom conversion. It is easy to develop your own converters and use them in pages with JSF. You simply have to write a class that implements the **javax.faces.convert.Converter** interface and register it with metadata. This interface has two methods:

```
Object getAsObject(FacesContext ctx, UIComponent component, String value)
String getAsString(FacesContext ctx, UIComponent component, Object value)
```

The getAsObject() method converts the string value of a UI component into the corresponding supported type and returns the new instance. This method throws a **ConverterException** if the conversion fails. Conversely, the getAsString() method converts the provided type to a string, to be rendered in markup language (such as XHTML).

Once the custom converter is developed, it must be registered to allow it to be used in the web application. One method is by declaring the converter in the **faces-config.xml** file; the other is to use the @FacesConverter annotation.

Listing 12-12 shows how to write a custom converter that converts a price from dollars to euros. It starts by associating this converter with the name euroConverter (**value = "euroConverter"**) using the @FacesConverter annotation, and implements the **Converter** interface. This example only overrides the getAsString() method, which returns a string representation of a given price in euros.

Listing 12-12. *A Euro Converter*

```
@FacesConverter(value = "euroConverter")
public class EuroConverter implements Converter {

    @Override
    public Object getAsObject(FacesContext ctx, UIComponent component, String value) {
        return value;
    }

    @Override
    public String getAsString(FacesContext ctx, UIComponent component, Object value) {
        float amountInDollars = Float.parseFloat(value.toString());
        double ammountInEuros = amountInDollars * 0.8;
        DecimalFormat df = new DecimalFormat("###,##0.##");
        return df.format(ammountInEuros);
    }
}
```

To use this converter, use either the **converter** attribute of the **<h:outputText>** tag or the **<f:converter>** tag. In both cases, you must pass the name of the custom converter defined in the **@FacesConverter** annotation (**euroConverter**). The following code displays two output texts, one representing the price in dollars and the other converting this price to euros:

```
<h:outputText value="#{book.price}"/> // in dollar
<h:outputText value="#{book.price}">  // converted in euro
    <f:converter converterId="euroConverter"/>
</h:outputText>
```

Or you can use the **converter** attribute of the **outputText** tag:

```
<h:outputText value="#{book.price}" converter="euroConverter"/>
```

Validators

When working with web applications, the accuracy of the user-entered data must be ensured. Enforcing the right values are entered can be done on the client side using JavaScript or on the server side using validators. JSF simplifies data validation through the use of standard and custom server-side validators. Validators act as a first level of control by validating the value of UI components before being processed by the managed bean.

UI components generally handle simple validation, such as whether or not a value is required. For example, the following tag would require that a value in the text field be entered:

```
<h:inputText value="#{bookController.book.title}" required="true"/>
```

If a value is not entered, JSF returns the page with a message indicating that a value should be entered (the page must have a **<h:messages>** tag). This uses the same message mechanism that I described before. But JSF comes with a set of richer validators that can be used (described in Table 12-4), which are defined in the **javax.faces.validator** package.

Table 12-4. Standard Validators

Converter	Description
DoubleRangeValidator	Checks the value of the corresponding component against specified minimum and maximum double values.
LengthValidator	Checks the number of characters in the string value of the associated component.
LongRangeValidator	Checks the value of the corresponding component against specified minimum and maximum long values.
MethodExpressionValidator	Performs validation by executing a method on an object.
RequiredValidator	This validator is equivalent to setting the **required** attribute on the input component to true.
RegexValidator	Checks the value of the corresponding component against a regular expression.

These validators are useful for generic cases like the length of a field or a number range and can be easily associated within a component, in the same way as converters are (both can be used on the same component). The following code ensures the book's title is between 2 and 20 characters in length and its price is from 1 to 500 dollars.

```
<h:inputText value="#{bookController.book.title}" required="true">
    <f:validateLength minimum="2" maximum="20"/>
</h:inputText>
<h:inputText value="#{bookController.book.price}">
    <f:validateLongRange minimum="1" maximum="500"/>
</h:inputText>
```

Custom Validators

Perhaps the standard JSF validators might not suit your needs; you may have data that has to follow certain business formats such as a ZIP code, a state, or an e-mail address. You must create your own custom validator to address these cases. Like converters, a validator is a class that needs to implement an interface and override some method. In the case of a validator, the interface is `javax.faces.validator.Validator`, which has a single `validate()` method:

```
void validate(FacesContext context, UIComponent component, Object value)
```

In this method, the `value` argument is the one that has to be checked, based on some business logic. If it passes the validation check, you can simply return from the method, and the life cycle of the page will continue. If not, you can throw a `ValidatorException` and include a `FacesMessage` with a summary and a detail message describing the validation error, and register the validator either in the `faces-config.xml` or by using the `@FacesValidator` annotation.

As an example, create an ISBN validator that ensures the ISBN entered by the user for the book follows a certain format. Listing 12-13 shows the code for the `IsbnValidator`.

Listing 12-13. An ISBN Validator

```
@FacesValidator(value = "isbnValidator")
public class IsbnValidator implements Validator {

  private Pattern pattern;
  private Matcher matcher;

  @Override
  public void validate(FacesContext context, UIComponent component, ➥
                       Object value) throws ValidatorException {

    String componentValue = value.toString();

    pattern = Pattern.compile("(?=[-0-9xX]{13}$)");
    matcher = pattern.matcher(componentValue);
```

```
    if (!matcher.find()) {
      String message = MessageFormat.format(↦
                       "{0} is not a valid isbn format", componentValue);

      FacesMessage facesMessage = new FacesMessage(SEVERITY_ERROR, message, message);
      throw new ValidatorException(facesMessage);
    }
  }
}
```

The code in Listing 12-13 starts by associating the validator with the name `isbnValidator`, to allow it to be used in a page. It implements the `Validator` interface and adds the validation logic to the `validate()` method. It checks, with a regular expression, that the ISBN has the right format. If not, it adds a message to the context and throws an exception. JSF will automatically resume the life cycle of the page, recall the page, and display the error message. You can employ this custom validator in your pages using the `validator` attribute or embedding a `<f:validator>` tag:

```
<h:inputText value="#{book.isbn}" validator="isbnValidator"/>
// or
<h:inputText value="#{book.isbn}">
    <f:validator validatorId="isbnValidator" />
</h:inputText>
```

Ajax

The HTTP protocol is based on a request/response mechanism: a client needs something, sends a request, and receives a response from the server, usually an entire web page. The communication follows this direction: a client requests something from the server, and not the other way around. However, web applications must provide rich and responsive interfaces and must react to server events, update parts of the page, aggregate widgets, and so on. In a normal request/response situation, the server would have to send the entire web page back even if only a small portion had to change. If the page has a significant size, you'll overload the bandwidth and have poor responsiveness as the browser would need to load the entire page. If you want to increase the browser's responsiveness and improve the user's browsing experience, you need to update only small portions of the page. And this can be done with Ajax.

Ajax (stands for Asynchronous JavaScript and XML) is a set of web development techniques used to create interactive web applications. Ajax allows web applications to retrieve portions of data from the server asynchronously without interfering with the display and behavior of the existing page. Once the data is received by the client, only the portions requiring updating using the Document Object Model (DOM) of the page and JavaScript are needed. There is also a mechanism called *Reverse Ajax* (or Comet programming) for pushing data from the server back to the browser. These mechanisms are used in most of our daily web applications, and JSF 2.0 has introduced support for them.

General Concepts

The term *Ajax* was coined in 2005 as a set of alternative techniques for loading asynchronous data into web pages. Back in 1999, Microsoft created the `XMLHttpRequest` object as an ActiveX control in Internet Explorer 5. In 2006, the World Wide Web Consortium (W3C) released the first specification draft for the

XMLHttpRequest object, which is now supported by most browsers. At the same time, several companies brainstormed about how to ensure that Ajax could be the industry standard for a rich application platform based on open technologies. The result of this work was the creation of the OpenAjax Alliance, which consists of vendors, open source projects, and companies using Ajax-based technologies.

As shown in Figure 12-7, in traditional web applications, the browser has to ask for the full HTML documents from the server. The user clicks a button to send or get the information, waits for the server to respond, and then receives the entire page that the browser loads. Ajax, on the other hand, uses asynchronous data transfer (HTTP requests) between the browser and the server, allowing web pages to request small bits of information (JSON or XML data) from the server instead of whole pages. The user stays on the same page while a piece of JavaScript requests or sends data to a server asynchronously, and only portions of the page are actually updated, making web application faster and more user friendly.

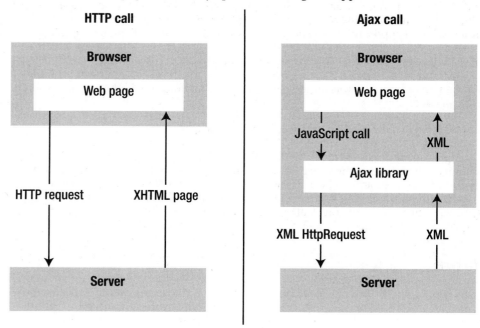

Figure 12-7. Plain HTTP calls vs. Ajax HTTP calls

In principle, Ajax is based on the following:

- XHTML and CSS for presentation.

- DOM for dynamic display and interaction with data.

- XML and XSLT for the interchange, manipulation, and display of XML data.

- The XMLHttpRequest object for asynchronous communication.

- JavaScript to bring these technologies together.

XMLHttpRequest is an important part of Ajax, as it's a DOM API used by JavaScript to transfer XML from the browser to the server. The data returned has to be fetched on the client side to update portions of the page dynamically with JavaScript. The data can have several formats such as XHTML, JSON, or even plain text.

Since JSF 2.0, Ajax is supported natively, so you don't have to develop JavaScript to handle the XMLHttpRequest, but you do need to use a JavaScript library that has been specified and shipped with JSF implementations.

Support in JSF

Previous versions of JSF offered no native Ajax solution, so third-party libraries had to be used to fill the gap. Sometimes this increased the complexity of the code at the expense of performance. With JSF 2.0, things are much easier, as Ajax support has been specified and is built into any JSF implementation.

First of all, there is a specified JavaScript library (jsf.js) for performing Ajax interaction, which means you don't have to develop your own scripts nor manipulate the XMLHttpRequest objects directly. Without developing any JavaScript, you can use a set of standardized functions to send asynchronous requests and receive data. In order to use this library in your pages, you need to add the jsf.js resource with the following line of code:

```
<h:outputScript name="jsf.js" library="javax.faces" target="head"/>
```

The <h:outputScript> tag renders a <script> markup element referring to the jsf.js JavaScript file in the javax.faces library (which follows the new resource management of JSF 2.0, meaning that the jsf.js file in under the META-INF/resources/javax/faces directory). Note that the top-level javax namespace is registered within the OpenAjax Alliance. This JavaScript API is used to initiate client-side interactions with JSF including partial tree traversal and partial page update. The function that we will be directly using in our pages is the request function, as it is responsible for sending an Ajax request to the server. Its signature follows:

```
jsf.ajax.request(ELEMENT, |event|, { |OPTIONS| });
```

ELEMENT is any JSF component or XHTML element from which you trigger the event. Typically, for submitting a form, the element would be a button. EVENT is any JavaScript event supported by that element, such as onmousedown, onclick, onblur, and so forth. The OPTIONS argument is an array that may contain the following name/value pairs:

- execute: '<space-separated list of UI component IDs>': Sends the list of component IDs to the server in order to be processed during the execute phase of the request.

- render:'<space-separated list of UI component IDs>': Renders the list of component IDs that have been processed during the render phase of the request.

As an example, the following code shows a button that calls asynchronously the doCreateBook method passing all the parameters of a book form (which will redraw the book list when the user adds a new book). The button calls the jsf.ajax.request function when the user clicks on it (onclick event). The this argument refers to the element itself (the button), and the options refer to components IDs (isbn, title, price...):

```
<h:commandButton value="Create a book" onclick="jsf.ajax.request(this, event,
        {execute:'isbn title price description nbOfPage illustrations',
          render:'booklist'}); return false;"
        actionListener="#{bookController.doCreateBook}" />
```

When the client makes an Ajax request, the page life cycle on the server side stays the same (it goes through the same six phases). The key benefit is that the response is simply the return of a small chunk of data rather than a large HTML page to the browser. The *Apply request* phase determines whether the current request is a "partial request" or not, and the `PartialViewContext` object is used throughout the page's life cycle. It contains methods and properties that pertain to partial request processing and partial response rendering. At the end of the life cycle, the Ajax response (or, strictly speaking, partial response) is sent to the client during the *Render response* phase. It usually consists of XHTML, XML, or JSON that the client-side JavaScript will parse.

JSF 2 also includes a declarative approach that is intended to be more convenient. This approach leverages the new `<f:ajax>` tag. Instead of manually coding the JavaScript for the Ajax request call, you can declaratively specify the same behavior without requiring any JavaScript code:

```
<h:commandButton value="Create a book" action="#{bookController.doCreateBook}">
    <f:ajax execute="@form" render=":booklist"/>
</h:commandButton>
```

In this example, `render` points to the component id we want to render back (the `booklist` component). The `execute` attribute refers to all the components that belong to the form. Table 12-5 shows all the possible values that the `render` and `execute` attribute can take:

Table 12-5. Possible Values of the Render and Execute Attribute

Value	Description
@all	Renders or executes all components in view.
@none	Renders or executes no components in view (this is the default value if `render` or `execute` is not specified).
@this	Renders or executes only this component (the component that triggered the Ajax request).
@form	Renders or executes all components within this form (from which Ajax request was fired).
Space separated list of IDs	One or more IDs of components to be rendered or executed.
Expression language	Expression which resolves to Collection of Strings.

Putting It All Together

The example shown in Listing 12-14 illustrates how to use this general background on Ajax and its support in JSF. The "Putting It All Together" section of Chapter 10 showed how to insert new books into the database using a BookController managed bean. The navigation was simple, as, once the book was created, you were redirected to the page displaying the list of the books. By clicking a link, you would go from the list back to the book form. Let's take this example and add some Ajax capabilities.

Now, you only want a single page that has a form at the top to enter the book data, and a list of books at the bottom (see Figure 12-8). Each time a new book is created by clicking the button, the list is refreshed, showing the newly created book.

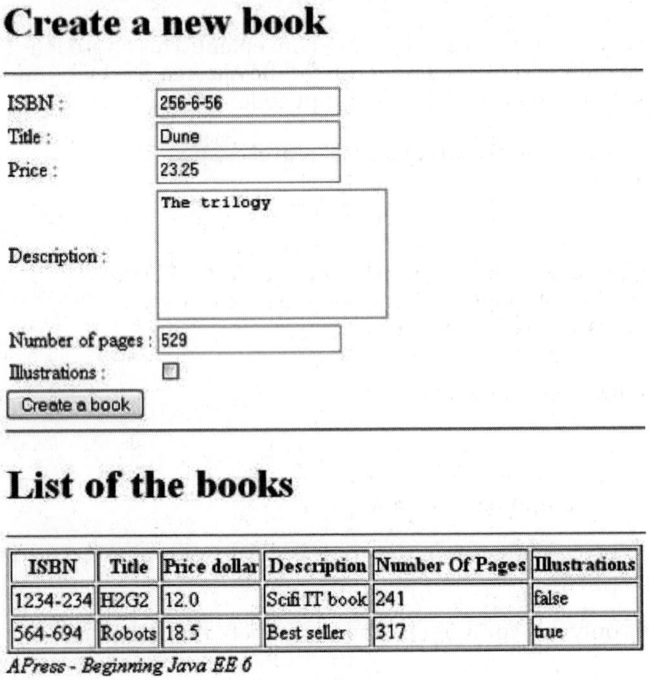

Create a new book

ISBN :	256-6-56
Title :	Dune
Price :	23.25
Description :	The trilogy
Number of pages :	529
Illustrations :	☐

[Create a book]

List of the books

ISBN	Title	Price dollar	Description	Number Of Pages	Illustrations
1234-234	H2G2	12.0	Scifi IT book	241	false
564-694	Robots	18.5	Best seller	317	true

APress - Beginning Java EE 6

Figure 12-8. A single page to create and list books

The form at the top of the page doesn't change, and only the list portion of the page needs to be refreshed. The code in Listing 12-14 is the first part of the page and represents the form. Nothing really changes from the code in Chapter 10. The bookCtrl variable refers to the BookController managed bean that is responsible for all the business logic (invoking an EJB to persist and retrieve books). Book is the entity, and its attributes are accessed using expression language (#{bookCtrl.book.isbn} binds to the ISBN). Each input component has an identifier (id="isbn", id="title", etc.). This is very important because it gives an identifier to each DOM node that needs to interact asynchronously with the server. Identifiers must be unique for the whole page, because the application must be able to map data to a specific component.

Listing 12-14. The Form Part of the newBook.xhtml Page

```
<!DOCTYPE html PUBLIC "-//W3C//DTD XHTML 1.0 Transitional//EN"
        "http://www.w3.org/TR/xhtml1/DTD/xhtml1-transitional.dtd">
<html xmlns="http://www.w3.org/1999/xhtml"
      xmlns:h="http://java.sun.com/jsf/html"
      xmlns:f="http://java.sun.com/jsf/core">

<h:head>
    <title>Creates a new book</title>
</h:head>
<h:body>

    <h1>Creates a new book</h1>
    <hr/>

    <h:form id="form" prependId="false">
        <h:panelGrid columns="2">
            <h:outputLabel value="ISBN : "/>
            <h:inputText id="isbn" value="#{bookCtrl.book.isbn}"/>

            <h:outputLabel value="Title :"/>
            <h:inputText id="title" value="#{bookCtrl.book.title}"/>

            <h:outputLabel value="Price : "/>
            <h:inputText id="price" value="#{bookCtrl.book.price}"/>

            <h:outputLabel value="Description : "/>
            <h:inputTextarea id="description" ➥
               value="#{bookCtrl.book.description}" cols="20" rows="5"/>

            <h:outputLabel value="Number of pages : "/>
            <h:inputText id="nbOfPage" value="#{bookCtrl.book.nbOfPage}"/>

            <h:outputLabel value="Illustrations : "/>
            <h:selectBooleanCheckbox id="illustrations" ➥
                              value="#{bookCtrl.book.illustrations}"/>
        </h:panelGrid>

        <h:commandButton value="Create a book" action="#{bookCtrl.doCreateBook}">
            <f:ajax execute="@form" render=":booklist"/>
        </h:commandButton>

    </h:form>
```

The `<h:commandButton>` tag represents the button where the Ajax call is made. When the user clicks the button, the `<f:ajax>` tag passes all the form parameters using the `@form` shortcut (instead, it could have passed the list of all the components identifiers of the form: `isbn`, `title`, etc.). The values of all the UI components that make up the form are then posted to the server. The `doCreateBook()` method of the managed bean is invoked, the new book is created, and the list of books is retrieved. The rendering of this list on the client side is made asynchronously thanks to Ajax. The **render** element refers to the **booklist** ID as the identifier of the data table displaying all the books (see Listing 12-15).

Listing 12-15. The List Part of the newBook.xhtml Page

```
<hr/>
  <h1>List of the books</h1>
  <hr/>
  <h:dataTable id="booklist" value="#{bookCtrl.bookList}" var="bk">
    <h:column>
      <f:facet name="header">
        <h:outputText value="ISBN"/>
      </f:facet>
      <h:outputText value="#{bk.isbn}"/>
    </h:column>

    <h:column>
      <f:facet name="header">
        <h:outputText value="Title"/>
      </f:facet>
      <h:outputText value="#{bk.title}"/>
    </h:column>

    <h:column>
      <f:facet name="header">
        <h:outputText value="Price"/>
      </f:facet>
      <h:outputText value="#{bk.price}"/>
    </h:column>

    <h:column>
      <f:facet name="header">
        <h:outputText value="Description"/>
      </f:facet>
      <h:outputText value="#{bk.description}" />
    </h:column>

    <h:column>
      <f:facet name="header">
        <h:outputText value="Number Of Pages"/>
      </f:facet>
      <h:outputText value="#{bk.nbOfPage}"/>
    </h:column>

    <h:column>
      <f:facet name="header">
        <h:outputText value="Illustrations"/>
      </f:facet>
      <h:outputText value="#{bk.illustrations}"/>
    </h:column>
```

```
    </h:dataTable>

    <i>APress - Beginning Java EE 6</i>
</h:body>
</html>
```

The partial response from the server contains the XHTML portion of the page to be updated. The JavaScript looks for the booklist element of the page and applies the changes needed. The partial response on Listing 12-16 is self-explanatory; it specifies that an update has to be made to the component identified by booklist (<update id="booklist">). The body of the <update> element is the fragment of XHTML that has to override the actual data table. Of course, this XML is handled automatically by the JSF Ajax handlers—the developer doesn't need to do anything with it manually.

Listing 12-16. The Partial Response Received by the Client

```
<?xml version="1.0" encoding="utf-8"?>
<partial-response>
    <changes>
        <update id="booklist">
            <table id="booklist" border="1">
                <tr>
                    <th scope="col">ISBN</th>
                    <th scope="col">Title</th>
                    <th scope="col">Price</th>
                    <th scope="col">Description</th>
                    <th scope="col">Number Of Pages</th>
                    <th scope="col">Illustrations</th>
                </tr>
                <tr>
                    <td>1234-234</td>
                    <td>H2G2</td>
                    <td>12.0</td>
                    <td>Scifi IT book</td>
                    <td>241</td>
                    <td>false</td>
                </tr>
                <tr>
                    <td>564-694</td>
                    <td>Robots</td>
                    <td>18.5</td>
                    <td>Best seller</td>
                    <td>317</td>
                    <td>true</td>
                </tr>
            </table>
        </update>
    </changes>
</partial-response>
```

Summary

The preceding chapter examined the graphical aspect of JSF, and this chapter focused on its dynamic side. JSF follows the MVC design pattern, and its specification ranges from creating user interfaces with components to processing data with managed beans.

Managed beans are at the heart of JSF as they are used to process business logic, call EJBs, databases, and so on, as well as navigating between pages. They have a scope and a life cycle (resembling stateless session beans), and they declare methods and properties that are bound to UI components using expression language. Annotations and configuration by exception have greatly simplified JSF 2.0, as most of the XML configuration is now optional.

I then showed how conversion and validation is handled on any input component. JSF defines a set of converters and validators for most common cases, but it also allows you to easily create and register custom ones.

While the Ajax technique has been around for some years, JSF 2.0 brings standard support, allowing web pages to invoke managed beans asynchronously. It defines a standard JavaScript library, and the developer doesn't need to write scripts but instead uses functions to refresh portions of pages.

The next three chapters will focus on how to interoperate with systems through messaging, SOAP web services, and RESTful web services.

■ ■ ■

CHAPTER 13

Sending Messages

Most of the communications between components that you have seen so far are synchronous: one class calls another, a managed bean invokes an EJB, which calls an entity, and so on. In such cases, the invoker and the target have to be up and running for the communication to succeed, and the invoker must wait for the target to complete before proceeding. With the exception of asynchronous calls in EJB (thanks to the `@Asynchronous` annotation), most Java EE components use synchronous calls (local or remote). When we talk about messaging, we mean loosely coupled, asynchronous communication between components.

Message-oriented middleware (MOM) is software (a provider) that enables asynchronous messages between heterogeneous systems. It can be seen as a buffer between systems that produce and consume messages at their own pace (e.g., one system is 24/7, the other runs only at night). It is inherently loosely coupled, as senders don't know who at the other end of the communication channel is going to receive the message and perform actions. The sender and the receiver do not have to be available at the same time in order to communicate. In fact, they do not even know about each other, as they use an intermediate buffer. In this respect, MOM differs completely from technologies, such as remote method invocation (RMI), which requires an application to know the signature of a remote application's methods.

Today, the typical organization has many applications, often written in different languages, that perform well-defined tasks. MOM allows these applications to work independently and, at the same time, form part of an information workflow process. Messaging is a good solution for integrating existing and new applications in a loosely coupled, asynchronous way, as long as the sender and receiver agree on the message format and the intermediate destination. This communication can be local within an organization or distributed among several external services.

Understanding Messages

MOM, which has been around for a while, uses a special vocabulary. When a message is sent, the software that stores the message and dispatches it is called a *provider* (or sometimes a *broker*). The message sender is called a *producer*, and the location where the message is stored is called a *destination*. The component receiving the message is called a *consumer*. Any component interested in a message at that particular destination can consume it. Figure 13-1 illustrates these concepts.

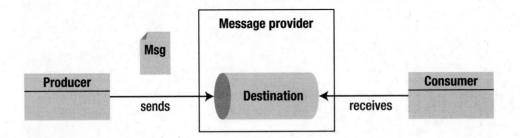

Figure 13-1. MOM architecture

In Java EE, the API that deals with these concepts is called Java Message Service (JMS). It has a set of interfaces and classes that allow you to connect to a provider, create a message, send it, and receive it. JMS doesn't physically carry messages, it's just an API; it requires a provider that is in charge of handling messages. When running in a container, Message-Driven Beans (MDBs) can be used to receive messages in a container-managed way.

JMS

JMS is a standard Java API that allows applications to create, send, receive, and read messages asynchronously. It defines a common set of interfaces and classes that allows programs to communicate with other message providers. JMS is analogous to JDBC: the latter connects to several databases (Derby, MySQL, Oracle, DB2, etc.), and JMS connects to several providers (OpenMQ, MQSeries, SonicMQ, etc.).

The JMS API covers all the required functionality for messaging, that is, sending and receiving a message through destinations. It provides:

- *Message producers*: JMS provides the API for clients to generate the message (a.k.a. senders and publishers).

- *Message consumers*: The API allows clients' applications to consume messages (a.k.a. receivers or subscribers).

- *Messages*: A message consists of a header, properties, and a body that contains different information (text, objects, etc.).

- *Connections and destinations*: The API has several factories where connections to providers can be obtained, as well as destinations (queues and topics).

MDB

MDBs are asynchronous message consumers that are executed inside an EJB container. As you've seen in Chapters 6 through 9, the EJB container takes care of several services (transactions, security, concurrency, message acknowledgement, etc.), while the MDB focuses on consuming JMS messages. MDBs are stateless, meaning that the EJB container can have numerous instances, executing concurrently, to process messages coming in from various JMS producers. Even if they look like stateless beans, client applications cannot access MDBs directly; the only way to communicate with an MDB is to send a message to the destination that the MDB is listening to.

In general, MDBs listen to a destination (queue or topic) and, when a message arrives, they consume and process it. They can also delegate business logic to other stateless session beans in a safe, transactional manner. Because they are stateless, MDBs do not maintain state across separate invocations from one message received to the next. MDBs respond to JMS messages received from the container, whereas stateless session beans respond to client requests through an appropriate interface (local, remote, or no-interface).

Messaging Specification Overview

Messaging in Java is mostly represented by JMS, which can be used in applications running in a standard (Java SE) or an enterprise (Java EE) environment. MDBs simply represent a way for stateless session EJBs to be message consumers and is bound to the EJB specification.

A Brief History of Messaging

Up until the late 1980s, companies did not have any easy way to link different applications. Developers had to write separate software adapters for systems to translate data from source applications into a format that the destination system could understand (and vice versa). Because of the disparity of servers' processing capabilities and availabilities, buffers were created to de-couple the processing so that the overall time wouldn't be prolonged. A lack of homogeneous transport protocols created low-level protocol adapters. Toward the end of the 1980s, middleware began to emerge, which solved these integration issues. The first MOMs were created as separate pieces of software that could sit in the middle of applications and manage the "plumbing" between systems. They were able to manage different platforms, different programming languages, various network protocols, and diverse hardware.

JMS 1.1

The JMS specification was first published in August 1998. It was created by the major middleware vendors to bring messaging capabilities to Java. JSR 914 went through minor changes (JMS 1.0.1, 1.0.2, and 1.0.2b) to finally reach the 1.1 version in April 2002. Since then, the specification hasn't changed. JMS 1.1 was integrated into J2EE 1.2 and has been a part of Java EE since. However, JMS and MDBs are not part of the Web Profile specification I described in the first chapter. This means they will only be available on application servers implementing the full Java EE 6 platform.

Although JMS is a verbose and low-level API compared to JPA or EJB, it does a very good job. Unfortunately, it has not been changed or improved in Java EE 5, nor in Java EE 6.

EJB 3.1

MDBs were introduced in EJB 2.0 and were improved with EJB 3.0 and the general Java EE 5 paradigm of "ease of use." They were not internally modified as they continued to be message consumers, but the introduction of annotations and configuration by exception made them much easier to write. The new EJB 3.1 specification (JSR 318) has no notable changes to MDBs.

As you've seen in Chapter 7, asynchronous calls are now possible within stateless session beans (using the @Asynchronous annotation). In previous versions of Java EE, it was impossible to have asynchronous calls between EJBs. Therefore, the only possible solution was to use JMS and MDBs—expensive, as many resources had to be used (JMS destinations, connections, factories, etc.) just to call a method asynchronously. Today, with EJB 3.1, asynchronous calls are possible between session beans without the need of MDBs, allowing them to focus on integrating systems through messaging.

Reference Implementation

Open Message Queue (OpenMQ) is the reference implementation of JMS. It has been open source since 2006 and can be used in stand-alone JMS applications or embedded in an application server. OpenMQ is the default messaging provider for GlassFish and, as this book is being written, is reaching version 4.5. It also adds many non-standard features such as the Universal Message Service (UMS), wildcard topic destinations, XML message validation, clustering, and more.

How to Send and Receive a Message

Let's take a look at a simple example to get an idea of JMS. JMS employs producers, consumers, and destinations. The producer sends a message to the destination, where the consumer is waiting for the message to arrive. Destinations can be of two kinds: queues (for point-to-point communication) and topics (for publish-subscribe communication). In Listing 13-1, a producer sends a text message to a queue to which the consumer is listening.

Listing 13-1. The Sender Class Produces a Message into a Queue

```java
public class Sender {

    public static void main(String[] args) {

        // Gets the JNDI context
        Context jndiContext = new InitialContext();

        // Looks up the administered objects
        ConnectionFactory connectionFactory = (ConnectionFactory)↪
                    jndiContext.lookup("jms/javaee6/ConnectionFactory");
        Queue queue = (Queue) jndiContext.lookup("jms/javaee6/Queue");

        // Creates the needed artifacts to connect to the queue
        Connection connection = connectionFactory.createConnection();
        Session session = connection.createSession(false, ↪
                                        Session.AUTO_ACKNOWLEDGE);
        MessageProducer producer = session.createProducer(queue);

        // Sends a text message to the queue
        TextMessage message = session.createTextMessage();
        message.setText("This is a text message sent at " + new Date());
        producer.send(message);

        connection.close();
    }
}
```

The code in Listing 13-1 represents a `Sender` class that has a `main()` method only. In this method, the first thing that occurs is that a JNDI context is instantiated and used to obtain a `ConnectionFactory` and a `Queue`. Connection factories and destinations (queues and topics) are called administered objects; they have to be created and declared in the message provider (in this case, OpenMQ). They both have a JNDI name (e.g., the queue is called `jms/javaee6/Queue`) and need to be looked up in the JNDI tree.

When the two administered objects are obtained, the `Sender` class uses the `ConnectionFactory` to create a `Connection` from which a `Session` is obtained. With this session, a `MessageProducer` and a message are created on the destination queue (`session.createProducer(queue)`). The producer then sends this message (of type text). The code is quite verbose, and in the example I've purposely omitted exception handling (catching JNDI and JMS exceptions).

Fortunately, once you've written this code to send a message, the code to receive the message looks almost the same. In fact, the first lines of the `Receiver` class in Listing 13-2 are exactly the same: create a JNDI context, lookup for the connection factory and the queue, and then connect. The only differences are that a `MessageConsumer` is used instead of a `MessageProducer`, and that the receiver enters an infinite loop to listen to the queue (you'll later see that this loop can be avoided by using the more standard message listener). When the message arrives, it is consumed and the content displayed.

Listing 13-2. The Receiver *Class Consumes a Message from a Queue*

```java
public class Receiver {

    public static void main(String[] args) {

        // Gets the JNDI context
        Context jndiContext = new InitialContext();

        // Looks up the administered objects
        ConnectionFactory connectionFactory = (ConnectionFactory) ↪
                jndiContext.lookup("jms/javaee6/ConnectionFactory");
        Queue queue = (Queue) jndiContext.lookup("jms/javaee6/Queue");

        // Creates the needed artifacts to connect to the queue
        Connection connection = connectionFactory.createConnection();
        Session session = connection.createSession(false, ↪
                                        Session.AUTO_ACKNOWLEDGE);
        MessageConsumer consumer = session.createConsumer(queue);
        connection.start();

        // Infinite loop to receive the messages
        while (true) {
            TextMessage message = (TextMessage) consumer.receive();
            System.out.println("Message received: " + message.getText());
        }
    }
}
```

Next, it's time to focus on the JMS API, define all the administered objects and classes that are used, and see how this translates to an MDB.

Java Messaging Service

At a high level, the JMS architecture consists of the following components (see Figure 13-2):

- *A provider*. JMS is only a specification, so it needs an underlying implementation to route messages, that is, the provider (aka a message broker). The provider handles the buffering and delivery of messages by providing an implementation of the JMS API.

- *Clients*: A client is any Java application or component that uses the JMS API to either consume or produce a JMS message. Such a client is known as a JMS client because it is a client of the underlying provider. "Client" is the generic term for producer, sender, publisher, consumer, receiver, or subscriber.

- *Messages*: These are the objects that clients send to or receive from the JMS provider.

- *Administered objects*: A message broker must provide administered objects to the client (connection factories and destinations) either through JNDI lookups or injection (as you'll see later).

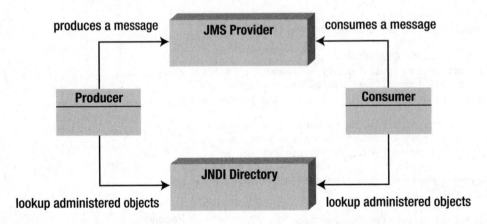

Figure 13-2. JMS architecture

The messaging provider enables asynchronous communication by providing a destination where messages can be held until they can be delivered to a client. There are two different types of destination, each applying to a specific messaging model:

- *The point-to-point (P2P) model*: In this model, the destination used to hold messages is called a *queue*. When using point-to-point messaging, one client puts a message on a queue, and another client receives the message. Once the message is acknowledged, the message provider removes the message from the queue.

- *The publish-subscribe (pub-sub) model:* The destination is called a *topic.* When using publish/subscribe messaging, a client publishes a message to a topic, and all subscribers to that topic receive the message.

The JMS specification provides a unified set of interfaces that can be used with both P2P and pub-sub messaging. Table 13-1 shows the generic name of an interface (e.g., Session) and the specific name for each model (QueueSession, TopicSession). Note also the different vocabulary; a consumer is called a receiver in P2P and a subscriber in pub-sub.

Table 13-1. Interfaces Used Depending on the Destination Type

Generic	Point-to-Point	Publish-Subscribe
Destination	Queue	Topic
ConnectionFactory	QueueConnectionFactory	TopicConnectionFactory
Connection	QueueConnection	TopicConnection
Session	QueueSession	TopicSession
MessageConsumer	QueueReceiver	TopicSubscriber
MessageProducer	QueueSender	TopicPublisher

Point-to-Point

In the P2P model, a message travels from a single producer (point A) to a single consumer (point B). The model is built around the concept of message queues, senders, and receivers (see Figure 13-3). A queue retains the messages sent by the sender until they are consumed, and a sender and a receiver do not have timing dependencies. This means that the sender can produce messages and send them in the queue whenever he likes, and a receiver can consume them whenever he likes. Once the receiver is created, it will get all the messages that were sent to the queue, even those sent before its creation.

Figure 13-3. P2P model

Each message is sent to a specific queue, and the receiver extracts the messages from the queue. Queues retain all messages sent until they are consumed or until they expire.

The P2P model is used if there is only one receiver for each message. Note that a queue can have multiple consumers, but once a receiver consumes a message from the queue, it is taken out of the queue, and no other consumer can receive it. In Figure 13-4, you can see one sender producing three messages.

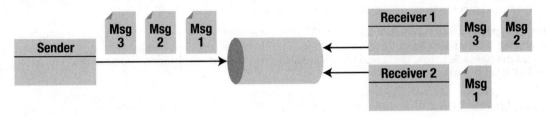

Figure 13-4. Multiple receivers

Note that P2P doesn't guarantee messages are delivered in any particular order (the order is not defined). A provider might pick them in arrival order, or randomly, or some other way.

Publish-Subscribe

In the pub-sub model, a single message is sent by a single producer to potentially several consumers. The model is built around the concept of topics, publishers, and subscribers (Figure 13-5). Consumers are called *subscribers* because they first need to subscribe to a topic. The provider manages the subscribing/unsubscribing mechanism as it occurs dynamically.

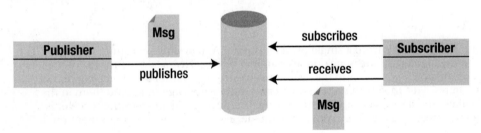

Figure 13-5. Pub-sub model

The topic retains messages until they are distributed to all subscribers. Unlike the P2P model, there is a timing dependency between publishers and subscribers; subscribers do not receive messages sent prior to their subscription, and, if the subscriber is inactive for a specified period, it will not receive past messages when it becomes active again. Note that this can be avoided, because the JMS API supports the concept of a durable subscriber, as you'll later see.

Multiple subscribers can consume the same message. The pub-sub model can be used for broadcast-type applications, in which a single message is delivered to several consumers. In Figure 13-6, the publisher sends three messages that each subscriber will receive (in an undefined order).

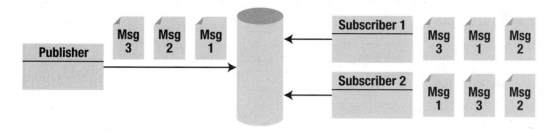

Figure 13-6. Multiple subscribers

JMS API

The JMS API is located under the `javax.jms` package and provides classes and interfaces for applications that require a messaging system (see Figure 13-7). This API enables asynchronous communication between clients by providing a connection to the provider, and a session where messages can be created and sent or received. These messages can contain text or other different kinds of objects.

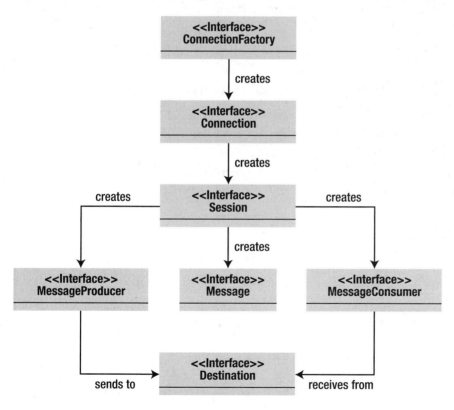

Figure 13-7. JMS API (derived from Figure 2-1 of the JMS 1.1 specification)

Administered Objects

Administered objects are objects that are configured administratively, as opposed to programmatically. The message provider allows these objects to be configured, and makes them available in the JNDI namespace. Like JDBC datasources, administered objects are created only once. The two types of administered objects for JMS are:

- *Connection factories*: Used by clients to create a connection to a destination.

- *Destinations*: Message distribution points that receive, hold, and distribute messages. Destinations can be queues (P2P) or topics (pub-sub).

JMS clients access these objects through portable interfaces by looking them up in the JNDI namespace. In GlassFish, there are several ways to create these objects: by using the administration console, the `asadmin` command line, or the REST interface.

ConnectionFactory

Connection factories are administered objects that allow an application to connect to a provider by creating a `Connection` object programmatically. A connection factory encapsulates the configuration parameters that have been defined by an administrator. There are three types of connection factories:

- `javax.jms.ConnectionFactory` is an interface that can be used for both P2P and pub-sub communications.

- `javax.jms.QueueConnectionFactory` is an interface that extends `ConnectionFactory` and is used for P2P communication.

- `javax.jms.TopicConnectionFactory` is an interface that extends `ConnectionFactory` and is used for pub-sub communication.

The program first has to get the connection factory by performing a JNDI lookup. For example, the following code fragment obtains the JNDI `InitialContext` object and uses it to look up a `QueueConnectionFactory` and a `TopicConnectionFactory` by its JNDI name:

```
Context ctx = new InitialContext();
QueueConnectionFactory queueConnectionFactory = ➥
                (QueueConnectionFactory) ctx.lookup("QConnFactory");
TopicConnectionFactory topicConnectionFactory = ➥
                (TopicConnectionFactory) ctx.lookup("TConnFactory");
```

Queue/Topic factories are needed when you need to access details specific to those messaging models (e.g., only topics can create durable subscribers). If not, you can also directly get a generic `ConnectionFactory` that can be used for both cases:

```
Context ctx = new InitialContext();
ConnectionFactory ConnectionFactory = ➥
                (QueueConnectionFactory) ctx.lookup("GenericConnFactory");
```

The only methods available in these three interfaces are `createConnection()` methods that return a `Connection` object. You can create a connection either with the default user identity or by specifying a username and password (see Listing 13-3).

Listing 13-3. ConnectionFactory Interface

```
public interface ConnectionFactory {

    Connection createConnection() throws JMSException;
    Connection createConnection(String userName, String password) ↩
                                            throws JMSException;
}
```

Destination

A destination is an administered object that contains provider-specific configuration information such as the destination address. But this configuration is hidden from the JMS client by using the standard `javax.jms.Destination` interface. There are two kinds of destinations, both interfaces that extend `Destination`:

- `javax.jms.Queue` objects used for P2P communication

- `javax.jms.Topic` objects used for pub-sub communication

These interfaces do not have any methods except one, which returns the name of the destination (`getQueueName()` for queues and `getTopicName()` for topics). Like the connection factory, a JNDI lookup is needed to return such objects.

Injection

Connection factories and destinations are administered objects that reside in a message provider and have to be declared in the JNDI namespace, which is why you use the JNDI API to look them up, or injection. When the client code runs inside a container, dependency injection can be used instead. Java EE 6 has several containers: EJB, servlet, and application client container (ACC). If code runs in one of these containers, the `@Resource` annotation (see the section "Dependency Injection" in Chapter 7) can be used to inject a reference to that resource by the container. With Java EE 6, using resources is much easier, as you don't have the complexity of JNDI or are not required to configure resource references in deployment descriptors. You just rely on the container injection capabilities.

Table 13-2 lists the elements that belong to the `@Resource` annotation.

Table 13-2. API of the @javax.annotation.Resource Annotation

Element	Description
name	The JNDI name of the resource (the name is implementation specific and not portable).
type	The Java type of the resource (e.g., `javax.sql.DataSource` or `javax.jms.Topic`).
authenticationType	The authentication type to use for the resource (either the container or the application).
shareable	Whether the resource can be shared.
mappedName	A product-specific name that the resource should map to.
lookup	The JNDI name of a resource that the resource being defined will be bound to. It can link to any compatible resource using the portable JNDI names.
description	Description of the resource.

To use this annotation let's take the example of a `Receiver` class with a `main()` method that receives text messages. In Listing 13-2, both the connection factory and the queue are looked up using JNDI. In Listing 13-4, the JNDI name is on the `@Resource` annotation. When this `Receiver` class is run into a container, it gets a reference of `ConnectionFactory` and `Queue` at initialization.

Listing 13-4. The Receiver Class Gets Injected References to JMS Resources

```java
public class Receiver {

    @Resource(lookup = "jms/javaee6/ConnectionFactory")
    private static ConnectionFactory connectionFactory;
    @Resource(lookup = "jms/javaee6/Queue")
    private static Queue queue;

    public static void main(String[] args) {

        // Creates the needed artifacts to connect to the queue
        Connection connection = connectionFactory.createConnection();
        Session session = connection.createSession(false, Session.AUTO_ACKNOWLEDGE);
        MessageConsumer consumer = session.createConsumer(queue);
        connection.start();

        // Loops to receive the messages
        while (true) {
            TextMessage message = (TextMessage) consumer.receive();
            System.out.println("Message received: " + message.getText());
        }
    }
}
```

For clarity, the code for exception handling is omitted. Note that the `@Resource` annotation appears on private attributes. Injection of resources occurs with different visibilities (private, protected, package, or public).

Connection

The `javax.jms.Connection` object, which you create using the `createConnection()` method of the connection factory, encapsulates a connection to the JMS provider. Connections are thread-safe and designed to be shareable, as opening a new connection is resource intensive. However, a session (`javax.jms.Session`) provides a single-threaded context for sending and receiving messages, using a connection to create one or more sessions.

Like connection factories, connections come in three forms: the generic `Connection` interface, the `QueueConnection` interface, and the `TopicConnection` interface that extends it. Depending on the connection factory object that you have, you can use it to create a connection:

```
Connection connection = connFactory.createConnection();
QueueConnection connection = queueConnFactory.createQueueConnection();
TopicConnection connection = topicConnFactory.createTopicConnection();
```

In Listing 13-4, before the receiver can consume messages, it must call the `start()` method. If you need to stop receiving messages temporarily without closing the connection, you can call the `stop()` method.

```
connection.start();
connection.stop();
```

When the application completes, you need to close any connections created. Closing a connection also closes its sessions and its producers or consumers.

```
connection.close();
```

Session

You create a session from the connection using the `createSession()` method. A session provides a transactional context in which a set of messages to be sent or received is grouped in an atomic unit of work, meaning that, if you send several messages during the same session, JMS will ensure that they either all arrive in the order they've been sent at the destination or none at all. This behavior is set at the creation of the session:

```
Session session = connection.createSession(true, Session.AUTO_ACKNOWLEDGE);
```

The first parameter of the method specifies whether or not the session is transactional. In the preceding code, the parameter is set to `true`, meaning that the request for sending messages won't be realized until either the session's `commit()` method is called or the session is closed. If the parameter was set to `false`, the session would not be transactional, and messages would be sent as soon as the `send()` method is invoked. The second parameter means that the session automatically acknowledges messages when they have been received successfully.

A session is single-threaded and is used to create messages, producers, and consumers. Like all the objects you've seen so far, sessions come in two different flavors: `QueueSession` and `TopicSession`. The more generic `Session` allows you to use either one with a unified interface.

Messages

To communicate, clients exchange messages; one producer will send a message to a destination, and a consumer will receive it. Messages are objects that encapsulate information and are divided in three parts (see Figure 13-8):

- A header contains standard information for identifying and routing the message.

- Properties are name-value pairs that the application can set or read. Properties also allow destinations to filter messages based on property values.

- A body contains the actual message and can take several formats (text, bytes, object, etc.).

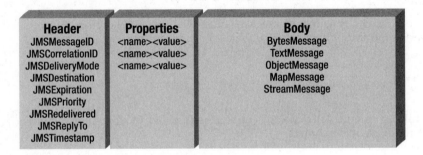

Figure 13-8. Structure of a JMS message

Header

The header has predefined name-value pairs, common to all messages that both clients and providers use to identify and route messages. They can be seen as message metadata as they give information about the message. Each field has associated getter and setter methods defined in the `javax.jms.Message` interface. Some header fields are intended to be set by a client, but many are set automatically by the `send()` or the `publish()` method.

Table 13-3 describes each JMS message header field.

Table 13-3. *Fields Contained in the Header**

Field	Description	Set By
JMSDestination	This indicates the destination to which the message is being sent.	send() or publish() method
JMSDeliveryMode	JMS supports two modes of message delivery. PERSISTENT mode instructs the provider to ensure the message is not lost in transit due to a failure. NON_PERSISTENT mode is the lowest-overhead delivery mode because it does not require the message to be logged to a persistent storage.	send() or publish() method
JMSMessageID	This provides a value that uniquely identifies each message sent by a provider.	send() or publish() method
JMSTimestamp	This contains the time a message was handed off to a provider to be sent.	send() or publish() method
JMSCorrelationID	A client can use this field to link one message with another such as linking a response message with its request message.	Client
JMSReplyTo	This contains the destination where a reply to the message should be sent.	Client
JMSRedelivered	This Boolean value is set by the provider to indicate whether a message has been redelivered.	Provider
JMSType	This serves as a message type identifier.	Client
JMSExpiration	When a message is sent, its expiration time is calculated and set based on the time-to-live value specified on the send() method.	send() or publish() method
JMSPriority	JMS defines a ten-level priority value, with 0 as the lowest priority and 9 as the highest.	send() or publish() method

* JMS 1.1 Specification, "3.4: Message Header Fields," (http://jcp.org/en/jsr/detail?id=914)

Properties

In addition to the header fields, the `javax.jms.Message` interface supports property values, which are just like headers, but explicitly created by the application, instead of being standard across messages. This provides a mechanism for adding optional header fields to a message that a client will choose to receive or not via selectors. Property values can be `boolean`, `byte`, `short`, `int`, `long`, `float`, `double`, and `String`. The code to set and get properties looks like this:

```
message.setFloatProperty("orderAmount", 1245.5f);
message.getFloatProperty("orderAmount");
```

Body

The body of a message is optional, and contains the data to send or receive. Depending on the interface that you use, it can contain different formats of data, as listed in Table 13-4.

Table 13-4. Types of Messages

Interface	Description
StreamMessage	A message whose body contains a stream of Java primitive values. It is filled and read sequentially.
MapMessage	A message whose body contains a set of name-value pairs where names are strings and values are Java primitive types.
TextMessage	A message whose body contains a string (for example, it can contain XML).
ObjectMessage	A message that contains a serializable object or a collection of serializable objects.
BytesMessage	A message that contains a stream of bytes.

It is possible to create your own message format, if you extend the `javax.jms.Message` interface. Note that, when a message is received, its body is read-only. Depending on the message type, you have different methods to access its content. A text message will have a `getText()` and `setText()` method, an object message will have a `getObject()` and `setObject()`, and so forth (check Listing 13-5 to see the `setText` method in context).

```
textMessage.setText("This is a text message");
textMessage.getText();
bytesMessage.readByte();
objectMessage.getObject();
```

MessageProducer

A message producer is an object created by a session and used to send messages to a destination. The generic `javax.jms.MessageProducer` interface can be used to get a specific producer with a unified interface. For the P2P model, a message producer is called a sender and implements the `QueueSender` interface. For the pub-sub model, it is called a publisher and implements `TopicPublisher`. Once you have created a message, depending on the interface you use, the producer can send it (P2P) or publish it (pub-sub):

```
messageProducer.send(message);
queueSender.send(message);
topicPublisher.publish(message);
```

A producer can specify a default delivery mode, priority, and time-to-live for messages sent. The following steps explain how to create a publisher that sends a message to a topic (see Listing 13-5):

1. Obtain a connection factory and a topic using injection (or JNDI lookup).

2. Create a `Connection` object using the connection factory.

3. Create a `Session` object using the connection.

4. Create a `MessageProducer` (or in this case it could have been a `TopicPublisher`) using the `Session` object.

5. Create one or more messages of any type (here I used a `TextMessage`) using the `Session` object. After creation, populate the message with the required data (this is done with the `setText()` method in this example).

6. Send one or more messages to the topic using the `MessageProducer.send()` method (or the `TopicPublisher.publish()` method).

7. Close the connection.

Listing 13-5. The Sender Class Sends a Message to a Topic

```
public class Sender {

    @Resource(lookup = "jms/javaee6/ConnectionFactory")        // 1
    private static ConnectionFactory connectionFactory;
    @Resource(lookup = "jms/javaee6/Topic")                    // 1
    private static Topic topic;

    public static void main(String[] args) {

        // Creates the needed artifacts to connect to the queue
        Connection connection = connectionFactory.createConnection();   // 2
        Session session = connection.createSession(false, ↪
                                    Session.AUTO_ACKNOWLEDGE);   // 3
        MessageProducer producer = session.createProducer(topic);  // 4

        // Sends a text message to the topic
        TextMessage message = session.createTextMessage();          // 5
        message.setText("This is a text message sent at " + new Date());
        producer.send(message);                                      // 6

        connection.close();                                          // 7
    }
}
```

MessageConsumer

A client uses a `MessageConsumer` to receive messages from a destination. A `MessageConsumer` is created by passing a `Queue` or `Topic` to the `Session`'s `createConsumer()` method. For the P2P model, a message consumer can implement the `QueueReceiver` interface, and, for the pub-sub model, it can implement `TopicSubscriber`.

Messaging is inherently asynchronous, in that there is no timing dependency between producers and consumers. However, the client itself can consume messages in two ways:

- *Synchronously.* A receiver explicitly fetches the message from the destination by calling the `receive()` method. Previous examples use an infinite loop that blocks until the message arrives.

- *Asynchronously.* A receiver decides to register to an event that is triggered when the message arrives. It has to implement the `MessageListener` interface, and, whenever a message arrives, the provider delivers it by calling the `onMessage()` method.

Figure 13-9 illustrates these two types of consumer.

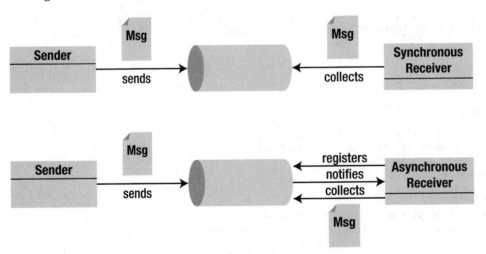

Figure 13-9. Synchronous and asynchronous consumers

Synchronous Delivery

A synchronous receiver needs to start a connection, loop to wait until a message arrives, and request the arrived message, using one of its `receive()` methods. There are several variations of `receive()` that allow a client to poll or wait for the next message. The following steps explain how you can create a synchronous receiver that consumes a message from a topic (see Listing 13-6):

1. Obtain a connection factory and a topic using injection (or JNDI lookup).

2. Create a `Connection` object using the connection factory.

3. Create a `Session` object using the connection.

4. Create a `MessageConsumer` (or in this case it could have been a `TopicSubscriber`) using the `Session` object.

5. Start the connection.

6. Loop and call the `receive()` method on the consumer object. The `receive()` method is blocked if the queue is empty and waits for a message to arrive. Here, the infinite loop waits for other messages to arrive.

7. Process the message returned by the `receive()` method using the `TextMessage.getText()` method (if it's a text message).

Listing 13-6. The Receiver Consumes Messages in a Synchronous Manner

```
public class Receiver {

    @Resource(lookup = "jms/javaee6/ConnectionFactory")            // 1
    private static ConnectionFactory connectionFactory;
    @Resource(lookup = "jms/javaee6/Topic")                        // 1
    private static Topic topic;

    public static void main(String[] args) {

        // Creates the needed artifacts to connect to the queue
        Connection connection = connectionFactory.createConnection();   // 2
        Session session = connection.createSession(false, ➥
                                    Session.AUTO_ACKNOWLEDGE);      // 3
        MessageConsumer consumer = session.createConsumer(topic);  // 4
        connection.start();                                        // 5

        // Infinite loop to receive the messages
        while (true) {
            TextMessage message = (TextMessage) consumer.receive();     // 6
            System.out.println("Message received: " + message.getText()); // 7
        }

    }
}
```

Asynchronous Delivery

Asynchronous consumption is based on event handling. A client can register an object (including itself) that implements the `MessageListener` interface. A *message listener* is an object that acts as an asynchronous event handler for messages. As messages arrive, the provider delivers them by calling the listener's onMessage() method, which takes one argument of type Message. With this event model, the consumer doesn't need to loop indefinitely to receive a message. MDBs use this event model.

The following steps describe the process used to create an asynchronous message listener (see Listing 13-7):

1. The class implements the javax.jms.MessageListener interface, which defines a single method called onMessage().

2. Obtain a connection factory and a destination using injection (or JNDI lookup).

3. Create a Connection object using the connection factory, create a Session object using the connection, and create a MessageConsumer using the Session object.

4. Call the setMessageListener() method, passing an instance of a MessageListener interface (in Listing 13-7, the Listener class itself implements the MessageListener interface).

5. After registering the message listener, call the start() method to start listening for message arrival. If you call start() before registering the listener, you are likely to miss messages.

6. Implement the onMessage() method and process the received message. Each time a message arrives, the provider will invoke this method, passing the message.

Listing 13-7. The Consumer Is a Message Listener

```
public class Listener implements MessageListener {            // 1

    @Resource(lookup = "jms/javaee6/ConnectionFactory")      // 2
    private static ConnectionFactory connectionFactory;
    @Resource(lookup = "jms/javaee6/Topic")                  // 2
    private static Topic topic;

    public static void main(String[] args) {

        // Creates the needed artifacts to connect to the queue
        Connection connection = connectionFactory.createConnection();   // 3
        Session session = connection.createSession(false, ↩
                                    Session.AUTO_ACKNOWLEDGE);
        MessageConsumer consumer = session.createConsumer(topic);
        consumer.setMessageListener(new Listener());         // 4
        connection.start();                                  // 5
    }

    public void onMessage(Message message) {                 // 6
        System.out.println("Message received: " + ↩
                        ((TextMessage) message).getText());
    }
}
```

Selectors

Some messaging applications need to filter the messages they receive. When a message is broadcast to many clients, it becomes useful to set criteria so that it is only consumed by certain receivers. This eliminates both time and bandwidth the provider would waste transporting messages to clients that don't need them.

You've seen that messages are composed of three parts: header, properties, and body. The header contains a fixed number of fields (the message metadata), and the properties are a set of custom name-value pairs that the application can use to set any values. Selection can be done on those two areas. Senders set one or several property values or header fields, and the receiver specifies message selection criteria using selector expressions. Only messages that match the selector are delivered. Message selectors assign the work of filtering messages to the JMS provider, rather than to the application.

A message selector is a string that contains an expression. The syntax of the expression is based on a subset of the SQL92 conditional expression syntax and looks like this:

```
session.createConsumer(topic, "JMSPriority < 6");
session.createConsumer(topic, "JMSPriority < 6 AND orderAmount < 200");
session.createConsumer(topic, "orderAmount BETWEEN 1000 AND 2000");
```

In the preceding code, a consumer is created, passing a selector string. This string can use header fields (JMSPriority < 6) or custom properties (orderAmount < 200). The producer sets these properties into the message as follows:

```
message.setIntProperty("orderAmount", 1530);
message.setJMSPriority(5);
```

Selector expression can use logical operators (NOT, AND, OR), comparison operators (=, >, >=, <, <=, <>), arithmetic operators (+, -, *, /), expressions ([NOT] BETWEEN, [NOT] IN, [NOT] LIKE, IS [NOT] NULL), and so on.

Reliability Mechanisms

You've seen how to connect to a provider, create different types of messages, send them to queues or topics, and receive them all or filter them with selectors. But what if you rely heavily on JMS and need to ensure reliability? JMS defines several levels of reliability to ensure your message is delivered, even if the provider crashes or is under load, or if destinations are filled with messages that should have expired. The mechanisms for achieving reliable message delivery are as follows:

- *Setting message time-to-live*: Set an expiration time on messages so they are not delivered if they are obsolete.

- *Specifying message persistence*: Specify that messages are persistent in the event of a provider failure.

- *Controlling acknowledgment*: Specify various levels of message acknowledgment.

- *Creating durable subscribers*: Ensure messages are delivered to an unavailable subscriber in a pub-sub model.

- *Setting priorities*: Set the priority for delivering a message.

Setting Message Time-to-Live

Under heavy load, a time-to-live can be set on messages to ensure that the provider will remove them from the destination when they become obsolete, by either using the `MessageProducer` API or setting the `JMSExpiration` header field.

The `MessageProducer` has a `setTimeToLive()` method that takes a number of milliseconds, or use the `send()` method for each message:

```
MessageProducer producer = session.createProducer(topic);
producer.setTimeToLive(1000);
// or
producer.send(message, DeliveryMode.NON_PERSISTENT, 2, 1000);
```

The first call sets the TTL for the producer overall and all messages it delivers, while the second call sets it for one message only. The second call sends a message specifying the delivery mode, the priority, and time-to-live (1000).

Specifying Message Persistence

JMS supports two modes of message delivery: persistent and nonpersistent. *Persistent delivery* ensures that a message is delivered only once to a consumer, whereas *nonpersistent delivery* requires a message be delivered once at most. Persistent delivery (which is the default) is more reliable, but at a performance cost, as it prevents losing a message if a provider failure occurs.

The delivery mode can be specified in two ways: by using the `setDeliveryMode()` method of the `MessageProducer` interface, or passing a parameter to the `send()` method:

```
MessageProducer producer = session.createProducer(topic);
producer.setDeliveryMode(DeliveryMode.NON_PERSISTENT);
// or
producer.send(message, DeliveryMode.NON_PERSISTENT, 2, 1000);
```

The first call sets the delivery mode for the producer overall and all messages it delivers, while the second call sets it for one message only.

Controlling Acknowledgment

So far, the scenarios we've explored have assumed that a message is sent and received without any acknowledgment. But sometimes, you will want a receiver to acknowledge the message has been received (see Figure 13-10). An acknowledgment phase can be initiated either by the JMS provider or by the client, depending on the acknowledgment mode.

Figure 13-10. *A receiver acknowledging a message*

In transactional sessions, acknowledgment happens automatically when a transaction is committed. If a transaction is rolled back, all consumed messages are redelivered. But in nontransactional sessions, an acknowledgment mode must be specified:

- AUTO_ACKNOWLEDGE: The session automatically acknowledges the reception of a message.

- CLIENT_ACKNOWLEDGE: A client acknowledges a message by explicitly calling the Message.acknowledge() method.

- DUPS_OK_ACKNOWLEDGE: This option instructs the session to lazily acknowledge the delivery of messages. This is likely to result in the delivery of some duplicate messages if the JMS provider fails, so it should be used only by consumers that can tolerate duplicate messages. If the message is redelivered, the provider sets the value of the JMSRedelivered header field to true.

The following code uses the explicit client acknowledgment mode by calling the acknowledge() method:

```
// Producer
connection.createSession(false, Session.CLIENT_ACKNOWLEDGE);
producer = session.createProducer(topic);
message = session.createTextMessage();
producer.send(message);
// Consumer
message.acknowledge();
```

Creating Durable Subscribers

The disadvantage of using the pub-sub model is that a message consumer must be running when the messages are sent to the topic; otherwise, it will not receive them. By using durable subscribers, the JMS API provides a way to keep messages in the topic until all subscribed consumers receive them. With durable subscription, the receiver can be offline for some time, but, when it reconnects, it receives the messages that arrived during its disconnection. To achieve this, the client creates a durable subscriber using the session.

```
session.createDurableSubscriber(topic,"javaee6DurableSubscription");
```

At this point, the client program starts the connection and receives messages. The name `javaee6DurableSubscription` is used as an identifier of the durable subscription. Each durable subscriber must have a unique ID, resulting in the declaration of a unique connection factory for each potential, durable subscriber.

Setting Priorities

You can use message priority levels to instruct the JMS provider to deliver urgent messages first. JMS defines ten priority values, with 0 as the lowest and 9 as the highest. You can specify the priority value by either using the `setPriority()` method or passing it as a parameter to the `send()` method:

```
MessageProducer producer = session.createProducer(topic);
producer.setPriority(2);
// or
producer.send(message, DeliveryMode.NON_PERSISTENT, 2, 1000);
```

Message-Driven Beans

This chapter shows how asynchronous messaging provides loose coupling and increased flexibility between systems, using the JMS API in a stand-alone environment with main classes, JNDI lookup, or resource injection using the ACC. MDBs provide this standard asynchronous messaging model for enterprise applications running in an EJB container.

An MDB is an asynchronous consumer that is invoked by the container as a result of the arrival of a message. To a message producer, an MDB is simply a message consumer, hidden behind a destination to which it listens.

MDBs are part of the EJB specification, and their model is close to stateless session beans as they do not have any state and run inside an EJB container. The container listens to a destination and delegates the call to the MDB upon message arrival. Like any other EJB, MDBs can access resources managed by the container (other EJBs, JDBC connections, JMS resources, etc.).

Why use MDBs when you can use stand-alone JMS clients, as you've seen previously? Because of the container, which manages multithreading, security, and transactions, thereby greatly simplifying the code of your JMS consumer. It also manages incoming messages among multiple instances of MDBs (available in a pool) that have no special multithreading code themselves. As soon as a new message reaches the destination, an MDB instance is retrieved from the pool to handle the message.

How to Write an MDB

MDBs can be transactional, multithreaded, and naturally consume JMS messages. With the JMS API thus far, you might expect factories, connections, sessions, consumers, user transactions, and so on. However, it is surprising to see that a simple consumer MDB can look like Listing 13-8.

Listing 13-8. A Simple MDB

```
@MessageDriven(mappedName = "jms/javaee6/Topic")
public class BillingMDB implements MessageListener {

    public void onMessage(Message message) {
        TextMessage msg = (TextMessage)message;
        System.out.println("Message received: " + msg.getText());
    }
}
```

The code in Listing 13-8 (omitting exception handling for clarity) shows that MDBs relieve the programmer of all mechanical aspects of processing the types of messages explained so far. An MDB implements the MessageListener interface and the onMessage() method, but no other code is needed to connect to the provider or start message consumption. MDBs also rely on the configuration-by-exception mechanism, and only a few annotations are needed to make it work (see the @MessageDriven annotation).

MDB Model

MDBs are different from session beans, as they do not implement a local or remote business interface, instead implementing javax.jms.MessageListener. Clients cannot invoke methods directly on MDBs; however, like session beans, MDBs have a rich programming model that includes a life cycle, callback annotations, interceptors, injection, and transactions. Taking advantage of this model provides applications with a high level of functionality.

It is important to be aware that MDBs are not part of the new EJB Lite model, meaning they cannot be deployed in a simple web application (in a war file), but still need an enterprise packaging (ear archive).

The requirements to develop an MDB class are as follows:

- The class must be annotated with @javax.ejb.MessageDriven or its XML equivalent in a deployment descriptor.

- The class must implement, directly or indirectly, the MessageListener interface.

- The class must be defined as public, and must not be final or abstract.

- The class must have a public no-arg constructor that the container will use to create instances of the MDB.

- The class must not define the finalize() method.

The MDB class is allowed to implement other methods, invoke other resources, and so on. MDBs are deployed in a container and can be optionally packaged with an ejb-jar.xml file. Following the "ease of use" model of Java EE 6, an MDB can be simply an annotated POJO, eliminating most of the configuration. However, if you still need to customize the JMS configuration, you can use the elements of the @MessageDriven and @ActivationConfigProperty annotations (or XML equivalent).

@MessageDriven

MDBs are one of the simplest kinds of EJBs to develop, as they support the smallest number of annotations. The @MessageDriven annotation (or XML equivalent) is mandatory, as it is the piece of metadata the container requires to recognize that the Java class is actually an MDB.

The API of the @MessageDriven annotation, shown in Listing 13-9, is very simple, and all elements are optional.

Listing 13-9. @MessageDriven Annotation API

```
@Target(TYPE) @Retention(RUNTIME)
public @interface MessageDriven {
    String name() default "";
    Class messageListenerInterface default Object.class;
    ActivationConfigProperty[] activationConfig() default {};
    String mappedName();
    String description();
}
```

The name element specifies the name of the MDB (which by default is the name of the class). messageListenerInterface specifies which message listener the MDB implements (if the MDB implements multiple interfaces, it tells the EJB container which one is the MessageListener interface). The mappedName element is the JNDI name of the destination that the MDB should be listening to. description is just a string, used to give a description of the MDB once deployed. The activationConfig element is used to specify configuration properties and takes an array of @ActivationConfigProperty annotations.

@ActivationConfigProperty

JMS allows configuration of certain properties such as message selectors, acknowledgment mode, durable subscribers, and so on. In an MDB, these properties can be set using the @ActivationConfigProperty annotation. This optional annotation can be provided as one of the parameters for the @MessageDriven annotation, and, compared to the JMS equivalent, the @ActivationConfigProperty is very basic, consisting of a name-value pair (see Listing 13-10).

Listing 13-10. ActivationConfigProperty Annotation API

```
@Target({}) @Retention(RUNTIME)
public @interface ActivationConfigProperty {
    String propertyName();
    String propertyValue();
}
```

The activationConfig property allows you to provide messaging system–specific configuration, meaning that it supports provider-specific properties. For OpenMQ, the code in Listing 13-11 sets the acknowledge mode and the message selector.

Listing 13-11. Setting Properties on MDBs

```
@MessageDriven(mappedName = "jms/javaee6/Topic", activationConfig = {
    @ActivationConfigProperty(propertyName = "acknowledgeMode", ↩
                              propertyValue = "Auto-acknowledge"),
    @ActivationConfigProperty(propertyName = "messageSelector", ↩
                              propertyValue = "orderAmount < 3000")
})
public class BillingMDB implements MessageListener {

    public void onMessage(Message message) {
        TextMessage msg = (TextMessage)message;
        System.out.println("Message received: " + msg.getText());
    }
}
```

Each activation property is a name-value pair that the underlying messaging provider understands and uses to set up the MDB. Table 13-5 lists some properties used by OpenMQ (you should consult the documentation if you use a different JMS provider).

Table 13-5. Activation Properties for OpenMQ

Property	Description
destinationType	The destination type, which can be TOPIC or QUEUE.
destination	The name of the destination.
messageSelector	The message selector string used by the MDB.
acknowledgeMode	The acknowledgment mode (default is AUTO_ACKNOWLEDGE).
subscriptionDurability	The subscription durability (default is NON_DURABLE).
subscriptionName	The subscription name of the consumer.

As in the API of the javax.jms.Session class, acknowledgment can take three different modes, but only two can be used with MDBs:

- AUTO_ACKNOWLEDGE: The session automatically acknowledges the reception of a message.

- DUPS_OK_ACKNOWLEDGE: This mode instructs the session to lazily acknowledge the delivery of messages (sometimes resulting in the delivery of duplicate messages).

- CLIENT_ACKNOWLEDGE: This mode is not permitted, as MDBs should not attempt to use the JMS API directly for message acknowledgment. Acknowledgment is handled automatically by the container.

Dependencies Injection

Like all the other EJBs that you've seen in Chapter 6, MDBs can use dependency injection to acquire references to resources such as JDBC datasources, EJBs, or other objects. *Injection* is the means by which the container inserts an object reference automatically for annotated attributes. These resources have to be available in the container or environment context, so the following code is allowed in an MDB:

```
@PersistenceContext
private EntityManager em;
@EJB
private InvoiceBean invoice;
@Resource(lookup = "jms/javaee6/ConnectionFactory")
private ConnectionFactory connectionFactory;
```

The MDB context can also be injected using the **@Resource** annotation:

```
@Resource private MessageDrivenContext context;
```

MDB Context

The `MessageDrivenContext` interface provides access to the runtime context that the container provides for an MDB instance. The container passes the `MessageDrivenContext` interface to this instance, which remains associated for the lifetime of the MDB. This gives the MDB the possibility to explicitly roll back a transaction, get the user principal, and so on. The `MessageDrivenContext` interface extends the `javax.ejb.EJBContext` interface without adding any extra methods.

If the MDB injects a reference to its context, it will be able to invoke the methods listed in Table 13-6.

Table 13-6. Methods of the `MessageDrivenContext` Interface

Method	Description
getCallerPrincipal	Returns the `java.security.Principal` associated with the invocation.
getRollbackOnly	Tests whether the current transaction has been marked for rollback.
getTimerService	Returns the `javax.ejb.TimerService` interface.
getUserTransaction	Returns the `javax.transaction.UserTransaction` interface to use to demarcate transactions. Only MDBs with bean-managed transaction (BMT) can use this method.
isCallerInRole	Tests whether the caller has a given security role.
Lookup	Enables the MDB to look up its environment entries in the JNDI naming context.
setRollbackOnly	Allows the instance to mark the current transaction as rollback. Only MDBs with BMT can use this method.

Life Cycle and Callback Annotations

The MDB life cycle (see Figure 13-11) is identical to the stateless session bean: either the MDB exists and is ready to consume messages or it doesn't exist. Before exiting, the container first creates an instance of the MDB and, if applicable, injects the necessary resources as specified by metadata annotations (@Resource, @EJB, etc.) or deployment descriptor. The container then calls the bean's @PostConstruct callback method, if any. After this, the MDB is in the ready state and waits to consume any incoming message. The @PreDestroy callback occurs when the MDB is removed from the pool or destroyed.

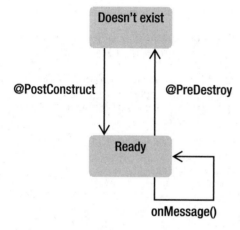

Figure 13-11. MDB life cycle

This behavior is identical to stateless session beans (see Chapter 8 for more details about callback methods and interceptors), and, like other EJBs, you can add interceptors with the @javax.ejb.AroundInvoke annotation.

MDB as a Consumer

As explained in the "JMS API" section earlier in the chapter, consumers can receive a message either synchronously, by looping and waiting for a message to arrive, or asynchronously, by implementing the MessageListener interface. By nature, MDBs are designed to function as asynchronous message consumers. MDBs implement a message listener interface, which is triggered by the container when a message arrives.

Can an MDB do synchronous consuming? Yes, but this is not recommended. Synchronous message consumers block and tie up server resources (the EJBs will be stuck looping without performing any work, and the container will not be able to free them). MDBs, like stateless session beans, live in a pool of a certain size. When the container needs an instance, it takes one out of the pool and uses it. If each instance goes into an infinite loop, the pool will eventually empty, and all the available instances will be busy looping. The EJB container can also start generating more MDB instances, growing the pool and eating up more and more memory. For this reason, session beans and MDBs should not be used as synchronous message consumers. Table 13-7 shows you the different receiving modes for MDBs and session beans.

Table 13-7. MDB Compared with Session Beans

Enterprise Beans	Producer	Synchronous Receiver	Asynchronous Receiver
Session beans	Yes	Not recommended	Not possible
MDB	Yes	Not recommended	Yes

MDB as a Producer

MDBs are capable of becoming message producers, something that often occurs when they are involved in a workflow, as they receive a message from one destination, process it, and send it to another destination. To add this capability, the JMS API must be used.

A destination and a connection factory can be injected by using the @Resource annotation or via JNDI lookup and then invoking methods on the javax.jms.Session object to create and send a message. The code of the BillingMDB (see Listing 13-12) listens to a topic (jms/javaee6/Topic), receives messages (onMessage() method), and sends a new message to a queue (jms/javaee6/Queue).

Listing 13-12. A MDB Consuming and Producing Messages

```
@MessageDriven(mappedName = "jms/javaee6/Topic", activationConfig = {
        @ActivationConfigProperty(propertyName = "acknowledgeMode", ↪
                                  propertyValue = "Auto-acknowledge"),
        @ActivationConfigProperty(propertyName = "messageSelector", ↪
                                  propertyValue = "orderAmount < 3000")
})
public class BillingMDB implements MessageListener {

    @Resource(lookup = "jms/javaee6/Queue")
    private Destination printingQueue;
    @Resource(lookup = "jms/javaee6/ConnectionFactory")
    private ConnectionFactory connectionFactory;
    private Connection connection;

    @PostConstruct
    private void initConnection() {
        connection = connectionFactory.createConnection();
    }

    @PreDestroy
    private void closeConnection() {
        connection.close();
    }

    public void onMessage(Message message) {
        TextMessage msg = (TextMessage)message;
        System.out.println("Message received: " + msg.getText());
```

```
        sendPrintingMessage();
    }

    private void sendPrintingMessage() throws JMSException {
        Session session = connection.createSession(true, Session.AUTO_ACKNOWLEDGE);
        MessageProducer producer = session.createProducer(printingQueue);
        TextMessage message = session.createTextMessage();
        message.setText("This message has been received and sent again");
        producer.send(message);
        session.close();
    }
}
```

This MDB uses most of the concepts introduced thus far. First, it uses the @MessageDriven annotation to define the JNDI name of the topic it is listening to (mappedName = "jms/javaee6/Topic"). In this same annotation, it defines a set of properties, such as the acknowledge mode and a message selector using an array of @ActivationConfigProperty annotations, and it implements MessageListener and its onMessage() method.

This MDB also needs to produce a message. Therefore, it gets injected with the two administered objects required: a connection factory and a destination (the queue named jms/javaee6/Queue). It can then create and close a shared javax.jms.Connection instance using life-cycle callbacks; although creating a connection is expensive, putting this code in the @PostConstruct and @PreDestroy annotated methods will ensure that it will be done only at creation and at destruction of the MDB.

Finally, the business method that sends messages (the sendPrintingMessage() method) looks like what you've seen earlier: a JMS session gets created and used to create a text message and a producer, and the message is then sent. For better readability, exception handling has been omitted in the entire class.

Transaction

MDBs are EJBs (see Chapter 9 for more information). MDBs can use BMTs or container-managed transactions (CMTs); they can explicitly roll back a transaction by using the MessageDrivenContext.setRollbackOnly() method, etc. There is some specificity about MDBs that is worth explaining.

When we talk about transactions, we always think of relational databases. However, other resources are also transactional, such as messaging systems. If two or more operations have to succeed or fail together, they form a transaction. With messaging, if two or more messages are sent, they have to succeed (commit) or fail (roll back) together. How does this work in practice? The answer is that messages are not released to consumers until the transaction commits. The container will start a transaction before the onMessage() method is invoked and will commit the transaction when the method returns (unless the transaction was marked for rollback with setRollbackOnly()).

Even though MDBs are transactional, they cannot execute in the client's transaction context, as they don't have a client. Nobody explicitly invokes methods on MDBs, they just listen to a destination and consume messages. There is no context passed from a client to an MDB, and client transaction context to the onMessage() method cannot be passed.

Table 13-8 compares CMTs with session beans and MDBs.

Table 13-8. *MDB Transactions Compared with Session Beans*

Transaction Attribute	Session Beans	MDB
NOT_SUPPORTED	Yes	Yes
REQUIRED	Yes	Yes
MANDATORY	Yes	No
REQUIRES_NEW	Yes	No
SUPPORTS	Yes	No
NEVER	Yes	No

In CMTs, MDBs can use the `@javax.ejb.TransactionAttribute` annotation on business methods with the two following attributes:

- `REQUIRED` *(the default)*: If the MDB invokes other enterprise beans, the container passes the transaction context with the invocation. The container attempts to commit the transaction when the message listener method has completed.

- `NOT_SUPPORTED`: If the MDB invokes other enterprise beans, the container passes no transaction context with the invocation.

Handling Exceptions

In the snippets of code in this chapter, exception handling has been omitted as the JMS API is very verbose in dealing with exceptions. The API defines 12 different exceptions, all inheriting from `javax.jms.JMSException`. Any method invocation on connections, sessions, consumers, messages, or producers will throw a `JMSException` or one of the subclasses.

It is important to note that `JMSException` is a checked exception (see the discussion on application exception in the "Exception Handling" section in Chapter 9). The EJB specification outlines two types of exceptions:

- *Application exceptions*: Checked exceptions that extend `Exception` do not cause the container to roll back.

- *System exceptions*: Unchecked exceptions that extend `RuntimeException` cause the container to roll back.

Throwing a `JMSException` will not cause the container to roll back. If a rollback is needed, the `setRollBackOnly()` must be explicitly called or a system exception (such as `EJBException`) rethrown:

```
public void onMessage(Message message) {
    TextMessage msg = (TextMessage)message;
    try {
        System.out.println("Message received: " + msg.getText());
```

```
        sendPrintingMessage();
    } catch (JMSException e) {
        context.setRollBackOnly();
    }
}
```

Putting It All Together

The most important concepts of messaging are P2P and pub-sub models, administered objects (connection factories and destinations), how to connect to a provider and produce or consume messages, some reliability mechanisms used by JMS, and how to use container-managed components (MDBs) to listen to destinations. So now let's see how these concepts work together through an example, compile and package it with Maven, and deploy it in GlassFish.

The example uses a stand-alone class (OrderSender) that sends messages to a queue (called jms/javaee6/Queue). These messages are objects representing a customer order of books and CDs. This object (OrderDTO) has several attributes, including the total amount of the order. On the other side of the queue, an MDB (OrderMDB) consumes only orders that have a total amount greater than $1,000. This amount is passed as a parameter to the OrderSender class.

Because Maven needs to structure the code based on the final packaging artifacts, the OrderSender will get deployed in one jar file, the OrderMDB in another one, and the OrderDTO class will be common to both jar files (for simplicity, just to avoid creating a third Maven module).

Writing the OrderDTO

The object that will be sent in the JMS message is a POJO that needs to implement the Serializable interface. The OrderDTO class, shown in Listing 13-13, gives some information about the order, including its total amount; it is the object that will be set into a JMS ObjectMessage and sent from the OrderSender to the OrderMDB.

Listing 13-13. The OrderDTO Is Passed in a JMS ObjectMessage

```
public class OrderDTO implements Serializable {

    private Long orderId;
    private Date creationDate;
    private String customerName;
    private Float totalAmount;

    // Constructors, getters, setters
}
```

Writing the OrderSender

The OrderSender, shown in Listing 13-14, is a stand-alone client that uses the JMS API to send an ObjectMessage to the jms/javaee6/Queue queue. It gets injected with the necessary connection factory and destination, and in the main() method creates an instance of an OrderDTO class. Note that the totalAmount of the order is an argument passed to the class (args[0]). An ObjectMessage is created from the Session, and, with the message.setObject(order) method, the order is set into the body of the message. Note that the total amount is set into a property (message.setFloatProperty()) for selection later.

Listing 13-14. The OrderSender Sends an OrderDTO in a Message

```
public class OrderSender {

    @Resource(lookup = "jms/javaee6/ConnectionFactory")
    private static ConnectionFactory connectionFactory;
    @Resource(lookup = "jms/javaee6/Queue")
    private static Queue queue;

    public static void main(String[] args) {

        // Creates an orderDto with a total amount parameter
        Float totalAmount = Float.valueOf(args[0]);
        OrderDTO order = new OrderDTO(1234l, new Date(), ⮐
                                     "Serge Gainsbourg", totalAmount);

        try {
            // Creates the needed artifacts to connect to the queue
            Connection connection = connectionFactory.createConnection();
            Session session = connection.createSession(false, ⮐
                                         Session.AUTO_ACKNOWLEDGE);
            MessageProducer producer = session.createProducer(queue);

            // Sends an object message to the queue
            ObjectMessage message = session.createObjectMessage();
            message.setObject(order);
            message.setFloatProperty("orderAmount", totalAmount);
            producer.send(message);
            connection.close();

        } catch (Exception e) {
            e.printStackTrace();
        }
    }
}
```

Writing the OrderMDB

The OrderMDB class (see Listing 13-15) is an MDB annotated with @MessageDriven that listens to the jms/javaee6/Queue destination. This MDB is only interested in orders greater than $1,000, using a message selector (orderAmount > 1000). At message arrival, the onMessage() method consumes it, casts it to an ObjectMessage, and gets the body of the message (msg.getObject()). For this example, only the message is displayed, but other processing could have also been done.

Listing 13-15. The OrderMDB Receives an ObjectMessage

```java
@MessageDriven(mappedName = "jms/javaee6/Queue", activationConfig = {
    @ActivationConfigProperty(propertyName = "acknowledgeMode", ↪
                            propertyValue = "Auto-acknowledge"),
    @ActivationConfigProperty(propertyName = "messageSelector", ↪
                            propertyValue = "orderAmount > 1000")
})
public class OrderMDB implements MessageListener {

    public void onMessage(Message message) {
        try {
            ObjectMessage msg = (ObjectMessage) message;
            OrderDTO order = (OrderDTO) msg.getObject();
            System.out.println("Order received: " + order.toString());
        } catch (JMSException e) {
            e.printStackTrace();
        }
    }
}
```

Compiling and Packaging with Maven

The sender and the MDB should be packaged in separate jar files and use different directory structures and different pom.xml files. The pom.xml of the OrderMDB, shown in Listing 13-16, is nearly the same as the OrderSender's.

Because MDBs use annotations from the EJB package (@MessageDriven), the javax.ejb dependency needs to be declared. The javax.jms dependency is for the JMS API (session, messages, etc.). Both dependencies have the scope provided because GlassFish, as an EJB container and a JMS provider, provides these APIs at runtime. Maven should be informed that you are using Java SE 6 by configuring the maven-compiler-plugin.

Listing 13-16. The pom.xml to Build and Package the MDB

```xml
<?xml version="1.0" encoding="UTF-8"?>
<project xmlns="http://maven.apache.org/POM/4.0.0" ↪
        xmlns:xsi="http://www.w3.org/2001/XMLSchema-instance"↪
        xsi:schemaLocation="http://maven.apache.org/POM/4.0.0 ↪
        http://maven.apache.org/xsd/maven-4.0.0.xsd">
    <modelVersion>4.0.0</modelVersion>
    <groupId>com.apress.javaee6</groupId>
    <artifactId>chapter13-MDB</artifactId>
    <version>2.0</version>
    <packaging>jar</packaging>

    <dependencies>
        <dependency>
            <groupId>org.glassfish</groupId>
            <artifactId>javax.ejb</artifactId>
```

411

```
            <version>3.0.1</version>
            <scope>provided</scope>
        </dependency>
        <dependency>
            <groupId>org.glassfish</groupId>
            <artifactId>javax.jms</artifactId>
            <version>3.0.1</version>
            <scope>provided</scope>
        </dependency>
        <dependency>
            <groupId>org.glassfish</groupId>
            <artifactId>javax.annotation</artifactId>
            <version>3.0.1</version>
            <scope>provided</scope>
        </dependency>
    </dependencies>

    <build>
        <plugins>
            <plugin>
                <groupId>org.apache.maven.plugins</groupId>
                <artifactId>maven-compiler-plugin</artifactId>
                <inherited>true</inherited>
                <configuration>
                    <source>1.6</source>
                    <target>1.6</target>
                </configuration>
            </plugin>
        </plugins>
    </build>

</project>
```

■ **Note** To get resource injection, both the MDB and the Sender use the @Resource annotation which is part of the Common Annotations (JSR 250). The problem is that JDK 1.6 bundles Common Annotations 1.0 instead of 1.1 (the lookup attribute was introduced in 1.1). For this example to work, we need to depend on version 1.1 of Common Annotations (that's why there is a Maven dependency on org.glassfish.javax.annotation) but also to override the one bundled in the JDK. This is called endorsement. The jar file of Common Annotations 1.1 has to be copied to the %JAVA_HOME%\lib\endorsed directory.

To compile and package the classes, open a command-line interpreter in the directory that contains the pom.xml file, and enter the following Maven command:

```
mvn package
```

Go to the `target` directory, where you should see the file `chapter13-MDB-2.0.jar`. If you open it, you will see that it contains the class file for the `OrderMDB`. For the `OrderSender`, you will get another jar file where the class is packaged: `chapter13-Sender-2.0.jar`.

Creating the Administered Objects

The administered objects required to send and receive messages need to be created by JMS. Each one has a JNDI name, allowing clients to obtain a reference of the object (injection is used in the example):

- The connection factory is called `jms/javaee6/ConnectionFactory`.

- The queue is called `jms/javaee6/Queue`.

As these objects are created administratively, GlassFish needs to be up and running as OpenMQ is running inside GlassFish. Once you've made sure that the `asadmin` command line is in your path, execute the following command in the DOS console:

```
asadmin create-jms-resource --restype javax.jms.ConnectionFactory↪
                                    jms/javaee6/ConnectionFactory
asadmin create-jms-resource --restype javax.jms.Queue jms/javaee6/Queue
```

The GlassFish's web console can be used to set up the connection factory and the queue. Note, however, that in my experience the easiest and quickest way to administer GlassFish is through the `asadmin` script. Use another command to list all the JMS resources and ensure that the administered objects are created successfully.

```
asadmin list-jms-resources
jms/javaee6/Queue
jms/javaee6/ConnectionFactory
```

Deploying the MDB on GlassFish

Once the MDB is packaged in a jar, it needs to be deployed into GlassFish. This can be done in several ways, including via the web administration console. However, the `asadmin` command line does the job simply: open a DOS console and go to the `target` directory where the `chapter13-MDB-2.0.jar` file is, make sure that GlassFish is still running, and enter the following:

```
asadmin deploy chapter13-MDB-2.0.jar
```

If the deployment is successful, the following command should return the name of the deployed jar and its type (`ejb` in the example):

```
asadmin list-components
chapter13-MDB-2.0 <ejb>
```

Running the Example

The MDB is deployed on GlassFish and is listening to the `jms/javaee6/Queue` destination, waiting for a message to arrive. It's time to run the `OrderSender` client. This is a stand-alone application and executes outside GlassFish, yet resources need to be injected into it (connection factory and queue). The ACC can be used to execute it. The ACC wraps a jar file and gives it access to the application server resources. To execute the ACC, use the `appclient` utility that comes with GlassFish, and pass the jar file as a parameter along with the parameters of our application (the order amount). Enter the following command to send a message with an order of $2,000:

```
appclient -client chapter13-Sender-2.0.jar 2000
```

Because the amount is greater than $1,000 (the amount defined in the selector message), the `OrderMDB` should receive and print the message. Check the GlassFish logs to confirm. If you pass a parameter lower than $1,000, the MDB will not receive the message.

```
appclient -client chapter13-Sender-2.0.jar 500
```

Summary

This chapter showed that integration with messaging is a loosely coupled, asynchronous form of communication between components. MOM can be seen as a buffer between systems that need to produce and consume messages at their own pace. This is different from the RPC architecture (such as RMI) where clients need to know the methods of an available service.

The first section of this chapter concentrated on the JMS API and its vocabulary. The asynchronous model is a very powerful API that can be used in a Java SE or Java EE environment, and is based on P2P and pub-sub, connection factories, destinations, connections, sessions, messages (header, properties, body) of different types (text, object, map, stream, bytes), selectors, and other reliability mechanisms such as acknowledgment or durability.

Java EE has a special enterprise component to consume messages: MDBs. The second section of this chapter showed how MDBs could be used as asynchronous consumers and how they rely on their container to take care of several services (life cycle, interceptors, transactions, security, concurrency, message acknowledgment, etc.).

This section also showed how to put these pieces together with Maven, GlassFish, and OpenMQ, and gave an example with a stand-alone sender and an MDB receiver.

The following chapters will demonstrate other technologies used to interoperate with external systems: SOAP web services and RESTful web services.

CHAPTER 14

■■■

SOAP Web Services

Formerly considered a buzzword, web services today form part of day-to-day architectural life. Web services applications can be implemented with different technologies such as SOAP or REST web services, or even XML-RPC.

SOAP (Simple Object Access Protocol) web services are said to be "loosely coupled" because the client of a web service doesn't have to know its implementation details (such as the language used to develop it or the method signature). The consumer is able to invoke a web service using a self-explanatory interface describing the available business methods (parameters and return value). The underlying implementation can be done in any language (Visual Basic, C#, C, C++, Java, etc.). A consumer and a service will still be able to exchange data in a loosely coupled way: using XML documents. A consumer sends a request to a web service in the form of an XML document, and, optionally, receives a reply, also in XML.

Web services are also about distribution. Distributed software has been around for a long time, but, unlike existing distributed systems, SOAP web services are adapted to the Web. The default network protocol is HTTP, a well-known and robust stateless protocol.

Web services are everywhere, and they can run on desktops or be used for business-to-business (B2B) integration so that operations that previously required manual intervention are performed automatically. Web services integrate applications run by various organizations through the Internet or within the same company (which is known as Enterprise Application Integration, or EAI). In all cases, web services provide a standard way to connect diverse pieces of software.

Understanding SOAP Web Services

Simply put, SOAP web services constitute a kind of business logic exposed via a service interface to a client application (i.e., a service consumer). However, unlike objects or EJBs, SOAP web services provide a loosely coupled interface using XML. SOAP web service standards specify that the interface to which a message is sent should define the format of the message request and response, and mechanisms to publish and to discover web service interfaces (a registry).

In Figure 14-1, you can see a high-level picture of a web service interaction. The web service can optionally register its interface into a registry (Universal Description Discovery, and Integration, or UDDI) so a consumer can discover it. Once the consumer knows the interface of the service and the message format, it can send a request and receive a response.

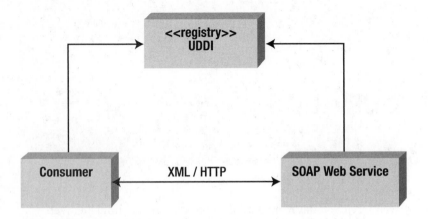

Figure 14-1. The consumer discovers the service through a registry.

SOAP web services depend on several technologies and protocols to transport and to transform data from a consumer to a service in a standard way. The ones that you will come across more often are the following:

- Extensible Markup Language (XML) is the basic foundation on which web services are built and defined (SOAP, WSDL, and UDDI).

- Web Services Description Language (WSDL) defines the web service interface, data and message types, interactions, and protocols.

- Simple Object Access Protocol (SOAP) is a message-encoding protocol based on XML technologies, defining an envelope for web services communication.

- Messages are exchanged using a transport protocol. Although Hypertext Transfer Protocol (HTTP) is the most widely adopted transport protocol, others such as SMTP or JMS can also be used.

- Universal Description Discovery, and Integration (UDDI) is a registry and discovery mechanism, similar to the Yellow Pages; it can be used for storing and categorizing web services interfaces.

With these standard technologies, web services provide almost unlimited potential. Clients can call a web service, which can be mapped to any program and accommodate any data type and structure to exchange messages through XML.

XML

XML is used in the Java EE platform for deployment descriptors, metadata information, and so on. For SOAP web services, XML is also used as an integration technology that solves the problem of data independence and interoperability. It is used not only as the message format, but also as the way the services are defined (WSDL) or exchanged (SOAP). Associated with these XML documents, schemas are used to validate exchanged data. Historically, SOAP web services evolved from the basic idea of "RPC (Remote Procedure Call) using XML".

WSDL

The UDDI registry points to a public WSDL file available on the Internet that can be downloaded by potential consumers. WSDL is the interface definition language (IDL) that defines the interactions between consumers and web services (see Figure 14-2). It is central to a web service as it describes the message type, port, communication protocol, supported operations, location, and what the client should expect in return. It defines the contract to which the web service guarantees it will conform. You can think of WSDL as a Java interface but written in XML.

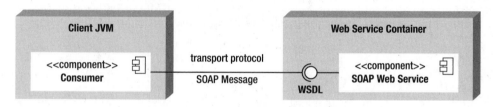

Figure 14-2. WSDL interface between the consumer and the web service

To ensure interoperability, a standard web service interface is needed for a consumer and a producer to share and understand a message. That's the role of WSDL. SOAP defines the way in which the message will be sent from one computer to another.

SOAP

SOAP is the standard web services application protocol. It provides the communication mechanism to connect web services exchanging formatted XML data across a network protocol, commonly HTTP. Like WSDL, SOAP heavily relies on XML because a SOAP message is an XML document containing several elements (an envelope, a header, a body, etc.).

SOAP is designed to provide an independent, abstract communication protocol capable of connecting distributed services. The connected services can be built using any combination of hardware and software that supports a given transport protocol.

UDDI

Programs that interact with one another over the Web need to be able to find information that allows them to interconnect. UDDI provides this standard approach of locating information about a web service and how to invoke it. It is optional as you can invoke a web service without UDDI if you already know the web service's location.

UDDI is an XML-based registry of web services, similar to a Yellow Pages directory, where businesses can register their services. This registration includes the business type, geographical location, web site, phone number, and so on. Other businesses can then search the registry and discover information about specific web services. This information provides additional metadata about the service, describing its behavior and the actual location of the WSDL document.

Transport Protocol

For a consumer to communicate with a web service, a way to send messages to each other is needed. SOAP messages can be transported over a network using a protocol that both parties can support. Given that web services are used mostly on the Web, they usually use HTTP, but they can also use other network protocols such as HTTPS (HTTP Secure), TCP/IP, SMTP (Simple Mail Transport Protocol), FTP (File Transfer Protocol), and so on.

SOAP Web Services Specification Overview

Persistence is mostly covered by one specification: JPA. For web services, the situation is more complex, as you have to deal with many specifications from different standards bodies. Moreover, because web services are used by other programming languages, these specifications are not all directly related to the Java Community Process (JCP).

A Brief History of SOAP Web Services

SOAP web services are a standard way for businesses to communicate over a network, and there were precursors before them: Common Object Request Broker Architecture (CORBA), initially used by Unix systems, and Distributed Component Object Model (DCOM), its Microsoft competitor. On a lower level, there is Remote Procedure Call (RPC) and, closer to our Java world, Remote Method Invocation (RMI).

Before the Web, it was difficult to get all major software vendors to agree on a transport protocol. When the HTTP protocol became a mature standard, it gradually became a universal business medium of communication. At about the same time, XML officially became a standard when the World Wide Web Consortium (W3C) announced that XML 1.0 was suitable for deployment in applications. By 1998, both ingredients, HTTP and XML, were ready to work together.

SOAP 1.0, started in 1998 by Microsoft, was finally shipped at the end of 1999, and modeled typed references and arrays in XML Schema. By 2000, IBM started working on SOAP 1.1, and WSDL was submitted to the W3C in 2001. UDDI was written in 2000 by the Organization for the Advancement of Structured Information Standards (OASIS) to allow businesses to publish and discover web services. With SOAP, WSDL, and UDDI in place, the de facto standards to create web services had arrived with the support of major IT companies.

Java introduced web services capabilities with the Java API for XML-based RPC 1.0 (JAX-RPC 1.0) in June 2002 and added JAX-RPC 1.1 to J2EE 1.4 in 2003. This specification was very verbose and not easy to use. With the arrival of Java EE 5 and annotations in Java, the brand-new Java API for XML-based Web Services 2.0 (JAX-WS 2.0) specification was introduced as the preferred SOAP web service model. Today Java EE 6 is shipped with JAX-WS 2.2.

Java EE Specifications

To master all web services standards, you would have to spend some time reading a bunch of specifications coming from the W3C, the JCP, and OASIS.

The W3C is a consortium that develops and maintains web technologies such as HTML, XHTML, RDF, CSS, and so forth and, more interestingly, for web services, XML, XML Schemas, SOAP, and WSDL.

OASIS hosts several web service-related standards such as UDDI, WS-Addressing, WS-Security, WS-Reliability, and many others.

Coming back to Java, the JCP has a set of specifications that are part of Java EE 6 and Java SE 6. They include JAX-WS 2.2 (JSR 224), Web Services 1.2 (JSR 109), JAXB 2.2 (JSR 222), Web Services Metadata 2.0 (JSR 181), and JAXR 1.0 (JSR 93). Taken together, these specifications are usually referred to by the informal term Java Web Services (JWS).

At first, these lists of specifications may make you think that writing a SOAP web service in Java would be difficult, especially when it comes to getting your head around the APIs. However, the beauty of it is that you don't need to worry about the underlying technologies (XML, WSDL, SOAP, HTTP, etc.), as just a few JWS standards will do the work for you.

JAX-WS 2.2

Since Java EE 5, JAX-WS (JSR 224) is the preferred technology to write SOAP web services. Prior to JAX-WS was JAX-RPC 1.0 (JSR 101). JAX-RPC has been pruned in Java EE 6, meaning that it is proposed to be removed from Java EE 7.

JAX-WS 2.2 defines a set of APIs and annotations that allow you to build and consume web services with Java. It provides the consumer and service facilities to send and receive web service requests via SOAP, masking the complexity of the protocol. Therefore, neither the consumer nor the service has to generate or parse SOAP messages, as JAX-WS deals with the low-level processing. The JAX-WS specification depends on other specifications such as Java Architecture for XML Binding (JAXB).

Web Services 1.2

JSR 109 ("Implementing Enterprise Web Services") defines the programming model and runtime behavior of web services in the Java EE container. It also defines packaging to ensure portability of web services across application server implementations.

JAXB 2.2

Web services send requests and responses exchanging XML messages. In Java, there are several low-level APIs to process XML documents and XML Schemas. The JAXB specification provides a set of APIs and annotations for representing XML documents as Java artifacts, allowing developers to work with Java objects representing XML documents. JAXB (JSR 222) facilitates unmarshalling XML documents into objects and marshalling objects back into XML documents. Even if JAXB can be used for any XML purpose, it is tightly integrated with JAX-WS.

WS-Metadata 2.0

Web Services Metadata (WS-Metadata, specification JSR 181) provides annotations that facilitate the definition and deployment of web services. The primary goal of JSR 181 is to simplify the development of web services. It provides mapping facilities between WSDL and Java interfaces, and vice versa, through annotations. These annotations can be used within simple Java classes or EJBs.

JAXR 1.0

The Java API for XML Registries (JAXR) specification defines a standard set of APIs that allow Java clients to access UDDI. Like JAX-RPC, JAXR (JSR 93) is the second web service-related specification to be pruned, with its removal proposed in the next version of Java EE. If the pruning is accepted, JAXR will still keep on evolving, but outside Java EE. You will still be able to use it with open source or commercial implementations.

Reference Implementation

Metro is not a Java EE specification, but rather the open source reference implementation of the Java web service specifications. It consists of JAX-WS and JAXB, and also supports the legacy JAX-RPC APIs. It allows you to create and deploy secure, reliable, transactional, interoperable web services and consumers. The Metro stack is produced by the GlassFish community, but it can also be used outside GlassFish in a Java EE or Java SE environment.

How to Invoke a SOAP Web Service

Despite all these specifications, concepts, standards, and organizations, writing and consuming a web service is very easy. Listing 14-1 shows you the code of a web service that validates a credit card.

Listing 14-1. The CardValidator Web Service

```
@WebService
public class CardValidator {

    public boolean validate(CreditCard creditCard) {
        Character lastDigit = creditCard.getNumber().charAt(↪
                            creditCard.getNumber().length() - 1);

        if (Integer.parseInt(lastDigit.toString()) % 2 != 0) {
            return true;
        } else {
            return false;
        }
    }
}
```

Like entities or EJBs, a web service uses the annotated POJO model with the configuration-by-exception policy. This means that a web service can just be a Java class annotated with @javax.jws.WebService if all the defaults suit you. This CardValidator web service has one method to validate a credit card. It takes a credit card as a parameter and returns true or false according to whether the card is valid or not. In this instance, it assumes that credit cards with an odd number are valid, and those with an even number are not.

A CreditCard object (see Listing 14-2) is exchanged between the consumer and the SOAP web service. When describing the web service architecture, the data exchanged needs to be an XML document, so a method to transform a Java object into an XML document is needed. This is where JAXB comes into play with its simple annotations and powerful API. The CreditCard object just has to be annotated with @javax.xml.bind.annotation.XmlRootElement, and JAXB will transform it back and forth from XML to Java.

Listing 14-2. The CreditCard Class with a JAXB Annotation

```java
@XmlRootElement
public class CreditCard {

    private String number;
    private String expiryDate;
    private Integer controlNumber;
    private String type;

    // Constructors, getters, setters
}
```

With JAXB annotations, you avoid developing all the low-level XML parsing, as it happens behind the scenes. The web service manipulates a Java object, and the same is true for the consumer. The consumer can be a main class, as shown in Listing 14-3, that creates an instance of **CreditCard** and then invokes the web service.

Listing 14-3. A Consumer Invoking the Web Service

```java
public class Main {

    public static void main(String[] args) {

        CreditCard creditCard = new CreditCard();
        creditCard.setNumber("12341234");
        creditCard.setExpiryDate("10/10");
        creditCard.setType("VISA");
        creditCard.setControlNumber(1234);

        CardValidator cardValidator = ↪
                    new CardValidatorService().getCardValidatorPort();

        cardValidator.validate(creditCard);

    }
}
```

The **CardValidator** web service is not directly invoked. The consumer uses a **CardValidatorService** class and calls the **getCardValidatorPort()** method to get a reference to a **CardValidator**. With this reference, the consumer can then call the **validate()** method and pass a credit card.

Although this code is straightforward, there's a lot of magic happening behind the scenes. Several artifacts have been generated to make this work: a WSDL file and client stubs, which contain all the information to connect to the URL where the web service is located, marshall the **CreditCard** object into XML, invoke the web service, and obtain a result.

The visible part of web services in Java doesn't deal directly with XML, SOAP, or WSDL and is very easy to understand. However, there are some invisible parts that are very important for interoperability.

Java Architecture for XML Binding

As you will understand by now, XML is used to exchange data and to define web services through WSDL and SOAP envelopes. But in Listing 14-3, which shows a consumer invoking a web service, there is no XML at all. That's because the consumer only manipulates Java interfaces and stubs, which in turn deal with all the XML plumbing and network wiring. At one point in the chain, you manipulate Java classes, and at another XML documents, with JAXB facilitating this bidirectional correspondence.

Java offers various ways to manipulate XML, from common APIs (`javax.xml.stream.XmlStreamWriter` and `java.beans.XMLEncoder`) to more complex and low-level models such as Simple API for XML (SAX), Document Object Model (DOM), or Java API for XML Processing (JAXP). JAXB provides a higher level of abstraction than SAX or DOM and is based on annotations.

JAXB defines a standard to bind Java representations to XML and vice versa. It manages XML documents and XML Schema Definitions (XSD) in a transparent, object-oriented way that hides the complexity of the XSD language.

Except for the `@XmlRootElement` annotation, Listing 14-2 shows the code of a normal Java class. With this annotation and a marshalling mechanism, JAXB is able to create an XML representation of a `CreditCard` instance, as shown in Listing 14-4.

Listing 14-4. An XML Document Representing Credit Card Data

```
<?xml version="1.0" encoding="UTF-8" standalone="yes"?>
<creditCard>
    <controlNumber>6398</controlNumber>
    <expiryDate>12/09</expiryDate>
    <number>1234</number>
    <type>Visa</type>
</creditCard>
```

Marshalling is the action of transforming an object into XML. The inverse is also possible with JAXB. Unmarshalling would take this XML document as an input and instantiate a `CreditCard` object with the values defined in the document. JAXB can also automatically generate the schema that would validate the credit card XML structure to ensure that it would have the correct structure and data types. Listing 14-5 shows the XML Schema Definition (XSD) of the `CreditCard` class.

Listing 14-5. XML Schema Validating the Previous XML Document

```
<?xml version="1.0" encoding="UTF-8" standalone="yes"?>
<xs:schema version="1.0" xmlns:xs="http://www.w3.org/2001/XMLSchema">

  <xs:element name="creditCard" type="creditCard"/>

  <xs:complexType name="creditCard">
    <xs:sequence>
      <xs:element name="controlNumber" type="xs:int" minOccurs="0"/>
      <xs:element name="expiryDate" type="xs:string" minOccurs="0"/>
      <xs:element name="number" type="xs:string" minOccurs="0"/>
      <xs:element name="type" type="xs:string" minOccurs="0"/>
    </xs:sequence>
  </xs:complexType>
</xs:schema>
```

This schema is made of simple elements (`controlNumber`, `expiryDate`, etc.) and a complex type (`creditCard`). Complex types model element content, that is, they determine the possible set of elements used in a document (here, a credit card).

Notice that all the tags use the `xs` prefix (`xs:element`, `xs:string`, etc.). This prefix is called a *namespace* and is defined in the `xmlns` (XML namespace) header tag of the document.

```
<xs:schema version="1.0" xmlns:xs="http://www.w3.org/2001/XMLSchema">
```

Namespaces create unique prefixes for elements in separate documents or applications that are used together. They are used primarily to avoid conflict problems that may be caused if the same element name appears in several documents (the `<element>` tag, for instance, could appear in several documents and have different meanings). This is a significant issue for web services, as they involve handling multiple documents at the same time (the SOAP envelope, the WSDL document, etc.). Namespaces are very important in web services.

Binding

The JAXB API, defined in the `javax.xml.bind` package, provides a set of interfaces and classes to produce XML documents and to generate Java classes; in other words, it binds the two models. The JAXB runtime framework implements the marshall and unmarshall operations. Marshalling is the process of converting instances of JAXB-annotated classes to XML representations. Likewise, unmarshalling is the process of converting an XML representation to a tree of objects.

This marshalled XML data can be validated by an XML Schema, and JAXB is able to automatically generate a schema from a set of classes and vice versa. Figure 14-3 shows the possible interactions that an application can have with JAXB.

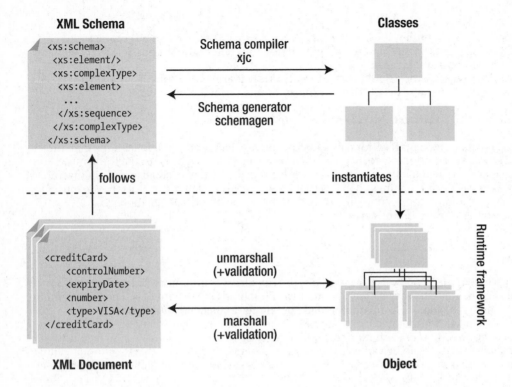

Figure 14-3. JAXB architecture (derived from Figure 1-1 of the JAXB 2.2 specification)

The center of the JAXB API is the `javax.xml.bind.JAXBContext` class. This abstract class manages the binding between XML documents and Java objects as it provides:

- An `Unmarshaller` class that transforms an XML document into an object graph and optionally validates the XML

- A `Marshaller` class that takes an object graph and transforms it into an XML document

For example, to transform our `CreditCard` object into an XML document (see Listing 14-3), the `Marshaller.marshal()` method must be used. This method takes an object as a parameter and marshals it into several supports (`StringWriter` to have a string representation of the XML document or `FileOutputStream` to store it in a file).

The code in Listing 14-6 creates an instance of `JAXBContext` by using the static method `newInstance()`, to which it passes the root class that needs to be marshalled (`CreditCard.class`). From the created `Marshaller` object, it then calls the `marshal()` method that generates the XML representation (shown previously in Listing 14-4) of the credit card object into a `StringWriter` and displays it. The same approach could be used to unmarshall an XML document into objects using the `Unmarshaller.unmarshal()` method.

Listing 14-6. A Main Class Marshalling a CreditCard Object

```
public class Main {

  public static void main(String[] args) {

    CreditCard creditCard = new CreditCard("1234", "12/09", 6398, "Visa");
    StringWriter writer = new StringWriter();

    JAXBContext context = JAXBContext.newInstance(CreditCard.class);
    Marshaller m = context.createMarshaller();
    m.marshal(creditCard, writer);

    System.out.println(writer.toString());
  }
}
```

Metro, the JAXB reference implementation, has other tools, specifically the schema compiler (`xjc`) and the schema generator (`schemaGen`); while marshalling/unmarshalling deals with objects and XML documents, the schema compiler and the schema generator deal with classes and XML Schemas. These tools can be used in the command line (they are bundled with Java SE 6) or as Maven goals.

With JAXB, you have two possible scenarios from which bindings arise:

- *Start from Java classes*: The Java classes exist and are used to generate an XML Schema.

- *Start from an XML Schema*: In this scenario, the schema exists, and the Java classes are created using a schema compiler.

These two scenarios are very important for web services. A SOAP web service can generate its WSDL files, and, based on that WSDL, a consumer can generate a set of Java classes, all in a transparent and portable way.

Annotations

JAXB is similar to JPA in many ways. However, instead of mapping objects to a database, JAXB does the mapping to an XML document. Also, like JPA, JAXB defines a set of annotations (in the `javax.xml.bind.annotation` package) to customize this mapping, and relies on configuration by exception to minimize the work of the developer. If persistent objects have to be annotated with `@Entity`, the correspondent in JAXB is `@XmlRootElement` (see Listing 14-7).

Listing 14-7. A Customized CreditCard Class

```
@XmlRootElement
@XmlAccessorType(XmlAccessType.FIELD)
public class CreditCard {
```

```
@XmlAttribute (required = true)
private String number;
@XmlElement(name = "expiry-date", defaultValue = "01/10")
private String expiryDate;
private String type;
@XmlElement(name = "control-number")
private Integer controlNumber;

// Constructors, getters, setters
}
```

The @XmlRootElement annotation notifies JAXB that the CreditCard class (shown earlier in Listing 14-2) is the root element of the XML document. If this annotation is missing, JAXB will throw an exception when trying to marshall it. This class is then mapped to the schema shown in Listing 14-5 using all the JAXB default mapping rules (each attribute is mapped to an element and has the same name).

With a Marshaller object, you can easily get an XML representation of a CreditCard object (shown earlier in Listing 14-4). The root element <creditCard> represents the CreditCard object, and it includes the value of each attribute.

JAXB provides a way to customize and control this XML structure. An XML document is made of elements (<element>value</element>) and attributes (<element attribute="value"/>). JAXB uses two annotations to differentiate them: @XmlAttribute and @XmlElement. Each annotation has a set of parameters that allows you to rename an attribute, allow null values or not, give default values, and so forth. Listing 14-7 uses these annotations to turn the credit card number into an attribute (instead of an element) and to rename the expiry date and control number.

This class will get mapped to a different schema in which the credit card number is represented as a required <xs:attribute>, and the expiry date renamed with a default value set to 01/10, as shown in Listing 14-8.

Listing 14-8. *The Credit Card Schema with Attributes and Default Values*

```xml
<?xml version="1.0" encoding="UTF-8" standalone="yes"?>
<xs:schema version="1.0" xmlns:xs="http://www.w3.org/2001/XMLSchema">

  <xs:element name="creditCard" type="creditCard"/>

  <xs:complexType name="creditCard">
    <xs:sequence>
      <xs:element name="expiry-date" type="xs:string" default="01/10" minOccurs="0"/>
      <xs:element name="type" type="xs:string" minOccurs="0"/>
      <xs:element name="control-number" type="xs:int" minOccurs="0"/>
    </xs:sequence>
    <xs:attribute name="number" type="xs:string" use="required"/>
  </xs:complexType>
</xs:schema>
```

The XML representation will also change (see Listing 14-9).

Listing 14-9. An XML Document Representing a Customized CreditCard Object

```xml
<?xml version="1.0" encoding="UTF-8" standalone="yes"?>
<creditCard number="1234">
    <expiry-date>12/09</expiry-date>
    <type>Visa</type>
    <control-number>6398</control-number>
</creditCard>
```

Table 14-1 lists the main JAXB annotations, most with elements that can be used; some can annotate attributes (or getters), others classes, and some can be used on an entire package (such as @XmlSchema).

Table 14-1. JAXB Annotations

Annotation	Description
@XmlAccessorType	Controls whether attributes or getters should be mapped (FIELD, NONE, PROPERTY, PUBLIC_MEMBER)
@XmlAttribute	Maps an attribute or a getter to an XML attribute of simple type (String, Boolean, Integer, and so on)
@XmlElement	Maps a nonstatic and nontransient attribute or getter to an XML element
@XmlElements	Acts as a container for multiple @XmlElement annotations
@XmlEnum	Maps an enum to an XML representation
@XmlEnumValue	Identifies an enumerated constant
@XmlID	Identifies the key field of an XML element (of type String), which can be used when referring back to an element using the @XmlIDREF annotation (XML Schema ID and IDREF concepts)
@XmlIDREF	Maps a property to an XML IDREF in the schema
@XmlList	Maps a property to a list
@XmlMimeType	Identifies a textual representation of the MIME type for a property
@XmlNs	Identifies an XML namespace
@XmlRootElement	Represents an annotation required by any class that is to be bound as the root XML element
@XmlSchema	Maps a package name to an XML namespace
@XmlTransient	Informs JAXB not to bind an attribute (analogous to the Java transient keyword or @Transient annotation in JPA)
@XmlType	Annotates a class as being a complex type in XML Schema
@XmlValue	Allows the mapping of a class to a simple schema content or type

When using these annotations, you can map objects to a specific XML Schema. And sometimes you need this flexibility with legacy web services. Referring to JPA, when you need to map entities to a legacy database, there is a set of annotations that allows customizing every part of the mapping (columns, table, foreign keys, etc.). With web services, it's similar: web services are described in a WSDL file written in XML. If it's a legacy web service, its WSDL cannot change. Instead, a mechanism to map it to objects must be used, which is why JAXB is used with web services.

■ **Note** In this section, I've mentioned JPA several times because both JPA and JAXB technologies heavily rely on annotations and are used to map objects to a different media (database or XML). In terms of architecture, entities should only be used to map data to a database, and JAXB classes to map data to XML. But sometimes you may want the same object to have a database representation as well as an XML one. It is technically possible to annotate the same class with @Entity and @XmlRootElement even if it's not really recommended.

The Invisible Part of the Iceberg

Even if you don't explicitly manipulate SOAP and WSDL documents when you develop with JAX-WS, it is important to have some understanding of their structure.

When developing SOAP web services, you can use WSDL to define their interface: the input and output parameters of the web service in terms of XML Schema. SOAP messages are used to carry the input and output parameters specified by the WSDL. SOAP web services provide two key ingredients: an interface definition language (WSDL) and a messaging standard (SOAP).

When a consumer wants to invoke the CardValidator web service (see Figure 14-4), it gets its WSDL to know the interface it can use, asks to validate a credit card (the validate SOAP message), and receives a response (the validateResponse SOAP message).

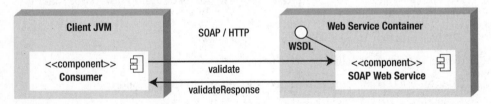

Figure 14-4. A consumer invoking a SOAP web service

WSDL

WSDL documents are hosted in the web service container and use XML to describe what a service does, how to invoke its operations, and where to find it. The XML document follows a fixed structure containing several parts (see Listing 14-10). The CardValidator web service is the example used to introduce the elements listed here:

- `<definitions>` is the root element of the WSDL, and it specifies the global declarations of namespaces that are visible through the document.

- `<types>` defines the data types to be used in the messages. In this example, it is the XML Schema Definition (`CardValidatorService?xsd=1`) that describes the parameters passed to the web service request (the `CreditCard` object) and the response (a `Boolean`).

- `<message>` defines the format of data exchanged between a web service consumer and the web service itself. Here you have the request (the `validate` method) and the response (`validateResponse`).

- `<portType>` specifies the operations of the web service (the `validate` method).

- `<binding>` describes the concrete protocol (here SOAP) and data formats for the operations and messages defined for a particular port type.

- `<service>` contains a collection of `<port>` elements, where each port is associated with an endpoint (a network address location or URL).

The following WSDL file will help you to better understand the information described in the `CardValidator` web service.

Listing 14-10. The WSDL File for the CardValidator Web Service

```
<definitions targetNamespace="http://chapter14.javaee6.org/" ➥
                       name="CardValidatorService">
  <types>
    <xsd:schema>
      <xsd:import namespace="http://chapter14.javaee6.org/" schemaLocation
        ="http://localhost:8080/chapter14/CardValidatorService?xsd=1"/>
    </xsd:schema>
  </types>
  <message name="validate">
    <part name="parameters" element="tns:validate"/>
  </message>
  <message name="validateResponse">
    <part name="parameters" element="tns:validateResponse"/>
  </message>
  <portType name="CardValidator">
    <operation name="validate">
      <input message="tns:validate"/>
      <output message="tns:validateResponse"/>
    </operation>
  </portType>
  <binding name="CardValidatorPortBinding" type="tns:CardValidator">
    <soap:binding transport="http://schemas.xmlsoap.org/soap/http" style="document"/>
```

```
      <operation name="validate">
        <soap:operation soapAction=""/>
        <input>
          <soap:body use="literal"/>
        </input>
        <output>
          <soap:body use="literal"/>
        </output>
      </operation>
    </binding>
    <service name="CardValidatorService">
      <port name="CardValidatorPort" binding="tns:CardValidatorPortBinding">
        <soap:address location = "http://localhost:8080/chapter14/CardValidatorService"/>
      </port>
    </service>
</definitions>
```

The `<xsd:import namespace>` element refers to an XML Schema that has to also be available on the network to the consumers of the WSDL. Listing 14-11 shows this schema defining the types used in the web service (the structure of the `CreditCard` object with number, expiry date, and so on).

Listing 14-11. The Schema Imported by the WSDL File

```
<xs:schema version="1.0" targetNamespace="http://chapter14.javaee6.org/">
  <xs:element name="creditCard" type="tns:creditCard"/>
  <xs:element name="validate" type="tns:validate"/>
  <xs:element name="validateResponse" type="tns:validateResponse"/>
  <xs:complexType name="validate">
    <xs:sequence>
      <xs:element name="arg0" type="tns:creditCard" minOccurs="0"/>
    </xs:sequence>
  </xs:complexType>
  <xs:complexType name="creditCard">
    <xs:sequence>
      <xs:element name="controlNumber" type="xs:int" minOccurs="0"/>
      <xs:element name="expiryDate" type="xs:string" minOccurs="0"/>
      <xs:element name="number" type="xs:string" minOccurs="0"/>
      <xs:element name="type" type="xs:string" minOccurs="0"/>
    </xs:sequence>
  </xs:complexType>
  <xs:complexType name="validateResponse">
    <xs:sequence>
      <xs:element name="return" type="xs:boolean"/>
    </xs:sequence>
  </xs:complexType>
</xs:schema>
```

This WSDL and schema are usually generated using tools that transform the web service metadata into XML. JAX-WS comes with utilities that automatically generate these artifacts.

SOAP

WSDL describes an abstract interface of the web service, while SOAP provides a concrete implementation, defining the XML structure of the messages exchanged. In relation to the Web, SOAP is a web service message structure that can be delivered over HTTP (or other communication protocols), and the HTTP binding of SOAP includes some standard HTTP extension headers. This message structure is described in XML. Instead of using HTTP to request a web page from a browser, SOAP sends an XML message via HTTP request and receives a reply via HTTP response. A SOAP message is an XML document containing the following elements:

- `<Envelope>`: Defines the message and the namespace used in the document. This is a required root element.

- `<Header>`: Contains any optional attributes of the message or application-specific infrastructure such as security information or network routing.

- `<Body>`: Contains the message being exchanged between applications.

- `<Fault>`: Provides information about errors that occur while the message is processed. This element is optional.

Only the envelope and the body are required. Using our example, a client application calls the web service to validate a credit card (one SOAP envelope for the request) and receives a Boolean informing whether the card is valid or not (another SOAP envelope for the response). Listings 14-12 and 14-13 show the structure of these two SOAP messages.

Listing 14-12. The SOAP Envelope for the Request

```xml
<soap:Envelope xmlns:soap="http://schemas.xmlsoap.org/soap/envelope/" ➥
               xmlns:cc="http://chapter14.javaee6.org/">
   <soap:Header/>
   <soap:Body>
      <cc:validate>
         <arg0>
            <controlNumber>1234</controlNumber>
            <expiryDate>10/10</expiryDate>
            <number>9999</number>
            <type>VISA</type>
         </arg0>
      </cc:validate>
   </soap:Body>
</soap:Envelope>
```

Listing 14-13. The SOAP Envelope for the Response

```xml
<soap:Envelope xmlns:soap="http://schemas.xmlsoap.org/soap/envelope/">
   <soap:Body>
      <ns2:validateResponse xmlns:ns2="http://chapter14.javaee6.org/">
         <return>true</return>
      </ns2:validateResponse>
   </soap:Body>
</soap:Envelope>
```

Java API for XML-Based Web Services

We have reviewed a simple WSDL document, a SOAP request, and a SOAP response. When web services have several operations with complex parameters, these XML documents can look daunting to a Java developer. The good news is that JAX-WS makes life easier by hiding the complexity of these XML documents. Unfortunately, sometimes you need to dive into the WSDL structure.

Because the WSDL document is the contract between the consumer and the service, it can be used to write the Java code for the consumer and the service. This is the *top-down approach*, also known as *contract first*. This approach starts with the contract (the WSDL) by defining operations, messages, and so forth. When both the consumer and provider agree on the contract, you can then implement the Java classes based on that contract. Metro provides some tools that generate classes from a WSDL.

With the other approach, called *bottom-up*, the implementation class already exists, and all that is needed is to create the WSDL. Again, Metro provides utilities to generate a WSDL from existing classes. In both cases, at times the code has to be adjusted to fit the WSDL or vice versa. That is when JAX-WS comes to your aid. With a simple development model and a few annotations, Java-to-WSDL mapping can be adjusted. The bottom-up approach can result in very inefficient applications, as the Java methods and classes have no bearing on the ideal granularity of messages crossing the network. If latency is high and/or bandwidth low, it pays to use the fewest, largest messages, and this can only be done by using the contract-first approach.

This chapter presented the general web services concepts and specifications, and then discussed JAXB, used for XML binding, and the surface of WSDL and SOAP documents. But web services follow the "ease of development" paradigm of Java EE 6 and do not require you to write any WSDL or SOAP. The web service is just an annotated POJO that needs to be deployed in a web service container. However, there is more to the web service programming model.

JAX-WS Model

Like most of the Java EE 6 components, web services rely on the configuration-by-exception paradigm, which specifies that configuring a component is the exception. Only one annotation is actually needed to turn a POJO into a web service: `@WebService`. The requirements to write a web service are as follows:

- The class must be annotated with `@javax.jws.WebService` or the XML equivalent in a deployment descriptor.

- To turn a web service into an EJB endpoint, the class has to be annotated with `@javax.ejb.Stateless` (as demonstrated in Chapter 7).

- The class must be defined as public, and it must not be final or abstract.

- The class must have a default public constructor.

- The class must not define the `finalize()` method.

- A service must be a stateless object and should not save client-specific state across method calls.

The WS-Metadata specification (JSR 181) says that, as long as it meets these requirements, a POJO can be used to implement a web service deployed to the servlet container. This is commonly referred to as a *servlet endpoint*. A stateless session bean can also be used to implement a web service that will be deployed in an EJB container (a.k.a. an EJB endpoint).

Web Service Endpoints

JAX-WS 2.2 allows both regular Java classes and stateless EJBs to be exposed as web services. Referring to the code for a POJO (Listing 14-1) and for an EJB web service (Listing 14-14) reveals hardly any differences, with the exception that the EJB web service has the extra annotation, @Stateless, although the packaging is different. A POJO web service is packaged in a web module (in a war file) and is called a servlet endpoint, whereas an EJB web service is packaged in a jar file and is called an EJB endpoint. One is deployed in a servlet container and the other in an EJB container.

Listing 14-14. The CardValidator Web Service

```
@WebService
@Stateless
public class CardValidator {

    public boolean validate(CreditCard creditCard) {
        Character lastDigit = creditCard.getNumber().charAt(↪
                              creditCard.getNumber().length() - 1);

        if (Integer.parseInt(lastDigit.toString()) % 2 != 0) {
            return true;
        } else {
            return false;
        }
    }
}
```

Both endpoints have almost identical behavior, but a few extra benefits are gained from using EJB endpoints. As the web service is also an EJB, the benefits of transaction and security managed by the container are automatic, and interceptors can be used, which is not possible with servlet endpoints. The business code can be exposed as a web service and as an EJB at the same time, meaning that the business logic can be exposed through SOAP and also through RMI by adding a remote interface.

Annotations

At the service level, systems are defined in terms of XML messages, WSDL operations, and SOAP messages. Meanwhile, at the Java level, applications are defined in terms of objects, interfaces, and methods. A translation from Java objects to WSDL operations is needed. The JAXB runtime uses annotations to determine how to marshall/unmarshall a class to/from XML. These annotations are typically hidden from the web service developer. Analogously, JWS uses annotations to determine how to marshall a method invocation to a SOAP request message and unmarshall a SOAP response into an instance of the method's return type.

The WS-Metadata specification (JSR 181) defines two different kinds of annotations:

- *WSDL mapping annotations*: These annotations belong to the `javax.jws` package and allow you to change the WSDL/Java mapping. The `@WebMethod`, `@WebResult`, `@WebParam`, and `@OneWay` annotations are used on the web service to customize the signature of the exposed methods.

- *SOAP binding annotations*: These annotations belong to the `javax.jws.soap` package and allow customizing of the SOAP binding (`@SOAPBinding` and `@SOAPMessageHandler`).

Like all the other Java EE 6 specifications, web services annotations can be overridden by an XML deployment descriptor (`webservices.xml`), which is optional. Let's take a closer look at the WSDL mapping annotations.

@WebService

The `@javax.jws.WebService` annotation marks a Java class or interface as being a web service. If used directly on the class (as in all examples so far), the annotation processor of the container will generate the interface, so the following snippets of code are equivalent. Following is the annotation on the class:

```
@WebService
public class CardValidator {...}
```

And this shows the annotation on an interface implemented by a class:

```
@WebService
public interface CCValidator {...}

public class CardValidator implements CCValidator {...}
```

The `@WebService` annotation has a set of attributes (see Listing 14-15) that allow you to customize the name of the web service in the WSDL file (the `<wsdl:portType>` or `<wsdl:service>` element) and its namespace, as well as change the location of the WSDL itself (the `wsdlLocation` attribute).

Listing 14-15. The @WebService API

```
@Retention(RUNTIME) @Target(TYPE)
public @interface WebService {
    String name() default "";
    String targetNamespace() default "";
    String serviceName() default "";
    String portName() default "";
    String wsdlLocation() default "";
    String endpointInterface() default "";
}
```

When you use the `@WebService` annotation, all public methods of the web service are exposed except when using the `@WebMethod` annotation.

@WebMethod

By default, all the public methods of a web service are exposed in the WSDL and use all the default mapping rules. To customize some elements of this mapping, you can apply the @javax.jws.WebMethod annotation on methods. The API of this annotation is quite simple as it allows renaming a method or excluding it from the WSDL. Listing 14-16 shows how the CardValidator web service renames the first method to ValidateCreditCard and excludes the second one.

Listing 14-16. One Method Is Renamed, the Other Excluded

```
@WebService
public class CardValidator {

    @WebMethod(operationName = "ValidateCreditCard")
    public boolean validate(CreditCard creditCard) {
        // business logic
    }

    @WebMethod(exclude = true)
    public void validate(String ccNumber) {
        // business logic
    }
}
```

@WebResult

The @javax.jws.WebResult annotation operates in conjunction with @WebMethod to control the generated name of the message returned value in the WSDL. In Listing 14-17, the returned result of the validate() method is renamed to IsValid.

Listing 14-17. The Return Result of the Method Is Renamed

```
@WebService
public class CardValidator {

    @WebMethod
    @WebResult(name = "IsValid")
    public boolean validate(CreditCard creditCard) {
        // business logic
    }
}
```

This annotation also has other elements to customize the XML namespace for the returned value, for example, and looks like the @WebParam annotation.

@WebParam

The @javax.jws.WebParam annotation, shown in Listing 14-18, is similar to @WebResult as it customizes the parameters for the web service methods. Its API permits changing of the name of the parameter in the WSDL (see Listing 14-19), the namespace, and the type. Valid types are IN, OUT, or INOUT (both), which determine how the parameter is flowing.

Listing 14-18. The @WebParam API

```
@Retention(RUNTIME) @Target(PARAMETER)
    public @interface WebParam {
    String name() default "";
    public enum Mode {IN, OUT, INOUT};
    String targetNamespace() default "";
    boolean header() default false;
    String partName() default "";
};
```

Listing 14-19. The Method Parameter Is Renamed

```
@WebService
public class CardValidator {

    @WebMethod
    public boolean validate(@WebParam(name = "Credit-Card") CreditCard creditCard) {
        // business logic
    }
}
```

@OneWay

The @OneWay annotation can be used on methods that do not have a return value such as methods returning void. This annotation has no elements and can be seen as a markup interface that informs the container the invocation can be optimized, as there is no return (using an asynchronous invocation, for example).

All Together

To have a better understanding of these annotations, I'll use them on the CardValidator web service (see Listing 14-20) and show you the impact they have on the WSDL document and the accompanying schema. You can compare the original WSDL document in Listing 14-10 with Listing 14-21, and the original schema in Listing 14-11 with Listing 14-22. The differences are highlighted.

Listing 14-20. The CardValidator Web Service with Annotations

```
@WebService(name = "CreditCardValidator", portName = "ValidatorPort")
public class CardValidator {

    @WebMethod(operationName = "ValidateCreditCard")
    @WebResult(name = "IsValid")
    public boolean validate(@WebParam(name = "CreditCard") CreditCard creditCard) {

        Character lastDigit = creditCard.getNumber().charAt(↪
                             creditCard.getNumber().length() - 1);
        if (Integer.parseInt(lastDigit.toString()) % 2 != 0) {
            return true;
        } else {
            return false;
        }
    }


    @WebMethod(exclude = true)
    public void validate(String ccNumber) {
        // business logic
    }
}
```

The `@WebService` annotation renames the `<portType name>` and `<port name>` elements of the WSDL. All the other annotations have an impact on the method, which is represented by the `<message>` element in the WSDL.

Listing 14-21. The WSDL Document After Customization

```
<definitions targetNamespace="http://chapter14.javaee6.org/" name="CardValidatorService">
  <types>
    <xsd:schema>
      <xsd:import namespace="http://chapter14.javaee6.org/" ↪
            schemaLocation="CardValidatorService_schema1.xsd"/>
    </xsd:schema>
  </types>
  <message name="ValidateCreditCard">
    <part name="parameters" element="tns:ValidateCreditCard"/>
  </message>
  <message name="ValidateCreditCardResponse">
    <part name="parameters" element="tns:ValidateCreditCardResponse"/>
  </message>
  <portType name="CreditCardValidator">
    <operation name="ValidateCreditCard">
      <input message="tns:ValidateCreditCard"/>
      <output message="tns:ValidateCreditCardResponse"/>
    </operation>
  </portType>
```

```
    <binding name="ValidatorPortBinding" type="tns:CreditCardValidator">
      <soap:binding transport="http://schemas.xmlsoap.org/soap/http" ↪
                             style="document"/>
      <operation name="ValidateCreditCard">
        <soap:operation soapAction=""/>
        <input>
          <soap:body use="literal"/>
        </input>
        <output>
          <soap:body use="literal"/>
        </output>
      </operation>
    </binding>
    <service name="CardValidatorService">
      <port name="ValidatorPort" binding="tns:ValidatorPortBinding">
        <soap:address location= "http://localhost:8080/chapter14/CardValidatorService"/>
      </port>
    </service>
</definitions>
```

The schema gets customized as both elements, the request and the response, are defined in the `<xs:complexType>` element. The returned value of the method is called `IsValid` and is of type `Boolean`.

Listing 14-22. The WSDL Schema After Customization

```
<?xml version="1.0" encoding="UTF-8" standalone="yes"?>
<xs:schema version="1.0" targetNamespace="http://chapter14.javaee6.org/"
  xmlns:tns="http://chapter14.javaee6.org/" ↪
  xmlns:xs="http://www.w3.org/2001/XMLSchema">

  <xs:element name="ValidateCreditCard" type="tns:ValidateCreditCard"/>

  <xs:element name="ValidateCreditCardResponse" ↪
              type="tns:ValidateCreditCardResponse"/>

  <xs:element name="creditCard" type="tns:creditCard"/>

  <xs:complexType name="ValidateCreditCard">
    <xs:sequence>
      <xs:element name="CreditCard" type="tns:creditCard" minOccurs="0"/>
    </xs:sequence>
  </xs:complexType>

  <xs:complexType name="creditCard">
    <xs:sequence>
      <xs:element name="controlNumber" type="xs:int" minOccurs="0"/>
      <xs:element name="expiryDate" type="xs:string" minOccurs="0"/>
      <xs:element name="number" type="xs:string" minOccurs="0"/>
      <xs:element name="type" type="xs:string" minOccurs="0"/>
    </xs:sequence>
  </xs:complexType>
```

```
<xs:complexType name="ValidateCreditCardResponse">
  <xs:sequence>
    <xs:element name="IsValid" type="xs:boolean"/>
  </xs:sequence>
</xs:complexType>
</xs:schema>
```

Life Cycle and Callback

Web services also have a life cycle that resembles the stateless and message-driven bean, as you can see in Figure 14-5. It is the same life cycle found for components that do not hold any state: either they do not exist or they are ready to process a request. This life cycle is managed by the container.

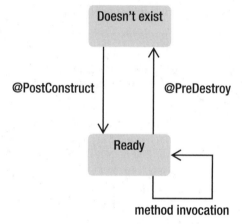

Figure 14-5. *Web service life cycle*

Both the servlet and EJB endpoint support dependency injection (because they run in a container) and life-cycle methods such as @PostConstruct and @PreDestroy. The container calls the @PostConstruct callback method, if any, when it creates an instance of a web service, and calls the @PreDestroy callback when it destroys it.

One difference between servlet and EJB endpoints is that EJBs can use interceptors. Interceptors are the Java EE implementation of the Aspect-Oriented Programming (AOP) concept described in Chapter 8.

Web Service Context

A web service has an environment context and can access it by injecting a reference of `javax.xml.ws.WebServiceContext` with a `@Resource` annotation. Within this context, the web service can obtain runtime information such as the endpoint implementation class, the message context, and security information relative to a request being served.

```
@Resource
private WebServiceContext context;
```

Table 14-2 lists the methods defined in the `javax.xml.ws.WebServiceContext` interface.

Table 14-2. Methods of the WebServiceContext Interface

Method	Description
getMessageContext	Returns the MessageContext for the request being served at the time this method is called. It can be used to access the SOAP message headers, body, and so on.
getUserPrincipal	Returns the Principal that identifies the sender of the request currently being serviced.
isUserInRole	Returns a Boolean indicating whether the authenticated user is included in the specified logical role.
getEndpointReference	Returns the EndpointReference associated with this endpoint.

Invoking a SOAP Web Service

With the WSDL and some tools to generate the Java stubs, you can invoke a web service. Invoking a web service is similar to invoking a distributed object with RMI. Like RMI, JAX-WS enables the programmer to use a local method call to invoke a service on another host. The difference is that, on the remote host, the web service can be written in another programming language (note that you can invoke non-Java code using RMI-IIOP). The WSDL is the standard contract between the consumer and the service. Metro provides a WSDL-to-Java utility tool (`wsimport`) that generates Java interfaces and classes from a WSDL. Such interfaces are called service endpoint interfaces (SEI) because it is a Java representation of a web service endpoint (servlet or EJB). This SEI acts like a proxy that routes the local Java call to the remote web service using HTTP.

When a method on this proxy is invoked (see Figure 14-6), it converts the parameters of the method into a SOAP message (the request) and sends it to the web service endpoint. To obtain the result, the SOAP response is converted back into an instance of the returned type. You don't need to understand the internal work of the proxy nor even look at the code. Before compiling your client consumer, you need to generate the SEI to get the proxy class to call it in your code.

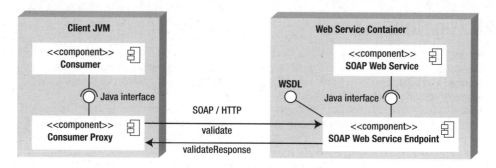

Figure 14-6. A consumer invoking a web service through a proxy

The consumer can get an instance of the proxy either through injection or by programmatically creating it. To inject a web service, you need to use the @javax.xml.ws.WebServiceRef annotation. It follows the @Resource or @EJB annotation pattern shown in previous chapters, but for the web service. When this annotation is applied on an attribute (or a getter method), the container will inject an instance of the web service when the application is initialized. The code would look like this:

```
@WebServiceRef
private CardValidatorService cardValidatorService;
// ...
CardValidator cardValidator = cardValidatorService.getCardValidatorPort();
cardValidator.validate(creditCard);
```

Note that the CardValidatorService class is the SEI, not the web service itself. We then have to get the proxy CardValidator class to invoke business methods locally. A local call is made on the validate() method of the proxy, which in turn will invoke the remote web service, create the SOAP request, marshall the messages, and so on. The proxy finds the target service because the default endpoint URL is embedded in the WSDL file, and is subsequently integrated into the proxy implementation.

For such injection to work, this code must be executed inside a container (servlet container, EJB container, or application client container). If not running inside a container, the @WebServiceRef annotation cannot be used. The classes generated by the wsimport tool can be used directly as follows:

```
CardValidatorService cardValidatorService = new CardValidatorService();
CardValidator cardValidator = cardValidatorService.getCardValidatorPort();
cardValidator.validate(creditCard);
```

In this code, an instance of CardValidatorService is created with the new keyword, and the rest of the code is similar.

■ **Note** The wsimport and wsgen tools are shipped with JDK 1.6 as well as GlassFish. wsimport takes a WSDL in input and generates JAX-WS artifacts, such as an SEI. wsgen reads a web service endpoint class and generates the WSDL. You can access these tools directly with a Java SE 6 installation, or through the GlassFish command-line interface (CLI), an Ant task, or a Maven plug-in.

441

Putting It All Together

By putting these concepts together, you can write a web service and a web service consumer, and deploy and test it all with GlassFish. You should use JAXB and JAX-WS annotations, as well as generate a service endpoint interface with the `wsimport` Maven goal. To write a web service, several steps are needed. I'll demonstrate these steps by revisiting the `CardValidator` web service.

The `CardValidator` SOAP web service checks that a credit card is valid. It has one method that takes a `CreditCard` object as a parameter, applies some algorithm, and returns `true` if the card is valid, `false` if not. Once this web service is deployed on GlassFish, `wsimport` is used to generate all the needed artifacts for the consumer. The consumer can then invoke the web service to validate credit cards.

You will use two Maven projects: one to package the web service into a war file (`chapter14-service-2.0.war`) and another to package the consumer into a jar file (`chapter14-consumer-2.0.jar`).

Writing the CreditCard Class

The `CreditCard` class, shown in Listing 14-23, is the POJO used as a parameter to the web service `validate()` method. SOAP web services exchange XML messages, not Java objects. The `CreditCard` class is annotated with the JAXB `@XmlRootElement` annotation to be marshalled into XML so it can be sent in a SOAP request. The `CreditCard` object has some basic attributes such as the credit card number, the expiry date (formatted as MM/YY), a credit card type (Visa, Master Card, American Express, etc.), and a control number.

Listing 14-23. The CreditCard Class with a JAXB Annotation

```
@XmlRootElement
public class CreditCard {

    private String number;
    private String expiryDate;
    private Integer controlNumber;
    private String type;

    // Constructors, getters, setters
}
```

Writing the CardValidator SOAP Web Service

The `CardValidator` (see Listing 14-24) is also a POJO with a JAX-WS `@WebService` annotation. It is not an EJB endpoint as it doesn't have the `@Stateless` annotation. The `CardValidator` web service is a servlet endpoint that will be deployed in a war file (`chapter14-service-2.0.war`). It has a `validate()` method that takes a `CreditCard` object as a parameter. The algorithm to check whether the card is valid or not is based on the card number: odd numbers are valid, even numbers are not. The method returns a `boolean`.

Listing 14-24. The CardValidator Web Service

```
@WebService
public class CardValidator {

    public boolean validate(CreditCard creditCard) {
        Character lastDigit = creditCard.getNumber().charAt(↪
                                 creditCard.getNumber().length() - 1);

        if (Integer.parseInt(lastDigit.toString()) % 2 != 0) {
            return true;
        } else {
            return false;
        }
    }
}
```

For simplicity, no extra Java-to-WSDL mapping is used, so there are no @WebMethod, @WebResult, or @WebParam annotations, allowing you to see how easy it is to write a web service using all the default mapping rules.

Compiling and Packaging with Maven

The CardValidator web service (shown previously in Listing 14-24) needs to be compiled and packaged in a war file (<packaging> war </packaging>). The pom.xml file (see Listing 14-25) declares the jaxws-rt dependency to use the 2.2 version of JAX-WS. Java SE 6 comes with a JAXB and JAX-WS implementation. Specifying the 1.6 version in the maven-compiler-plugin should be enough as you explicitly specify you want to use Java SE 6 (<source> 1.6 </source>). But if you want to control your dependency versions and absolutely want JAX-WS 2.2, it's better to explicitly add the jaxws-rt dependency to the project.

Listing 14-25. The pom.xml File to Compile and Package the Web Service

```
<?xml version="1.0" encoding="UTF-8"?>
<project xmlns="http://maven.apache.org/POM/4.0.0" ↪
         xmlns:xsi="http://www.w3.org/2001/XMLSchema-instance"↪
         xsi:schemaLocation="http://maven.apache.org/POM/4.0.0 ↪
         http://maven.apache.org/xsd/maven-4.0.0.xsd">
    <modelVersion>4.0.0</modelVersion>
    <groupId>com.apress.javaee6</groupId>
    <artifactId>chapter14-service</artifactId>
    <version>2.0</version>

    <packaging>war</packaging>

    <dependencies>
        <dependency>
            <groupId>com.sun.xml.ws</groupId>
            <artifactId>jaxws-rt</artifactId>
```

```
            <version>2.2</version>
            <scope>provided</scope>
        </dependency>
    </dependencies>

    <build>
        <plugins>
            <plugin>
                <groupId>org.apache.maven.plugins</groupId>
                <artifactId>maven-war-plugin</artifactId>
                <version>2.1</version>
                <configuration>
                    <failOnMissingWebXml>false</failOnMissingWebXml>
                </configuration>
            </plugin>

            <plugin>
                <groupId>org.apache.maven.plugins</groupId>
                <artifactId>maven-compiler-plugin</artifactId>
                <inherited>true</inherited>
                <configuration>
                    <source>1.6</source>
                    <target>1.6</target>
                </configuration>
            </plugin>
        </plugins>
    </build>
</project>
```

With Java EE 6, deployment descriptors are optional; therefore, you don't need a `web.xml` or `webservices.xml` file. However, as Maven still obliges you to add a `web.xml` file into a war, you need to change the `failOnMissingWebXml` attribute of the `maven-war-plugin` to `false`; otherwise, Maven will fail the build.

To compile and package the web service, open a DOS command line in the root directory containing the `pom.xml` file and enter the following Maven command:

```
mvn package
```

Go to the `target` directory, where you should see a file named `chapter14-service-2.0.war`. If you open it, you will see that both `CardValidator.class` and `CreditCard.class` are under the `WEB-INF\classes` directory. The war file doesn't contain anything else, not even a WSDL file.

Deploying on GlassFish

Once the web service is packaged in the war file, it needs to be deployed into GlassFish. This can be done using the `asadmin` command line. Open a DOS console and go to the `target` directory where the `chapter14-service-2.0.war` file is, make sure GlassFish is running, and enter the following:

```
asadmin deploy chapter14-service-2.0.war
```

If the deployment is successful, the following command should return the name of the deployed components and their types:

```
asadmin list-components
chapter14-service-2.0 <webservices, web>
```

It's interesting to note that GlassFish recognizes the web module (the war file could have contained web pages, servlets, and so on) as being a web service. If you go to the GlassFish administration console shown in Figure 14-7 (`http://localhost:4848/`), you will see that `chapter14-service-2.0` is deployed under the Applications menu.

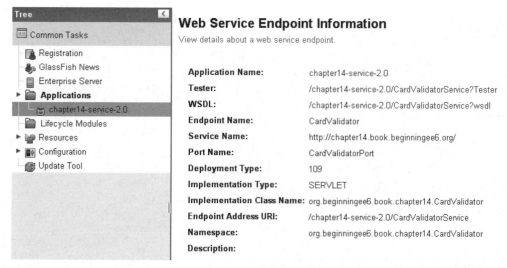

Figure 14-7. Web services deployed in the GlassFish administration console

On this page, if you click the WSDL link, it will open a browser at the following URL and show the WSDL of the web service (see Figure 14-8):

```
http://localhost:8080/chapter14-service-2.0/CardValidatorService?wsdl
```

```
– <definitions targetNamespace="http://chapter14.book.beginningee6.org/" name="CardValidatorService">
   – <types>
      – <xsd:schema>
           <xsd:import namespace="http://chapter14.book.beginningee6.org/" schemaLocation="http://localhost:8080/chapter14-service-2.0/CardValidatorService?xsd=1"/>
         </xsd:schema>
      </types>
   – <message name="validate">
        <part name="parameters" element="tns:validate"/>
      </message>
   – <message name="validateResponse">
        <part name="parameters" element="tns:validateResponse"/>
      </message>
   – <portType name="CardValidator">
      – <operation name="validate">
           <input wsam:Action="http://chapter14.book.beginningee6.org/CardValidator/validateRequest" message="tns:validate"/>
           <output wsam:Action="http://chapter14.book.beginningee6.org/CardValidator/validateResponse" message="tns:validateResponse"/>
         </operation>
      </portType>
   – <binding name="CardValidatorPortBinding" type="tns:CardValidator">
        <soap:binding transport="http://schemas.xmlsoap.org/soap/http" style="document"/>
      – <operation name="validate">
           <soap:operation soapAction=""/>
         – <input>
              <soap:body use="literal"/>
           </input>
         – <output>
              <soap:body use="literal"/>
           </output>
         </operation>
      </binding>
   – <service name="CardValidatorService">
      – <port name="CardValidatorPort" binding="tns:CardValidatorPortBinding">
           <soap:address location="http://localhost:8080/chapter14-service-2.0/CardValidatorService"/>
         </port>
      </service>
   </definitions>
```

Figure 14-8. *The WSDL has been generated by Metro*

It is interesting to note that you didn't create this WSDL nor deploy it in the war file. The Metro stack automatically generates the WSDL based on the annotations contained in the web service.

Writing the Web Service Consumer

The web service is now online, and you know where to find the WSDL. Thanks to this WSDL, the consumer will be able to generate the artifacts necessary to invoke the web service with the `wsimport` tool. First, write the code of the consumer as shown in Listing 14-26.

Listing 14-26. *The Main Class Invokes the Web Service Using Injection*

```
public class Main {

    @WebServiceRef
    private static CardValidatorService cardValidatorService;

    public static void main(String[] args) {
```

```
    CreditCard creditCard = new CreditCard();
    creditCard.setNumber("12341234");
    creditCard.setExpiryDate("10/10");
    creditCard.setType("VISA");
    creditCard.setControlNumber(1234);

    CardValidator cardValidator = cardValidatorService.getCardValidatorPort();

    System.out.println(cardValidator.validate(creditCard));
  }
}
```

This `Main` class creates an instance of the `CreditCard` object, sets some data, gets injected a reference of the web service, invokes the `validate()` method, and displays the result (`true` or `false` depending on whether the credit card is valid). The interesting thing is that the consumer does not have any of these classes. The `CardValidatorService`, `CardValidator`, and `CreditCard` are totally unknown to the consumer. This code will not compile until all these classes are generated.

Generating Consumer's Artifacts and Packaging with Maven

Before compiling the consumer `Main` class, you need to generate the artifacts with the `wsimport` tool. The good news is that Maven has a `wsimport` goal, and this goal is executed automatically during the `generate-sources` life-cycle phase. As described in Chapter 1, Maven uses a rich life cycle to build applications. The `generate-sources` phase is used to generate code and is executed before compilation. The only thing to do is tell this `wsimport` goal where to find the WSDL document. You know this information because you've deployed the web service into GlassFish, and you have displayed the content of the WSDL. Its location is at:

`http://localhost:8080/chapter14-service-2.0/CardValidatorService?wsdl`

The `pom.xml` file in Listing 14-27 also specifies the needed dependencies, the `jaxws-rt` version (2.2), as well as the JDK version (1.6). The `Main` class is packaged in a jar file, and, like every jar file, it has a `META-INF\MANIFEST.MF` file. This file can be used to define some metadata about the jar, and that's what you do when you use the `maven-jar-plugin`. You add a `Main-Class` element to the `MANIFEST` pointing to the consumer `Main` class. This will allow execution of the jar file.

Listing 14-27. The pom.xml File Generates the Consumer Artifacts and Packages

```
<project xmlns="http://maven.apache.org/POM/4.0.0" ↪
        xmlns:xsi="http://www.w3.org/2001/XMLSchema-instance"↪
        xsi:schemaLocation="http://maven.apache.org/POM/4.0.0 ↪
        http://maven.apache.org/xsd/maven-4.0.0.xsd">
    <modelVersion>4.0.0</modelVersion>
    <groupId>com.apress.javaee6</groupId>
    <artifactId>chapter14-consumer</artifactId>
    <packaging>jar</packaging>
    <version>2.0</version>
```

```xml
<dependencies>
    <dependency>
        <groupId>com.sun.xml.ws</groupId>
        <artifactId>jaxws-rt</artifactId>
        <version>2.2</version>
        <scope>provided</scope>
    </dependency>
</dependencies>

<build>
    <plugins>
        <plugin>
            <groupId>org.apache.maven.plugins</groupId>
            <artifactId>maven-jar-plugin</artifactId>
            <version>2.2</version>
            <configuration>
                <archive>
                  <manifest>
                <mainClass>com.apress.javaee6.chapter14.Main</mainClass>
                  </manifest>
                </archive>
            </configuration>
        </plugin>

        <plugin>
            <groupId>org.codehaus.mojo</groupId>
            <artifactId>jaxws-maven-plugin</artifactId>
            <executions>
                <execution>
                    <goals>
                        <goal>wsimport</goal>
                    </goals>
                    <configuration>
                        <wsdlUrls>
                            <wsdlUrl>
http://localhost:8080/chapter14-service-2.0/CardValidatorService?wsdl
                            </wsdlUrl>
                        </wsdlUrls>
                        <keep>true</keep>
                    </configuration>
                </execution>
            </executions>
        </plugin>

        <plugin>
            <groupId>org.apache.maven.plugins</groupId>
            <artifactId>maven-compiler-plugin</artifactId>
            <inherited>true</inherited>
            <configuration>
                <source>1.6</source>
                <target>1.6</target>
```

```
            </configuration>
         </plugin>
      </plugins>
   </build>
</project>
```

To have a better understanding of what happens behind the scenes, first generate the artifacts by entering the following Maven command:

`mvn clean generate-sources`

This command executes the Maven **generate-sources** life-cycle phase, and thus the **wsimport** goal that is defined with it. **wsimport** connects to the web service WSDL URL, downloads it, and generates all the artifacts. Here is the output of the Maven command:

```
[INFO] [clean:clean]
[INFO] [jaxws:wsimport {execution: default}]
[INFO] Processing: http://localhost:8080/chapter14-service-2.0/ CardValidatorService?wsdl
[INFO] jaxws:wsimport args: [-s, D:\Chapter14-Consumer\target\jaxws\wsimport\ ↪
     java, -d, D:\Chapter14-Consumer\target\classes, -Xnocompile, ↪
     http://localhost:8080/chapter14-service-2.0/CardValidatorService?wsdl]


parsing WSDL...
generating code...


[INFO]----------------------------------------
[INFO] BUILD SUCCESSFUL
[INFO]----------------------------------------
```

If you are curious, you can go to the **target\jaxws\wsimport\java** directory and check the classes that have been generated. You will find the **CardValidator**, **CardValidatorService**, and **CreditCard** classes, of course, but also one class for the SOAP request (**Validate**) and another one for the response (**ValidateResponse**). These classes are full of JAXB and JAXW annotations as they marshall the **CreditCard** object and connect to the remote web service. You don't have to worry about the generated code. The jar file can be compiled and packaged:

`mvn package`

This creates the **chapter14-consumer-2.0.jar** file, which contains the **Main** class that you wrote plus all the generated classes. This jar is self-contained and can now be run to invoke the web service.

Running the Main Class

Remember that the consumer **Main** class uses the **@WebServiceRef** annotation to get a reference of the web service endpoint interface injected. This means that the code needs to be executed in the application client container (ACC). Also remember that the **chapter14-consumer-2.0.jar** file is executable, as you've added a **Main-Class** element to the **MANIFEST.MF** file. The only thing that you have to do is to invoke the **appclient** utility that comes with GlassFish and pass it the jar file as follows:

```
appclient -client chapter14-consumer-2.0.jar
```

This will invoke the web service through HTTP and get a response back telling you whether the credit card is valid or not.

Summary

Web services are used for business-to-business (B2B) integration and are crucial technology for SOA. Amazon, eBay, Google, Yahoo!, and many others provide web services for the use of their customers. And many organizations use web services heavily in house. This chapter has introduced some relevant standards (UDDI, WSDL, SOAP, XML, etc.) and focused on the Java EE specifications that cover these standards (JAX-WS, JAXB, WS-Metadata, etc.).

Java Architecture for XML Binding (JAXB) defines a standard to bind Java representations to XML and vice versa. It provides a high level of abstraction, as it is based on annotations. Even if JAXB can be used in any kind of Java application, it fits well in the web service space because any information exchanged is written in XML.

After JAXB, we looked at WSDL and SOAP. These specifications are vital to web services as they describe the web service interface and the messages exchanged, respectively.

Leaving these specifications behind, JAX-WS follows a simple development model and uses only a small set of annotations to adjust the Java-to-WSDL mapping. It is then easy to write a web service (servlet or EJB endpoint) or a web service consumer as simple annotated POJOs with optional deployment descriptors.

This chapter ended with an example of how to write a web service, compile and package it with Maven, and generate the consumer's artifact with the wsimport utility.

CHAPTER 15

■ ■ ■

RESTful Web Services

The SOAP web services stack (SOAP, WSDL, WS-*) described in the previous chapter delivers interoperability in both message integration and RPC style. With the rise of Web 2.0, new web frameworks such as Rails have emerged, and a new kind of web service has gained in popularity: the RESTful web service.

Many key web players like Amazon, Google, and Yahoo! have deprecated their SOAP services in favor of RESTful resource-oriented services. Many factors must be taken into account when making a choice between SOAP web services and RESTful web services.

Representational State Transfer (REST) is an architectural style created based on how the Web works. Applied to web services, it tries to put the Web back into web services. To design a RESTful web service, you need to know Hypertext Transfer Protocol (HTTP) and Uniform Resource Identifiers (URIs), and to observe a few design principles. You need to think in terms of resources so as not to betray the principles of REST.

This chapter focuses on REST, its architecture, and the HTTP protocol. In Java EE 6, REST has been specified through Java API for RESTful Web Services (JAX-RS), used in this chapter.

Understanding RESTful Web Services

In the REST architectural style, every piece of information is a resource, and these resources are addressed using Uniform Resource Identifiers (URIs), typically links on the Web. The resources are acted upon by using a set of simple, well-defined operations. The REST client-server architectural style is designed to use a stateless communication protocol, typically HTTP. In REST, clients and servers exchange representations of resources using a defined interface and protocol. These principles encourage RESTful applications to be simple and lightweight, and have high performance.

Resources and URIs

Resources are given a central role in RESTful architectures. A resource is anything the client might want to reference or interact with, any piece of information that might be worthwhile referencing in a hyperlink. It can be stored in a database, a file, and so forth. Avoid as much as possible exposing abstract concepts as a resource; favor simple objects. Some resources used in the CD-BookStore application could be:

- A list of Apress Java books

- The book *The Definitive Guide to Grails*

- Ola Bini's résumé

Resources on the Web are identified by a URI. A URI is a unique identifier for a resource, made of a name and a structured address indicating where to find this resource. Various types of URIs exist: WWW addresses, Universal Document Identifiers, Universal Resource Identifiers, and finally the combination of Uniform Resource Locators (URLs) and Uniform Resource Names (URNs). Examples of resources and URIs are listed in Table 15-1.

Table 15-1. Examples of Resources and URIs

Resource	URI
The catalog of Apress books	`http://www.apress.com/book/catalog`
The cover of the Java EE 6 book	`http://www.apress.com/book/catalog/beginning-javaee6.jpg`
Information about jobs at Apress	`http://www.apress.com/info/jobs`
The weather in Paris for 2008	`http://www.weather.com/weather/2008?location=Paris,France`
Interesting photos on Flickr for January 1st, 2009	`http://www.flickr.com/explore/interesting/2009/01/01`
Interesting photos on Flickr for the last 24 hours	`http://www.flickr.com/explore/interesting/24hours`
The list of adventure movies	`http://www.movies.com/categories/adventure`

URIs should be as descriptive as possible and should target a unique resource. Note that different URIs identifying different resources may lead to the same data. Actually, at some point in time, the list of the interesting photos uploaded to Flickr on 01/01/2009 was the same as the list of the uploaded photos in the last 24 hours, but the information conveyed by the two corresponding URIs is not the same.

Representations

You might want to get the representation of an object as text, XML, a PDF document, a JPG image, or another data format. When the client deals with a resource, it is always through its representation; the resource itself remains on the server. *Representation* is any useful information about the state of a resource. For example, the list of Java books mentioned previously has at least two representations:

- The HTML page rendered by your browser:
  `http://www.apress.com/book/catalog?category=32`

- The comma-separated value (CSV) file better suited to compute the total number
  of books: `http://www.apress.com/resource/csv/bookcategory?cat=32`

How do you choose between the different representations of a given resource? Two solutions are possible. The service could expose one URI per representation. That's what the Apress web site does for the list of Java books. However, the two URIs are really different and do not seem directly related. Following is a neater set of URIs:

- `http://www.apress.com/book/catalog/java`

- `http://www.apress.com/book/catalog/java.csv`

- `http://www.apress.com/book/catalog/java.xml`

The first URI is the default representation of the resource, and additional representations append their format extension to it: `.csv` (for `text/csv`), `.xml`, `.pdf`, and so on.

Another solution is to expose one single URI for all representations (e.g., `http://www.apress.com/book/catalog/java`) and to rely on the mechanism called *content negotiation*, which I'll discuss in more detail a little later in this chapter.

WADL

While SOAP-based services rely on WSDL to describe the format of possible requests for a given web service, Web Application Description Language (WADL) is used to expose the possible interactions with a given RESTful web service. It eases client development, which can load and interact directly with the resources. This book will not cover WADL, as it is not mandatory for REST services and is not widely used.

HTTP

HTTP, a protocol for distributed, collaborative, hypermedia information systems, led to the establishment of the World Wide Web together with URIs, HTML, and the first browsers. Coordinated by the World Wide Web Consortium (W3C) and Internet Engineering Task Force (IETF), HTTP is the result of several Requests For Comment (RFC), notably RFC 216, which defines HTTP 1.1. HTTP is based on requests and responses exchanged between a client and a server.

Request and Response

A client sends a request to a server, expecting an answer (see Figure 15-1). The message exchanges are made of an envelope and a body, also called a document or representation.

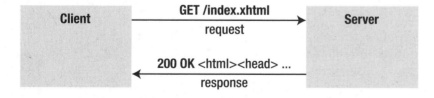

Figure 15-1. HTTP request and response

453

For instance, here is a type of request sent to a server:

```
$> curl -v http://www.apress.com/book/catalog?category=32
> GET /book/catalog?category=32 HTTP/1.1
> User-Agent: curl/7.19.3 (i586-pc-mingw32msvc) libcurl/7.19.3 zlib/1.2.3
> Host: www.apress.com
> Accept: */*
```

This request has several pieces of information sent from the client:

- The HTTP method, here GET

- The path, here /book/catalog?category=32

- Several other request headers

Notice that there is no body as part of the request. Actually, a GET never has a body. To the request, the server will send the following response:

```
< HTTP/1.1 200 OK
< Date: Mon, 23 Feb 2009 07:28:09 GMT
< Server: Apache/2.0.63 (Unix) PHP/5.2.6
< X-Powered-By: PHP/5.2.6
< Set-Cookie: PHPSESSID=b9ae64b800781d9761670fcf6067a317; path=/
< Expires: Thu, 19 Nov 1981 08:52:00 GMT
< Cache-Control: no-store, no-cache, must-revalidate, post-check=0, pre-check=0
< Pragma: no-cache
< Transfer-Encoding: chunked
< Content-Type: text/html
<!DOCTYPE HTML PUBLIC "-//W3C//DTD HTML 4.01 Transitional//EN">
<html>
  <head>
  <title>
...
```

This response is made up of the following:

- *A response code*: In this case, the response code is 200 OK.

- *Several response headers*: In the preceding code, the response headers are Date, Server, Content-Type. Here the content type is text/html, but it could be any other media such as XML (application/xml) or images (image/jpeg).

- *Entity body, or representation*: The content of the returned web page is the entity body in this example (here I just showed a fragment of an HTML page).

■ **Note** Here I am using cURL (`http://curl.haxx.se/`) as a client, but I could have used Firefox or any other web client that deals with HTTP requests. cURL is a command-line tool for transferring files with URL syntax via protocols such as HTTP, FTP, Gopher, SFTP, FTPS, SCP, TFTP, and many more. You can send HTTP commands, change HTTP headers, and so on. It is a good tool for simulating a user's actions at a web browser.

HTTP Methods

The Web consists of well-identified resources linked together and accessed through simple HTTP requests. The main types of requests standardized in HTTP are `GET`, `POST`, `PUT`, `DELETE`. These are also called verbs, or methods. HTTP defines four other methods that are less frequently used: `HEAD`, `TRACE`, `OPTIONS`, `CONNECT`.

GET

`GET` is a simple read that requests a representation of a resource. `GET` should be implemented in a safe way, meaning it shouldn't change the state of the resource. In addition, `GET` must be idempotent, which means it must leave the resource in the same state when called once, twice, or more. Safety and idempotence bring greater stability. When a client does not get a response (e.g., due to a network failure), it might renew its requests, and those new requests will expect the same answer it should have received originally, without corrupting the resource state on the server.

POST

Given a representation (text, XML, etc.), calling a `POST` method creates a new resource identified by the requested URI. Examples of `POST` could be appending a message to a log file, a comment to a blog, a book to a booklist, and so on. Consequently, `POST` is not safe (the resource state is updated) nor idempotent (sending the request twice will result in two new subordinates). If a resource has been created on the origin server, the response should be status 201 (Created). Most modern browsers generate only `GET` and `POST requests`.

PUT

A `PUT` request is intended to update the state of the resource stored under a given URI. If the request URI refers to a nonexistent resource, the resource will be created under this same URI. Examples of `PUT` could be updating the price of a book or the address of a customer. `PUT` is not safe (because the state of the resource gets updated), but it is idempotent: you can send the same `PUT` request many times, and the final resource state will always be the same.

DELETE

A `DELETE` request deletes the resource. The response to a `DELETE` may be a status message as part of the body or no status at all. `DELETE` is also idempotent but not safe.

Others

As mentioned previously, other HTTP methods exist, even if they are less used:

- HEAD is identical to GET except that the server doesn't return a message body in the response. HEAD might be useful for checking the validity of a link or the size of an entity without transferring it.

- When a server receives a TRACE request from the client, it echoes back the received request. This can be useful to see what intermediate servers, proxies or firewalls are adding or changing in the request.

- OPTIONS represents a request for information about the communication options available on the request/response chain identified by the URI. This method allows the client to determine the options and/or requirements associated with a resource, or the capabilities of a server, without implying a resource action or initiating resource retrieval.

- CONNECT is used in conjunction with a proxy that can dynamically switch to being a tunnel (a technique by which the HTTP protocol acts as a wrapper for various network protocols).

Content Negotiation

Content negotiation, described in section 12 of the HTTP standard, is defined as "the process of selecting the best representation for a given response when there are multiple representations available." Clients' needs, desires, and capabilities vary; the best representation for a mobile-device user in Japan might not be the best for a feed-reader application in the US.

Content negotiation is based on, but not limited to, the HTTP request headers Accept, Accept-Charset, Accept-Encoding, Accept-Language, and User-Agent. For example, to get the CSV representation of Apress Java books, the client application (the user agent) will request http://www.apress.com/book/catalog/java with a header Accept set to text/csv. You could also imagine that, based on the Accept-Language header, the server selects the proper CSV document to match the corresponding language (Japanese or English).

Content Types

HTTP uses Internet media types (originally called MIME types) in the Content-Type and Accept header fields in order to provide open and extensible data typing and type negotiation. Internet media types are divided into five discrete, top-level categories: text, image, audio, video, and application. These types are further divided into several subtypes (text/plain, text/xml, text/xhtml, etc.). Some of the most common public content types are as follows:

- `text/html`: HTML has been in use in the World Wide Web information infrastructure since 1990 and specified in various informal documents. The `text/html` media type was first officially defined by the IETF HTML working group in 1995. For a complete definition of the media type, refer to RFC 2854.

- `text/plain`: This is the default content type, as it's used for simple text messages.

- `image/gif`, `image/jpeg`, `image/png`: This image top-level media type requires a display device (such as a graphical display, a graphics printer, etc.) to view the information.

- `text/xml`, `application/xml`: The W3C issued Extensible Markup Language (XML) 1.0 in February 1998. For a complete definition of the media type, refer to RFC 3023.

- `application/json`: JavaScript Object Notation (JSON) is a lightweight data-interchange text format independent of the programming language.

Status Codes

Each time a response is received, an HTTP code is associated with it. The specification defines around 60 status codes. The `Status-Code` element is a three-digit integer that describes the context of a response and is part of the response envelope. The first digit specifies one of five classes of response:

- *1xx*: Informational. The request was received, and the process is continuing.

- *2xx*: Success. The action was successfully received, understood, and accepted.

- *3xx*: Redirection. Further action must be taken in order to complete the request.

- *4xx*: Client Error. The request contains bad syntax or cannot be fulfilled.

- *5xx*: Server Error. The server failed to fulfill an apparently valid request.

Following are some status codes you might have already come across:

- *200 OK*: The request has succeeded. The entity body, if any, contains the representation of the resource.

- *301 Moved Permanently*: The requested resource has been assigned a new, permanent URI and any future reference to this resource should use one of the returned URIs.

- *404 Not Found*: The server has not found anything matching the request URI.

- *500 Internal Server Error*: The server encountered an unexpected condition that prevented it from fulfilling the request.

Caching and Conditional Requests

In most distributed systems, caching is crucial. Caching aims at improving performance by avoiding unnecessary requests or by reducing the amount of data in responses. HTTP provides mechanisms to allow caching and make sure cached data is correct. But, if the client decides not to use any caching mechanism, it will always need to request data even if it hasn't been modified since the last request.

When a response to a GET is sent, it could include a Last-Modified header indicating the time that the resource was last modified. The next time the user agent requests this resource, it can pass this date in the If-Modified-Since header. The web server (or a proxy) will compare this date with the latest modification date. If the date sent by the user agent is equal or newer, a 304 Not Modified status code with no response body is returned. Otherwise, the requested operation is performed or forwarded.

But dates can be difficult to manipulate and imply that all the interacting agents are, and stay, synchronized. The ETag response header solves this issue. The easiest way to think of an ETag is as an MD5 or SHA1 hash of all the bytes in a representation; if just one byte in the representation changes, the ETag will change.

Figure 15-2 gives an example of how to use ETags. To get a book resource, you use the GET action and give it the URI of the resource (GET /book/12345). The server will return a response with the XML representation of the book, a 200 OK status code, and a generated ETag. The second time you ask for the same resource, if you pass the ETag as a value in an If-None-Match header, the server will not send the representation of the resource assuming the resource has not actually changed since the earlier request. This will instead return a 304 Not Modified status code informing the client that the resource hasn't changed since last access.

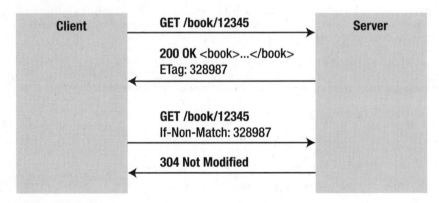

Figure 15-2. Using caching and the 304 Not Modified status code

Requests using the HTTP headers If-Modified-Since, If-Unmodified-Since, If-Match, If-None-Match, and If-Range are said to be conditional. Conditional requests can save bandwidth and CPU (on both the server and client side) by avoiding unnecessary round-trips or data transmissions. The If-* headers are most often used for GET and PUT requests.

RESTful Web Services Specification

Contrary to SOAP and the WS-* stack, which rely on W3C standards, REST has no standard and is just a style of architecture with design criteria. REST applications rely heavily on many other standards:

- HTTP

- URI, URL

- XML, JSON, HTML, GIF, JPEG, and so forth (resource representations)

The Java side has been specified through JAX-RS, but REST is like a design pattern: a reusable solution to a common problem that can be implemented by several languages.

A Brief History of REST

The term REST was first introduced by Roy Thomas Fielding in Chapter 5 of his PhD thesis, *Architectural Styles and the Design of Network-based Software Architectures* (University of California, Irvine, 2000, `http://www.ics.uci.edu/~fielding/pubs/dissertation/top.htm`). The dissertation is a retrospective explanation of the architecture chosen to develop the Web. In his thesis, Fielding takes a look at the parts of the World Wide Web that work very well and extracts design principles that could make any other distributed hypermedia system—whether related to the Web or not—as efficient.

The original motivation for developing REST was to create an architectural model of the Web. Roy T. Fielding is also one of the authors of the HTTP specification, so it's not surprising that HTTP fits quite well the architectural design he described in his dissertation.

JAX-RS 1.1

To write RESTful web services in Java, you only need a client and a server supporting HTTP. Any browser and an HTTP servlet container will do the job at the cost of some XML configuration and glue-code pain. At the end, this code may be barely readable and maintainable. This is when JAX-RS comes to the rescue. The first version of the JAX-RS specification, finalized in October 2008, defines a set of APIs that promotes the REST architecture style. It is the JCP standard for RESTful web services (JSR 311). Through annotations, it simplifies the implementation of RESTful web services. The specification only covers the server-side aspect of REST.

What's New in JAX-RS 1.1?

JAX-RS 1.1 is a maintenance release focusing on integration with Java EE 6 and its new features. The major new features of JAX-RS 1.1 are as follows:

- It provides support for stateless session beans as root resources.

- JAX-RS annotations can be applied to a bean's local interface or directly to a no-interface bean.

- External resources (persistence manager, data sources, EJBs, etc.) are allowed to be injected into a REST resource.

- `web.xml` is optional to configure a web container to serve REST requests.

Reference Implementation

Jersey is the reference implementation of JAX-RS. It is an open source project under dual CDDL and GPL licenses. Jersey is extensible through its API and also provides a client API (which is not covered by the specification).

Other implementations of JAX-RS are also available such as CXF (Apache), RESTEasy (JBoss), and Restlet (a senior project that existed even before JAX-RS was finalized).

The REST Approach

As I mentioned before, REST is a set of general design constraints based on HTTP. However, this chapter focuses on web services, and, since REST is derived from the Web, I'll start with a real-life web-browsing experience before going over the principles that drive the Web. The Web has become a main source of information and is part of our everyday tool set. You are probably very familiar with it, and this familiarity should help you in understanding REST concepts and properties.

From the Web to Web Services

We know how the Web works, so why should web services behave differently? After all, services also often exchange uniquely identified resources, linked with others like hyperlinks. Web architecture has proven its scalability for years; why reinvent the wheel?

To create, update, and delete a book resource, why not use the common HTTP verbs? For example:

- Use POST on data (in XML, JSON, or text format) to **create** the book resource with the URI http://www.apress.com/books/. Once created, the response sends back the URI of the new resource: http://www.apress.com/books/123456.

- Use GET to **read** the resource (and possible links to other resources from the entity body) at http://www.apress.com/books/123456.

- Use PUT on data to **update** the book resource at http://www.apress.com/books/123456.

- Use DELETE to **delete** the resource at http://www.apress.com/books/123456.

By using HTTP verbs, we have access to all possible Create, Read, Update, Delete (CRUD) actions on a resource.

A Web-Browsing Experience

How would you proceed to reach the list of Java technology books at Apress? You point your browser to the Apress web site: http://www.apress.com. Although it is likely that this page will not contain the exact information you're seeking, you're expecting it to give you access in one way or another to the Java book list. The home page offers a search engine on all Apress books, but there is also a book directory sorted by technologies. Click the Java node, and the hypermedia magic happens: here is the full list of Apress Java books. Quite a long list actually, and, although the number is not provided, the link to the CSV format and your command-line skills will do the math in a few clock cycles (there are 144 books under the Java category):

```
curl http://www.apress.com/resource/csv/bookcategory?cat=32 | ↩
        sed -n 2~1p | wc -l
(..)
144
```

Say that you save the link in your favorite bookmark manager, and, as you go through the book list, *The Definitive Guide to Grails, Second Edition* by Graeme Rocher and Jeff Brown captures your attention. The hyperlink on the book title takes you to the book page where you can read the abstract, author biography, and so on, and you notice one of the books listed in the Related titles section might be as valuable for your current project. You would like to compare Graeme Rocher's book with *Practical JRuby on Rails Web 2.0 Projects: Bringing Ruby on Rails to Java* by Ola Bini. Apress book pages give you access to a more concrete representation of its books in the form of online previews: open a preview, go through the table of contents, and make your choice.

Here is what we do on a day-to-day basis with our browsers. REST applies the same principles to your services where books, search results, a table of contents, or a book's cover can be defined as resources.

Uniform Interface

One of the main constraints that make an architecture RESTful is the use of a uniform interface to manage your resources. Pick whatever interface suits you, but use it in the same way all across the board, from resource to resource, from service to service. Never stray from it or alter the original meaning. By using a uniform interface, "the overall system architecture is simplified and the visibility of interactions is improved" (Roy Thomas Fielding, *Architectural Styles and the Design of Network-based Software Architectures*). Your services become part of a community of services using the exact same semantic.

The de facto web protocol is HTTP, which is a document-based standardized request/response protocol between a client and a server. HTTP is the uniform interface of RESTful web services. Web services built on SOAP, WSDL, and other WS-* standards also use HTTP as the transport layer, but they leverage only a very few of its capabilities. You have to discover the semantic of the service by analyzing the WSDL and then invoke the right methods. RESTful web services have a uniform interface (HTTP methods and URIs), so, once you know where the resource is (URI), you can invoke the HTTP method (GET, POST, etc.).

In addition to familiarity, a uniform interface promotes interoperability between applications; HTTP is widely supported, and the number of HTTP client libraries guarantees that you won't have to deal with communication issues.

Addressability

The second tenet to follow when designing RESTful web services is addressability. Your web service should make your application as addressable as possible, which means that every valuable piece of information of your application should be a resource and have a URI, making that resource easily reachable. It is the only piece of data you need to publish to make the resource accessible, so your business partner won't have some guesswork to do in order to reach the resource.

For example, you're dealing with a bug in your application, and your investigations lead you to line 42 of the class `CreditCardValidator.java` as the place where the bug occurs. Because you're not responsible for this domain of the application, you want to file an issue so a qualified person will take care of it. How would you point her to the incriminating line? You could say, "Go to line 42 of the class `CreditCardValidator`," or, if your source code is addressable through a repository browser, you could save the URI of the line itself in the bug report. This raises the issue of defining the granularity of your RESTful resources in your application: it could be at the line, method, or class level, and so forth.

Unique URIs make your resources linkable, and, because they are exposed through a uniform interface, everyone knows exactly how to interact with them, allowing people to use your application in ways you would have never imagined.

Connectedness

In graph theory, a graph is called connected if every pair of distinct vertices in the graph can be connected through some path. It is said to be strongly connected if it contains a direct path from u to v and a direct path from v to u for every pair of vertices u,v. REST advocates that resources should be as connected as possible. As the now famous formulation goes: "Hypermedia as the engine of application state."

Once again, this daunting statement resulted from an examination of the success of the Web. Web pages embed links to navigate through pages in a logical and smooth manner and, as such, the Web is very well connected. If there is a strong relationship between two resources, they should be connected. REST states that web services should also take advantage of hypermedia to inform the client of what is available and where to go. It promotes the discoverability of services. From a single URI, a user agent accessing a well-connected web service could discover all available actions, resources, their various representations, and so forth.

For instance, when a user agent looks up the representation of a CD (see Listing 15-1), this representation could have not only the names of the artist, but also a link, or a URI, to the biography. It's up to the user agent to actually retrieve it or not. The representation could also link to other representations of the resource or available actions.

Listing 15-1. A CD Representation Connected to Other Services

```
<cd>
  <title>Ella and Louis</title>
  <year ref="http://music.com/year/1956">1956</year>
  <artist ref="http://music.com/artists/123">Ella Fitzgerald</artist>
  <artist ref="http://music.com/artists/456">Louis Armstrong</artist>
  <link rel="self" type="text/json" href="http://music.com/album/789"/>
  <link rel="self" type="text/xml" href="http://music.com/album/789"/>
  <link rel="http://music.com/album/comments" type="text/xml" ↪
      href="http://music.com/album/789/comments"/>
</cd>
```

Another crucial aspect of the hypermedia principle is the state of the application, which must be led by the hypermedia. In short, the fact that the web service provides a set of links enables the client to move the application from one state to the next by simply following a link.

In the preceding XML snippet, the client could change the state of the application by commenting on the album. The list of comments on the album is a resource addressable with the URI `http://music.com/album/789/comments`. Because this web service uses a uniform interface, once the client knows the URI format, the available content types and the data format, it will know exactly how to interact with it: a `GET` will retrieve the list of existing comments, a `POST` will create a new comment, and so on. From this single initial request, the client can take many actions: the hypermedia drives the state of the application.

Statelessness

The last feature of REST is statelessness, which means that every HTTP request happens in complete isolation, as the server should never keep track of requests that were executed. For the sake of clarity, resource state and application state are usually distinguished. The resource state must live on the server and is shared by everybody, while the application state must remain on the client and is its sole property. Going back to the example in Listing 15-1, the application state is that the client has fetched a representation of the album *Ella and Louis*, but the server should not hold onto this information. The resource state is the album information itself; the server should obviously maintain this information. The client may change the resource state. If the shopping cart is a resource with restricted access to just one client, the application needs to keep track of the shopping cart ID in the client session.

Statelessness comes with many advantages such as better scalability: no session information to handle, no need to route subsequent requests to the same server, failure handling, and so on. If you need to keep state, the client has to do extra work to store it.

Java API for RESTful Web Services

Some of the low-level concepts (such as the HTTP protocol) might have you wondering how the code would look when developing a resource; you don't have to write plumbing code to digest HTTP requests, nor create HTTP responses by hand. JAX-RS is a very elegant API allowing you to describe a resource with only a few annotations. Resources are POJOs that have at least one method annotated with @javax.ws.rs.Path. Listing 15-2 shows a typical resource.

Listing 15-2. A Simple Book Resource

```
@Path("/book")
public class BookResource {

    @GET
    @Produces("text/plain")
    public String getBookTitle() {
        return "H2G2";
    }
}
```

The BookResource is a Java class annotated with @Path, indicating that the resource will be hosted at the URI path /book. The getBookTitle() method is marked to process HTTP GET requests (using @GET annotation) and produces text (the content is identified by the MIME Media text/plain; I could have also used the constant MediaType.TEXT_PLAIN). To access this resource, you need an HTTP client such as a browser and an HTTP GET method to point to the URL http://www.myserver.com/book.

As writing a resource with JAX-RS is easy, let's explore further the JAX-RS API.

The JAX-RS Model

From Listing 15-2, you can see that the REST service doesn't implement any interface nor extend any class; the only mandatory annotation to turn a POJO into a REST service is `@Path`. JAX-RS relies on configuration by exception, so it has a set of annotations to configure the default behavior. Following are the requirements to write a REST service:

- The class must be annotated with `@javax.ws.rs.Path`.

- To add EJB capabilities to a REST service, the class has to be annotated with `@javax.ejb.Stateless`.

- The class must be defined as public, and it must not be final or abstract.

- Root resource classes (classes with a `@Path` annotation) must have a default public constructor. Non-root resource classes do not require such a constructor.

- The class must not define the `finalize()` method.

JAX-RS is HTTP-centric by nature and has a set of clearly defined classes and annotations to deal with HTTP and URIs. A resource can have several representations, so the API provides support for a variety of content types and uses JAXB to marshall and unmarshall XML and JSON representations from/into objects. JAX-RS is also independent of the container, so resources can be deployed in GlassFish, of course, but also in a variety of servlet containers.

How to Write a REST Service

Listing 15-2 shows how to write a very simple REST service. But most of the time you need to access a database, retrieve or store data in a transactional manner. You can have stateless session beans functionalities on REST services, by adding the `@Stateless` annotation allowing transactional access to a persistent layer (JPA entities), as shown in Listing 15-3.

Listing 15-3. A Book Resource Creating and Retrieving Books from the Database

```
@Path("books")
@Stateless
@Produces({"application/xml", "application/json"})
@Consumes({"application/xml", "application/json"})
public class BookResource {

    @Context
    private UriInfo uriInfo;
    @PersistenceContext(unitName = "chapter15PU")
    private EntityManager em;
```

```
@GET
public List<Book> getAllBooks() {
    Query query = em.createNamedQuery("findAllBooks");
    List<Book> books = query.getResultList();
    return books;
}

@POST
public Response createNewBook(JAXBElement<Book> bookJaxb) {
    Book book = bookJaxb.getValue();
    em.persist(book);
    URI bookUri = uriInfo.getAbsolutePathBuilder().path(↪
                        book.getId().toString()).build();
    return Response.created(bookUri).build();
}
}
```

The code in Listing 15-3 represents a REST service that can consume and produce XML and JSON representations of a book. The `getAllBooks()` method retrieves the list of books from the database and returns an XML or a JSON representation (using content negotiation) of this list, accessible through a `GET` method. The `createNewBook()` method takes an XML or a JSON representation of a book and persists it to the database. This method is invoked with an HTTP `POST` and returns a `Response` with the URI (`bookUri`) of the new book as well as the `created` status. This code follows a very simple JAX-RS model and uses a set of powerful annotations.

URI Definition

The `@Path` annotation's value is a relative URI path. When used on classes, these are referred to as *root resources*, providing the roots of the resource tree and access to subresources.

```
@Path("/customers")
public class CustomerResource {

    @GET
    public List getCustomers() {
        // ...
    }
}
```

You can also use URI path templates with variables embedded within the URI syntax. Those variables are evaluated at runtime. The Javadoc for the `@Path` annotation describes the template syntax.

```
@Path("/customers/{customername}")
```

`@Path` may also be used on methods of root resources, which can be useful to group together common functionalities for several resources as shown in Listing 15-4 (you may ignore for the moment the `@GET`, `@POST`, and `@DELETE` annotations in the listing, as they will be described later in the "Methods or the Uniform Interface" section).

Listing 15-4. An Item Resource with Several @Path Annotations

```java
@Path("/items")
public class ItemResource {

    // URI : /items
    @GET
    public List<Item> getListOfItems() {
        // ...
    }

    // URI : /items/1234
    @GET
    @Path("{itemid}")
    public Item getItem(@PathParam("itemid") String itemid) {
        // ...
    }

    // URI : /items/1234
    @DELETE
    @Path("{itemid}")
    public void deleteItem(@PathParam("itemid") String itemid) {
        // ...
    }

    // URI : /items/books
    @GET
    @Path("/books/")
    public List<Book> getListOfBooks() {
        // ...
    }

    // URI : /items/books/1234
    @GET
    @Path("/books/{bookid}")
    public Book getBook(@PathParam("bookid") String bookid) {
        // ...
    }
}
```

If @Path exists on both the class and method, the relative path to the resource method is a concatenation of the class and method. For example, to get a book by its ID, the path will be /items/books/1234. When requesting the root resource /items, the only method without @Path will be selected (getListOfItems()). When requesting /items/books, the getListOfBooks() method will be invoked. If @Path("/items") only existed on the class, and not on any methods, the path to access each method would be the same. The only way to differentiate them would be the HTTP verb (GET, PUT, etc.) and the content negotiation (text, XML, etc.).

Extracting Parameters

You need to extract information about URIs and requests when dealing with them. Listing 15-4 showed how to get a parameter out of the path with @javax.ws.rs.PathParam. JAX-RS provides a rich set of annotations to extract the different parameters that a request could send (@QueryParam, @MatrixParam, @CookieParam, @HeaderParam, and @FormParam).

The @PathParam annotation is used to extract the value of a URI template parameter; the following code allows you to extract the customer ID (98342) out of the http://www.myserver.com/customers/98342 URI:

```
@Path("/customers")
public class CustomerResource {
    @GET
    public Customer getCustomer(@PathParam("customerId") customerId) {
        // ...
    }
}
```

The @QueryParam annotation extracts the value of a URI query parameter. For example, the following code allows you to extract the ZIP code parameter (19870) out of the http://www.myserver.com/customers?zip=19870 URI:

```
@Path("/customers")
public class CustomerResource {
    @GET
    public Customer getCustomerByZipCode(@QueryParam("zip") Long zip) {
        // ...
    }
}
```

The @MatrixParam annotation acts like @QueryParam, except it extracts the value of a URI matrix parameter (; is used as a delimiter instead of ?). For example, you'll be able to extract the author's name (Goncalves) out of this URI: http://www.myserver.com/products/books;author=Goncalves.

Two other annotations are related to the innards of HTTP, things you don't see directly in URIs: cookies and HTTP headers. @CookieParam extracts the value of a cookie, while @HeaderParam extracts the value of a header field. The following code extracts the session ID from the cookie:

```
@Path("/products")
public class ItemResource {
    @GET
    public Book getBook(@CookieParam("sessionid") int sessionid) {
        // ...
    }
}
```

The @FormParam annotation specifies that the value of a parameter is to be extracted from a form in a request entity body. @FormParam is not required to be supported on fields or properties.

With all these annotations, you can add a @DefaultValue annotation to define the default value for a parameter you're expecting. The default value is used if the corresponding metadata is not present in the request. In the following code, if the query parameter age is not in the request, the default value 50 is set:

```
@Path("/customers")
public class CustomerResource {
  @GET
  public Response getCustomers(@DefaultValue("50") @QueryParam("age") int age) {
    // ...
  }
}
```

Consuming and Producing Content Types

With REST, a resource can have several representations; a book can be represented as a web page, XML data, or an image showing the album cover. JAX-RS specifies a number of Java types that can represent a resource such as `String`, `InputStream` and JAXB beans. The `@javax.ws.rs.Consumes` and `@javax.ws.rs.Produces` annotations may be applied to a resource where several representations are possible. It defines the media types of the representation exchanged between the client and the server. JAX-RS has a `MediaType` class that acts like an abstraction for a MIME type. It has several methods and defines the constants listed in Table 15-2.

Table 15-2. MIME Types Defined in `javax.ws.rs.core.MediaType`

Constant name	MIME type
APPLICATION_ATOM_XML	"application/atom+xml"
APPLICATION_FORM_URLENCODED	"application/x-www-form-urlencoded"
APPLICATION_JSON	"application/json"
APPLICATION_OCTET_STREAM	"application/octet-stream"
APPLICATION_SVG_XML	"application/svg+xml"
APPLICATION_XHTML_XML	"application/xhtml+xml"
APPLICATION_XML	"application/xml"
MULTIPART_FORM_DATA	"multipart/form-data"
TEXT_HTML	"text/html"
TEXT_PLAIN	"text/plain"
TEXT_XML	"text/xml"
WILDCARD	"*/*"

Using the `@Consumes` and `@Produces` annotations on a method overrides any on the resource class for a method argument or return type. In the absence of either of these annotations, support for any media type (*/*) is assumed. By default, `CustomerResource` produces plain text representations that are overridden in some methods (see Listing 15-5).

Listing 15-5. A Customer Resource with Several Representations

```java
@Path("/customers")
@Produces(MediaType.TEXT_PLAIN)
public class CustomerResource {

    @GET
    public String getAsPlainText() {
        // ...
    }

    @GET
    @Produces(MediaType.TEXT_HTML)
    public String getAsHtml() {
        // ...
    }

    @GET
    @Produces(MediaType.APPLICATION_JSON)
    public List<Customer> getAsJson() {
        // ...
    }

    @PUT
    @Consumes(MediaType.TEXT_PLAIN)
    public void putBasic(String customer) {
        // ...
    }

    @POST
    @Consumes(MediaType.APPLICATION_XML)
    public Response createCustomer(InputStream is) {
        // ...
    }
}
```

If a resource is capable of producing more than one Internet media type, the resource method chosen will correspond to the most acceptable media type, as declared by the client in the Accept header of the HTTP request. For example, if the Accept header is:

```
Accept: text/plain
```

and the URI is /customers, the getAsPlainText() method will be invoked. The client could have used the following HTTP header:

```
Accept: text/plain; q=0.8, text/html
```

This header declares that the client can accept media types of `text/plain` and `text/html` but prefers the latter using the quality factor (or preference weight) of 0.8 ("I prefer `text/html`, but send me `text/plain` if it is the best available after an 80% markdown in quality"). By including such a header and pointing at the `/customers` URI, the `getAsHtml()` method will be invoked.

In Listing 15-5, the `getAsJson()` method returns a representation of type `application/json`. JSON is a lightweight data-interchange format that is less verbose and more readable than XML. It is also directly consumable by JavaScript code in web pages, this being the major reason for using JSON over other representations. Listing 15-6 shows a list of customers in JSON.

Listing 15-6. A JSON Representation of Customers

```
{"customers": {
  "id": "0",
  "version": "1",
  "customer": [
    {
      "firstName": "Alexis",
      "lastName": "Midon",
      "address": {
        "streetAddress": "21 2nd Street",
        "city": "New York",
        "postalCode": 10021
      },
      "phoneNumbers": [
        "212 555-1234",
        "646 555-4567"
      ]
    },
    {
      "firstName": "Sebastien",
      "lastName": "Auvray",
      "address": {
        "streetAddress": "2 Rue des Acacias",
        "city": "Paris",
        "postalCode": 75015
      },
      "phoneNumbers": [
        "+33 555-1234",
      ]
    }
  ]
}}
```

Jersey will convert the list of customers into JSON for you, using the built-in `MessageBodyReader` and `MessageBodyWriter`, which are entity providers.

■ **Note** Jersey adds a BadgerFish mapping of JAXB XML to JSON. BadgerFish (`http://badgerfish.ning.com/`) is a convention for translating an XML document into a JSON object so it's easy to manipulate within JavaScript.

Entity Provider

When entities are received in requests or sent in responses, the JAX-RS implementation needs a way to convert the representations to a Java type and vice versa. This is the role of entity providers that supply mapping services between representations and their associated java types. An example is JAXB, which maps an object to an XML representation and vice versa. If the default XML and JSON providers are not sufficient, then you can develop your own custom entity providers. Entity providers come in two flavors: `MessageBodyReader` and `MessageBodyWriter`.

To map a request body to a Java type, a class must implement the `javax.ws.rs.ext.MessageBodyReader` interface and be annotated with `@Provider`. By default, the implementation is assumed to consume all media types (`*/*`). The annotation `@Consumes` might be used to restrict the supported media types. The code in Listing 15-7 takes an XML stream (represented by a `javax.xml.bind.Element` object) and converts it into a `Customer` object.

Listing 15-7. A Provider Reading an XML Stream and Creating a Customer Entity

```java
@Provider
@Consumes(MediaType.APPLICATION_XML)
public class CustomerReader implements MessageBodyReader<Element> {

  @Override
  public boolean isReadable(Class<?> type, Type genericType, Annotation[] annotations, ↪
                                                    MediaType mediaType) {
      return Element.class.isAssignableFrom(type);
  }

  @Override
   public Element readFrom(Class<Element> customer, Type genericType, ↪
        Annotation[] annotations, MediaType mediaType, MultivaluedMap<String, String> ↪
        httpHeaders, InputStream inputStream) throws IOException, WebApplicationException {
      Document doc = getParser().parse(inputStream);
      Element node = doc.getDocumentElement();
      if (node.getLocalName().equals("customer")) {
          return node;
      } else {
          throw new IOException("Unexpected payload!");
      }
  }
}
```

In the same way, a Java type could be mapped to a response body. A class willing to do that must implement the `javax.ws.rs.ext.MessageBodyWriter` interface and be annotated with `@Provider`. The annotation `@Produces` specifies the supported media types. Listing 15-8 is a snippet showing how to convert a `Customer` entity into a plain text HTTP body.

Listing 15-8. A Provider Producing a Text Representation of a Customer Entity

```java
@Provider
@Produces(MediaType.TEXT_PLAIN)
public class CustomerWriter implements MessageBodyWriter<Customer> {

    @Override
    public boolean isWriteable(Class<?> type, Type genericType, Annotation[] annotations, ↪
                            MediaType mediaType) {
        return Customer.class.isAssignableFrom(type);
    }

    @Override
    public void writeTo(Customer customer, Class<?> type, Type genericType, ↪
                    Annotation[] annotations, MediaType mediaType, ↪
                    MultivaluedMap<String, Object> httpHeaders, OutputStream outputStream) ↪
                    throws IOException, WebApplicationException {
        outputStream.write(customer.getId().byteValue());
        // ...
    }
}
```

MessageBodyReader and MessageBodyWriter implementations may throw a WebApplicationException if they can't produce any representation. For common cases, the JAX-RS implementation comes with a set of default entity providers (see Table 15-3).

Table 15-3. Default Providers of the JAX-RS Implementation

Type	Description
byte[]	All media types (*/*).
java.lang.String	All media types (*/*).
java.io.InputStream	All media types (*/*).
java.io.Reader	All media types (*/*).
java.io.File	All media types (*/*).
javax.activation.DataSource	All media types (*/*).
javax.xml.transform.Source	XML types (text/xml, application/xml, and application/-*+xml).
javax.xml.bind.JAXBElement	JAXB class XML media types (text/-xml, application/xml, and application/*+xml).
MultivaluedMap<String,String>	Form content (application/x-www-form-urlencoded).
javax.ws.rs.core StreamingOutput	All media types (*/*), MessageBodyWriter only.

Methods or the Uniform Interface

You've seen how the HTTP protocol works with its requests, responses, and action methods (GET, POST, PUT, etc.). JAX-RS defines these common HTTP methods using annotations: @GET, @POST, @PUT, @DELETE, @HEAD, and @OPTIONS. Only public methods may be exposed as resource methods. Listing 15-9 shows a customer resource exposing CRUD methods. Note that the createCustomer and updateCustomer methods take an InputStream as a parameter which represents the HTTP request body.

Listing 15-9. A Customer Resource Exposing CRUD Operations

```
@Path("/customers")
public class CustomerResource {

  @GET
  public List<Customer> getListOfCustomers() {
      // ...
  }

  @POST
  @Consumes(MediaType.APPLICATION_XML)
  public Response createCustomer(InputStream is) {
      // ...
  }

  @PUT
  @Path("{customerId}")
  @Consumes(MediaType.APPLICATION_XML)
  public Response updateCustomer(@PathParam("customerId") String customerId,↪
                                  InputStream is) {
      // ...
  }

  @DELETE
  @Path("{customerId}")
  public void deleteCustomer(@PathParam("customerId") String customerId) {
      // ...
  }
}
```

When a resource method is invoked, parameters annotated with one of the extractor annotations seen previously are filled. The value of a nonannotated parameter (called an *entity parameter*) is mapped from the request entity body and converted by an entity provider.

Methods may return void, Response, or another Java type. Response is used when additional metadata needs to be provided; for example, when you create a new customer, you might need to send back the URI of this customer.

Contextual Information

When a request is being processed, the resource provider needs contextual information to perform the request properly. The @javax.ws.rs.core.Context annotation is intended to inject into an attribute or a method parameter the following classes: HttpHeaders, UriInfo, Request, SecurityContext, and Providers. For example, Listing 15-10 shows the code that gets injected a UriInfo so it can build URIs.

Listing 15-10. A Customer Resource Getting a UriInfo

```
@Path("/customers")
public class CustomerResource {

    @Context
    UriInfo uriInfo;
    @EJB
    CustomerEJB customerEJB;

    @GET
    @Produces(MediaType.APPLICATION_JSON)
    public JSONArray getListOfCustomers() {
        JSONArray uriArray = new JSONArray();
        for (Customer customer : customerEJB.findAll()) {
            UriBuilder ub = uriInfo.getAbsolutePathBuilder();
            URI userUri = ub.path(customer.getId().toString()).build();
            uriArray.put(userUri.toASCIIString());
        }
        return uriArray;
    }
}
```

■ **Note** The JSONArray object returned by the getListOfCustomers() is part of the Jettison open source project hosted at Codehaus. It is a collection of Java APIs (like STaX and DOM) which read and write JSON.

Headers

As you saw earlier with HTTP, information is transported between the client and the server not only in the entity body, but also in the headers (Date, Server, Content-Type, etc.). HTTP headers take part in the uniform interface, and RESTful web services use them in their original meanings. As a resource developer, you may need to access HTTP headers; that's what the javax.ws.rs.core.HttpHeaders interface serves. An instance of HttpHeaders can be injected into an attribute or a method parameter using the @Context annotation, as the HttpHeaders class is a map with helper methods to access the header values in a case-insensitive manner.

If the service provides localized resources, the Accept-Language header can be extracted as follows:

```
@GET
@Produces(MediaType.TEXT_PLAIN)
public String get(@Context HttpHeaders headers) {
    List<java.util.Locale> locales = headers.getAcceptableLanguages()
    // or headers.getRequestHeader("accept-language")
    // or headers.getRequestHeader(HttpHeaders.ACCEPT_LANGUAGE)
    ...
}
```

Building URIs

Hyperlinks are a central aspect of REST applications. In order to evolve through the application states, RESTful web services need to be agile at managing transition and URI building. JAX-RS provides a `javax.ws.rs.core.UriBuilder` that aims at replacing `java.net.URI` for making it easier to build URI in a safe manner. `UriBuilder` has a set of methods that can be used to build new URIs or build from existing URIs. The code in Listing 15-10 returns an array of URIs.

UriBuilder can also be used to easily translate URI templates. For example, the URI `http://www.myserver.com/products/books?author=Goncalves` can be obtained as follows:

```
UriBuilder.fromUri("http://www.myserver.com/")
         .path("{a}/{b}").queryParam("author", "{value}")
         .build("products", "books", "Goncalves");
```

Exception Handling

The code so far was executed in a happy world where everything goes fine and no exception management has been necessary. Unfortunately, life is not that perfect, and sooner or later you have to face a resource being blown up either because the data you receive is not valid or because pieces of the network are not reliable.

In a resource provider, at any time you can throw a `WebApplicationException` or subclasses of it (see Listing 15-11). The exception will be caught by the JAX-RS implementation and converted into an HTTP response. The default error is a 500 with a blank message, but the class `javax.ws.rs.WebApplicationException` offers various constructors so you can pick a specific status code (defined in the enumeration `javax.ws.rs.core.Response.Status`) or an entity. In this example, we use a builder to create a 400 response with a message ("Id must be a positive integer!") in the `Response` body.

Listing 15-11. A Method Throwing Exceptions

```
@Path("customers/{customerId}")
public Customer getCustomer(@PathParam("customerId") Long customerId) {
    if(id < 1)
        throw new WebApplicationException(
            Response.status(400).entity("Id must be a positive integer!").build());

    Customer customer = em.find(Customer.class, customerId);
    if (customer == null)
        throw new WebApplicationException(Response.Status.NOT_FOUND);
    return customer;
}
```

To keep your code DRY (which stands for Don't Repeat Yourself), you can supply exception mapping providers. An exception mapping provider maps an exception to a **Response**. If this exception is thrown, the JAX-RS implementation will catch it and invoke the corresponding exception mapping provider. An exception mapping provider is an implementation of ExceptionMapper<E extends java.lang.Throwable>, annotated with @Provider (see Listing 15-12).

Listing 15-12. An Exception Mapping

```
@Provider
public class EntityNotFoundMapper implements
        ExceptionMapper<javax.persistence.EntityNotFoundException> {

 public Response toResponse(javax.persistence.EntityNotFoundException ex){
   return Response.status(404). entity(ex.getMessage()).↪
        type(MediaType.TEXT_PLAIN).build();
 }
}
```

Unchecked exceptions and errors that do not fall into the two previous cases will be rethrown like any other normal Java unchecked exception.

Life Cycle

When a request comes in, the targeted resource is resolved, and a new instance of the matching root resource class is created. Thus, the life cycle of a root resource class is per request. As a result, a resource class does not have to worry about concurrency and can use instance variables safely.

If deployed in a Java EE container (servlet or EJB), JAX-RS resource classes and providers may also make use of the JSR 250 life-cycle management and security annotations: @PostConstruct, @PreDestroy, @RunAs, @RolesAllowed, @PermitAll, @DenyAll, and @DeclareRoles. The life cycle of a resource can use @PostConstruct and @PreDestroy to add business logic after the resource is created or before it is destroyed. Figure 15-3 shows the life cycle that is equivalent to all stateless components in Java EE.

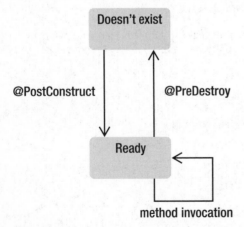

Figure 15-3. Resource life cyle

Putting It All Together

Let's put these concepts together and write a book resource, package and deploy it in GlassFish, and test it with cURL. The idea is to have a **Book** entity that maps to a database and a **BookResource** that gives a RESTful representation of the book. The **BookResource** is also a stateless session bean that allows transactional demarcation with the entity manager for CRUD operations. Once deployed, you will be able to create, retrieve, or delete books using HTTP methods with cURL and have both XML and JSON representations.

The example follows the Maven directory structure and packages all the classes into a war file (`chapter15-resource-2.0.war`). The classes have to be placed in the following directories:

- `src/main/java`: The directory for the **Book** entity and **BookResource** RESTful web service

- `src/main/resources`: The `persistence.xml` file used by the resource that maps the **Book** entity to the Derby database

- `pom.xml`: The Maven Project Object Model (POM) describing the project and its dependencies

Writing the Book Entity

By now, you understand the code of the **Book** entity, but there is one very important element to notice: this entity is also annotated with the JAXB `@XmlRootElement` annotation (see Listing 15-13), which allows it to have an XML representation of a book.

Listing 15-13. A Book Entity with a JAXB Annotation

```
@Entity
@XmlRootElement
@NamedQuery(name = "findAllBooks", query = "SELECT b FROM Book b")
public class Book {

    @Id @GeneratedValue
    private Long id;
    @Column(nullable = false)
    private String title;
    private Float price;
    @Column(length = 2000)
    private String description;
    private String isbn;
    private Integer nbOfPage;
    private Boolean illustrations;

    // Constructors, getters, setters
}
```

This entity also has to be packaged with a `persistence.xml` file (not shown here for simplicity).

Writing the BookResource

The BookResource is a RESTful web service, implemented as a stateless session bean, using an entity manager to create, delete, and retrieve books.

Header

The header of the BookResource is important as it uses several metadata annotations. In JAX-RS, users can access resources by publishing a URI. The @Path("books") annotation indicates the path of the resource (the URL used to access it)—in this case, it's something like http://localhost:8080/books.

The @Produces and @Consumes annotations define the default content type that this resource produces or consumes: XML and JSON. You can override this content type on a per-method basis. Finally, we find the @Stateless annotation that you've seen in Chapter 7, which informs the container that this resource should also be treated as an EJB and allows transaction demarcation when accessing the database. This resource gets injected a reference to an entity manager and a UriInfo.

```
@Path("books")
@Produces({MediaType.APPLICATION_XML, MediaType.APPLICATION_JSON})
@Consumes({MediaType.APPLICATION_XML, MediaType.APPLICATION_JSON})
@Stateless
public class BookResource {

    @PersistenceContext(unitName = "chapter15PU")
    private EntityManager em;
    @Context
    private UriInfo uriInfo;
```

Creating a New Book

Following the REST semantic, we use an HTTP POST method to create a new resource in XML or JSON, as specified in the header with the @Consumes annotation. By default, every method consumes XML or JSON, and this is true for the createNewBook() method. As already seen in Listing 15-3, this method takes a JAXBElement as a parameter; remember that the Book entity is also a JAXB object, and, once the XML has been unmarshalled to a Book object (bookJaxb.getValue()), the entity manager is used to persist the book.

This method returns a Response, which is the URI of the newly created book. We could return a status code of 200 OK (Response.ok()), indicating the creation of the book was successful, but, following the REST principles, the method should return a 201 (or 204), specifying the request has been fulfilled and resulting in the creation (Response.created()) of a new resource. The newly created resource can be referenced by the URI returned in the response.

```
@POST
public Response createNewBook(JAXBElement<Book> bookJaxb) {
    Book book = bookJaxb.getValue();
    em.persist(book);
```

```
        URI bookUri = uriInfo.getAbsolutePathBuilder().↪
                      path(book.getId().toString()).build();
        return Response.created(bookUri).build();
}
```

To create a resource with the previous code, we have the choice of sending either XML or JSON. JSON is less verbose. The cURL command line uses a **POST** method and passes data in a JSON format that must follow the JSON/XML mapping used in Jersey (remember that the XML in turn is mapped from the **Book** object using JAXB rules):

```
curl -X POST --data-binary ↪
"{ \"title\":\"H2G2\", \"description\":\"Scifi IT book\", ↪
\"illustrations\":\"false\",\"isbn\":\"134-234\",\"nbOfPage\":\"241\",↪
\"price\":\"24.0\" }" -H "Content-Type: application/json" ↪
http://localhost:8080/chapter15-resource-2.0/rs/books -v
```

The verbose mode of cURL (the **-v** argument) displays the HTTP request and response (as shown in the following output). You can see in the response the URI of the created book resource with an ID set to 601:

```
> POST /chapter15-resource-2.0/rs/books HTTP/1.1
> User-Agent: curl/7.19.0 (i586-pc-mingw32msvc) libcurl/7.19.0 zlib/1.2.3
> Host: localhost:8080
> Accept: */*
> Content-Type: application/json
> Content-Length: 127
>
< HTTP/1.1 201 Created
< X-Powered-By: Servlet/3.0
< Server: Server Open Source Edition 3.0.1
< Location: http://localhost:8080/chapter15-resource-2.0/rs/books/601
< Content-Type: application/xml
< Content-Length: 0
```

Getting a Book by ID

To retrieve a book resource by its identifier, the request must have a URL of the form **/books/{id of the book}**. The id is used as a parameter to find the book in the database. In an HTTP GET request to **/books/601**, the getBookById() method will return an XML or a JSON representation of the book with ID 601.

```
@GET
@Path("{id}/")
public Book getBookById(@PathParam("id") Long id) {
    Book book = em.find(Book.class, id);
    return book;
}
```

The @Path annotation indicates the subpath within the already specified path at the class level. The use of the {id} syntax binds the URL element to the method parameter. Let's use cURL to access resource 601 and get a JSON representation:

```
curl -X GET -H "Accept: application/json" ↦
              http://localhost:8080/chapter15-resource-2.0/rs/books/601
```

```
{"description":"Scifi IT book","illustrations":"false",↦
"isbn":"1234-234","nbOfPage":"241","price":"24.0","title":"H2G2"}
```

By just changing the Accept header property, the same code will return the XML representation of book 601:

```
curl -X GET -H "Accept: application/xml" ↦
              http://localhost:8080/chapter15-resource-2.0/rs/books/601
```

```
<?xml version="1.0" encoding="UTF-8" standalone="yes"?>
<book><description>Scifi IT book</description>
<illustrations>false</illustrations><isbn>1234-234</isbn>
<nbOfPage>241</nbOfPage><price>24.0</price><title>H2G2</title></book>
```

Deleting a Book

The deleteBook() method follows the format of the getBookById() method because it uses a subpath and an ID as a parameter, with the only difference being the HTTP request used. We need an HTTP DELETE method that takes a URL and deletes the content associated with that URL.

```
@DELETE
@Path("{id}/")
public void deleteBook(@PathParam("id") Long id) {
    Book book = em.find(Book.class, id);
    em.remove(book);
}
```

If we use the verbose mode of cURL (-v argument), we'll see the DELETE request is sent, and the 204 No Content status code appears in the response to indicate that the resource doesn't exist anymore.

```
curl -X DELETE http://localhost:8080/chapter15-resource-2.0/rs/books/601 -v
```

```
> DELETE /chapter15-resource-2.0/rs/books/601 HTTP/1.1
> User-Agent: curl/7.19.0 (i586-pc-mingw32msvc) libcurl/7.19.0 zlib/1.2.3
> Host: localhost:8080
> Accept: */*
>
< HTTP/1.1 204 No Content
< X-Powered-By: Servlet/3.0
< Server: Server Open Source Edition 3.0.1
```

Configuring Jersey

Before deploying the `BookResource` and `Book` entity, we need to register a url pattern in Jersey to intercept HTTP calls to RESTful services. This way the requests sent to the `/rs` path will get intercepted by Jersey. You can either set this url pattern by configuring the Jersey servlet in the `web.xml` file, or use the `@ApplicationPath` annotation (see Listing 15-14).

Listing 15-14. The `ApplicationConfig` Class Declaring the /rs URL Pattern

```
import javax.ws.rs.ApplicationPath;
import javax.ws.rs.core.Application;

@ApplicationPath("rs")
public class ApplicationConfig extends Application {
}
```

This class has to be somewhere in your project (no particular package) and, thanks to the `@ApplicationPath` annotation, it will map the requests to the `/rs/*` URL pattern. This means, each time a URL starts with `/rs/`, it will be handled by Jersey. And indeed, in the examples that I have used with cURL, all the resource URLs start with `/rs`:

```
curl -X GET -H "Accept: application/json" ➥
            http://localhost:8080/chapter15-resource-2.0/rs/books

curl -X DELETE http://localhost:8080/chapter15-resource-2.0/rs/books/601
```

Compiling and Packaging with Maven

The web application needs to be compiled and packaged in a war file (`<packaging>war</packaging>`). The `pom.xml` in Listing 15-15 declares all necessary dependencies to compile code (`jsr311-api`, `javax.ejb`, and `javax.persistence`). Remember that JAXB is part of Java SE, so we don't need to add this dependency.

Listing 15-15. The Maven `pom.xml` File for Compiling and Packaging the Web Application

```
<?xml version="1.0" encoding="UTF-8"?>
<project xmlns="http://maven.apache.org/POM/4.0.0" ➥
         xmlns:xsi="http://www.w3.org/2001/XMLSchema-instance"➥
         xsi:schemaLocation="http://maven.apache.org/POM/4.0.0 ➥
         http://maven.apache.org/xsd/maven-4.0.0.xsd">

    <modelVersion>4.0.0</modelVersion>
    <groupId>com.apress.javaee6</groupId>
    <artifactId>chapter15-resource</artifactId>
    <packaging>war</packaging>
    <version>2.0</version>
    <name>Chapter 15 - REST Resource</name>
```

```xml
<dependencies>
    <dependency>
        <groupId>javax.ws.rs</groupId>
        <artifactId>jsr311-api</artifactId>
        <version>1.1</version>
        <scope>provided</scope>
    </dependency>
    <dependency>
        <groupId>org.glassfish</groupId>
        <artifactId>javax.ejb</artifactId>
        <version>3.0.1</version>
        <scope>provided</scope>
    </dependency>
    <dependency>
        <groupId>org.eclipse.persistence</groupId>
        <artifactId>javax.persistence</artifactId>
        <version>2.0.0</version>
        <scope>provided</scope>
    </dependency>
</dependencies>

<build>
    <plugins>
        <plugin>
            <groupId>org.apache.maven.plugins</groupId>
            <artifactId>maven-compiler-plugin</artifactId>
            <inherited>true</inherited>
            <configuration>
                <source>1.6</source>
                <target>1.6</target>
            </configuration>
        </plugin>
    </plugins>
</build>
</project>
```

To compile and package the classes, open a DOS command line in the root directory containing the pom.xml file and enter the following Maven command:

```
mvn package
```

Go to the target directory, look for a file named chapter15-resource-2.0.war, and open it. Notice that Book.class, ApplicationConfig.class and BookResource.class are under the WEB-INF\classes directory. The persistence.xml file is also packaged in the war.

Deploying on GlassFish

Once the code is packaged, make sure GlassFish and Derby are up and running and deploy the war file by issuing the asadmin command-line interface. Open a DOS console, go to the target directory where the chapter15-resource-2.0.war file is located, and enter:

```
asadmin deploy chapter15-resource-2.0.war
```

If the deployment is successful, the following command should return the name of the deployed component and its type:

```
asadmin list-components
chapter15-resource-2.0 <ejb, web>
```

Running the Example

Once the application is deployed, you can use cURL in a command line to create book resources by sending POST requests and get all or a specific resource with GET requests. DELETE will remove book resources. Following are some commands you can use:

```
// Creates a book
curl -X POST --data-binary ↪
"{ \"title\":\"H2G2\", \"description\":\"Scifi IT book\", ↪
\"illustrations\":\"false\",\"isbn\":\"134-234\",\"nbOfPage\":\"241\",↪
\"price\":\"24.0\" }" -H "Content-Type: application/json" ↪
http://localhost:8080/chapter15-resource-2.0/rs/books

// Returns all the books
curl -X GET -H "Accept: application/json" ↪
             http://localhost:8080/chapter15-resource-2.0/rs/books

// Returns the book with ID 601 in JSON
curl -X GET -H "Accept: application/json" ↪
             http://localhost:8080/chapter15-resource-2.0/rs/books/601

{"description":"Scifi IT book","illustrations":"false",↪
"isbn":"1234-234","nbOfPage":"241","price":"24.0","title":"H2G2"}

// Returns the book with ID 601 in XML
curl -X GET -H "Accept: application/xml" ↪
             http://localhost:8080/chapter15-resource-2.0/rs/books/601

<?xml version="1.0" encoding="UTF-8" standalone="yes"?>
<book><description>Scifi IT book</description>
<illustrations>false</illustrations><isbn>1234-234</isbn>
<nbOfPage>241</nbOfPage><price>24.0</price><title>H2G2</title></book>

// Deletes the book with ID 601
curl -X DELETE http://localhost:8080/chapter15-resource-2.0/rs/books/601
```

Summary

The previous chapter explained SOAP web services. They use a special envelope (described using WSDL) and can be invoked by several protocols, HTTP being one of them. In this chapter, I've explained RESTful web services, and you should now know how different JAX-WS and JAX-RS are to implement.

This chapter commenced with a general introduction to REST. With simple verbs (GET, POST, PUT, etc.) and a unified interface, you learned how you can access any resource deployed on the Web. The chapter then zoomed in on HTTP, a protocol based on a request/response mechanism using content negotiation to choose appropriate content type from a request. Caching can be employed to optimize network traffic with conditional requests using dates and ETags. This optimization can also be used with REST as it is based on HTTP.

JAX-RS is a Java API, shipped with Java EE 6, that simplifies RESTful web service development. With a set of annotations, you can define the path and subpaths of your resource, extract different kinds of parameters, or map to HTTP methods (@GET, @POST, etc.). When developing RESTful web services, you must think about resources, how they are linked together, and how to manage their state using HTTP.

Index

Symbols

. (dot operator), to access object attributes , 313
${expr}, 312, 324
<% and %> (scriptlet tags), 312
#{expr}, 312, 324

A

abstract entity, 118
Abstract Window Toolkit (AWT), 283
ACC. *See* application client container (ACC)
access type
    for annotations, 78–81
    of embeddable class, 89
@AccessTimeout annotation, 213
ACID (Atomicity, Consistency, Isolation, Durability) properties, 254
acknowledgment of messages, 397, 398
action elements (JSP), 309
activation, 206, 239
@ActivationConfigProperty annotation, 402–3
addMessage() method (FacesContext), 349
Address entity, 66
addToCache() method, 207
admin console for GlassFish, 36, 37

administered objects, 382, 386–89
    connection factories, 386
    connection object, 389
    creating, 413
    destination, 387
    injection, 387
    MessageConsumer, 394
    MessageProducer, 392
    messages, 390
    selectors, 397
    session, 389
@AfterClass annotation, 58
Ajax, 279, 282
    in CD_BookStore application, 372–75
Ajax (Asynchronous JavaScript and XML), 368–71
    support in JSF, 370–71
@all, 371
ALL cascade type, 141
anchor element, <h:outputLink> tag for, 328
AND logical operator, in JPQL queries, 148
annotations
    access type, 78–81
    for metadata format, 46
    vs. XML descriptors, 84
AOP (Aspect-Oriented Programming), 243
Apache Ant, 21

■ G

Gamma, Erich, 27

@GeneratedValue annotation, 51, 68

generateReport() method, 233

GET method (HTTP), 455

getAllBooks() method, 465

getApplication() method (FacesContext), 349

getAsHtml() method, 470

getAsJson() method, 470

getAsObject() method, 365

getAsString() method, 365

getAttributes() method (FacesContext), 349

getCallerPrincipal() method
(MessageDrivenContext), 404

getCallerPrincipal() method
(SessionContext), 221, 274

getContextData() method
(InvocationContext), 245

getCurrentInstance() method
(FacesContext), 349

getELContext() method (FacesContext), 349

getElementById() method, 305

getEndpointReference() method
(WebServiceContext), 440

getMaximumSeverity() method
(FacesContext), 349

getMessageContext() method
(WebServiceContext), 440

getMessages (FacesContext), 349

getMethod() method (InvocationContext), 245

getParameters() method
(InvocationContext), 245

getPartialViewContext() method
(FacesContext), 350

getProperty action (JSP), 310

getReference() method (EntityManager), 132,
135

getResultList() method, 153

getRollbackOnly() method
(MessageDrivenContext), 404

getRollbackOnly() method
(SessionContext), 221

getSingleResult() method, 153, 154

getTarget() method (InvocationContext), 245

getter method, 78

getTimer() method (InvocationContext), 245

getTimerService() method
(MessageDrivenContext), 404

getTimerService() method
(SessionContext), 221

getUserPrincipal() method
(WebServiceContext), 440

getUserTransaction() method
(MessageDrivenContext), 404

getUserTransaction() method
(SessionContext), 221

getViewRoot() method (FacesContext), 350

GlassFish, 34–41, 189

administration, 37

architecture, 34

customization of EJB pool parameters, 239

deploying application on, 196, 482

deploying MDBs on, 413

deploying web service on, 444

history, 34

installing, 39

subprojects, 36

update center, 36

web application deployment on, 294

global navigation rules in XML, 359

granularity of RESTFUL resources, 462

graphics in JSF, 330

grid, in JSF, 330–32

Grizzly framework, 35

GROUP BY construct (JPQL), 150

■ H

HAVING clause (JPQL), 150

<h:body> tag (JSF), 333

You Need the Companion eBook

Your purchase of this book entitles you to buy the companion PDF-version eBook for only $10. Take the weightless companion with you anywhere.

We believe this Apress title will prove so indispensable that you'll want to carry it with you everywhere, which is why we are offering the companion eBook (in PDF format) for $10 to customers who purchase this book now. Convenient and fully searchable, the PDF version of any content-rich, page-heavy Apress book makes a valuable addition to your programming library. You can easily find and copy code—or perform examples by quickly toggling between instructions and the application. Even simultaneously tackling a donut, diet soda, and complex code becomes simplified with hands-free eBooks!

Once you purchase your book, getting the $10 companion eBook is simple:

1. Visit **www.apress.com/promo/tendollars/**.

2. Complete a basic registration form to receive a randomly generated question about this title.

3. Answer the question correctly in 60 seconds, and you will receive a promotional code to redeem for the $10.00 eBook.

THE EXPERT'S VOICE™

233 Spring Street, New York, NY 10013

Offer valid through 2/11.